RACIAL POLICIES AND PRACTICES OF
REAL ESTATE BROKERS

RACIAL POLICIES AND PRACTICES OF REAL ESTATE BROKERS

by ROSE HELPER

UNIVERSITY OF MINNESOTA PRESS
Minneapolis

To the memory of
MY PARENTS AND MY BROTHER

Foreword

COLLECTIVE manifestations of race relations have been too often simplistically interpreted from a perspective of the individuals who make up the community. The consequence of this substantial and far-reaching assumption has been to overlook the fact that the individual members of the community are participating in its social life, not merely as individuals giving expression to their personal attitudes and feelings, but as persons playing specifically differentiated roles, such as homeowners, workers, merchants, members of professions, realtors, and members of other organized interest groups. The roles played by individuals are less and less acted out under the definitions provided by the traditional folkways and mores of the community.

The behavior of the average citizen is increasingly structured and defined instrumentally by the demands and requirements of organizations set up with the purpose of realizing quite specific interests and/or objectives. More often than not, preferences of individuals within the community reflect not only their private interests as they see them, but willy-nilly the subordination of their distinctively individual attitudes and views to the definition of organizations and structures that have been deliberately set up to effect specific economic and social purposes. What we identify as the sentiment and feelings of individuals is more frequently than not a function of organizations responding to specific needs and acting toward the realization of specific interests. The structure and organization of racial practices are held together and reinforced by influences beyond the informal understandings, beliefs, and practices of the individuals concerned. Society is increasingly characterized by groupings, deliberate in nature, responding to specific needs and acting toward the realization of specific

vii

interests. Furthermore, we are increasingly dependent in modern society upon such organized groups. Social life under the conditions of our current "mass society" exhibits a constant flux, mobility, and change. The community gives the appearance of a shapeless heterogeneous mass whose form, organization, and purpose are given specific meaning and direction through the agency of deliberate and calculated association. It is within the framework of these developments that specific race relations of the present day need to be examined.

The present volume underlines the shortcomings and limitations of the view of our racial relations which is confined to the individual attitudes found within the population. Although there are some situations in which the behavior of persons toward one another can be explained *qua* individuals in terms of their sentiments and attitudes in the major and significant areas of our social life — namely, jobs, business, and housing — this conception is woefully inadequate. Increasingly, contact and interaction of racial groups in our population are defined by organizations with collectively asserted interests of those groups and are not merely projections of the individuals who make up the community. Hence, in the market for residential housing, we find the locale in which individuals attempt to realize their personal needs for social deference and the protection of their property values. It is interests of this kind that are served by organizations and professional groups and that cause their members to reflect in themselves the raison d'être of those organizations.

As this author's insightful empirical research makes clear, it is within the framework of the real estate institution that the real estate policies and practices with reference to Negroes take place and are maintained. The association of real estate men structures and defines the situation for its members, and through them offers ready and available patterns of race relations in the community. Distinctly personal attitudes toward members of minority groups recede and are seen as of lesser consequence in explaining racial practices. The reality is the *social fact*. The key to an understanding of racial practices in the United States, and hence a necessary condition for social policy formulation, is to be found in the present study. The framework of the real estate institution and the policies and practices of real estate brokers supply the individual realtor with a well-formulated rationale which makes meaningful and justifies to him his activity — that is, the acceptance and/or rejection of minority groups. This study is a significant contribution to the understanding of the increasing influence in

Foreword

our social life of the policies, stratagems, and tactics of deliberately organized interest groups. The pressing problems of racial tension and conflict must be seen in a more formidable context than merely individual dimensions of personal prejudice and racial enmity.

JOSEPH D. LOHMAN
School of Criminology, University of
California, Berkeley

Preface

ANY inquiry into the housing of minority groups cannot neglect the role of the real estate broker, who has been looked upon for a number of years as a main source of discrimination in housing. "Minority group" in this book refers primarily to Negroes, since they compose the largest minority group in the United States. Their housing conditions have probably received more intensive study than those of any other minority group, yet some facets remain to be explored. The studies which have dealt totally or partly with the housing of Negroes fall into two main categories—those describing the physical conditions of this housing and those taking to task the groups considered responsible for discriminatory practices. The latter studies approach minority housing problems in a way exterior to the group blamed for such practices.

In contrast, I attempted to find out how real estate men themselves regard their racial practices. Two premises underlie this approach—that the real estate man is a focal point in the whole problem of residential segregation, and that only by understanding the thinking of the real estate man can the problem be clarified and more constructively attacked. To a large extent, the real estate broker stands between the supply of housing and its potential buyer in a minority group.

A particular feature of the study is an analysis of the ideology of the real estate broker, which explains and supports his racial practices. Other factors affecting brokers' practices were also examined—the real estate board, the community, the lending agency, and particular sources of pecuniary gain present in certain real estate transactions. In this study, the real estate man is considered a member of the real estate collectivity, learning and drawing upon its principles, its outlook and values, and its definitions for his decision-making. He also operates in a community and is subject to the wishes of its residents.

The primary data were obtained from real estate brokers in Chicago; these have been supplemented with evidence of real estate practices in other cities of the United States and with an examination of the ideology and practice of the real estate board. Since Chicago has had to absorb as many or more Negroes moving from the rural South as any other northern city, since rather similar discrimination against Negroes by real estate men has been reported in different parts of the country, and since the problems in housing for minority groups have not been more prominent in any other city than in Chicago, it is likely that the conclusions of this study would apply in considerable measure to other cities of the United States.

This work grew out of a doctoral dissertation completed in the Department of Sociology, University of Chicago, in 1958. A follow-up study of less extensive proportions made during 1964–1965 ascertained that the practices of real estate brokers and the supporting ideology had remained substantially unchanged.

Because it departs from the more usual approach of blaming the real estate man for discriminatory practice against Negroes, and instead attempts an objective, nonpartisan analysis of how real estate men view their own practices, this work brings out facts that may seem unfavorable both to real estate men and to Negroes. Therefore, I may be subject to "the hazard of institutional crossfire," to use Merton's phrase. Since the aim of this research was to discover and shed light on the factors contributing to the exclusion of Negroes from white areas, more attention was given to those brokers who practice exclusion than to those who do not. I hope that this approach will lead to a better understanding of the problem of segregation than has hitherto been attained.

When I undertook the present study, I used the word *Negro* throughout, since black Americans did not object to it then. I express here recognition of the standpoint supporting the use of the term *black*, but owing to the pressure of work and publication schedules, the substitution in deference to this standpoint was not possible.

ROSE HELPER

The University of Toledo, Toledo, Ohio
April, 1966; April, 1969

Acknowledgments

MY INITIAL interest in minority problems was heightened through association with Louis Wirth, a prime source of insight and clarification in this area of study. I was fortunate to have the advice and assistance of Joseph D. Lohman, Donald Horton, the late William C. Bradbury, and Peter H. Rossi in the development of the original dissertation. Valuable help in criticism of the Interview Schedule and at other stages of the study was given by Philip M. Hauser, Otis D. Duncan, Peter M. Blau, Clyde W. Hart, Donald J. Bogue, Leo A. Goodman, and the late Kermit Eby. I acknowledge gratefully the helpful counsel and interest of Ernest W. Burgess at crucial points in the work.

I cannot thank sufficiently all the real estate men and women — the respondents — who gave generously of their time and experience. To assure their anonymity, they will remain unnamed.

A special expression of appreciation is due Rachael M. Roberts, real estate saleswoman of Chicago, who gave valuable counsel from the beginning of the study, who was a constant source of information on real estate principles and practice, and who was always available for the solving of the day-by-day problems that arose as the study progressed.

In revising the dissertation for publication, I have received much important help from Janina M. Adamczyk, of the University of Toledo, who read with great care most of the manuscript, gave discerning criticisms, and made constructive suggestions. I am also much indebted to William H. Leckie, of the same university, who read most of the manuscript and gave valuable advice.

I wish to thank Mollie Helper Fleysher, Dorothy Milton, Margaret Pahlman Sering, and Albert Weisbord for their careful reading and criticism of Chapters I and II.

I thank the National Association of Real Estate Boards and the Chicago Real Estate Board, and acknowledge gratefully their generous cooperation and assistance in supplying important information and making necessary documents available for both the original dissertation and the present study. Members of these organizations gave willingly of their time and knowledge.

I appreciate the cooperation of the following organizations: the California Real Estate Association, the Ohio Commission on Civil Rights, the Illinois Commission on Human Relations, the Chicago Urban League, and the Chicago Commission on Human Relations.

I acknowledge gratefully the generous assistance and helpfulness of Mr. William F. Harrah, Council Committee Secretary and Sergeant at Arms of the Chicago City Council, who made available the records of the hearings on the 1963 Fair Housing Ordinance and other related documents.

I am indebted to Alderman Leon M. Despres of Chicago for a helpful conference and for allowing me to obtain information from files in his office.

I thank Sidney J. Kaplan, past Chairman, Department of Sociology and Anthropology, University of Toledo, for his encouragement and his helpfulness in making available the services of office personnel.

I wish to express appreciation to Mrs. Maybelle E. Jones for her careful typing of six chapters and other parts of the manuscript and her cooperation at every point.

The index was prepared by Mrs. Norma Yarde.

R. H.

Table of Contents

RACIAL POLICIES AND PRACTICES OF
REAL ESTATE BROKERS

The Problem in National Perspective

"IT's getting worse. I don't know what we're going to do about it. I mean Negroes coming up to Chicago from the South every day. They crowd in with their relatives. They don't have work. Then you get these hold-ups and rapes. Some here are just as bad. And all the moving. A Negro family buys a house in a nice neighborhood. Soon there are three families in that house. It's noisy, not kept up, and the white people don't like it and move away. What's going to become of Chicago? Some people say there'll be a black mayor. What are we going to do?"

Thus a white resident of Chicago expresses his point of view. Now a Negro resident speaks his mind: "These real estate men keep us out of homes we want to buy. We can pay for them. We've got a right to buy them. We've got to have housing. Why should we pay sky high rents for slum property or even better property when the white man pays less? Why can't we live where we want to? They tell us lies, 'It's rented,' 'It's sold.' Some come out and say, 'We can't sell to a Negro here. It's white.' The real estate man is to blame for all this discrimination. Either he won't let you in at all or he lets you in and soaks you in the price or rent."

Housing for Negroes in the North became a problem with their movement out of the South during and after World War I. Negro workers and their families flocking to industrial centers like Chicago, Detroit, Cleveland, and Buffalo crowded Negro areas of residence. The Negroes' need to spread into adjoining white neighborhoods and the efforts of white residents to keep them out through restrictive covenants and other means are well known. This tug of war continues although the restrictive covenant can no longer be legally enforced.

The real estate man's means of livelihood is deeply involved in this situation. In Chicago in 1917, the Real Estate Board decided upon a policy

3

toward the movement of Negroes to offset its effect on property values. The policy was to keep Negroes from moving into white residential areas haphazardly and to see to it that they filled a block solidly before being allowed to move into the next one.[1] A set of practices designed to keep Negroes out of white residential areas became established and has continued to the present. At the same time some real estate men violate this policy and facilitate the entry of Negroes into white neighborhoods. Thus, two sets of real estate practices in regard to Negroes exist in Chicago and other cities of the United States. Both sets, the restrictive and the unrestrictive, have given rise to serious problems.

This book attempts to ascertain more precisely than has been done hitherto the practices of real estate men in dealing with Negroes — especially those involving restriction — and to reveal some of the factors that contribute to these practices and result in exclusion of Negroes from white residential areas.

CONSEQUENCES OF RESTRICTIVE AND UNRESTRICTIVE PRACTICES IN REAL ESTATE

Owing to exclusion practices, well-to-do Negroes are hampered in their efforts to obtain better housing. They are not allowed to compete in an open housing market, and only older housing is open to them. Negroes with low incomes are compelled to accept the most dilapidated housing at rentals often far too high. Overcrowding frequently results. For many, low-rent public housing is the only solution. News of children's dying from fires or rat bites from time to time shocks public-minded citizens into a flurry of committee meetings, visits to the city fathers, writing of articles and making of speeches — all of which soon subsides with little accomplished until the next catastrophe makes headlines. Gradually, programs of slum clearance and urban renewal are eliminating some of the firetraps, but in relocating, the Negro family again encounters the difficulty of securing a home at a fair rental or price, in addition to suffering the upset of moving to a new neighborhood. The individual Negro citizen and leaders of organizations representing Negro interests voice much dissatisfaction and protest about the harmful results of restrictive practices. Some improvement has taken place, but in the main, the problem exists now as it did in preceding decades.

The U.S. Housing and Home Finance Agency wrote of the situation in 1950 as follows:

In acquiring decent housing, Negro and other racial minorities experience special difficulties beyond those which confront others. Census data of 1950, while indicating significant improvements in the housing conditions of nonwhites since 1940, reveal that 26.6 percent of nonfarm homes of nonwhites were dilapidated as compared to 5.4 percent for whites. Not only was the proportion of overcrowding in dwellings occupied by nonwhites four times as high as that for whites in 1950, but the extent of overcrowding among nonwhites had actually increased in 1950 over 1940 . . . Census data also attest that nonwhites have actually received less housing value and less home financing service per dollar spent by them for shelter than do whites and also less favorable home financing terms. These are the inevitable results of practices which have differentiated local housing markets and supplies on the basis of race and have tended generally to restrict or exclude nonwhites from the better housing and newly developed neighborhoods and thus constrict them generally into the poorer housing and largely within the more crowded, blighted, and slum areas.[2]

The situation in 1960 still revealed restrictive practices and inadequate housing for nonwhites. Robert C. Weaver, formerly administrator of the U.S. Housing and Home Finance Agency, writes in the foreword of the Agency's report, "Gains were made in nonwhite housing conditions, it is true, between 1950 and 1960. Yet a look at the facts makes it clear that as a group the nonwhites remain far less satisfactorily housed than whites."[3] The existence of restrictive practices is acknowledged in the same report as follows:

It was suggested earlier that the concentration of nonwhites in central cities, in contrast with the white families who are moving more and more to the suburbs, was not necessarily entirely voluntary. In part, it no doubt reflects the necessity of the nonwhites with their lower level of income to seek out older housing within their price range. Much of such housing is in central cities. Unquestionably another factor involved was the general lack of open occupancy during the 1950's in most of the new housing built in the suburbs . . . This tendency to move into older units certainly has been a factor associated with the lower quality of the nonwhite housing.[4]

By 1960, there had been some decrease in the amount of overcrowding in nonwhite dwelling units, but the overcrowding in dwellings occupied by nonwhite families was still over three times as high as that in those occupied by white families — 27 per cent against 8 per cent.[5] The contrast between white and nonwhite families is sharpened when the comparison is limited to seriously overcrowded units — units with 1.51 or more persons per room. In 1960, 13 per cent of all nonwhite units were seriously over-crowded, but only 2.4 per cent of all white units were.[6]

A crucial question for many years has been whether Negroes are paying more rent than white people for the same kind of accommodation. An authoritative yes was given in 1946,[7] and the situation remained the same in 1960. The report of the U.S. Housing and Home Finance Agency states,

Here again the lower level of rents and values is a reflection of the poorer quality of much of the housing in which nonwhite families are still obliged to live. These disparities in rents and values in 1950 and again in 1960 do not, however, fully reflect differences in the quality of the housing occupied by the two races. Because of limitations in the availability of housing to nonwhites, the rents and values of units they occupy often tend to run well above the levels at which houses of comparable quality can be obtained by white families.[8]

Two studies in Chicago confirm this statement. Duncan and Duncan point out that during the 1940–1950 decade rents rose for both whites and non-whites as the general level of consumer prices rose, but that in both absolute and relative terms the increase was greater for nonwhites than for whites. They conclude, "One thing seems quite clear: non-whites get less desirable housing for a given rent than do whites."[9] Duncan and Hauser found, in comparing white and nonwhite families with the same incomes, that the proportion of families in substandard dwellings was consistently higher for nonwhites than for whites. Twelve per cent of the white families as compared with 33 per cent of the nonwhite families who reported their family income for 1956 were living in substandard units.[10] When the rentals for substandard dwellings were considered, the median rental for white households in substandard units was $50, as compared with a median rental of $65 for nonwhite households in substandard units. "On the average, then, a $15 'bonus' is found," the authors say. If comparisons are restricted to substandard dwellings of the same size — that is, with the same number of bedrooms — nonwhites "consistently pay higher rents than whites, and the differential apparently increases as size of unit increases."[11] The authors state, "In sum, it is clear that nonwhite families receive less 'quality' per dollar spent on housing than do white families."[12]

In a study in Chicago completed in 1953, Wallace found that residential segregation of Negroes had increased rather than decreased.[13] In a study published in 1965, the Taeubers found high levels of residential segregation throughout the country. By an index of segregation developed in the latter study, a rating of 70 would indicate that 70 per cent of the non-white population of a city would have to move to other blocks to obtain an unsegregated distribution of population in the city. Indexes of residential segregation between whites and nonwhites were computed for 207 cities for 1960. The index values range from 60.4 to 98.1. Half the cities have values above 87.8 and a fourth above 91.7. The most striking finding is the universally high degree of segregation of the residences of whites and Negroes in all regions of the country and for all kinds of cities — large and small, industrial and commercial, metropolitan and suburban.[14] In Chicago the segregation index was found to be 92.6.[15]

Separate residential areas for Negroes and white people establish the basic structure for other forms of segregation, as Charles S. Johnson, Gunnar Myrdal, and other researchers in race relations have demonstrated.[16] Residential segregation in the North has led particularly to segregated schools. Grodzins has written, "If segregation is defined not in legal terms but in the numbers of students who attend all-Negro schools, then it is undoubtedly true that more Negro students are segregated in the schools of New York and Chicago than in any other cities or some states."[17] Although it is true that these cities have the problem in an accentuated form, practically all the large cities in the North have a pattern of segregated schools. In its report on segregation in the Chicago public schools, the U.S. Commission on Civil Rights found overcrowded schoolrooms, classes on double shifts, inexperienced teachers, inadequate psychological help, unimaginative curricula, and freezing of the Negro school population in zones of residential segregation. The neighborhood school policy — that is, the assumption that school attendance must conform to residential zones and that neighborhood schools most readily fulfill the educational needs of the community — was considered in the report as a factor perpetuating the pattern of racial segregation.[18]

Schools have been boycotted because of de facto school segregation in New York, Chicago, Boston, Buffalo, and Milwaukee.[19] As a result of the boycotts in New York and Chicago, plans have been advanced for experimenting with possible changes in the neighborhood policy.[20] In the meantime, the boycotts, although considered a success by the civil rights groups who promoted them, have apparently made the situation in the schools worse. In Chicago, teachers conceded that both Negro and white pupils had shown violence toward them before the stay-home boycotts of October 22, 1963, and February 25, 1964, but they contended that "a growing spirit of resentment, rage and rebellion has accompanied the bitter battle here against 'Jim Crow' schools." [21] Attacks on teachers by pupils and parents have been reported in both Chicago and New York.[22]

In the many cities where de facto school segregation is being fought, there is growing recognition that such segregation cannot be overcome until residential segregation is substantially reduced. The New York City Board of Education pointed out that "de facto segregation in housing exists on such a wide scale" that it could not possibly produce racial balance in all schools without wholesale shifts of school populations. The Board indicated that, much as it might favor integration, it is not the function of the schools to resolve what is basically a neighborhood housing problem.[23] Dan Dodson, consultant to the Board and student of intergroup relations, declared that there was presently no feasible way to desegregate many of the schools in the ghetto areas of large northern cities.[24] In a Gary, Indiana, case in which civil rights groups were attacking de facto segregation, the United States Supreme Court declined to review a lower court ruling that school boards have no constitutional duty to end racial imbalance resulting from housing patterns.[25]

The Negro protest against de facto school segregation is combined in some cities with protest against other inequities. In Chester, Pennsylvania, the Negroes began their revolt against school segregation and other alleged denials of civil rights, such as crowded, slum living conditions and unemployment, in the fall of 1963. A report states that "the local police contained the pressures for a while, but by April the State Police had been called in four times." [26] Again the segregated housing pattern accounted for the school pattern of de facto segregation and was at the root of other problems.

School integration alone is insufficient. The effects of long denial of equal opportunity in education and of a culturally deprived homelife make it imperative that many Negro children be given extra training so that they can catch up and benefit from integration with more fortunate white children.[27] The Head Start programs may be a beginning in this direction.

There are other consequences of housing segregation. The relation of housing to health and social adjustment has long been a topic of interest among lay and professional groups. Some cross-sectional studies have been made, but because of the numerous variables, it has been difficult to

8

evaluate accurately the effects of improved housing. In one study, the researchers took advantage of a unique opportunity to observe simultaneously a Negro population moved from substandard slum areas to a new public housing project (test group) and a similar population different only in that it continued to live in substandard housing (control group). The study followed approximately 1,000 Negro families (5,000 persons) over a 3-year period (1955–1958); all names were obtained from the Baltimore Housing Authority. Test rates of the incidence of illness were, in general, found to be lower than control rates for persons under 35 and especially for children.[28] In a 2-year "after" period, test children were considerably more likely to be promoted at a normal pace in school, whereas control children were held back more often for one or more semesters.[29] Among important housing items considered in the study which showed differences in quality of housing between test and control groups were the following: density and crowding, hot water and other facilities for cleanliness, toilet, sharing of facilities, window screening, rodent infestation, food storage, and refrigeration.[30]

Much evidence substantiates the relation between overcrowding and the incidence of communicable diseases, as can be seen from the outbreaks of poliomyelitis in 1952 and 1956. In 1956, the largest concentration of poliomyelitis in the United States occurred in Chicago, where more than 1,100 cases were reported, and the high rates were in the nonwhite areas.[31] In 1952, the cases had been scattered evenly throughout the city, and in 1956 early cases were also scattered widely, but "as the outbreak progressed, high rates developed only in those areas of the city characterized by a particularly dense population, a low socioeconomic status, and a high proportion of nonwhites."[32] In 1952, cases among nonwhites constituted 14 per cent of the total number of cases, as compared with 61 per cent in 1956.[33] The increase in nonwhite population over the 1952–1956 period cannot account for the large increase in the percentage of cases among nonwhites. The nonwhite population of Chicago increased from 14.1 per cent of the total population in 1950 to an estimated 18.9 per cent of the total in 1956.[34]

Overcrowding is a demonstrable factor in the spread of tuberculosis, says M. R. Lichtenstein, who states, "Tuberculosis is a disease of congested city areas in general, and death rates are twice as high in the nonwhite group all over the country."[35] This statement is amply attested to by a governmental report which states that for 1960 there were 5.1 deaths

9

per 100,000 of white and 13.1 per 100,000 of nonwhite population caused by tuberculosis, and there were 24.4 new active cases per 100,000 of white and 80.6 per 100,000 of nonwhite population.[36] In Chicago, the rates of tuberculosis are much higher in the overcrowded Negro areas than in the outlying districts where the housing is much better.[37]

As a consequence of segregation, public facilities for nonwhite neighborhoods tend to be neglected. Myrdal, writing of the South, says, "Virtually the whole range of . . . publicly administered facilities — such as hospitals, libraries, parks, and similar recreational facilities — are much poorer for Negroes than they are for whites . . ."[38] And again, "[Negroes] are segregated into districts where public services of water provision, sewage and garbage removal, street cleaning, street lighting, street paving, police protection and everything else is neglected or withheld while vice is often allowed."[39] In the North and West, where Negroes usually live in the oldest districts, the school buildings and other public institutional structures are old, parks and playgrounds are few, and the same neglect is found.[40] The continuing migration of Negroes from the South has contributed to the congestion of the old neighborhoods. Another problem for the resident of segregated, minority group areas is the difficulty of obtaining credit for mortgages. A man who tries to improve his house or to buy a house in a run-down district finds his path blocked by lending agencies.[41]

Lack of space in the home puts various strains upon family life. The maintenance of cleanliness, order, and privacy is difficult in cramped quarters. The unpleasantness of a crowded and dilapidated dwelling paves the way for family disorganization. The house becomes a place from which to escape.[42]

Students of race relations have long recognized that enforced segregation prevents understanding between dominant and minority groups and is harmful to both in a number of ways. There is the psychological interpretation of segregation by dominant and minority group members — in both groups it is assumed that enforced segregation connotes the inferiority of the segregated group. This assumption may and often does result in a lesser effort by members of minority groups and hence in lesser achievement, so that the effects of imposed segregation upon members of minority groups reinforce the original assumption of their inferiority. This meaning of enforced segregation was the crucial factor in the unanimous decision of the United States Supreme Court declaring segregation in public schools to be unconstitutional. Chief Justice Warren, writing the decision, said,

> To separate them [Negroes] from others of similar age and qualifications solely because of their race generates a feeling of inferiority as to their status in the community that may affect their hearts and minds in a way unlikely ever to be undone . . .

> A sense of inferiority affects the motivation of a child to learn. Segregation . . . has a tendency to retard the educational and mental development of Negro children and to deprive them of some of the benefits they would receive from a racially integrated school system. . . .

> We conclude that in the field of public education the doctrine of "separate but equal" has no place. Separate educational facilities are inherently unequal.[43]

Apart from the psychological effects of the interpretation of enforced segregation, the social isolation resulting from segregation deprives the minority group of socially useful associations and cultural stimulation. Segregation, by reducing social intercourse between members of dominant and minority groups, strengthens the tendency of white people to see Negroes in the mass instead of as individuals, perpetuates ignorance and stereotyping, and leads to misunderstanding, mistrust, and hostility between the racial groups.[44]

There are marked effects of enforced segregation on the members of the dominant group themselves. In a social-psychological survey, 849 social scientists who possessed special qualifications in the field of race relations were asked their views on enforced segregation. Eighty-three per cent of the 517 who replied said they believed segregation had detrimental effects on the group that enforced it. Among these effects were the anxiety aroused lest the segregated people revolt and get out of hand, and also the self-deception those who enforce segregation have to practice to square their behavior with the democratic creed.[45] This conclusion is akin to the one reached by Myrdal. He interprets the problem of race relations in the United States as a moral conflict in the heart of the American. The American is torn between the valuations of the "American Creed" — where he "thinks, talks, and acts under the influence of high national and Christian precepts" — and the valuations on specific planes of individual and group living — where considerations of community prestige, conformity, and group prejudice against particular persons or types of people influence him.[46] Ninety per cent of the 517 social scientists said they believed en-

11

forced segregation had detrimental effects on the segregated group, even if equal facilities were provided.

Segregation leads to the development of a social climate within which racial tensions are likely to break out into violence. During and just after World War I, there were a number of race riots in northern cities, largely owing to the heavy migration of Negroes from the South and the consequent displacement of some whites in jobs and residences.[47] There was some recurrence of riots at the beginning of World War II, in particular, the Detroit riot. Recently violence on the part of Negro youth appears to be largely a direct consequence of discrimination and of the misery of life in the segregated slum area and in a deprived home. In addition to teachers, other persons and establishments have been attacked. In Chicago, a gang of at least 30 students from three high schools went on the rampage after being released from classes for the summer. They beat and robbed a number of persons, threatened others with gun and knife, took money and cases of pop from a store, and hurled pop bottles at a bus and a policeman.[48] In New York City, attacks on white persons by bands of young Negroes created an atmosphere of crisis. During one weekend, marauding gangs of Negro youths terrorized whites on four subway trains and a ferryboat.[49] In Ypsilanti, Michigan, Negro youths smashed car windows and double-paned glass windows in a drive-in and threw rocks at a police patrol car, but a gang of white youths also broke car windows in the Negro area.[50]

More general rioting broke out in Harlem and Brooklyn in New York City, in Rochester, in Jersey City, Elizabeth, and Paterson, New Jersey, in Dixmoor, a suburb of Chicago, and in Philadelphia.[51] Perhaps the most telling account to date of the consequences for the minority group of residential segregation and other discrimination is the study of Harlem by Harlem Youth Opportunities Unlimited (HARYOU).

This study revealed that the average resident of Harlem is in a low income bracket and resides in an unsafe, deteriorated, and overcrowded tenement. It also indicated "massive deterioration of the fabric of society and its institutions" and warned that unless something were done to correct the situation, the residents of Harlem might resort to violence in their frustration.[52] Violence and rioting did erupt in Harlem. Also, because of the intolerable housing conditions there, more than 13,000 persons living in more than 250 substandard tenements staged a rent strike dramatized by "rat marches" on City Hall.[53] A past president of the New York chapter

of the National Association for the Advancement of Colored People predicted that riots and trouble will continue in Harlem "until the Negroes
are allowed to break out of their slum." [54] The situation in Cleveland was
described as being similar to that in New York by the executive secretary
of the local NAACP chapter. "On the East Side in Cleveland, as in Harlem,"
he said, "Negroes are packed into a slum from which they are not allowed to escape, and are oppressed by a city administration which employs
the tactics of police brutality." He saw similar conditions all over the
country.[55] In 1965 there was the serious rioting in Watts in Los Angeles,
California,[56] and about the same time Chicago also had an evening of rioting.[57] In the summer of 1967, rioting and violence broke out in Fresno,
Sacramento, Long Beach, Los Angeles, and San Bernardino, California;
Tampa, Florida; Atlanta, Georgia; Durham, North Carolina; Memphis,
Tennessee; Kansas City, Missouri; Waterloo, Iowa; Detroit, Flint, Grand
Rapids, Lansing, Benton Harbor, and Saginaw, Michigan; Minneapolis,
Minnesota; Milwaukee, Wisconsin; Cairo, Chicago, East St. Louis, Elgin,
and Peoria, Illinois; South Bend, Indiana; Cincinnati, Cleveland, Dayton,
Youngstown, Toledo, Hamilton, Lorain, Sandusky, and Springfield, Ohio;
Buffalo, New York, Poughkeepsie, Albany, Mount Vernon, Newburgh,
and New Rochelle, New York; Newark, Plainsfield, Jersey City, Paterson,
Montclair, Elizabeth, New Brunswick, Palmyra, Passaic, and Camden,
New Jersey; Erie and Philadelphia, Pennsylvania; Cambridge, Maryland;
Wilmington, Delaware; Hartford, Connecticut; Providence, Rhode Island;
Boston, Massachusetts; and other communities.[58] The violence in Detroit,
Newark, and Milwaukee, was particularly intense.

Harmful consequences of the pattern of residential segregation have
been noted in the urban economic and political life of Chicago and other
cities of the North. Some students of urban affairs foresee a black Chicago
and a white periphery, with a decline in the standards of retail business in
the city and the replacement of white by Negro city fathers, a situation
which could intensify the troubled relations between the races.[59]

Finally, residential segregation has unfavorable consequences for the
international relations of the United States. Any form of discrimination
against nonwhite people has an incalculably adverse effect on the position
of the United States as a leader in world affairs. Discrimination is an
Achilles' heel in which barbs of criticism from nonwhite and white coun-
tries alike find their mark.

Just as the restrictive practices have given rise to many troubles in the lives of the Negro population, so the set of practices that facilitate the entry of Negroes into white areas creates serious problems for the white population. What white people think, feel, and say about the movement of Negroes into their neighborhoods has been recorded in a systematic way in only a few studies,[60] but their moving away from many of such areas has been widely observed and in one case carefully studied.[61]

All in all, the exclusion of Negroes from white areas and their entry into certain white neighborhoods have resulted in a number of severe problems for white and Negro citizens alike and for the United States as a whole, both internally and in the world at large. Disturbing events point to the crucial importance of the problem of residential segregation for the welfare of the country; residential segregation in the North has been labeled "our most serious of human problems." [62]

Purpose and Method of the Study

NEGROES generally have put much of the blame for discrimination in housing on the white real estate man because he channels the property in white neighborhoods to the buyer or renter. He is also accused of influencing white people against living with Negroes and thus of promoting racial residential segregation. Others, too, are blamed, but he is presented as the chief villain.

More objective observers who have written about the problem of discrimination in housing for minority groups, and particularly for the Negro group, have also treated the real estate man as a culprit and condemned him without giving him an opportunity to present his own point of view. On the basis of their kind of research and analysis, they have assumed that they know what ideas and motives underlie his racial policies and practices, but they have not let him explain his practices as he sees and understands them in the context of his years of experience in dealing with the people of white neighborhoods. In a number of surveys on minority housing, real estate men have been questioned, but incompletely and superficially.* Statements of the National Association of Real Estate Boards (NAREB) have been published, and books have been written by individual real estate men, usually in high positions in real estate organizations, but the ideas and convictions of the ordinary real estate brokers have not been heard. It seems to be generally assumed that the statements of policy of NAREB are identical with the beliefs of the men and women practicing in real estate. Actually, there is much likeness, but differences have been completely disregarded.

* The surveys sought to ascertain incidence and types of discriminatory practices. Few asked for the reasons underlying the practices. These surveys are reported in Chapter III. See p. 55.

In addition, although the beliefs, feelings, and wishes of white people about the movement of Negroes into their residential areas are of great importance in this whole question, not only have few studied them, but the writers on discrimination in housing have paid little attention to the findings of what studies there have been.

What actually are the real estate broker's policies and practices, especially where restriction is involved? How does he think about them and explain them according to his own experiences and convictions? What are the factors that affect his practices and help maintain them? Even such serious students of problems in minority housing as Robert C. Weaver, Charles Abrams, Herman H. Long, and the late Charles S. Johnson criticize the role of the real estate broker as promoter of residential segregation without firsthand research about how it is that the real estate broker acts as he does.[1] The sincerity and scholarly contributions of those who have concerned themselves with the problem of minority housing must be recognized, but a new approach to the problem seems indicated.

The present study is an attempt to answer these questions. It lets the real estate man speak for himself. To this end a research technique had to be developed that would elicit what the real estate man thinks and give him an opportunity to express *his* point of view. A second technique was an independent study of the real estate board itself. In the examination of previous research, no study was found that attempted to uncover the basic racial policies and practices of real estate men, as does this study. Furthermore, as the real estate man has revealed his practices and given his reasons for their being what they are, he has also disclosed what, in his experience, are the feelings, wishes, and beliefs of white people about Negroes and segregation.

THE REAL ESTATE INSTITUTION

To understand the real estate man's racial practices as he himself understands them, it is necessary to see him and his beliefs and practices in the larger context of his societal setting. Two important facts, themselves interrelated, need now to be taken into consideration.

First, insofar as the relations between white and Negro groups are being investigated, race relations are the frame of reference. Because it is a minority group * in the United States, the Negro group must be studied

* Louis Wirth defined a minority group as a "group of people who, because of their physical or cultural characteristics, are singled out from the others in the so-

through its relation to the dominant, white group, and thus, dominant-minority group relations become the second frame of reference. To understand the relations between Negro and white people, one must recognize that dominant-minority group relations develop and exist largely within the institutional framework of the dominant group, and one must also possess a thorough knowledge of the social structure and the particular institutions within which and through which these relations came to be what they are. This approach is amply supported by a number of sociologists.[2]

Second, the present analysis focuses on the restrictions that the dominant group imposes upon the residential movement of the minority group. Particularly, the aim in this study is to explore and reveal some of the factors that keep Negroes from white residential areas. One concerned with the racial policies and practices of real estate men cannot avoid being concerned with the real estate institution, for it is within the framework of the institution that the racial policies and practices of real estate men took shape and are maintained. And it is through the real estate men, the practitioners of the institution, that these racial policies and practices have to be understood. Thus, the study of the restriction on housing of the minority group becomes largely the study of the real estate institution, the third and most relevant frame of reference. This institution is the force operating behind the real estate man's practices.

To show the relation between the two facts presented above, it can be said that dominant-minority group relations arise and exist in the social structure of the dominant group, and that the racial practices of real estate men develop in the real estate institution within the context of the dominant-minority group relations present in the society. Although the primary purpose here is to understand a problem in dominant-minority group relations between groups differing in race, the approach most fruitful in yielding insight into the problem channels the research through the institution.

The procedure, then, was to investigate racial policies and practices among real estate men, particularly those of a restrictive nature, in the context of the totality of the real estate institution — that is, as an integral part of the total "life" of the institution. This involved ascertaining the rela-

ciety in which they live for differential and unequal treatment, and who therefore regard themselves as objects of collective discrimination" ("The Problem of Minority Groups," p. 347).

17

tion of the racial policies and practices to the main goals of the institution, and discovering how these are the racial policies and practices of real estate firms and independent brokers. The real estate institution is understood here to mean the whole set of arrangements in daily operation that meet, more or less adequately, the need of shelter — in other words, all the established forms of the real estate business. The unit organizations in the real estate institution are the individual businesses. The concern of this study is with the real estate institution in its aspects of brokerage and management only, and with the policies and practices of real estate brokers and management agents toward a racial minority group, the Negroes.

THE PRELIMINARY INTERVIEWS

Factors Affecting the Broker's Racial Policies and Practices

The question investigated in this study arose from a project in New York City in 1951 in which 30 interviews were held with real estate and real estate investment men. Questions about the reasons for excluding Negroes from white residential areas brought a variety of answers and raised another question, How much did different outlooks and different external conditions have to do with this practice? Ten exploratory interviews in Chicago in 1953 strengthened the impression that a number of factors were involved, the most outstanding of which was the broker's way of thinking about Negroes in relation to real estate interests. A whole set of conceptual formulations came to light in each real estate man's replies, and, after expressing these as apparently his own convictions, he would mention certain situational elements bearing on the question and speak of these as outside forces compelling him to act in a prescribed way.

From the 40 interviews and from previous research in Negro and other minority housing, it became clear that, to understand how it is that the racial policies and practices of real estate men are what they are, it is necessary to know what the content of the broker's thinking is which leads to his decisions about Negroes. Here a distinction needs to be made between, on the one hand, the broker's own convictions as a factor influencing his decisions — whether these convictions are the result of personal and business experience or are internalized judgments accepted from others — and, on the other hand, situational elements on which he depends and which he therefore must take into account in his decisions, regardless of what he himself believes. The situational elements may support his convictions or conflict with them and may outweigh them by appeal or by threat. They

18

may include real estate transactions or other events over which he has no control that affect his business, and may include the actions or known stand of persons or organizations as they pertain to him. Also related to the broker's decisions are his personal sentiments toward Negroes and the community in which he works.

THE BROKER'S IDEOLOGY

The concept of ideology is central to this study. Sociologists have given different meanings to this concept, depending on the frame of reference in which they analyzed it. A meaning relevant here is Mannheim's "total conception" of ideology — the "ideology of an age or of a concrete historico-social group . . . when we are concerned with the characteristics and composition of the total structure of the mind of this epoch or of this group." [3] Parsons initially defines an ideology as "a system of beliefs, held in common by the members of a collectivity . . ." [4] In spite of the differences in the definitions and interpretations of different sociologists, the concept itself has been recognized as a useful analytic tool. The working definition of ideology used in this study combines common elements of several definitions proposed by sociologists: "a set of related beliefs shared by the members of an organized group." It is necessary to include in the definition of institutional ideology the notion that the ideas and beliefs of the ideology are related to values that inhere in and grow out of the purpose of the institution and, when realized, benefit in some way the adherents of the institution and also the society. The ideology of an institution might be considered a core of beliefs and values established early in its development, around which a body of policy appropriate for the realization of the goals consonant with these beliefs and values has grown up, and in the light of which new policy is formed in answer to changes in the social situation affecting the institution. Changes in beliefs at the core may take place over a period of time.

The specific task of both the preliminary and the main studies was the search for the ideology of real estate men and particularly for those aspects of it which underlie their racial policies and practices — that is, their real estate ideology and their racial real estate ideology. For purposes of analysis, each will be considered alone as well as in relation to the other.

The real estate ideology and the racial real estate ideology of the real estate institution, insofar as these can be determined, must be distinguished from those of the practicing real estate man. Variations and divergences

19

from the accepted institutional ideology must be taken into account for the real estate man interpreting and applying the institutional ideology day by day.

In most of the 40 preliminary interviews, the real estate men expressed the exclusion ideology. It contains judgments mostly unfavorable to Negroes and supports a policy and practice of exclusion of Negroes from white residential areas — with all its ramifications of beliefs, attendant ideas, and arguments. In several interviews, the respondents were mostly favorable toward Negroes in relation to real estate and leaned toward the possibility and the advantages of residential integration; the set of beliefs behind this kind of response is called here the integration ideology. Variations were found in addition to these two types. For example, in some preliminary interviews, the judgments balanced between favorable and unfavorable views, and the set of beliefs behind these responses is called the intermediate ideology. These three ideologies are discussed in detail in Chapter IX in connection with the study proper.

The three racial real estate ideologies include five distinct components — namely, the real estate broker's beliefs about Negroes in relation to real estate; his beliefs about Negroes as people; his beliefs about the beliefs, feelings, and wishes of white people about Negroes; his beliefs about the consequences of certain lines of action in his business operations with regard to Negroes; and his idea of the function that his racial practices serve in his business, in his immediate community, and in the city at large.

RELATION BETWEEN IDEOLOGY, POLICY, AND PRACTICE

It is a leading idea of the present study that the racial real estate ideology of the real estate brokers in the selected community areas contributes to their racial policies and practices. In the analysis of the relation between belief and action, it must not be assumed that thought and action are independent of one another, for there is a constant interweaving of them in every person. A policy is a potential action, and the acting out of a policy is directed from moment to moment by judgments, assessments, and possible reappraisals. An interplay of thought and action is part of the interaction of the person with others and with himself.[5] Here the continuous interplay between reflection and action in the mind is distinguished from the significance for action of certain strongly held beliefs that refer to an ideology and become a directive for action in the person's most significant relations. Such strongly held beliefs may transcend all other con-

20

siderations, and they appeared to enter into the preliminary respondents' decision-making in transactions with Negroes.

A number of sociologists and other thinkers have affirmed that ideas and beliefs have a motivational effect on social action. Although some, such as Marx [6] and Pareto, belittle the effect of ideas on action, there are others, Weber in particular, who look upon ideas as powerful, driving forces in the historical processes. However, Weber is careful not to ascribe a direct or full causal relation between them, attempting only to clarify the part that religious motives have played in the "developing web" of modern culture.[7] Dewey posits a close relation between belief and action, defining belief as the outcome of inquiry in a condition so settled that it carries with it a readiness to act on the basis of the belief, overtly or in imagination.[8]

To Parsons, the essential feature of an ideology is as a directive for action in accord with the belief system and thereby contributing to the welfare of the collectivity. An ideology, he says, is directed toward, and is consistent with, the values on the continued fulfillment of which the integration of the collectivity depends.[9] Parsons finds that ideologies have functions directly homologous with those of rationalization in the personality system, in that the ideology will gloss over and play down any conflicting elements in the value system of the society that threaten its stability.[10] He does not equate ideology with rationalization — a position entirely in keeping with my own view, which is that an ideology may or may not include elements of rationalization.

Copeland, Johnson, and Myrdal have dealt with ideology and its relation to social conduct in race relations in the United States. All three assign great importance to ideology for its effect on action, but at the same time insist upon its character as rationalization. Copeland says that, once having arisen, as in the South, the ideology becomes a creative factor in the social process — its adherents apply it to new situations, using new fictions, and constantly present new rationalizations.[11] Charles S. Johnson applies the important relation he sees between belief and action to the race system and states that in its total effect the racial ideology of the dominant society defines the color line more certainly than either the laws or the customs. "It is in this sphere," he says, "that we must seek the explanation of the behavior of whites in their social relations with Negroes." [12] Myrdal, too, speaks of the ideology that developed in the South to defend slavery, that was retained to justify the social organization of Negro-white relations which succeeded slavery, and that was used also in the North to justify its course after the national compromise of the 1870's. He concludes, from the actual power structure in the United States, that what white people think about Negroes forms part of the vicious circle keeping Negroes down.[13] In particular, he draws attention to the need for studying the relation between belief and action, saying that "there have been many studies of the type of racial beliefs held and of the extent to which they are held, but few attempts to show their relation to the functioning of society." [14]

Whether they judge it rationalization or real motive, a number of sociologists believe that ideology has an important effect upon action. A similar recognition of the relation between ideology and action rose in the course of the analysis of the preliminary interviews. This relation was observed in the early respondents' statements in which a group of strongly held beliefs — linked, it seemed, to an ideology — were brought forward to explain choices of action.

The preliminary interviews point to a close relation between the broker's racial real estate ideology and his racial policies and practices and suggest that the racial ideology enters into the formation of these policies and practices. This seems true particularly of the exclusion ideology. It appears that the business acts of the real estate man who holds this ideology are in large part determined by it, whether in his consideration of requests from Negroes or in his refusal to consider their requests at all. Some of the beliefs involved in the exclusion ideology may be shown to be myth, whereas others have a realistic basis. However, when the question of a Negro as a prospective tenant or buyer comes up, these beliefs rise in the real estate man's mind to play a definite part in his decision, and to clarify this part became the primary task of this investigation. On the basis of the preliminary interviews, it was hypothesized that the holding of the exclusion ideology and the practice of exclusion of Negroes from white residential areas would be positively associated.

External Influences

The racial real estate ideology is not the only thing that affects the broker's racial policies and practices. There are external influences and conditions that the broker recognizes as important for his business. Just as any individual in defining a situation must, to use Thomas and Znaniecki's phrase, "take social meanings into account, interpret his experience not exclusively in terms of his own needs and wishes, but also in terms of the traditions, customs, beliefs, aspirations of his social milieu," [15] so the broker defines the elements in his business situation by interpreting them in the light of real estate tenet and tradition, community expectations, and his own business needs, and he acts in accord with his definition of the situation.

From among the external influences and conditions affecting the broker's racial policies and practices as revealed in the 40 preliminary interviews, four were selected for investigation. They are the real estate board; the lending agency; the community — including events, organizations, and persons; and particular sources of economic gain related both to a policy of exclusion and to racial change in the community. These four external factors will be considered in this study as they are experienced by the broker in the operation of his business. The real estate men and women in this book express conclusions which are considered judgments formed over years of practice and arrived at in circumstances when the prospering of the business depended on their accuracy.

THE REAL ESTATE BOARD

A distinction must be made among the real estate institution (in its brokerage and management aspects), the real estate board, the practitioners of the real estate institution, and the members of the board. The real estate board represents the real estate business in the economic organization of the country at large, but it is separate and distinct from the individual real estate businesses considered as economic units. Insofar as it can exert pressure, direct or indirect, on the broker to pursue or to desist from some line of action, the real estate board is an external influence for the broker. However, the preliminary interviews indicated that the board wields a particular kind of influence — one of professional and moral authority. The board defines and represents real estate interests locally and nationally. It is the trade association of real estate men and the center of information about real estate affairs. The board reserves for itself the right to define the broker's role in the community and seeks to raise his status to that of a professional. Over the years it has set up standards and rules that its members are expected to observe both for the sake of real estate interests and for their own good; these have been unified into a Code of Ethics by NAREB and are accepted by the local real estate boards. This Code was the result of much discussion and of consensus through all the levels of NAREB.

A relatively small proportion of the participants in the real estate institution are members of boards.[16] The board controls its members more directly than nonmembers. It can expel members who violate the Code. But the individual broker also affects the institution. He makes the day-by-day decisions through which the institutional values are realized and re-created. The present-day brokers did not create the racial practices of the institution, but received them along with all the other practices of the real estate business. However, they maintain these practices, their actions to meet new demands could change the practices, and their conception of the practices could alter the institutional ideology itself.

The questions here are what kind of influence the board has over its members and nonmembers and what the relation is between the board and its members and the board and nonmembers, so that we may know in what way the board affects the broker's racial policies and practices.

THE COMMUNITY

The broker exercises control over the community* in some matters and it controls him in others. His control over the community resides initially in the functions he fulfills, particularly in the advisory role which he, as an expert, performs in each of his functions. The preliminary interviews reveal the complex and special relation of the real estate broker with his community. He deals with people about their homes, which are of great meaning in their lives, and thus he is related to the community more closely than most other businessmen. Generally speaking, people ask for and follow the broker's advice when buying, selling, renting, altering, insuring, trading, and appraising property. He can determine some of the occupants of the neighborhood dwellings. He can help to change land use, standards of occupancy, and the racial and ethnic pattern of occupancy in the area.

On the other hand, the real estate broker is dependent on the people of his community — whether they are his clients or not — and also on the people of adjoining areas. His clients can withdraw their patronage, but in this his position is like that of other business and professional men. The mere rumor of the entry of "undesirable occupancy" can damage his business. Much of the transferring of property in the community is outside his con-

---

* The term community is used here to mean "community area" — that is, a division of a city — and refers specifically to the community area in which the broker operates. He usually has his office in the community area in which he operates, and sometimes lives in the area as well. A broker often operates in more than one community area.

trol. His feeling of identification with his community appears also to be of importance; data from the preliminary interviews pointed to the broker's social integration into and sense of identification with the community as a possible reason for his maintenance of a policy of exclusion. The present study investigates the pressures and powers involved in the broker-community relation to clarify the question of how the community may affect the broker's racial policies and practices.

ECONOMIC GAIN

The policy of exclusion has been called a source of moneymaking for those who own or manage deteriorated or slum property. It is said that, if Negroes had access to an open housing market, much of slum property that they now occupy because of restriction would cease to bring high returns to the owners of such property. This may well be true, but the preliminary data revealed that such management is not rewarding to the real estate agents who do it. Only the broker-investor who charges high rents and encourages overcrowding profits from this situation.

The real estate men recognized a more profound aspect of economic gain as a factor in exclusion, the primary control of land and property. They were of the opinion that, when property is transferred from white to Negro hands, it is lost to the white group forever. Hence the opportunities for future gain that that property might offer to white buyers are lost, and all possibilities for future control in the community by ownership of the land and property are also lost. The conclusion was based on the view that Negroes resell property less often than do white people, and that the white people seldom buy and live in property that has been occupied by Negroes. In addition, when such property is sold, the broker in charge is usually Negro. The question of restriction, Negro occupancy of slum property, and economic gain therefrom will be considered to some extent in this study (see pp. 185–186).

THE LENDING AGENCY

The lending agency may be defined here as a situational element contributing to the maintenance of a policy of exclusion by real estate brokers. According to the preliminary interview data, lending agencies, by refusing to make loans in certain areas, have kept brokers from making sales to Negroes or to white people in that area. This study investigates the

25

broker's experience with the lending agency in obtaining mortgages on sales to Negroes and in the ways in which it may restrain or coerce the broker in his racial policy.

ADVANTAGES OF DEVIANT BEHAVIOR

The influx of Negroes during and after World War I led to the Chicago Real Estate Board to lay down a policy of block-by-block concentration of Negroes (see pp. 4, 224–226). Since the Board has not affirmed any change in this policy, the term "deviant behavior" is properly applied to the actions of brokers that in any way contribute to Negroes' buying or renting in white residential areas of standard housing, and the adjective "deviant" is properly applied to such action or to the broker who so acts, whatever his motive may be.

The deviant broker may be acting earnestly and consistently in accord with a genuine integration ideology — that is, he may look upon the integration of Negroes in the white community as a social good and may even exercise moral courage to help bring about harmonious interracial living. A more common factor in brokers' deviant behavior is pecuniary gain. This study seeks to examine how it is that there are brokers who regularly or at certain times sell property in white residential areas to Negro citizens.

THE PLAN OF THE STUDY

The Areas Selected

It was beyond the scope of the study to include areas that would encompass the gamut of racial change — at one extreme, an area relatively distant from the line of movement of the Negro population; at the other extreme, an area which has been predominantly Negro for many years. Therefore, it was decided to select three areas in which the main effects and problems for the real estate man and the community are imminent: Area A, an area of recent and current settlement by Negroes; Area B, an area of fairly established Negro settlement; and Area C, an area of possible settlement by Negroes — that is, one adjacent to an area which Negroes have already entered. The three areas adjoin one another, in the order named, on the South Side of Chicago. The real estate men who took part in the study are identified only by number (to protect their anonymity) and by area.

Purpose and Method of the Study

Area A (recent and current settlement by Negroes) has had Negro residents for at least fifty years, but mostly because they worked in the neighborhood and lived near the hotels, private homes, and other places where they worked. There had long been five little pockets of Negro residence in the area, according to respondents 41A and 56A. Citizen groups have been and are attempting to stabilize Area A as interracial and to curb illegal conversions in it. Sections of the area are still white. Apart from the established Negro residents, Negroes began to move into the area in considerable numbers from 1948 on. An urban renewal program is under way.

In 1956, a survey [17] of Area A summarized the total white and nonwhite population for 1950 and 1956:

	U.S. Census of 1950	Survey in 1956	Change, 1950–1956 No.	%
White	67,349	47,360	−19,989	−29.7
Nonwhite	4,340	27,502	23,162	533.4
Total	71,689	74,862	3,173	4.4

The nonwhite population, 6.1 per cent of the total population of Area A in 1950, increased to 36.7 per cent. The estimated ethnic composition of the nonwhite population of Area A is also given in the survey:

	No.	%
Negro	24,399	89.0
Mexican and Puerto Rican	718	2.6
Oriental	1,545	5.6
Other	758	2.8
Total ....,, ...	27,420	100.0

Obviously, the Negro group constituted the major portion of the nonwhite population of Area A in 1956: 32.6 per cent of the total population of the area. However, it is hardly possible to speak of Area A as a whole with reference to its percentage of Negro or nonwhite population, because the percentage distribution of nonwhite population in the 19 tracts of the area ranged from less than 1 per cent to over 75 per cent, and 9 of the tracts had a nonwhite population of under 15 per cent. Several of the respondents looked upon Area A as consisting of several areas — 2 white, 2 mixed, and 2 predominantly Negro.

A survey of 15 of the 19 tracts in Area A found that the total population had decreased from 55,206 in 1950 to 45,577 in 1960, and the white population from 52,375 to 27,214, but the Negro population had increased from 1,757 (3.2 per cent) to 17,163 (37.7 per cent) and the other races from 1,074 (1.9 per cent) to 1,200 (2.6 per cent).[18] The authors state, "Though the total population of [Area A] declined markedly during the 1950's as a result of demolition for urban renewal projects, the Negro population increased until it comprised 38 per cent of the total by 1960. Germans and Russians (Jews) were still the predominant groups of foreign stock in 1960. A small group of Puerto Ricans also resided in the community in 1960." [19]

AREA B

Area B (relatively established Negro settlement) had in 1950 a total population of 80,699, a white population of 48,368 (60.0 per cent), a Negro population of 31,329 (38.8 per cent), and a total of other races of 1,002 (1.2 per cent). Negroes had been coming into this area for some years before 1948, and from 1948 on, the Negro population grew much more rapidly in Area B than in Area A. The rapid increase was due partly to the dilapidation of a number of its many apartment buildings and rooming houses and partly to their owners' readiness to sell. In 1960, the total population was 81,279, but the white population had declined to 8,450 (10.4 per cent), the Negro population had increased to 72,397 (89.1 per cent), and the total of other races had declined to 432 (0.5 per cent).[20] Although Area B, unlike Area A, is looked upon as a largely Negro area, it is not so old an area of Negro settlement as other Negro areas in the city.

AREA C

Area C (the area of possible settlement by Negroes) had in 1950 a total population of 79,336, almost all white. The Negro population numbered 182 (0.2 per cent). By 1960, the total population had decreased to 73,086, and the Negro population had increased to almost 10 per cent of the total population, numbering 7,018.[21] Area C is still largely a white area, except for a small part, Area CX, at its northwestern extremity; Negroes entered this corner in considerable numbers in the early 1950's. Area CX is separated from Area C proper by a major traffic artery. Directly east of Area CX, and on the other side of the traffic artery, are choice homes and a border of good apartment buildings — Area CY. There have been sales to Negroes in CY and apartments have been occupied by them. This has happened also, to a lesser extent, in more southerly parts of the area. The respondents consider Areas CX and CY to be special areas within Area C

28

because of their history and particular situation. In C, as in Area A, there are many good homes and apartment buildings.

The Respondents

The characteristics of the universe were: White real estate brokers engaged in the selling and/or managing of property wholly or partly residential in one or more of the three areas selected for the study (managing includes the renting of property). For purposes of random selection, a real estate firm of any size and an independent broker were considered equal, each counting as one. If he was inactive or spent over half his time on other business in or out of the city, an independent broker was excluded (this applied to very few).

The real estate section of the telephone directory of the three areas for 1954 was used as a guide to obtain the universe. Inquiry by telephone revealed who in the real estate section did not possess the necessary characteristics; their names were deleted. In Areas A and B, firms and independent brokers who were found in the course of the study to be operating in these areas were included, even though their names did not appear in the directory list. This could not be done in Area C because of the samples drawn. Using the boundaries of the three areas as determined by the *Local Community Fact Book for Chicago 1950* (except for the northern boundary of Area A), I divided the names in the tentative universe into three groups according to the area where the firm or broker was located.[22]

Because the total number of real estate men in Area A and the total in Area B were both smaller than that of Area C, I decided to interview all the real estate men in Areas A and B and to follow this design for Area C: a sample of 50 per cent of the Board members, a sample of 50 per cent of the nonmembers, the three branch firms (separately, since they are in a position somewhat different from that of the independent firm), and the six firms of Area CX (separately, because their situation is different from that of the rest of the real estate men in Area C). The two samples of 50 per cent were drawn from their respective universes after the names of the branch firms and the firms in Area CX had been withdrawn. In the analysis of the data, the two samples of 50 per cent were combined for certain questions. The totals for Areas A and B underwent some change because names were eliminated and others added in accordance with the criteria for the inclusion and exclusion of firms and brokers.

29

The Interviews

The primary method of obtaining data on racial practices, ideology, and other factors affecting practice was the interview, following the Interview Schedule reproduced in Appendix A. Various kinds of documentary data — such as letters, circulars, newspapers, governmental reports, and published literature — were also used, particularly for information about the Board. Before the study was undertaken, 10 exploratory interviews were held with leading real estate men in Chicago and 2 with heads of lending agencies. Since these interviews were favorably received, the study was planned, and a schedule was tested in 9 interviews in areas similar to those of the study. The Interview Schedule contains 43 main questions; with subquestions there are 120 questions in all. Those questions eliciting data about policy, practice, and personal background are structured, and those on ideology are open-ended.

The Interview Schedule contained few questions about personal background, because the study did not address itself to analyzing the relation between personality variables and ideology. This study was designed to investigate the racial practices of real estate men and some of the factors contributing to these practices — in particular, ideology. However, the Interview Schedule was constructed to invite the expression of all considerations touching on Negroes and real estate interests.

Although the Interview Schedule was designed to reduce evasion, I also showed each respondent a letter from the Chairman of the Department of Sociology at the University of Chicago assuring him that his anonymity would be protected, and I reassured him of this when I asked for the interview and again at the beginning of the interview. In the Interview Schedule, interlocking questions and the same question in somewhat different forms directed to the more sensitive points under investigation were introduced at certain intervals and in certain positions among the questions of the Schedule. The consistency of answers could then be checked. In addition, I probed at length to draw out the respondent's meaning and watched for unwitting revelations in answers to other questions.

The interviews were held with the chief executive (president, vice-president, or manager) of the firm or with a member of the firm authorized to represent it. Only in two cases was the interview held with a junior member of the firm. The interview was held directly with independent brokers in all cases. The interviewing went on from May 15, 1955, to approximately March 15, 1956.

Purpose and Method of the Study

It was very difficult to obtain the interviews. Real estate brokers are very active and often out of their offices. It took four or five telephone calls to reach many of the brokers. Letters and visits to the broker's office became necessary when I could not get an appointment for an interview by telephoning. There was fear and suspicion to overcome, a lack of interest in social research, and an unwillingness to spend time in a financially unproductive activity. Because the purpose of the interview was stated frankly to each broker, the assurance of anonymity was important — it was on the strength of this assurance that the majority of the real estate brokers granted an interview. A few said they did not care if what they revealed was printed, but others warned, "If you tell anyone I said this, I'll deny it." Once the broker was convinced that he would not be betrayed and granted the interview, he took the questions seriously and answered them with care. There were often strong reactions from the respondents. They spoke openly and emotionally, pounding on the desk at times and swearing. One man said after he had been unburdening himself for almost three hours, "You've been writing. You could ruin me with this," and drew his forefinger across his throat from ear to ear.

There were many respondents who, of their own accord, expressed a certain satisfaction over giving the interview during or at the end of it. Two or three were pleased to participate in research; a few believed it a public duty to assist in the study of an important subject. A considerable number were glad to speak freely about the question of race and about their particular problems with it without fear of repercussion or retaliation. Some appreciated the fact that someone from the University of Chicago had come to them for information — it was made clear that the respondent was the authority in the interview. Some admitted that they enjoyed the interview because the questions challenged them and made them think. For some, the interview was a diversion from the daily real estate activities. Some were glad simply to have an opportunity to express themselves and be listened to — one man said, "I enjoyed this. My wife doesn't give me a chance to talk."

There were a total of 90 interviews from the samples and 121 interviews in all.[23] The 90 interviews were distributed as follows: Area A, 37; Area B, 23; Area C, 21 (Board members, 10, and nonmembers, 11); Area CX, 6; and Area C branch offices, 3. The median length of the 90 interviews was 2½ hours. The study took 4 years to complete.

Racial Policies and Practices

THE respondents vary both in the combination of business functions they perform and in the emphasis upon a particular function. Most respondents stress the functions of sales, management, and insurance or the functions of sales and management. In Area A, 8 firms provide service in sales, management, insurance, mortgages, and appraisal. A few firms in Areas A, B, and C build and act as consultants. (See Tables 2 and 9, Appendix C.)

The businesses of the study are mostly seasoned enterprises. Four were operating before 1900; approximately half of those in Area A and close to a half in Areas B and C are over 25 years old. Almost a quarter in Area A and somewhat under a third in Areas B and C are 10 years old or less. (See Table 1, Appendix C.) The respondents have dealt with Negroes between 1 and 50 years, but a good many began in 1951 or shortly after. Of the respondents who deal with Negroes, almost one third in Area A, one half in Area B, over three quarters in Area C, and 4 out of 5 in Area CX began during the period 1951–1955. During the years 1945–1955, almost one half of the respondents in Area A, three quarters of those in Area B, and almost all in Area C began to deal with Negroes. In Area A, 13 out of 31 (42 per cent) have dealt with Negroes 18–50 years,* and in Area B, 4 out of 20 have. (See Table 3, Appendix C.) Twelve out of 30 (40 per cent) in Area A and 8 out of 20 (40 per cent) in Area B, but only 2 out of 13 (15 per cent) in Area C and none in Area CX began to deal with Negroes at the very beginning of their business (Tables 4 and 9, Appendix C). Almost half the respondents in Area A and fully half in Area B

---

* When numbers are given, the total for each area may differ from one question to another, because it was not possible to obtain an answer from every respondent to every question, and sometimes the question did not apply to a respondent.

first dealt with Negroes in their home area, whereas all 13 in Area C and 3 out of 4 in Area CX first dealt with them in other areas.[1] Some respondents in Areas A, B, and CX first dealt with Negroes in other than their home area, some began from their offices in other areas, and some from their offices in the home area. Then, when Negroes began to enter Areas A, B, and CX, most of these respondents continued their policy of dealing with them. (See Table 4, Appendix C.)

THE TREND

Many of the respondents themselves introduced the "trend" as immediately related to the formation of their racial policies as Negroes move closer to their area of operation. Trend is a familiar concept in real estate, as it is in other businesses. Real estate appraisers must know about general trends, trends affecting the specific area where a property is to be appraised, the direction of the trend and its limit, and what effect it will have on the property.

In addition to its usual meaning to the real estate man, and clearly distinguished from it, "trend" has a special sense, referring to the movement of Negroes as they approach and enter white neighborhoods and to what may affect its direction. Real estate men cannot know which way the trend will go or what may happen to send it in a particular direction, although they can expect it to go in a certain direction on the basis of experience and the situation in a given area. Neither can they know whether change in racial occupancy, if it comes, will be slow or fast.

Many factors enter into the trend — for example, the presence of a natural boundary, the kind of property in a street, the attractiveness of one neighborhood over another, or someone's need to sell in a certain block. Real estate men influence the trend and are influenced by it — some make it their business to anticipate it, or, by soliciting and making a few sales, help to turn it in a certain direction. The trend includes also what is done by residents of a community to facilitate or obstruct the entry of Negroes. A social and economic upheaval underlies the trend — the struggle of the Negro people for a better standard of living and their ability to pay for better quarters.

Twenty real estate men specifically mentioned trend in the interviews:

Others feel as I do, but most feel they are obliged to accept and go on with the trend. . . . I don't think the development . . . will bring back the neighborhood. I think the colored will go in there and the whites will be pushed out. (33A)*

There are brokers who follow the trend. That's their kind of business. As soon as they find it's a possibility to break in, for example, in X [area mostly white]. They're looking on the perimeter for a chance to break in. (35A)

We advised some to sell and some to wait according to the trend. (52A)

It was the condition of the time, the trend of the times. Apartments were becoming available, and there weren't any white applicants and there were colored applicants. (57A)

The Negro family I put in a house at X [near Area B] was the first in the block. No, I wouldn't do it in Area C, but here, yes, because it is the inevitable trend. (69B)

Some real estate men notice the trend sooner than others, depending on their location and policy. A firm at some distance from entering Negroes does not have to meet the problem and may ignore it. A firm so conservative in policy that no one would approach it may not hear readily what is happening, whereas a firm with an approachable policy would. The location of the real estate man's office in relation to the trend is significant for change in his policy and practice. The broker's office is often in the midst of the business district of his area. As Negroes come closer, he is compelled to make certain decisions if he is to continue dealing in that area. One respondent described this crisis:

When they were coming closer — 2 years or more ahead, the people who had the means to move, they moved as far as 2 or more years ahead of time. . . . The Negroes were a mile or 2 miles away. Well, then we were forced. During the OPA, a lot of people would have moved long before this, but since there were no available quarters elsewhere a good percentage remained. After that most of them moved away to other neighborhoods. This is about Area B, yes. We were compelled then to rent to inferior tenants — inferior type of people, still white. While this was happening, the other races came closer. They kept approaching and approaching so that all of a sudden when the Puerto Ricans came in, that was the climax of happenings here. We were definitely compelled to rent. Otherwise there would have been vacancies. We were compelled to rent to them. To rent

* In all quotations from interviews, the respondent has been given a number, immediately followed by the letter of his area. Unless another meaning is indicated, the statement refers to that area. All words that might reveal the identity of the respondents have been omitted; some times an omission has been indicated by ellipses, and some times a letter has been substituted for a name. When the respondent spoke of his area, Area A, B, or C has been substituted for the real name.

to an inferior type of tenant meant lower rents and more destruction. These are facts. . . . The Negroes entered Area B in 1953, when the loop came close to the neck — not that I'm against any race or nationality but speaking of the real estate business. It affected not only my business but others. (5B)

The effects of Negroes' approach and entry upon the real estate man's business as experienced by him in his situation were described by the respondents.

The Approach and Entry of Negroes

As the Negro movement comes closer, as rumors circulate about their having bought or being about to buy in the area, and as Negroes walk or drive up and down the streets, the people of the area become "concerned," "excited," "jittery," "disturbed," "troubled," "worried," "apprehensive," and "up in the air." Some owners and tenants leave. White people who ordinarily would buy in the area begin to hesitate. The broker's sales decrease or stop. This is the "doldrums," "twilight zone," "stagnation period," "stalemate period" — when white people will not buy and Negroes are not yet buying. Speculators begin to buy. Then a house or property is sold to a Negro, and the block is "broken." The exodus begins. Negroes may now occupy only two or three properties in the block, but, since probably a larger number of families are living there than before, there seem to be many Negroes in the area. White people become alarmed, put properties up for sale, and vacate housing. Some people cannot leave. Some remain on principle — those who will not sell their properties to Negroes, and those who see social good in an interracial community. Others who remain believe that they can "manage" the area so it will not go Negro or hope that some quota can be maintained.

Speculators continue to buy properties in the area and to resell to Negroes. Outside brokers enter to make sales to Negroes, and some set up offices. Some older firms and brokers of the area also begin to sell to Negroes. Others hold back, losing business, as new and old competitors reap the harvest. Still others move away. Vacancies increase and income falls: the loop has come close to the neck. Finally, most of the brokers begin to sell and rent to Negroes. For some, it is a new experience, and they must adjust to it. But for others, it is an old one: they left other areas when Negroes entered or they have already dealt with both whites and Negroes. It is against the backdrop of the continually changing situation and the need to cope with it that the broker's racial policies and practices need to be seen.

Confronted with the approach and entry of Negroes into his home area, the real estate broker must decide on his policy about dealings with them. The respondents decided in these ways: (1) A long-held policy for or against dealing with Negroes is continued. Some firms may already be dealing with them in adjacent areas or in other parts of the city. (2) A long-held policy is changed. The firm begins to sell to Negroes or to manage buildings with Negro tenants. (3) A policy is adopted where there had been no occasion for one before. (4) The policy is to go along with the trend. The broker makes no policy for himself. (5) The policy is to have no policy. The broker will do whatever the particular situation requires. As 47A said, "I can't afford to have a policy." (6) There is no awareness of any need for forming a policy. The broker has an opportunity to make a sale to a Negro, he takes it and goes on to make other such sales. A new area of business has opened for him.

Respondents' Adjustments

In Area A (14), Area B (9), Area C (2, not home area), and Area CX (3), the respondents' main reason for beginning to sell to Negroes was necessity: "They came in; you couldn't sell to anyone else." Other reasons were the opportunity to make money as Negroes entered (Area A, 5), the listing of property by white owners (Area B, 4, and Area C, 4), and helping a white client leave the area (Area C, 4). Except for "to make money," there is no evidence that the respondents deliberately sought dealings with Negroes. (See Table 5, Appendix C.)

In Areas A, B, and CX, necessity (vacancies; could not rent to whites any more) was again the chief reason that the respondents began to manage buildings with Negro tenants. Some respondents qualified their answer by saying that *good* white tenants could no longer be had and that it was difficult to replace those who had moved out. Some respondents took over buildings already occupied by Negroes. One in Area A described the circumstances: "In regard to these properties, for the most part the owners were already doing business with us on white property. When they found out we would take colored property, they turned them over to us.

36

(38A)" Some respondents (Area A, 4; Area B, 3; Area C, 1; Area CX, 1) were given the management of Negro-occupied buildings because they were the brokers for the sale. New owners included white and Negro buyers, so that the respondent sometimes began to manage buildings with Negro tenants for a Negro owner and sometimes for a white owner. Four respondents of Area A stated that Negro owners simply came to ask them to manage the property. One of these said, "They came to us and said they were not getting the kind of service from their Negro real estate people they wanted. They wanted to give it to us because they thought we would serve to the owners' advantage. We have never solicited any Negro owners, but we would not refuse any business unless it was a slum property . . . (38A)" Only 2 respondents of Area A and 1 of Area C (not in home area) deliberately acquired buildings for management as Negroes entered, regarding this as a profitable investment. (Table 5, Appendix C.)

Respondents' reactions to Negroes' entering Areas A and B varied considerably.[2] Some developed a policy gradually as they watched the changes in the area. Others decided quickly whether to deal with Negroes in their home area or not. Some respondents held out much longer than others, depending on location, kind of property handled, and diversification of business function, apart from outlook on the race question.

In Area A 31 out of 37 (84 per cent) and in Area B 20 out of 23 (87 per cent) deal with Negroes. Of the 31 respondents in Area A dealing with Negroes, 12 (39 per cent) had been unwilling to begin but finally had to do so. Ten, almost a third, either extended a policy begun in other areas or initiated a new policy with little resistance. In Area B, 12 out of 20 (60 per cent) had opposed such dealing but finally began, 4 were interested in such dealing, and 4 continued or soon initiated it. In Area CX, 5 out of 6 had been opposed but finally began to deal with Negroes. All those who were opposed finally began, making one or more of these adjustments: extending their business operation into other areas or throughout the city, concentrating on white purchasers, and opening a branch office in a suburb. Six out of 37 (16 per cent) in Area A and 3 out of 23 (13 per cent) in Area B avoid dealing with Negroes by managing buildings in a part of the area still white, managing buildings in other areas, changing business function or area, extending their business operation throughout the city, and beginning an operation in a new subdivision. One respondent of Area B and 2 of Area CX were considering leaving the area.

Of 9 offices set up in Area A in order to deal with Negroes, 1 was opened by an old firm with offices in other parts of the city, 1 was moved from another area into Area A, 4 were opened largely for purposes of management, and 1 is operated in the broker's home. One respondent took over the office of an old firm and continued its policy of dealing with Negroes; he was planning to open a suburban office as well. The reason for opening the ninth office is undetermined. (Table 6, Appendix C.)

POLICIES AND PRACTICES

Almost half (16/34) of the respondents in Area A and almost half (8/19) in Area B manage property for Negro owners. Such factors as the opening of Negro real estate businesses in Area B, which has a heavier Negro concentration, would explain the smaller proportion of white agents. However, a considerable number of the respondents manage property for Negro owners. (See Table 7, Appendix C.) Approximately three quarters (23/30) of the respondents in Area A and four fifths (12/15) in Area B manage properties owned by white persons but tenanted partly or wholly by Negroes. Four respondents of Area A and 4 of B own and manage such property themselves. Even in Area C, 2 out of 15 manage property for Negro owners (tenant-owners of cooperative apartments), and 2 manage for white owners property partly or wholly occupied by Negroes. In Area CX, 1 out of 6 manages property for a Negro owner, and 4 manage for white owners property tenanted partly or wholly by Negroes. (Table 7, Appendix C.)

In each area, except for the branch offices of Area C, a majority of the respondents sell to Negroes — in Area A 24 out of 36 (67 per cent), in Area B 16 out of 21 (76 per cent), in Area C 12 out of 21 (57 per cent), and in Area CX 4 out of 6 (67 per cent) (Table 9, Appendix C). Most respondents in Areas A, B, and CX both sell and manage with regard to Negroes, but in Area C the majority sell only (Table 9, Appendix C).

Of the 24 respondents in Area A who sell to Negroes, one third make at least 75 per cent of their sales to Negroes. However, 3 of these are management firms that make 10 or fewer sales a year to Negroes. For 10 of the 24 (42 per cent), 50 per cent or more of their sales are made to Negroes. In Area B, 6 out of 16 (38 per cent) make 50 per cent or more of their sales to Negroes. The smaller percentage of sales in Area B may be due to the operation of Negro real estate firms in the area or to fewer re-sales among Negro owners. Five out of 12 in Area C make 10–50 per cent of their sales to Negroes. (Table 10, Appendix C.)

38

Racial Policies and Practices

In Area A, 12 out of 27 respondents (44 per cent) and in Area B half of the respondents (8/16) manage units of which over half are occupied by Negroes (see Table 11, Appendix C). The management of property for Negro owners constitutes a noticeable proportion of the total management business of the respondents of Areas A and B. Of the 16 in Area A who manage properties for Negro owners, 4 have 25–50 per cent of their clients among Negro owners, 5 have 10–25 per cent, and 5 have under 10 per cent. Of the 8 in Area B, 2 have 10–25 per cent of their clients among Negro owners. Even some respondents in Areas C and CX manage property for Negro owners. (See Table 7, Appendix C.) However, 18 out of 29 respondents in Area A and some in each of the other areas lost the management of buildings sold to Negroes (Table 8, Appendix C). Many complained that Negro owners turn the management over to Negro firms or manage their buildings themselves. Some asserted that a property sold to a Negro loses its resale value to the white broker, because frequently any further transactions with that property will be handled by a Negro broker.

Restrictions in Selling

Of the firms and independent brokers that deal with Negroes, few will deal with them without some form of restriction (Table 12, Appendix C) — the main restriction being their unwillingness to sell property in a white area or block to a Negro. ("Block" was defined in an interview with a high official of the Chicago Real Estate Board as "from one corner to the next on only one side of the street," there being about 15 houses on a block, or 30 for both sides of the street.) All the respondents, whether actually selling to Negroes or not, were asked Question 16, "Would you sell (or rent) property to Negroes in an area where there are no Negroes?" (for complete question, see Appendix A). Most respondents first gave a flat no. Twenty-seven out of 35 (77 per cent) in Area A, 17 out of 22 (77 per cent) in Area B, 20 out of 21 (95 per cent) in Area C, 5 out of 6 (83 per cent) in Area CX, and the 3 Area C branch offices refused outright to sell in this way. Seven in Area A and a few in the other areas emphasized their unwillingness, stating that they had *lost* sales because they would not participate in such transactions. Only 2 respondents would not take a stand. A few gave a qualified yes. Only 4 out of 35 in Area A and 3 out of 22 in Area B will sell to a Negro without any kind of restriction; none will do so in Area C or in any of its parts. (Table 12, Appendix C.)

39

If the respondent answered no to Question 16, he was asked when he thought he could make a sale to a Negro. Question 16 asked about the area only, but many of the respondents brought up restriction in the block. Some respondents limit their conditions to the neighborhood or area, others to the block, and a few to a combination of area and block (Table 13, Appendix C). In Areas A and B, the respondents most strongly emphasize the block restriction in selling, whereas in Area C they emphasize the area. This difference may be due to the fact that the real estate brokers of Area C can still consider Area C as a whole (except for Area CX) because the area proper is still largely white, but they can no longer consider Areas A and B white. Hence, the respondents of these areas, especially of Area A, would watch streets and blocks.

There is a wide range of restrictive conditions both for the area and the block. Among those respondents who stressed the area, there were a few adherents to each of the following conditions for selling to a Negro: (1) when the residents of the area are prepared to accept them; (2) when some Negroes are already in the neighborhood, and there is no trouble; (3) when there are 5 or 6 in the area, and people put their properties up for sale to any desirable family; (4) when the neighborhood is 25 per cent Negro, and the owners ask the broker to sell; (5) when the neighborhood is 50 per cent Negro; (6) when the neighborhood is at least 60 per cent Negro; (7) when the neighborhood is 75 per cent Negro; and (8) when the neighborhood is 100 per cent Negro.

This answer exemplifies some of these conditions:

When you can put a sign in front of a building and the sellers have no reluctance whatsoever in selling to colored and the people up and down the block are in accord with the idea, know that the situation is evident and there is no resentment to the seller of the property and you can have the colored drive up in front of the house at high noon and inspect the property, and there would be no reaction heard from the people in the area to the agency that has the sign on the property, at that time you know that the community has accepted the situation of a transition. . . . If I get a call from a colored party in regard to a piece of property adjacent to a colored area or an area going colored, but it is not salable to colored because the community doesn't wish to have colored, I don't sell. (65C)

A number of respondents who stress the area or the area and block hold similar views. Their underlying condition for selling to Negroes is their inference that Negroes are accepted by the members of the community.

Some respondents stated a condition for the area as well as for the block before they will sell to a Negro. These conditions are: (1) when the residents of the block and of the area are prepared to accept them; (2) after 1 house or building is sold to Negroes, and when there are other Negro owners in the vicinity (and there is police protection and the trend is inevitable); (3) when the neighborhood is partly Negro, the residents are resigned to the fact that the neighborhood is going colored, and there are 2 or more Negro families in the block; (4) when there are 3 or 4 Negro families in the block, tenants give notice, and enough Negroes have moved in to indicate a trend; and (5) when there are 4 or 5 Negro families in the block, the neighborhood is obviously changing, and the people know it's inevitable and list their properties for sale.

Among the respondents who stress the block, there are adherents for each of the following conditions for selling property to a Negro: (1) after 1 Negro family is in the block; (2) after 2 or 3 Negro families are in the block; (3) after 3 or 4 Negro families are in the block; (4) after 4 or 5 Negro families are in the block; (5) when the block is 50 per cent Negro [3]; and (6) when the block is predominantly Negro. The first and second conditions have more adherents than the others.

The respondents who stress the block are aware of the trend in the area, and those who stress the neighborhood are aware of the significance of 1 or more sales in a block. Respondents do not draw a sharp line between the block and the area or neighborhood. Those who stress the neighborhood recognize that the total trend, the larger area, has primarily to be taken into account.[4]

A few answers will illustrate the condition of 1 Negro family in the block. The respondents express this condition or some other, but also in many cases they reveal indirectly and unwittingly their attitudes toward the Negroes:

I wouldn't be the first one to do it. If there was a nigger in the block, I'd be tickled pink to sell to another nigger. (3B)

The firm has a policy where they won't sell to a Negro in an area where Negroes are not resident. . . . The general public, white, yes, is not willing to accept the Negro as a neighbor. That's the basis for our not selling to Negroes in this type of an area unless 1 Negro family is already in the block. You can't be censured then. A silly idea but that's life. (36A)

I would say when the whites have permitted their property to go to decay, to deteriorate without keeping up property and making repairs, then those properties are subject to sale to any one as a rule. When colored do

41

buy, they repair and keep the properties up better than the old owners. I would not be the first! (43A)

The answers of those respondents who sell to Negroes in a block after 2 or 3 sales do not differ greatly from the answers stipulating 1 sale:

When 2 or 3 sales have been made in a *block*, that is, from one corner to the next on only one side of the street. This holds in our office. . . . We had to have some measure and this is really that the people have considered that when 2 are sold, well, that block's gone, and they don't hold any animus against the broker after that. (13CX)

We don't sell to colored in any but already established colored areas — blocks with 3 or 4 families living in the block. (90A)

One respondent who does not sell at all to Negroes expressed this position: "We wouldn't consider selling property to a Negro buyer as an office operation under any circumstances. (66C)"

The distribution of the respondents' conditions for selling property to Negroes is given in Table 13, Appendix C. I concluded from these conditions that restrictions run the gamut from no to full exclusion, and that there is no uniform view about when selling to Negroes may begin. Respondent 83C took it upon himself to state such a view: "Real estate men have discussed the subject and have concluded that when there are 3 in the block or more, it would then be open for sales. In other words, if it has already gone colored, there would be no use in insisting. You can't do anything about it. No amount of resistance would withhold the tide. It requires a lot of mental adjustment on the part of the whites." It has been difficult to take into account all the differences in combinations of restrictive conditions required by the respondents. However, there is one chief point of agreement among them: do not sell property to a Negro in an area or block where there are no Negroes. And one theme underlying all the restrictions cropped up in most of the interviews, "At what point in the entry of Negroes will the community not hold it against me if I sell property to a Negro?" (This will be discussed in Chapter V.)

Treatment of Negro and White Buyers

I asked respondents who said they would not sell to Negroes in an area where there are none how, if the occasion arose, they refused to sell a property to a Negro. Their methods are: give a blunt refusal without explanation; say no and blame the owner; say no, accept the blame, and admit the racial difficulty; warn the Negro he will be unwelcome in such an area and advise him not to try to buy; and deceive the Negro — misrepresenting in one way or another to avoid a direct refusal. Twice as many brokers avoid misrepresentation as use it in Areas A and C, and almost twice as many in Area B (Table 14, Appendix C). Examples of 3 methods follow. In the first method, the broker accepts the blame and admits the racial difficulty:

Well, there was a case. I was very frank. I said to a colored buyer, "I can't sell that building to colored." "Why not?" he said. "I'll tell you," I said. "We still represent a lot of white owners of property. Ninety per cent of our business is with white owners, and frankly, if I sold you that property, I would hurt the neighbors. I'd depreciate their properties. The next fellow — he would want to sell. Pretty soon a lot of buildings would be thrown on the market and they'd have to sell at a discount. And furthermore, we represent a lot of white owners. That's with whom we're doing business, 90 per cent of them. We've a few colored owners, not many. If you were in my place, would you cater to 90 per cent or 10 per cent? After all, yes, your money is as good as the white man's, but, after all, the colored group as a group are not in the financial position that the white people are in, and, if we should throw down the bars and sell to colored, we would soon not have as good a market as we have now. Look at it from the practical business standpoint." (51A)

The second method is a warning: "I've had that a lot of times. I just explain to them that I do not think they would be welcome. It would be impossible for them to be happy living some place where they knew they were not welcome. (82C)" The third method is misrepresentation: "I tell them the property has been sold. They usually understand. (61C)" Or, "I just say I don't have anything for sale. If my sign is on a building, I say, 'The salesman is out. I will phone you.' I phone him or he phones. I say a contract is already under way, in the making. He usually catches on. (12A)" An indirect method of refusing to sell a property to a Negro is raising the price beyond his reach, and several respondents have done this.

The respondents who said that Negroes do not try to buy such property referred to 2 types in the Negro population. The first type considers it best to keep away from the white area — "I've never had any problem that way. The people I've been dealing with have been people of good will who wanted to do the right thing, who seemed to understand and were more interested in the common good than their own self-interest. (54C)" The second type has a white man buy for him — "You don't have to say anything to the Negro. They know themselves that they can't go in there. They'll let a white fellow buy for them and put it in trust with a Negro's name. So it's an unknown party until such time that they can take possession. (75C)"

The respondents who admitted differences in the way they show property to white and Negro prospective buyers said some of them are: holding open house on Sunday for inspection, because Negroes do not keep appointments; taking the Negro through the basement so as not to antagonize tenants; saying the Negro is a decorator; bringing the Negro at night (or in the daytime) so as not to upset the tenants; and questioning the Negro more thoroughly to see if he has the means to buy and checking his financial qualifications. Most of the respondents proceeded no differently with Negro than with white buyers. (Table 15, Appendix C.)

A few respondents in Areas A and C gave the impression that they were trying to hide or keep in the background their dealings with Negroes. One in Area C said that he makes his appointments with Negro clients by telephone and calls for them at their place of business or house in order to show them a property. Most of the time, he manages to do business with them outside his office. Another in Area C stated that the building manager collects the rent from his Negro tenants and that "no Negro comes in here [his office]." One in Area A expressed his displeasure over Negro tenants' coming to his office to pay their rent instead of mailing a check, as white tenants do: "It's harder to handle cash. A lot of Negroes don't have bank accounts. There is also the risk of holdup. Actually we have more white than Negro, but the whites don't come into the office as much. They mail in their checks. They phone about things. So there are more Negroes coming to the office. It's not too good. (53A)"

Two respondents hinted that some white real estate brokers are uneasy and wish to hide their dealing with Negroes. One in Area B spoke defiantly of not caring who knew that he deals with Negroes and scorned a broker who had set up an office for dealing with Negroes under another name.

I will not misrepresent. I do not hide the fact that I sell to Negroes. My future reputation depends on that type of business. I won't resort to that type of stuff. I won't do it. [Answer to Question 21, "How does the Board look upon a broker who sells property in a white area to a Negro buyer?"] This is my personal opinion. The majority of them are two-faced and misrepresent. All say they're not going to sell to Negroes and say of a broker who does, "He's a nigger-lover," but underhandedly they're all open to a buck and will sell to them. Two years ago only about 3 of us were in it. A certain concern opened another office under another name. . . . [He revealed the true and the assumed names.] I sell to Negroes. If anyone doesn't do it, I don't care, I don't give a damn! (69B)

One from Area C pointed out that he makes no secret of dealing with Negroes and answered the question on differences in procedures:

Oh, very little, if you could construe it as a different procedure. We put chairs and a desk in one of the apartments and made an office in the building. Many people were coming and looking at apartments. It was more convenient than having them come to this office. But now that they're in, they come here. They sit in the front window and it doesn't bother me. No neighbor has mentioned it to me, no. You saw one the other day, you remember? (83C)

A few respondents who are not dealing with Negroes stated that they do not want to deal with them partly because they would not want the people of the neighborhood to see Negroes coming into their office. One in Area C said he would be open to criticism because people would think he was trying to bring colored to the neighborhood. However, there are respondents like 69B and 83C above — among them members and officials of the Chicago Real Estate Board — who are dealing with Negroes and making no secret of it.

Financing of the sale is the crucial part of the whole transaction. The only difference in procedure at this point is the greater effort which the respondents on the whole must make to obtain a loan for a Negro buyer. Most respondents consider the land contract for a deed to be more common among Negro buyers than among white buyers. (Table 15, Appendix C.) One reason for this is that many Negroes cannot make a large enough down payment in cash to obtain a mortgage.[5] Another is the resistance of lending agencies to Negroes. At times, the broker has to go from one lending agency to another before he can obtain a loan for a Negro buyer, whereas usually he does not have such trouble with a white buyer. (This problem will be discussed more fully in Chapters IV and VI.)

The refusal of respondents to sell a house to a Negro in a white area or block is not related to their opinion of Negroes as homeowners. In each area a majority of the respondents consider that the Negro owner cares for his home as well as or better than the white owner. (Table 20, Appendix C.)

Restrictions in Management

Real estate men look upon management as the backbone of their business, because it represents steady earning. Firms that have never had Negro tenants must seriously consider what will happen to their management business if they take on properties with Negro tenants. Some of the respondents who made the change are pleased, and others gave up buildings rather than have Negro tenants. Still others had been ready to continue managing buildings sold to Negroes and converted to Negro occupancy, but the new, Negro owner decided to manage it himself or hired a Negro real estate agent. Some respondents have been managing buildings with Negro tenants in other areas for many years.

The respondents' answers to Question 16h (see Appendix A) indicate that, in most cases, the selling and the managing policies are the same. Twenty-nine out of 35 (83 per cent) in Area A, 15 out of 20 (75 per cent) in Area B, 11 out of 12 (92 per cent) in Area C, 5 out of 6 (83 per cent) in Area CX, and the 3 Area C branch offices will not rent to Negroes in an area where there are no Negroes. A few respondents gave a qualified yes.[6] Only 3 out of 35 in Area A and 4 out of 20 in Area B said they would do so. (Table 12, Appendix C.)

Negro and White Tenants

TREATMENT

The respondents avoid renting an apartment to a Negro in ways largely similar to those they use in selling property. These ways are: say no; say no and blame the owner; accept the blame and admit the racial problem — building cannot be turned yet, or area or block still white; warn the Negro that it may be unpleasant if he moves in where he is not wanted and suggest apartment buildings where Negroes are already living; evade and misrepresent. Almost three times as many respondents in Area A and fully three times as many in Area B avoid misrepresentation as use it. In Area C, almost all respondents to whom the question applied avoided misrepresentation. Some suggested several ways to avoid renting an apartment to a Negro. (Table 16, Appendix C.)

Many respondents stress the security deposit as an important part of their management practice with Negro tenants. The tenant pays in advance the rent for the last month of the year along with the rent for the first month. Sometimes the tenant pays a security deposit of two months' rent, for the last two months of the year. This is a security deposit because it secures the owner against loss of rent, damage to the apartment, or theft by the tenant. When he knows that the security deposit will be used to pay for any damage, the tenant is likely to take better care of the apartment. The security deposit is also a screening device — an applicant who has saved enough money to pay two months' rent in advance probably can be relied upon to pay his rent regularly.

The deposit is required usually of new tenants, unknown except by references. Since the new tenants for white real estate agents and white owners in Areas A and B have been chiefly Negroes, Negroes mostly pay the security deposit. In many cases, if the tenant pays his rent regularly and cares satisfactorily for property, no security deposit is required after the first year.

In Area A, of the 17 respondents who require a security deposit, 8 require it from all *Negro* tenants, whereas 9 require it from all tenants, Negro and white. In Area B, 6 require it from Negroes only and 5 from both Negro and white tenants. Thus, about half in each area require the deposit from Negroes only. In Area B, wage assignment appears as a guarantee of rent for Negro tenants only. In Area CX, 4 firms require the security deposit from white and Negro tenants. Some owners require it only from those tenants, white or Negro, whose credit is unsatisfactory. Some respondents always require it unless the owner is unwilling, and others act entirely according to the wishes of the owner. (Table 18, Appendix C.) A few answers illustrate the use of the security deposit:

> Yes, we require a security deposit of one month's rent. . . . It's required from all Negro tenants, but we also require it from some white tenants. [Why from all Negro tenants?] Because by and large the Negro tenants' incomes and stability-in-the-job records indicate that it is advisable to have some security. . . . Many get pretty heavily into debt. . . . Even if they have been a long time on the job, we require a security deposit because of our general experience, yes. It may not be necessary in some cases, but rather than qualify each one, we do it as a matter of policy. Many of those people that have come into our buildings have been accustomed to paying rent by the week. Here they pay monthly. That is contrary to their usual habits. They live from day to day. They have never been accustomed to accumulate money to pay a bill. (88A, 125 Negro tenants)

Yes, we require a security deposit of one month. Just from the colored tenants. Why? I think that possibly through education or some reason there seems to be a lack of responsibility at the end of something like that. We just had the experience. About the fifteenth of the month, we found they had moved out. If there is a 2-year lease, I have let the deposit apply to the last month. After that I don't require a security deposit. Individual owners have different ideas about that. In most cases they leave it up to us. My policy is to get it, and if they want a lease, to apply it to the last month. If it is a month-to-month tenant, they use it for the last month's rent. . . . Sometimes Negro tenants have been rooming. They lived with another family and shared the rent. They may have never been responsible for rent before, never had the experience, the education of that responsibility. That makes the security deposit necessary. As soon as they show they're responsible, there is no more security deposit. (22B, 624 Negro tenants)

Guarantee rent? We do by wage assignment. They sign a paper giving us the authority to garnishee their wages for not paying. We insist on leases. We can get the same on the lease, but wage assignment is stronger. There is a psychological effect. It gets across to them. Their wages will be held up — assigned. This applies only to Negro tenants. (2B, 1,150 Negro tenants)

Somewhat over half the respondents in Areas A and B and half in Areas C and CX screen Negro applicants more carefully than white. In Area A, 13 out of 24 (54 per cent) screen Negroes more carefully, whereas 10 screen them as they do the white. In Area B, 7 screen more carefully, and 6 use the same procedures. A respondent of Area A who screens Negro applicants less carefully does so because he finds fewer good Negro tenants and has to be less particular. Some respondents encountered difficulties in checking the references supplied by Negro applicants. (Table 18, Appendix C.) Here are a few examples of respondents' screening procedure and experience:

We screen them closer. We look for education and a sense of responsibility. A certain person can be of the middle class in income and still not correspond to another of the same income. (22B, 624 Negro tenants)

We check much further back, where they lived, the last 2 places. We check with their supervisor on the job. We verify their employment and seniority. [More intensively?] Yes, definitely. On the last 3 years of the job and the last 3 jobs. (53A, 325 Negro tenants)

I am amazed utterly at the absence of reliable references — even regarding the applicants that are tip-top academically, courteously, and economically. It is manifestly clear to me that these nonwhites desire to deal in a manner that will not permit you to penetrate the good truth about them. To wit: bank references are practically nonexistent. Most — 98 per cent — of their rent is paid in cash — checking accounts are virtually nonexistent. Savings accounts in large Loop banks are given as references. It is this that is disconcerting because the policy of virtually all banks is to make no disclosures as to the contents of a savings account. . . . Therefore, on too many occasions have we found that such a savings account exists with the sum of $1.00 in it. On account of the foregoing, we are obliged to impose conditions for security purposes to our owners that embody the requirement that an applicant for apartments renting for more than $75.00 a month deposit the last two months' rent and the first month's rent as security rent, which places a burden upon these renters not normally asked of whites, all occasioned by the inability and perhaps unwillingness of the nonwhite tenant to make honest and full disclosures. (47A, about 500 Negro tenants)

A number of respondents spoke of a useful clause in the lease preventing overcrowding of Negro tenants. The clause limits the occupancy of the dwelling unit to the number written in the contract by the signer.

RENT

Almost half the respondents (15/31) managing buildings with Negro tenants in Area A stated that their Negro tenants pay just as promptly as white and one considered them more prompt, but almost half (15/31) considered them not so prompt. In Area B, more (10 as against 6) considered them to be as prompt. The results for Areas C and CX are similar. Some of those who thought their Negro tenants just as prompt added that white and Negro tenants of the same socioeconomic status are equally prompt. (Table 19, Appendix C.)

Well, if you have picked your tenant carefully enough, they compare favorably. In a corresponding neighborhood, corresponding tenants of the middle class, both are about equal. (22B, 624 Negro tenants)

The majority are much slower. It's all right when they're working, but their employment is frequently interrupted — strikes, the Harvester's strike, for example, and then there are delinquencies. They never catch up. They suffer lack of employment as itinerant workers. Even the steady jobs give out. For example, they had good jobs on the Pullman trains, but the competition between the planes and the trains knocked that out. . . . (37A, 449 Negro tenants: 99 tenants, 350 tenant-owners of cooperative apartments)

Slightly more difficult — not as easy to collect from them. There is slightly more rent loss. Not at the beginning, but now since there is more Negro housing available, we find a change in the collection of rental. At the beginning they were fearful of losing the thing they had just obtained. (73A, 309 Negro tenants)

You have more difficulty making collections. You are more likely to receive partial payments on rent from Negro than from white. (6B, 200 Negro tenants)

That's our big problem — rent collection. We spend more time on rent collection than on any other single factor. (2B, 1,150 Negro tenants)

In Area A, 15 out of 26 (58 per cent) respondents maintained that Negroes are not paying more rent than white tenants for the same kind of apartment, and 2 claimed they are paying even less; only 9 out of 26 (35 per cent) stated that Negroes are paying more. In Area B, 6 out of 16 (38 per cent) said that Negro tenants pay the same amount as white, 1 claimed that they pay less, and 9 out of 16 (56 per cent) insisted that they pay more. (Table 18, Appendix C.) The question applied to few respondents in Areas C and CX — 3 in each of these areas stated that Negroes pay as much as or more than whites.

A study of housing in Chicago in 1960 found that the median rental for white households in substandard units was $50, as compared with a median rental of $65 for nonwhite households in substandard units.[7] In view of this finding and of the fact that there are more deteriorated properties in Area B than in Area A, it is understandable that there is a larger percentage of respondents in Area B than in Area A who say that Negroes pay higher rent. Furthermore, some respondents pointed out that Negroes pay higher rent than white people in the rundown districts, and my findings corroborated this.

Among the respondents' reasons for the Negroes' higher rent are the increased expense in the upkeep of the building when it is changed to frequently overcrowded Negro occupancy and the Negro's willingness to pay more — because he has no alternative or because of the prestige value of the neighborhood. Respondents estimate the difference in rent at 10–25 per cent. Those who maintain that Negroes do not pay more point out that the difference in rent disappears as more areas are opened to Negroes.

The Negro tenants do not pay more rent. They pay less for the best type of dwelling. They underpay for the top apartment and overpay for the cheap apartment. In the slums they pay through the nose . . . (53A)

There has been the charge that they pay more. Here is my answer. The difference comes in this respect. If you allow overcrowding in an apartment, they'll pay more. If you get the same high class of tenant, you won't get more. Certainly a landlord in a free market is going to charge as much as he can get. (13CX)

Yes, they do pay more rent, but there are more in the family. There are maybe 2 families. More hot water is used. There is more wear and tear. There is more garbage. So naturally you have to get more. The scavenger companies have to raise their rates for a building turned colored, because there is more garbage to handle. The cost of operation is a little more. More heat is needed. The water bill is higher. (28A)

One of the reasons [for higher rent] is the increase in the upkeep of the building. They use more of the utilities because of the greater occupancy — stoves, refrigerators, stair-carpeting, these do not have as long a life. That may be it. Then again, the prime reason is they're willing to pay it. The landlord can get it from them. (38A)

Do Negroes pay more rent? It was true in the past. However, in the last 3 years with the advent of more locations open to the Negro, it has brought the rent down to comparable rents of any other district. In fact, I would say, as of today, the rents in Negro areas comparable to those in white sections are cheaper, because the areas that have been opened to the Negro have been closed to the white, making a situation of supply and demand which is one of the most important of our business. (46A)

Yes, they pay more rent in this respect, when you consider high class, middle class, and low class, white and Negro, consider this area [A], when the upper grade in any race or creed, when a white upper class might consider this neighborhood a lower class neighborhood, whereas an upper class Negro might consider it a high class neighborhood. A Negro might think . . . [streets in Area A] was the highest grade neighborhood so far he has been permitted to live in and therefore he is willing to pay higher rent. To him, his apartment is worth $300 a month, but not to white. (48A)

MAINTENANCE

The respondents disagree in their judgments of Negro and white tenants' care of property, and again Area A differs from Area B. In Area A, 20 out of 31 (65 per cent) consider their Negro tenants not so good at maintenance as their white tenants, and 11 (35 per cent) consider them as good or better. In Area B, 7 out of 16 (44 per cent) consider their Negro tenants not so good as their white tenants, whereas 9 out of 16 (56 per cent) believe they are just as good or better. Three out of 4 in Area C and 2 out of 3 in Area CX consider them as good or better. (Table 20, Appendix C.) On the whole, Negro tenants receive a less favorable report on care of property than do Negro homeowners or white tenants: white and Negro tenants of the same socioeconomic standing look after their apartments equally well; care of property depends on fairness of rent, restrictions against overcrowding, the kind of service provided by the owner, and the type of building; and no matter how much screening the agent does, white tenants still care for property better than do Negro tenants.

If you can get the better class of Negro tenant, they take care of property equally well with the white, *if you can get them.* It is more difficult to get good Negro tenants. There are more good white tenants than good Negro tenants. There are more educated among the white. Even a good colored tenant may not have as much education as a good white tenant. We have some white tenants who get nasty. She lets her sink run over. It floods the people out below, or the radiator is turned on and spots the ceiling below. The white are bad too at times. The bad colored tenant gets drunk. They have no respect even for their own kind in the building. They break the marble in the hallway. They scratch up the halls newly decorated. They pull up, tear the stair-carpets up. They throw lit cigarettes on the nice stair-carpets. This is a little less likely to happen among the white. They are not quite as destructive. Of that class, there are perhaps more colored. It's a toss-up. (23A, 1,335 Negro tenants)

The ones we know personally and look into are the equal of the white. [There are two kinds of colored?] I should say there are! The colored do the same as the white. The better class move immediately when the undesirable element comes in. When a Negro owner buys a nice building and has his family there, and a tenant moves in across the street and soon there are five tenants instead of one, he moves. (79A, 97 Negro tenants)

I can't see any difference. If properties are operated fairly, if tenants are properly screened, and the building properly *managed* with no overcrowding and no rent gouging, there is no difference. We have managed colored property in this office for 30 years. We always did. That's the reason why we can't see any difference. (56A, 156 Negro tenants)

In regard to the better tenants of both groups, in general the white tenants are better. (36A, 300 Negro tenants)

Again, it's like the rent. Those in the better buildings have lived longer in the city. They are better wage earners, better tenants than the new migrants. (18B, 275 Negro tenants)

The respondents in Areas A and B agree about increased costs for maintenance and operation of a building when Negroes move in. In Area A, two thirds (18/27) stated that the cost of maintenance for Negro-occupied buildings is higher than that in similar white-occupied ones. In Area B, almost twice as many (11/6) considered cost of maintenance higher in Negro-occupied buildings. Most of the few in Areas C and CX to whom the question applied thought the cost was the same. (Table 20, Appendix C.)

Those who complained of increased costs attributed them to Negroes' greater carelessness and destructiveness, larger families, and overcrowding. A few quickly pointed out that the higher cost of operation applied especially to older buildings; others saw it as a general condition.

They're hard on property. They cause a fast depreciation. The maintenance costs are high. That's why buildings occupied by them as a rule are neglected because you can't keep up with repairs. The public areas, the stair halls are so abused. We would feel any money spent on the inside of most of those apartments would be a useless expense. I want to qualify that. The cooperative buyers take care of their apartments. They pay $500 down. That makes a difference. (37A, 449 tenants: 99 tenants and 350 tenant-owners)

There's no question but that the Negro as a group is much more careless. Now, there again, that's a generalization. *As a group*, they're much more careless than white people. Our plumbing bills are considerably higher, because things are continually being thrown into the toilets. They get stopped up. At the end of the year, the apartments require considerably more decorating to make them habitable. The white too, but less so. We have to do more plastering on the walls in the Negro-occupied buildings, and they deface the front hallways, so that our expense in decorating our hallways is . . . considerably more than among the white, in looking over the operating statements of the buildings. (13CX, 65 Negro tenants)

Yes, it costs a little more. We used to get the cream of the Negroes, but they're buying their own homes. While I was away, one Negro tenant sold a couch and sent it down the front hallway. It caused some damage. The colored are a little less reliable. They're here today and gone tomorrow. A lease doesn't mean too much to them. If the *Chicago Defender* [Negro newspaper] would do half the job of educating their readers as to proper housing procedures and practices instead of inciting them against vested interests. [What, for example?] What not to let go down the kitchen sink. When they move out, to sweep the apartment and leave it neat. Under what conditions they forfeit a deposit. The *Defender* could be an instrument for tremendous good, if they would just get the chip off their shoulder and say, "Let's go halfway to do the right thing according to the precepts of our society." If there is a prohibition against dogs, not to go and bring one in. (53A, 325 Negro tenants)

Negroes are not as careful. That's why the maintenance is higher. They move in and out the front stairway. They break the plaster. . . . The electrical fixtures, the plumbing fixtures — they'll pull the electrical wires out of the walls. Broken toilet bowls are frequent — a common finding. We replace quite a few. The faucets in the bath and kitchen become inoperative, whether they swing them around or whatever they do to them, but no water comes. . . . The stair-carpeting — it's impossible to keep the stair-carpets in the Negro-occupied buildings. They tear off the carpeting. They tear it right off the stairs. These conditions are fairly general regardless of rent. (2B, 1,150 Negro tenants)

. . . there is a tremendous increase in operational maintenance. And in our business, everything is percentage-wise, and to an owner who looks for profit from any enterprise, whether real estate or any other type of business, it is a noticeable amount. I must . . . answer that there would be an increase of operational expense to the astounding figure of 30 per cent. By that expense I mean various items, such as electricity and gas, furniture, decorating, plastering, water, etc. I'll go so far as to say that boiler repairs seem to be increased. This statement to the mind of any person who reads this must sound prejudiced, but I am sure that if one searches the records of various other companies who wish to maintain their Negro properties in any semblance of order, they will testify that the figures and facts I've given you are right. (46A, almost 2,000 Negro tenants)

THE CHANGE FROM WHITE TO NEGRO OCCUPANCY

The question has been raised whether the agent influences the owner in turning the building from white to Negro occupancy. Nine out of 17 in Area A, 10 out of 11 in Area B, 2 out of 3 in Area C, and 3 out of 4 in Area CX said the owner changed occupancy on their advice, and only 5 in Area A and 1 in Area B said the owner changed against or without their advice. In a number of cases, the agent manages his own property, and in a few cases, the agent and the owner decided between them. When white tenants are leaving, vacancies are increasing, and Negroes are applying for apartments, the owner and agent find themselves in agreement about the trend, and it is hard to say who finally decides that the building should turn. I conclude that the real estate agents in the three areas have more to do with the change in racial occupancy than the owners. (Table 17, Appendix C.)

Question 32 (Do you plan to continue your business in this area?) was designed to discover the respondent's direction of policy about dealing with Negroes, particularly in Areas A, B, and CX, although this was revealed in answers to other questions as well. Twenty-four out of 37 respondents (65 per cent) in Area A, 13 out of 23 (57 per cent) in Area B, 9 out of 21 (43 per cent) in Area C, 2 out of 6 (one third) in Area CX, but none of the 3 Area C branch offices intend to continue dealing with Negroes. (Table 21, Appendix C.)

RESTRICTIVE RACIAL PRACTICES IN OTHER CITIES
OF THE UNITED STATES

Many studies and reports reveal that, although there are variations in practice, most real estate men exclude Negroes from white areas, and this exclusion is widespread in the cities of the United States, including Chicago, and has existed for many years.[8] President Harris of the Negro organization, the National Association of Real Estate Brokers, said (in interview on September 20, 1956), "It's a gentlemen's agreement between all the facets of housing. It's an ordinary practice throughout the country, in the North, East, and West particularly."

The Broker's Conception of His Racial Policies and Practices, Part I

To UNDERSTAND the broker's racial practices, particularly those of restriction, my task is to bring to light the factors that enter into his decisions in dealing with Negroes. Among the factors revealed in the 40 preliminary interviews, the most prominent were the real estate man's own ideas and beliefs about selling or renting to Negroes in the white area or block, and their influence became apparent as the preliminary study progressed. The interviews indicated to me that the respondents' racial practices are the logical outcome of a group of related ideas, values, beliefs, and principles — that is, the racial real estate ideology. Most respondents' racial real estate ideology was largely unfavorable to Negroes and supported exclusion of Negroes from white areas; I named this the exclusion ideology. The questions then arose, Will a similar set of ideas be found among the respondents of the study proper? and Will a similar relation between exclusion ideology and exclusion practice be discovered? In addition to the exclusion ideology common to most of the preliminary respondents, I also found a set of ideas favorable to Negroes and supporting unrestricted sales — the integration ideology — and a third set of ideas balanced between favorable and unfavorable views about Negroes — the intermediate ideology. (On the three ideologies in the preliminary interviews, see pp. 18–20, 22.)

Now I shall set forth what I discovered in the study proper about the respondent's conception of his racial practices, particularly with respect to the practice of exclusion, and about the relation of this conception to his practices. I found in these respondents' conceptions of their racial practices the same components that I had found among the preliminary respondents (see p. 20) and some others, ten in all. These components reveal the broker's ideas and convictions about: (1) Negroes as people; (2) white people's attitudes toward Negroes; (3) Negroes' effect on property values; (4) Negroes' effect on neighborhoods; (5) the possibility of residential integration; (6) the consequences to others of his selling or renting property in the white area to Negroes; (7) justifications of racial policy; (8) his own values and wishes concerning a sale in a white area to a Negro; (9) the consequences to himself of unrestricted selling; and (10) the results of his racial policies and practices.

The components of the broker's ideology are not separate in his mind but linked in various ways — they are simply different aspects of his beliefs about Negroes. However, for purposes of analysis, I discuss them separately. A distinction must be made between components 1–8 and components 9 and 10: components 1–8 express the real estate man's ideas and convictions about Negroes and about real estate practice with them as it affects the world around him, whereas component 9 and, to some extent, 10, express the consequences of such practice to himself and include external influences.

First, component 9 — the consequences to himself of selling to Negroes in the white area that the real estate man foresees — is part of his racial ideology insofar as he is convinced that selling unrestrictedly to Negroes will bring him harm. This belief in dire consequences appeared among the related beliefs of most of the preliminary respondents opposed to unrestricted selling, although they had not made such sales and knew of brokers who had become rich through such sales. The few men who were not opposed to such selling did not hold this belief. Second, the broker's beliefs about consequences to himself of unrestricted selling belong within the ideology because they are related to his basic goal as a businessman, making a living. Any effects for this goal can hardly be divorced from his thinking as a real estate man, particularly in questions of actions unbecoming a real estate man. Third, component 9 belongs in the ideology because it reveals the real estate man's philosophy of life and hence presents an important contrast to components 6 and 7, in which he proclaims what he should or should not do because of his concern for the world at large. In components 6 and 7, he takes his stand on the basis of the principles he has internalized, and to this extent, he is Riesman's "inner-directed" man,[1] whereas in component 9, he is "other-directed,"[2] and conforms because he needs the others' approval or fears harm to himself. If he has his own convictions, he is afraid to declare them because others may consider them too conservative or too radical.

Components 9 and 10, beliefs about consequences of the broker's racial practices to himself, have a place within the ideology, but they arise out of pressures from the outside. Because I wanted to find out whether the real estate man's own convictions rather than outside pressures prompted his racial policies, and to ascertain the relation between his convictions about proper racial policy and his actual policy, I have considered the first 8 components by themselves. Thus, the 10 components are the broker's comprehensive ideology, and the first 8 components are the racial real estate ideology. From a long-range perspective, it may be said that the racial real estate ideology has arisen out of the cultural background of the real estate man and out of his total experience as a real estate broker. Its sources are many and its roots are deep in the historical development of the country itself. The Interview Schedule sought to draw out the experiential basis of his ideas and beliefs in order to uncover all possible factual support for his ideology.

For convenience, the components are discussed in two chapters. This chapter deals with the first five, and Chapter V with the last five.

COMPONENT 1. BELIEFS ABOUT NEGROES

The Interview Schedule contained no direct question on the broker's ideas and beliefs about Negroes, but these emerged spontaneously in the interviews. Respondents' beliefs about Negroes fall into three categories: Negroes as citizens; Negroes' actions and attitudes toward the white people; and Negroes' treatment of Negroes.

Negroes as Citizens
CLASS AND OTHER DIFFERENCES

Most respondents recognize differences among Negroes. Many distinguish between white and Negro groups, usually unfavorably to the Negro. Others believe that there are all kinds of Negroes and of white people — good and bad in both races — and that Negroes are also human beings. These respondents deal with Negroes as individuals, noting differences among them as they do with white people.

We deal with these people [Negroes] as individuals. We don't treat whites as a race. There's good and bad in all races. It boils down to the individual that has to be considered rather than people as a race. (2B)

If I had something to say, I'd say to the white people, "Why are you running away? For what? The colored people are humans the same as we are with the exception of some who are undesirable, but that is true with some individual whites too." I would have no objection if colored people live next door and are nice people. I take them as they come. Just because they're colored, that wouldn't change me. (5B)

Some respondents realize that there are social classes — upper, middle, and lower — among Negroes as among white people. Most speak of a "good" and a "bad" class, or of a "high" and a "low" class. Class distinctions are based on social, economic, and occupational differences, with much emphasis on educational differences.

I've come to realize that there are definite classes of colored just like there are classes of white. (17B)

We have white and Negro from the very lowest class to the upper middle class economically, laborers and all kinds. (67A)

The educated Negro of a higher social standard is on a par with the better class of whites, and the same is true with the lower class of white as compared with the lower class of Negro. (38A)

In Table 22 (Appendix C) on distinctions among Negroes, the largest category for Areas A, C, and CX and the Area C branch offices, and the second largest for Area B is the one in which the respondents are aware of two groups of Negroes of different educational and economic levels — the small well-educated, "fine" group and the large uneducated "lower element," whose manner of living, as far as they can observe, is unacceptable to white people.

We have some very fine colored here in Area A. Directly opposite me there is a prominent surgeon and his wife. They're good neighbors, but it's just as if you're asked about the human race and you talk about Lincoln and Washington. But the majority act differently, and it's the majority we're objecting to. (25A)

Many colored people are respectable and prosperous and take care of their property but they are few in proportion. (60C)

In dealing with them I've dealt with colored lawyers and have found out there are very intelligent, well-bred ones. The majority you hear about are the poorer, ill-mannered ones . . . the majority are of the lower class economically. In other words, they didn't have the opportunity. (72C)

Almost every respondent spoke well at some point in the interview of certain Negroes, and many spoke of the "better class," the "best element"

59

among Negroes. One said his Negro tenants are pleased that he does not permit overcrowding in his buildings. Another stated that a Negro rapist makes many innocent Negroes suffer.

Some respondents take the extreme view that the Negro race is inferior and will take a long time to improve. One said:

Certainly there is no advantage in renting to colored unless you have to. Property begins depreciating immediately on colored occupancy. If colored have lived in a building for 10 years, it has depreciated 15 per cent. They are much harder on the building. They have no regard for property values. They have no control over their children. They destroy property in occupying it. This applies to all except the very top grade of tenant, the high economic standard college graduate — to about 90 per cent of them. They've got another hundred years to go before they'll be at the point of being civilized. I've been in business for 25 years, and the more I see of them, the more I think they just climbed out of the trees. Of course, that's making a generalization you can't do. As a race, that's what I think of them, not individually. I didn't always have that attitude. The more you do business with them, the more you have to come around to that attitude. . . . I definitely consider them inferior as a race. I feel superior to them *as a race*. There are many, many cases of very intelligent people among them, no nicer anywhere, the educated. There are some uneducated ones, poor economically, whom I consider very fine people. . . . That's how I feel about them as a race, but there are a lot of them I wouldn't mind living next door to, not on a social basis, but as neighbors. (67A)

MANNER OF LIVING

Most respondents who compare white people and Negroes refer principally to the uneducated majority of Negroes. They observe in this group a manner of living and thinking different from that of the average white man. Some call this a different "psychology," "ethics," "outlook," or "sense of values." Twenty-eight respondents of Areas A, B, CX, and the Area C branch offices and 7 of Area C found a number of faults with Negroes' conduct. They say the Negro family is noisier than the white family, stays up later at night, and is less tidy and careful in housekeeping. Negro families are generally larger than white families, and in addition, they often bring in another family to help pay the rent, so that their dwelling is crowded. The Negro tenant is on the whole more destructive than the white tenant. Prospective Negro tenants and buyers are unreliable, not keeping appointments or coming late, paying the deposit on an apartment and then not appearing again. One respondent described his solution to this kind of behavior:

We have had to change some of our operating techniques. One example, in coming in to rent. The colored guy might not show up at the appointed hour. A white woman says she likes an apartment and she fills out an application. The rental is $80 and the deposit is $20. I process the application and call you in 2 days, and say that you are to come in and pay the $60. You come in and the deal is made. We started doing that. In 3 out of 4 cases, we couldn't find them again. *Now*, if a colored guy wants to rent an apartment with us, he pays 1 month's rent on filling out the application. That usually keeps him in touch with us. It's called security deposit. (17B)

A somewhat similar experience was reported in Interview J. This interview of Area B was not included in the sample because the interviewee is not a real estate broker, but an operator only. He has 96 Negro tenants in his buildings.

Different problems arise in regard to character, in regard to ethical behavior. An apartment is for rent. The first man [Negro] comes and says he'll bring his wife. She comes to look at the apartment. She says the furniture may not fit in it. Two days later, they come in and decide to take it. "Have you got the rent deposit?" He says, "No," and turning to his wife, asks, "Have you got it?" She says, "No, I left it on the dresser." They go and never did come back. That's an example of how this type of people will behave. You can't rely too much on what they say.

Negro applicants for apartments have been found to give false references. Sometimes, the name of a person who has good references is given, and later a different person moves into the apartment. Charge accounts given as references are found to be accounts for jewelry on credit, not standard accounts at Marshall Field.

A number of respondents have found some prospective Negro buyers also to lie about the amount of money they could invest in a home:

I enjoy selling to them, even though it's more difficult to sell to them, because they are so appreciative of what they get. [Why is it more difficult?] Because of the financing and because the prices asked are much higher and many of the Negroes imagine they have more money than they actually have, and when we get a building for them, we find they have only $3,000 when they said they had $5,000. (9B)

With the colored customer, you have to have a lot of patience. If they have $2,000 in their pocket, they're looking for a 3-flat. If they have $5,000, they're looking for a 6-flat. . . . If you do show them a piece of property they like, and the down payment is $5,000, if they have $3,000 they give you different stories. They want to buy but they have to take a trip to see their father or a sick brother, or mother or sister. Meantime they're trying to get money. They'll string you along. They just got back. They keep telling you so many stories, just lies. I just got sick and tired of it. . . . They did not keep appointments, yes, but that is not too important. White clients were much better, much easier to deal with. If they couldn't raise the down payment, if that building was out of their reach, they came out and said so, and the property was forgotten about. . . . (Interview O, left real estate business in Area B)

About a dozen respondents spoke of the improvidence of Negroes. They said that Negroes do not look ahead: they live from day to day, buy more than they can pay for, and get heavily into debt. They are not concerned about the total price of a house, car, or washing machine, so long as the down payment is within their reach. The first collector gets their money, and the rest have to wait. Coupled with this improvidence is a generally unstable mode of life. Many are insecure in their jobs; when they lose a job, they cannot pay the rent, and so they move. Most are not established, although real estate men are aware that there are the settled ones with good jobs. Many, like children, do not take care of things. One respondent described average Negroes: "They don't take care of property, their autos, their clothes, but there are 1 in 10 of them that do take pretty good care of things. In your white people, there are probably 7 in 10, a much bigger percentage who take care of things. (17B)"

Seven respondents of Areas A and B, and 2 of Area C, most of whom deal extensively with Negroes, spoke strongly of the lack of conventional morality among Negroes. They maintain that there is more marital infidelity among Negroes than among white people, more unmarried couples living together, and greater acceptance of the bearing of illegitimate children.

They are working people. Ninety-eight per cent of them, the man and wife both work. In many cases they live together as man and wife and are not married. They live in a sort of partnership way. The man pays half and the woman pays half. We don't know whether they're married or not. Lots of them don't bother to get a marriage license and when they decide to dissolve, they just dissolve. They come down and say, "Mr. So-and-so is moving out of my apartment." She'll still go by that name, but she has her maiden name on the letter box. That's not too uncommon. That's right. A man moved in, a Mr. and Mrs. X. All of a sudden she comes down and says, "Mr. X is moving out." I said, "Shall I change your name to your maiden name?" "Oh, no," she said, "He might come back." He did. They're nice people. They pay their rent promptly. (Interview J)

There is no common ground of understanding between the colored man and his wife as to family life. The respect of womanhood is somehow not there. They are a race which respects not the sanctity of thy neighbor's wife, which again makes for loose morals. Who is to blame I know not, but the morals of the Negro male and the female have been the same in regard to lack of fidelity. Both are of the same character. (46A, almost 2,000 Negro tenants)

The colored are different. Take even the most educated. They're different from white. They have no morals. Marriage means nothing to them. . . . They'll have children from different men and the children see that in the home. Marriage means nothing. Their morals are terrible. . . . These lawyers and doctors I haven't come close to know how they live, but the majority are like that. They'll sit in church, then steal. They're much more immoral than the white. Colored ministers are corrupt. I think colored women are even more immoral than the colored men, both married and unmarried. There is no fidelity to husband or wife. It makes me sick when I think of them building these projects, and cheap rents, and here they have men coming in. They give them the preference to white people who are in need and who are moral, who are really married and have legitimate children. . . . Their morals are not what they should be. A child has a baby. They take her in. Everything is fine. (75C, 90 per cent of sales business with Negroes)

A few respondents reported some crime among their Negro tenants — stealing from furnished apartments or from other tenants, using and selling of narcotics.

A large number of them are narcotics addicts. We've had to put 8 tenants out of that one building on X street [Area A] alone. The police have been in there at least 6 times, following up, trying to locate sellers of drugs. They found people buying from people in our building. . . . We've been thinking of doubling it [security deposit] because they take things from the apartment. They steal. The last 3 tenants who left our apartments had taken pictures, lamps, bedroom furniture, bedspreads, mattress pads, pillows, all the bedroom rugs. . . . This never happened with white tenants, and I've been having tenants since 1937. (33A)

We put special locks on all apartments in this building because they have a tendency of robbing each other. They blame one another. We have found this to happen a lot of times, but since we put the locks on, we're all right. They themselves began to secure themselves, protecting themselves with extra locks. So we put locks on ourselves. White people don't secure themselves that much. Sometimes there may be an intruder, but, if there are easy pickings, someone in the building will take a chance. In other words, they don't trust each other. (Interview J)

A considerable number of the respondents agree that the undesirable manner of living among Negro families is attributable largely to too little education. The Negroes newly arrived from the South receive much of the criticism from the respondents, who find them illiterate, unfamiliar with the requirements of urban home management, and untrained for maintaining an acceptable level of cleanliness. Their cultural standards are far below those of Negroes who have grown up and gone to school in Chicago. They do not look after property or behave properly away from home. Neither white nor Negro residents welcome them — only the industries are glad to have the labor of those who do not go on relief and who will do work white men will not. Respondents blame these Negroes for much of the crime committed by Negroes in Chicago. They liken Negroes to European immigrants of the nineteenth and early twentieth centuries who could not perform according to the cultural standards of the United States. A few respondents are aware that the southern Negroes have not had the opportunities of northern Negroes.

If we could eliminate or retard, rather, the immigration from the South, we'd have little problem here. That's the main point. We're not ready to absorb them. Those that come up here are not ready for our culture. We should absorb them slower. . . . When they first come up, they seem to go wild with enthusiasm and whiskey. Go down to X and Y [streets in Negro area] and see how they carry on. They don't know how to use modern buildings, plumbing. You'll find bottles in there. You can find anything. I know of one elevator building where they use the window. . . . They're not educated. That's where the trouble lies. (83C)

If we provide public housing, it will bring in more and more Negroes. I don't think even the Negroes want that to happen in Chicago, because the Negroes coming in from the South are just as different from the Negroes of the North in culture that they seem to belong to 2 different races. (62BOC)

You have a low class of colored and the high class of colored, the better class of colored. The low ones are those that come from the South. They never had a chance. We have 1 tenant. He worked in the South. He practically ran the place, a cleaning plant. He was paid $9.00 a week. Here he is working for $95.00 a week. (28A)

SOCIAL RESPONSIBILITY

Although the respondents blame the Negroes from the South for much unacceptable behavior, complaints about lack of social responsibility are addressed to the Negro group in Chicago as a whole. These complaints come most strongly from 19 in Areas A, B, and CX, and 7 in Area C. Specific complaints have to do with Negroes as tenants. Some respondents find that the Negro tenant will not accept responsibility for damage in his apartment. Even screened Negro tenants commit careless and destructive acts and will not admit them. Many Negro tenants pay their rent late. One respondent described their behavior, "During the occupancy of the white people, if there was any damage done to the property in the building, usually the white people admitted and agreed to pay for such damages, where the colored deny everything about the damage and they will not agree to pay for such damages. (5B)" And another said, "White people, tenants, that is, will admit they can't pay when they can't, but colored people threaten you. They're very nasty when we put them out. 'I'll take care of you personally,' they say. (37A)" Other Negro tenants move out in the middle of the night and do not pay their rent at all (see pp. 47–48, respondent 22B).

General complaints deal with housing, the treatment of criminal offenders, welfare services, and so forth. The real estate men maintain that Negroes get too much for nothing and thus come to believe that they are entitled to medical and other services. Negroes demand respect without having earned it. They should carry their own load, do something for themselves — build some housing instead of expecting the white people to do it for them, shoulder their financial responsibilities, and assume responsibility for their actions instead of shouting "discrimination" while many of their number violate certain standards of community life. Before making demands for acceptance, they should have less arrogance and a greater sense of civic duty: they should take wrongdoers among them to task instead of defending them; they should develop a sense of concern for property, in particular, other people's property. The respondents point to exceptions, but they emphasize that there are too many of the other kind.

The Negro needs education and knowledge so that he can assume the responsibilities that equality requires. He must be able to assume his financial responsibilities. . . . He has come along too fast and expects everything to be handed to him on a silver platter. . . . They want all the benefits that society gives but they don't want to pay the price. ["They have come along too fast." What do you mean by that?] Groups of so-called intellectuals in the Negro group are in the minority amongst their own people and they must learn that instead of hammering away at the white people they better begin teaching the rudiments and the fundamentals of what equality means to the colored people. (71C)

The Negroes are getting too much. They're being given too much. Then they think it's coming to them. Since the Supreme Court decisions about housing and school segregation, the Negroes in the North have become very bold, very arrogant. (75C)

They want more and more. They read in the Negro newspapers about discrimination, and they want their rights, but have no idea of the responsibility, of the obligation that go with rights. (1B)

I made a study of this. I find out that it's hard along certain lines to get a conviction of the colored person committing a crime unless it's iron-clad evidence. Their usual defense is that they are picked upon because of the racial question. . . . You will find a lot of our people who are not bigoted and charitable at heart that have made and would have continued to make contributions toward helping the unfortunates into betterment providing the organized attitude of the colored or the attitude of the colored organizations would try and help clean their own house . . . (4B)

Let the Negro earn his reputation with the public and there won't be any trouble. I was raised in a neighborhood where there were Negroes 50 years ago. I played ball with them and went to school with them. So did the rest of the people because they earned the respect of their neighbors. So there is too much coddling of them today because of the fact that they are Negroes, and the ones that are not worthy of respect presume that it is their right although they don't deserve it. . . . (84C)

POLITICAL INFLUENCE

A small number of respondents attributed the problems of the changing neighborhood to the political influence of Negroes in Chicago and decried the consequences of such influence. They claimed that because political parties depend on the Negro vote, Negroes get public housing projects, free welfare services, and extra police protection when entering white areas. These respondents said that Negroes are encouraged to come to Chicago for political reasons.

Here Negroes get police protection as long as they need it. Just you go down to X [Negro area] to live, and try to get police protection there. Well, just try. You won't get it. Why? Politics. The Negro vote. If it weren't for the politicians, there wouldn't be any problem. (17B)

That [coming of Negroes from the South] is due to the fact that they get everything. They come up here from the South sick. They go to the County Hospital and get all these things through politics. (25A)

Do you know what the colored population increase has been? It was

485,000 in 1949. Now it is over 1,000,000. That's where the political pressure comes in. They have to please these guys. (63C)

The politicians will do anything to get the Negro vote. They all depend on it. That's why you have Trumbull Park and all the public housing projects for Negroes. (75C)

A few respondents relate the political influence of the Negro population in Chicago to race consciousness. They point out that Negroes vote as a block for Negro candidates. Many respondents noted that Negroes favor Negroes in business and in other situations as well; only two added that any racial or ethnic group favors its own.

PROGRESS

A small number of respondents — 13 of Areas A, B, and CX and 3 of Area C — spoke of the progress Negroes have made in education, business, home ownership, and political and community participation. Some of these spoke unfavorably of Negroes in other parts of the interview, and a few considered them inferior to white people. This group emphasized the recency of Negro freedom — Negroes have done well to have come as far as they have — and intimated superiority, calling as much attention to Negroes' recent slavery as to their progress. Other respondents said that Negroes had no opportunities in the past but now are progressing rapidly.

The colored man's money is just as good to me as anyone else's. It's a positive crime to take money and not give proper service. He's one degree removed from slavery. If we think we're a superior race, we should show that we are. They're human beings. . . . [Toward the middle of the interview] I see a wonderful uplift in the colored race here. They're trying to get an education, a home, to give their children more than they had themselves. They're really trying. . . . [Toward the end of the interview] If these colored people are human beings I better try and treat them as human beings. Let me try and help them. I didn't feel that way at one time, maybe because I'm older, but you can do just so much. You have 20 Negroes coming to you. You have to slough them off. (42A)

If I were a Negro leader, I'd be fighting hard. They've come a long way. Why, 10 years ago they couldn't buy a house. Now they can go anywhere. (24B)

The Negro has made rapid strides in the last 50 years. They will make more rapid strides in the next 50 years. Probably the Irish, the Polish immigrants that came to this country at the turn of the century were in about the same position as the Negro today. . . . I've been in contact with them for the last 25 years, and I've noticed a big improvement in them in a business way, their way of doing business. Because of the rise in their economic conditions, they have branched out more, they are doing more, they are buying more. They are more a part of the community. (38A)

There has been a greater increase in ownership of property by colored in the past 15 years than by any group. Their desire for homes has been great. It's a natural expression of their trying to improve themselves. They have done a terrific job in trying to improve their position. (41A)

Negroes' Actions and Attitudes
PLANNED ACTION TO FORCE WHITE PEOPLE TO MOVE

A considerable number of respondents — 21 of Areas A, B, and CX, 4 of Area C, and 1 from an Area C branch office — stated that Negroes try to get into white areas and that Negroes seem to plan action to force white people to move from an area they wish to enter. Some explained that Negroes want to move into nice areas, and nice areas happen to be those where white people are living. Negroes' action may be nonviolent: spreading rumors that Negroes have bought or are on the point of buying in the area, walking and driving up and down the streets of the area, and approaching owners to see if they will sell their property. Or it may be violent: elbowing people off the street, throwing bricks through windows, and slugging people over the head. Either way, the Negroes' intention is clear.

The root of the evil [of sale of property to Negro in white area] is the fact that the Negro is not accepted in the white neighborhood and that's where he wants to get in. I've had it said to me many times by Negroes, "I want to buy in a white neighborhood. Haven't you got something in a white neighborhood?" We've taken it up with the Urban League, and they say, "Why shouldn't they?" We tell them, it destroys values. They say, it shouldn't destroy values. (35A)

Apartment buildings are what the colored would want first for income and to take over the neighborhood, to take the block over. Once they got an apartment building or 3 small buildings, the block would be gone. Yes, it is the colored man's intention, his intention, to take over the block, because when they take this apartment building, then they will buy up all the small stuff, the buildings right next, those under $10,000. Then the rest will fall in to colored people. . . . I have a lot of colored people come in and want to get an apartment in a white area. (78B)

Let's have harmony without violence, pressing, like saying, "We're going to put so many in each block." They've come in and said so. Yes, I've heard that from colored people. (83C)

There is a certain period of fear. It seems like a calculated procedure that's followed by the colored people before they break into a neighborhood — such things as shopping in the target neighborhood. Yes, Negroes come in deliberately to shop in the stores. They also drive up and down the streets for no apparent reason. They'll also utilize some of the public playgrounds on a limited scale once in a while, and parks if there are any. Yes, this has happened in all of those areas. . . . The whole thing is predicated on that psychosis of fear which has been produced by this softening up period. Yes, I've the impression that this is a planned thing. I've been told by colored real estate men that colored were going to occupy a certain neighborhood before any attempt to purchase any property in that neighborhood was made. (74CX)

In our experience in the X [citizens' organization], we can tell that they — the colored groups — would plan an attack on a given area, first, by circulating rumors through plants and by knocking on doors in the area and asking if the property was for sale. They would answer all advertising in that area. They would offer exorbitantly high prices for the first building in any general area. We also noticed that, without exception, there seemed to be colored people walking through an area which they were ready to attack. We came to the opinion that it was a planned approach to break the morale of the white people. (90A)

I've been told by owners that a nigger broker would come into Area A to the owners, certain owners, and say, "Do you want to sell your building?" and try to get the listing to sell. "If you won't sell, you'll have to sell because the people next door have sold to a Negro." . . . The Negro broker was trying to frighten them. (29A)

I've seen Negro women jostle white women on the street. They'll come along and give them a shove off the street. (69D, area Negroes are entering)

When they buy a building, they want the whites to get out. They make things very, very uncomfortable for the whites. You've seen these colored auto drivers on the street, haven't you? They don't give the white man a chance. I know a building where a colored man bought and he imposed conditions on the white tenants so that they had to get out . . . (31A)

They seem to try to get the white tenants out. They try to annoy the white tenants, their white neighbors. How? By profanity, obscenity, throwing of stones and other objects, pushing whites off the street, insulting whites in every way. (30A)

There are many things they've been doing to scare white people . . . That is a certain element that are trying to get the white people out of the neighborhood. How do they annoy white people to get them out? By breaking into their cars, getting into their garages, burglarizing. (33A)

There is intolerance amongst Negroes against the white. I have 2 white sales ladies living at X and Y [streets in largely Negro area]. It's better than 50 per cent Negro now. A bunch of Negro teen-agers chased her, threw bottles, hit her with one bottle, and told her to get out of the area. Two weeks ago they threw bricks through a front window when she was telephoning. (9B)

At . . . [area adjoining Area B] there is a property we manage. . . . We had no vacancies. We had white shopkeepers. It was fully occupied. We were the last to go colored. The people would be sleeping and a brick would come through their windows. That happened frequently, so they said, "We're getting out." [Is throwing of bricks frequent?] Oh, yes, all over, as soon as one building is left white, they throw bricks through the windows. (23A)*

A few respondents spoke of a different experience: 1 of Area A knew of cases where Negroes bought a building and did all they could to keep the white tenants, and 2 of Area A and 1 of Area B reported that the Negro owners for whom they were managing buildings kept their tenants white.

NEGROES' ATTITUDES TOWARD WHITE PEOPLE

Six respondents of Areas A and B stated that there is hatred of or prejudice against white people among Negroes, and 3 believe that Negroes are more prejudiced against white people than white people are against Negroes.

If a white broker has his office in an area that has become Negro, he'll have to move. Prejudice operates both ways. There's no evidence in any of my own studies that there is any less prejudice on one side than on the other. It's probably more universal on the minority side than in the majority group, as witness the fact that in politics in the over-all picture we have many members of minority groups who are representatives of all the people, but in no colored area do we have any member of the majority group elected to represent the people where they would have a chance to elect a minority group member. People get all excited and begin to think unrealistically. They think race prejudice operates only one way. It operates both ways with equal force and even more force from the minority group. (34A)

Six respondents claim that Negroes want social recognition from white people. The real estate men say this detracts from the Negro's dignity and lessens the likelihood of his being accepted and respected; the Negroes'

* In Pretest Interview C, the hitting of white people over the head and the throwing of bricks through the windows of white people's homes in the partly or largely Negro area was also reported.

best chance of acceptance lies in his development as a distinct person rather than in an aping of the white man.

The Negro seeks white relations, but the white does not seek Negro relations. It's a social problem. It's an evolutionary problem. (19B)

The main thing is the education of the Negro into becoming a reliable, self-sustaining individual. The Negro must learn to solve his own problems, to build his own homes, . . . and primarily the Negro must learn to find reasons to be happy that he is a Negro, rather than to ape every ambition, whim, desire, of the white man and to attach himself to the white man. The Negro should be proud of being a Negro. (69B)

Still other respondents speak of Negroes' friendliness and kindness, of their housing problem, and the difference between "good" Negroes and troublemakers. "Good" Negroes do not go where they are not accepted, do not try to break into white neighborhoods, do not want to create a disturbance, and are not aggressive or arrogant. The troublemakers are just the opposite.

The good Negro is a substantial, well-employed citizen and a guy that doesn't want to make trouble. (66C)

The Negro that wants to pioneer is usually of the leftist element, the Negro that pushes into a white area. Most of your Negro clients want to know if they would be acceptable in the area. (9B)

Colored people are not trying to break into white neighborhoods. It is only where they have been so exploited in other neighborhoods, that . . . they bust into other neighborhoods. They live in terribly overcrowded quarters. (58C)

You'd drop in your tracks if you saw how some Negroes live. No X [community improvement organization in Area A] coming down there. Well, in some cases with the horrible conditions under which some of them live, you can figure why they have to expand in some manner. . . . In the Black Belt there is a 2-mile stretch where there are terrible conditions — cubicles where people sleep in shifts. (21B)

A few respondents point out that the Negro, like the white man, is trying to better himself, and that what he wants is equal opportunity and treatment as a citizen, not as a servant.

NEGROES' TREATMENT OF NEGROES

Fifteen respondents of Areas A, B, and CX, and 2 of Area C maintained that Negro owners do not treat their Negro tenants so well as white owners do. They charge higher rents, encourage overcrowding, and withhold standard services (maintenance, equipment, and so forth). Some stated that Negroes expect a better deal from the white man. Respondents said that some Negro real estate brokers have swindled their own people and that a few of these are serving prison terms. In some ways Negroes are thought to be more guilty of discrimination against Negroes than white people — some Negro owners will not rent to Negroes from certain states or even from certain parts of the city; rich Negroes have objected to the building of a project for Negroes near their home.

There are classes in the Negro group as in the white group. There is a Negro that wants to make the dollar. He also buys buildings and moves 3 times as many people into it as a white man would. If there are 6 apartments with 6 rooms each, the Negro puts in about 3 times as many people to occupy the premises as a white man does, by using bunk beds and by a series of sleeping shifts. He's doing it to make a lot of money fast. (27A)

Negroes say that the worst landlord in the world is the Negro landlord. The Negro will exploit his own. The most ruthless landlord is the Negro landlord. They exploit to the nth degree. (69B)

The majority of Negro owners gouge their own people in regard to rent in order to make money fast. They don't give them any service. They don't give them the things they're entitled to. Negro people get fairer treatment from the white landlords. The Negro owners run their own buildings and that's why you get the "gouge." (56A)

I would say the colored are very much more severe on their own tenants than white landlords by far in regard to rents and otherwise. The colored person is more afraid of colored police than of white police. That's true of the schools. Colored children are more in fear of Negro teachers because they beat them up in the schools. . . . I would say the colored expect a better deal out of the whites than they do out of their own. They don't trust their own. (83C)

The Negro himself has not done anything — very few Negroes have done anything to benefit their own people. When they get a few dollars ahead, they are not satisfied nor do they want to live among their own people. The proof of that has been the so-called housing project at X, where numerous Negroes tried to prevent the building of that project for fear that poorer class Negroes might get in there. Yet the Negro will resent the white man having any opinion as to who he would like to have for a neighbor. (32CX)

Most of the respondents criticized the majority of Negroes chiefly for the difference in manner of living of Negro families as compared with white families and for their lack of social responsibility. The important implication is that the majority of Negroes would not make desirable neighbors.

COMPONENT 2. BELIEFS ABOUT WHITE PEOPLE'S ATTITUDES TOWARD NEGROES

The majority of the respondents believe that most white people entertain unfavorable images and beliefs about Negroes and do not wish to have Negroes as neighbors in the same building or even in the same neighborhood. The real estate brokers reach this conclusion on the basis of what the white people say and do.

Twenty five out of 35 respondents (71 per cent) in Area A, 15 out of 23 (65 per cent) in Area B, 19 out of 21 (91 per cent) in Area C, 4 out of 6 in Area CX, and 1 of 2 Area C branch offices claimed that all or the majority of white people say they do not want to have Negro neighbors. The percentage is smallest in Area B, where there is the largest proportion of Negroes and where the remaining white people have experienced living near them the longest; the percentage is largest in Area C, where white people have not lived next to Negroes at all or not so long. (Table 23, Appendix C.)

What white people say they will do and what they in fact do have turned out to be different, not only in cases where people had said they would not move if Negroes entered their area or block, but also in certain cases where people had said they would move but did not do so — at first because they could not and later because the new situation was not so unpleasant as they had expected.

In reply to Question 22, "What do the white people of this community say about having Negroes as neighbors?" respondents gave favorable, partly favorable, and unfavorable answers.

The favorable statements are in the form of surprise over how all right they are, how they are nicer people than those that were there before, lovely, quiet. (22B)

At first they say, "I won't live with colored." After they get in, they seem to change because they take care even better than the white people. They even remodel flats. (78B)

That is hard to say. There are some who don't mind, some who think they're very good, better than the white people who were there before. There are some who just can't stand them or won't ever try to. It all depends on the person and his particular upbringing, his outlook on life. If you have an individual who is not prejudiced, should I say, that type of individual will be a lot more likely to go along. (41A)

It seems to me that the more common the white person, the worse is said about the Negro. They're the ones that talk about the "nigger." Not that the white of any degree of intellect want to be closely associated in their living with them. (37A)

They absolutely would move. . . . I get their animosity. (49A)

You may indeed conclude that they are not desirous of having them as neighbors, most decisively. This immediate area is of the same character as Trumbull Park. They aren't in the Back-of-the-Yards area, are they? Yet, it's a working-class area. The people have enough political power and ready physical power, if necessary, to keep them out. (66C)

White people's actions reveal even more than their words that they do not want Negroes as neighbors. When Negroes approach a white area, some white owners put their property up for sale and some white tenants leave. As soon as Negroes enter, many houses are thrown on the market, and a panic often ensues, with people selling at whatever price they can get and leaving as soon as possible. Over a dozen respondents spoke of the white people's running away or fleeing when Negroes enter an area. Some "stick with their property," but the pattern has been that the majority do leave.[3] Several respondents stated that there is not so much panic-selling in Area A as there has been in other areas; people are holding out for their price.

When Negroes approach an area, actions of white people outside the area are also affected. The white people who ordinarily would buy residences stop buying in that area, and the white people who would ordinarily rent apartments hesitate for fear that Negroes will enter.[4] The same holds true when Negroes have already entered.

When 1 Negro moves in, the whole area becomes alarmed. I don't think they have cause for alarm until more have moved in. The homes it hurts the most are those that are nearest. The people may want a bigger home — the Negro's presence may not be the reason for moving — but, when they go to sell, the whites won't buy and they can sell only at a depressed price. There is an immediate influence. Maybe only one block is touched, but the whole community becomes alarmed. "I'm going to get out wherever I can," and the sales begin. In 1 case, a neighborhood meeting was held and all said they would hold the line. Within 2 weeks, 1 sold in the X block, another in the Y block. In 1 week's time, 3 dozen for-sale signs had sprung up in those 2 or 3 blocks. (67A)

There follow respondents' statements stressing the effects of the approach of Negroes and the entry of Negroes. Upon the approach of Negroes:

The sales peter out as soon as Negroes are within the next half mile. (9B)

All I can do is to keep my head above water, because I cannot get the whites to buy where there is the remotest chance that it will become colored. (32CX)

Today the influx of non-Caucasians has caused considerable distress in our business because of vacancies that are multiplying in solid white neighborhoods that are on the fringe through the refusal of people to either rent or buy for fear that the foreseeable future will show inroads of so-called undesirable elements. . . . White people wouldn't buy property. They would drive through, see some colored [walking down the street], and they would decide they didn't want to live in that neighborhood. (35A)

Upon the entry of Negroes:

Frankly, that's the case why I'm building, because owners of property in this neighborhood want cash for property which should be sold to colored on time, and there are a great number of people in the neighborhood who do not want to sell to colored and whites will not buy. (31A)

We always carried about 3 salesmen in this office. In the last years they've all quit. They say they can't sell, because we don't allow them to sell to colored and whites are hard to sell to. (51A)

But if you're talking about homes, as they approach on the fringe, selling or renting become very difficult, *as they approach,* yes. It is even more difficult afterwards, no question about it. Negroes have made great strides. This will taper off in time. But so far whites just run away. . . . If there are already 2 or 3 in a block, the remaining sales from then on out for the most part will go to Negroes. The only exception is the speculator for resale for profit. (27A)

Some white people remain when Negroes enter, and some buy or rent residences for their own use in an area where Negroes are living. Ten respondents of Area A, 5 of Area B, and 3 of Area C spoke of owners who remained in Areas A and B or in some other area after Negroes had entered, and 8 respondents of Area A, 2 of Area B, and 2 of Area CX spoke of white tenants who remained in a building after Negroes moved into it. The owners' reasons for remaining are the desire to remain in long-time homes, the financial inability to move, loyalty to the neighborhood, and the gradual adjustment to living in an interracial community.

I know of a lot of cases of people staying in the area . . . [where Negroes have moved in]. It doesn't make any difference to them as long as the neighborhood remains nice — no hold-ups, a safe neighborhood. (14B)

People that have investments, homes in the area, those that have remained, have more or less adjusted to having an interracial community, to get along. (57A)

In X [largely Negro area] where you have wide streets and more single and 2-family dwellings, there has been a completely mixed reaction. The first bunch fly. Then some hang about for maybe 3, 4, 5 years. Those that hang back are mostly older people without children. They stay for various reasons. They are not active in churches and are not anxious to go with their friends in their congregation. They love their home, have lived in it a long time. They'll tell you that the new Negro neighbors are better neighbors than the white. They spend more money in cleaning, tuck-pointing, etc. (53A)

The tenants' reasons for remaining are the physical and cultural advantages of the area, cheaper rents in some cases, freedom to move because of month-to-month tenancy, and the real estate agent's care in selecting Negro tenants. In some cases, the respondents are referring largely to white people without children.

At X [Area A], there were 7 or 8 remaining. I was amazed when they renewed their leases. Of course, they pay cheaper rents than the colored would pay. (47A)

However, it became obvious that the advantages and physical facilities of the neighborhood [part of Area A] were such that they were able to hold a high proportion of the old tenants. (39A)

In the 72-apartment building, it is 90 per cent Negro and 10 per cent white. . . . Because of the nice living accommodations and the nice neighborhood they will remain regardless of the color of the occupants, as long as we continue to remain very selective in our tenancy by social standard. (88A)

At . . . we have a 32-apartment building. It is 4 years since the first Negro moved into the building. There are 4 or 5 white tenants still there. Evidently they intend to remain. They asked for leases. We have a building at . . . a 24-flat building. It is 2 years since the first Negro tenant moved in. About 6 white tenants don't show any signs of moving. One thing we do is equalize the rents. (22B)

Question 23b (see Appendix A) was set up to find out whether there are exceptions to the rule that white people do not buy residences for themselves in an area after Negroes have moved into it. The respondents who said there were exceptions usually mentioned Area A, but 3 other areas were also mentioned. Approximately one half of the respondents of Areas A and C knew of such purchases or had heard of them, and 2 Area C branch offices knew of them; the much smaller proportion of respondents (less than one quarter) in Areas B and CX may be due partly to the fact that these real estate men deal largely in areas or parts of areas of preponderantly Negro occupancy or are interested primarily in selling to Negroes. (Table 24, Appendix C.) The respondents gave 3 reasons for such purchases: (1) necessity, such as location of business, nearness to employment or school, inability to buy or move elsewhere; (2) willingness to live in the area, provided it remains a good neighborhood, coupled with the belief that it will remain so; and (3) low prices.

The only reason the white person buys today in the changing area is because the property is less in that area. Some buy for necessity to live in the area. Their business is there or they are [educational institution] people. Generally speaking, 95 per cent of the white will not buy in the colored area. (42A)

[Prices go down in an area] because of the white resident seller being in such a terrific hurry to get out of the community that has already been penetrated. He don't want any association at all with the colored, so no sale to white, *except* in the small area I mentioned [near CX and part of Area C] where 6 buildings have been sold to colored already I was able to sell 4 homes to good bonafide white buyers for residential purposes, in the same pocket where Negroes have come in in the last 8 months. Why? These people — the new buyers — resented the colored, but they got such a terrific buy and felt within themselves that we might possibly be able to hold the community down to those initial 6 colored buyers, that they bought. So the low price plus the possibility of keeping the neighborhood so made those sales possible. The main reason for the low price is that white people are not willing to buy. (61C)

White people's unwillingness to have Negro neighbors has been expressed in certain areas by damage to the properties bought by Negroes and, at times, to the offices of the real estate brokers who participated in these transactions. In addition, there is danger of physical harm to the white broker, the white seller, and the Negro buyer or renter. The Interview Schedule contains no question about violence by white people to keep Negroes from entering their areas, but 9 respondents of Area A, 12 of Area B, and 10 of Area C spoke of white people's hostile acts against Negroes and white real estate brokers — breaking windows, arson, bombing, and rioting. Although such acts had not occurred in Areas A, B, and

CX, some respondents referred to them as a possibility and as a reason for not selling to Negroes in an all-white block.

In business the main thing is to stay out of trouble in the first place, and one sure way of getting into trouble is to put 1 Negro in a white building. The Chicago Housing Authority can do it but we can't. It's a matter of being realistic about it. There would be no limit to the trouble you could get. The minute you do that you are inviting so much trouble. I could get killed. My wife and children could get killed, and it's no exaggeration whatsoever. (10B)

That happened to me last week [asked to manage first Negro-occupied building in the block.] I told the fellow no. . . . I drove by later. There were two police cars there and all the windows were busted out. It was the first building, but I wouldn't have taken it, I'll be honest with you, because of the girls in the office. If there is such animosity, if it is running that high — most of that is done by teen-agers, punks. Intelligent white people pick up and move. . . . These teen-age punks might come by and throw a rock and hurt these girls. (22B)

In the fringe blocks that have been opened, good Negro families hesitate. The broker puts in a poor family just in from the South who don't understand the situation. . . . There has been a blackout on news in the last 6 months. There were 2 bombings at X [area of recent Negro entry]. We don't hear about it. Go look at the *Defender*. (39A)

In an area where it is all white, I would not put a colored family. First, because of the safety of my own skin. Second, I would not want to inflict any personal hard feelings, any hardships on a white or a colored family. After all, any colored person going into an area where there is a crystallized feeling, he is taking his life in his hands, and for me to be a part of that just wouldn't make sense. . . . I wouldn't want to get my head blown off, I wouldn't want the colored man to get his head blown off, or the white seller to get his head blown off. (71C)

White People's Reasons for Not Wanting Negroes as Neighbors

The respondents were asked why white people do not want Negro neighbors. They gave various answers: white people in the North are not used to living near Negroes, do not understand them, are prejudiced against them, or want to live with their own kind; white people and Negroes, like oil and water, just do not mix socially; white people do not want to live with Negroes because their standards are lower; and white people *fear* to live with Negroes. White people's fear received the greatest emphasis.

When it is known that Negroes are approaching an area, a vague fear of what might happen sets in, a fear with which one cannot reason: "There's a lot of things that I've heard — pros and cons. I would say that in the majority they don't like them as neighbors for some reason or other. Sometimes they have a basis for this anti-feeling, but some people just don't have any pinpointed reason. It's just that they're afraid of what they imagine might happen or have heard happened. They're afraid if they should happen to come into the neighborhood, others would follow and the ones that followed would be the less desirable. (52A)"

The white people also have specific fears. They fear that their neighborhood will deteriorate if Negroes come because of their manner of living in other areas: they associate Negroes with the undesirable slum (dirt, noise, squalor, stealing, vice), something to be avoided if possible. If one Negro enters the area, they see the beginning of the breakdown, the decline of their home neighborhood. People are afraid that they will not have a market for the sale of their property, that its value will decline, and that they will lose money. Owners of apartment buildings are afraid that Negro tenants will wreck them. People fear, too, the lack of liquidity of colored property.

White people fear loss of social status if Negroes enter their area ("Even if they were willing to remain in an area in which some Negro families live, they find that their friends are curious to know why they will remain in such an area. (73A)") and fear harm to their children's chances for social advancement ("The fundamental point in the life of the country is the ambition, the desire to improve one's position. A man gets married and has 2 kids. Some kids come to court them. 'Oh, I see you have colored kids next door.' They're embarrassed. People don't say anything. They just move. (70C)").

More widespread is the fear of assault and crime if Negroes enter. White people fear that the worst, criminal element will come in and the neighborhood will become unsafe. Crime increases in the areas where Negroes have entered, and people move because of it. A feeling of insecurity prevails.

They do have a terrific impact on the white neighbor. They scare the whites to death when they move in. They're afraid of the police problems that arise when we have a change in population. (38A)

Well, some [white people] don't mind as long as they behave, and some don't like it. They just don't want to live among the Negroes. They're afraid of them. Some of them say they're afraid of going out on the street alone at night. They're afraid of being held up and other things. I think that's been proven. X [Area A] has more crime than any other area in Chicago. I'm not sure, but it's been publicized. (55C)

White people are afraid to come home at night. If you met one in the hall on coming home you'd be scared to death, because you don't know whether he lives there or is there to hold you up. Most colored people look dangerous. They scare you when you look at them. They scare you when you're not used to them. Even to me they look dangerous at times, just to look at them, and I'm used to them. They seem to carry a hand in the pocket as if they had a gun. They frighten people. [Is it the color that is frightening?] The expression is frightening more so than the color. If you met colored at night, you'd be fearful. If you met one in a white neighborhood, you'd wonder, is he there to hold you up or not. (Interview J)

People fear that the schools will become undesirable — this, say respondents, is the main reason why white people do not want Negroes to come into their area. People fear danger to their children and eventual intermarriage, to which they are strongly opposed. White people with children definitely will not buy property or rent apartments in an area where Negroes are likely to enter or where Negro children are already attending the public schools, and in such an area white people with children sell their homes, give up their apartments (especially if Negroes with children move into their building), and move away because they do not want their children to associate with Negro children in play or in school. Two respondents reported friction between white and Negro children in a high school in Area B and the beating of white students by Negro students. One reported crime in the same high school, where there had been no crime before. One respondent moved his family out of the area because he thought the standard of work at the high school had fallen with the entry of Negroes. Another stated that a white family had moved out of the area because their child had learned undesirable habits of play from Negro children. A third said that white people do not want their children exposed to the morals of Negro people. The respondents, on the basis of their experience with and knowledge of the white people in their communities of operation, consider the school to be the basic problem in the relations between the white and Negro groups.

Now you've got this in your schools. You've got this right in X High School. You've got dope-selling and liquor. . . . I do know a lot of people who won't send their children to X High School. There's crime there. You'll find cuttings. You'll find rape. Don't ask me to prove them. I'd rather you verified them through police records. (4B)

Where we have sold property where there are still white tenants in there, they come to respect each other more, although the thing that pulls them away they get worried about their children, particularly in high school, even in grammar school. They worry about their children merging with them in school. They worry about marriage. In discussing with white people, *invariably* you find the problem about the children. (18B)

I do believe that most of them don't want colored to come in. They want to live by themselves. If the colored live with the white, then the children are together at school. That's what worries them, that later those children will marry, and the parents don't want it. (28A)

Ninety per cent of the people that move, move because of the schools. Sure, absolutely! If you had a lot of colored and white people without children, they'd stay. That's one of the most basic things in the whole business. They don't want their children to mingle. (56A)

[Re white people's reactions to having Negroes as neighbors;] They don't want them. . . . The school. That's the greatest problem of them all. That's basic. (62BOC)

As their children go to X High School and they don't want them to go there, they want to sell and move. Each sale I know of there is difficulty in selling. These are larger homes for families with children, and families with children don't want to move in where their children will have to go to X High School. (73A)

A considerable number of respondents believe that the white people are being forced out of their neighborhoods by the entering Negroes, and that they resent it. They do not want to sell their homes or leave, but they have to because, for the reasons stated above, they will not live in the same area with Negroes. The terms used by the respondents express this compulsion; they speak of the white people as being "uprooted," "pushed out," "forced out," "crowded out," "driven from," and "forced to move." The white people look upon their moving out in this way.

If you have to move from a home in which you have lived for 25 or 45 years because of the influx of people you never mixed with and won't mix with, you lose that enjoyment of your property. You feel you've been pushed out. It's hard to give up your own house. You're still enjoying it. (25A)

Of course, there is a natural resentment of property owners when they [Negroes] come in. They say it's unfair. They say that they're being crowded out of their own neighborhoods. (85CX)

One respondent said, "Well, I meet people on the street. I think I can say there is a kind of feeling of defeatism on a part of them in a way. Most of them will say to me, 'I heard that building went to colored. Oh, I heard the X Hotel was sold to colored.' I try to play it down. Most of them will say, 'Isn't that terrible! Isn't that too bad!' Some will say, 'Well, after all, what can you do about it?' The rumor stuff is accentuated. That's bad. That hurts. (51A)"

In sum, according to the experience and knowledge of the respondents, most white people have an unfavorable conception of Negroes. They do not want Negroes to come into their neighborhood, most of all because they fear deterioration, decline of property values and financial loss, loss of social status, crime and assault, and, particularly, danger to their children through their mingling with Negro children in school and at play, and the possibility of intermarriage. Most respondents maintained that the majority of white people do not want to live in the same building or even in the same neighborhood with Negroes.

COMPONENT 3. BELIEFS ABOUT NEGROES' EFFECT
ON PROPERTY VALUES

"Value" is defined by the Federal Housing Administration as "the price which typical buyers would be warranted in paying for the property for long-term use or investment, if they were well informed, acted intelligently, voluntarily and without necessity." [5] According to the same source, "value" also refers to the capability of useful things to produce benefits that persons need or desire. The future usefulness of a property is the only source of any value it may have. The expectations or forecasts of intelligent buyers and sellers in the market about the extent, quality, and duration of the future benefits from occupancy or rental income of property are translated into present prices. In similar vein, value has been defined by the American Institute of Real Estate Appraisers as "the present worth of all rights to future benefits arising from ownership." [6] Another definition states that value is concerned with "how people think, rather than with physical facts." [7] This refers particularly to the amenities – all those attributes over and above the bare necessities that make a home pleasant. Land and improvements in themselves have no value; value exists only in the minds of the human beings that desire or covet a particular object, and the object in itself has no other value.

Value is established over a relatively long period of time. There are certain situations that disrupt values, but these situations are relatively temporary. Price can vary from value, but it does not do so consistently over a long period of time — eventually value comes to the price, and most of the time, price is the expression of value.

In the light of the foregoing definitions, to consider the effects of movement of Negroes into an area upon price alone would be to omit the most fundamental point in the analysis of this aspect of the subject under consideration — namely, the valuation which white people and Negroes put upon property in an area which concerns them both. Whatever affects their home is of vital concern to people, especially people with families. What respondents understand to be white people's and Negroes' ideas about property valuation affects what they do about real estate transactions involving both races.

Patterns of Effect

The movement of Negroes into an area is seen here as a process in which different effects are produced in the area as the movement progresses. According to the respondents, distinctions should be made among the periods *before*, *during*, and *after* entry. A number of the men draw distinctions among the periods *just after* entry, *after* or *following* entry, and *later*.

Almost all the respondents find that property values are affected when Negroes enter an area, but most of them consider that the major changes in value occur *after* the entry of Negroes rather than during the period of their approach. They are aware that values in certain areas, like Area B, were declining before the entry of Negroes. Their judgments on the effect of Negro movement on property values apply to the better residential areas. Although most respondents report a downward effect on property values as the final outcome of the entry of Negroes into a white area, they also report different patterns of effect both for the *period* when effect takes place and for the *kind of property*. Some report decline in value before entry followed by increase upon or after entry followed by decline; others report decline in value before entry followed by increase after entry. Some report the same effect on both houses and apartment buildings, whereas others report different effects on different kinds of residential property in the same period or in different periods of the movement. A few report no effect. (See Tables 25 and 26, Appendix C.)

Despite the various patterns of effect on values, there are enough similarities among them to permit summarization. The percentage of respondents who maintained that decrease in value of residential property is the

83

final outcome of Negro entry is: Area A, 75; Area B, 72; Area C, 81. In Area CX, 5 of 6 and in the Area C branch offices 1 of 2 respondents also indicated that decrease in value finally results. These respondents hold one or the other of two views: values continue to go down for certain reasons, or values go down to a certain extent and then level off lower than before entry. Thirteen per cent of the respondents in Area A and 11 per cent in Area B maintain that increase in value is the final outcome. Some of these respondents were uncertain whether the higher prices paid would last, whereas others stated that how long they lasted would depend on upkeep of property and on a continuing strong demand by Negro buyers. No respondent in Area C and 1 in Area CX believed values would increase.

The percentage of respondents maintaining that value decreases *at some time* during approach and entry of Negroes is: Area A, 89; Area B, 81; Area C, 95; Area CX, 83; and 2 Area C branch offices. The percentage of respondents who maintain that value does not decrease *at any time* during the entry is: Area A, 11; Area B, 19; Area C, 5; and Area CX, 17 (1/6).

A few respondents believe prices return to normal, are not affected at all, or are affected *either* upward or downward depending on amount of use, upkeep and improvement, the physical condition of adjacent properties, and the general condition of the neighborhood. (Tables 25 and 26, Appendix C.)

TIME PERIODS

The Interview Schedule contained no question about how long each period of Negro entry lasted. However, I estimate from the respondents' statements that the period of approach (when sales to white people become difficult, prices begin to fall, and people start moving away) varies from 6 months to 4 years, and a few respondents emphasized 2 years or more. Several respondents said that the kind of neighborhood would determine how close Negroes would come before it would begin to be hard to sell residences to white people — it varies from a mile, a half mile, or just a block away. One man explained, "It isn't a question of distance. It's the impending threat. Here near this office, it was very difficult to sell any property here to white buyers for normal use. It became difficult about 3 years ago. (74CX)"

Respondents reported that the period of entry of 1, 2, or 3 Negro families into the block may last a few weeks or months. The period of entry of more Negroes may vary according to how eager the white owners are to sell and how eager the Negro buyers are to enter, how greatly they need housing, and how well off they are. Area B was taken over rapidly by Negro buyers and tenants; respondents explained that Negro owners had had to leave properties in another area condemned for a housing project and that the prices they got were high enough so that they could purchase other properties. Respondents spoke also of an area taken over relatively fast because of its desirable housing. Two respondents looked upon the whole "transition" as a 10-year period.

CHANGES IN PRICE

Inflation, government policies, employment trends and wages, rent control and its removal, policies of lending agencies, the real estate business cycle itself, economic conditions within region and municipality, and building obsolescence and deterioration all affect values in real estate aside from Negro entry. The respondents stress the contribution of these factors to changes in price of residential property. Although respondents find it difficult to distinguish the effect of Negro entry from that of general factors on an *increase* in price, they usually attribute a *decrease* in price solely to Negro approach and entry. The two major reasons for lower price on Negro entry are an oversupply of houses when all white residents want to sell at once and a limited market of white speculators and Negroes.

Respondents stated that the prices for residential property, particularly houses, including all periods of entry dropped 10–50 per cent — most dropped 20–25 per cent. (See Table 38 for an array of buying and selling prices.) A number of respondents would not estimate any percentage but gave examples of decline in price.*

* In his study of the movement of house prices in 20 neighborhoods entered by nonwhites and 19 matching all-white neighborhoods in *Property Values and Race* (Berkeley and Los Angeles: University of California Press, 1960; Chs. 6–10), Luigi Laurenti compares average price before entry with average price after entry. He points out the figure after entry and spotlights the difference between it and the figure before entry, but he does not examine the latter figure. According to my respondents, the figure before entry should be emphasized because the *first* change in values and prices of residential real estate takes place in the period of Negroes' approach. Laurenti's comparison does not take into account the effect of Negroes' *approach* on values and prices. Only a comparison of prices during the approach (3–4 years) with prices during the *preceding* period (also 3–4 years) could give meaning to the price figures in the period of approach. Of course, one must also take the precaution of considering other possible influences on prices.

I saw a 2-flat drop in value, because the price offered one year was $22,000, and, the following year, after having it on the market for 4 months, he accepted $12,500. This was in an area where Negroes were approaching. (80C)

A beautiful 3-apartment building, with 6 rooms each, which normally would have sold for $35,000 cash, if the community had remained white, in turn sold for $22,000 on a partial cash basis. (61C)

I sold a home at X [Area A] which, if located in Area C would have brought $65,000 to $75,000 or more. We sold it for $33,000. (39A)

The whites are not buying in here any more, you know. One of these houses I sold last week was worth $17,000. I had to sell it for $13,500, because the niggers haven't got the money, and the white people won't buy because there are niggers on both sides. (3B)

Individual homes, bungalows, are affected more than multiple dwellings. A lady was offered $19,000 for an 8-room house. She waited. Her advisers said to wait until the area was all Negro. It took one year. She wanted $21,000. It is [near Area B]. She got $12,000. I sold it. (69B)

The amount of decline in price depends on how much owners panic and how quickly they want their houses sold. The frequently fast sales when Negroes first enter catch people unprepared — homeowners feel that suddenly the whole neighborhood is going and that they must hurry to sell. This urgency floods the market with houses and affects prices. The amount of decline in price depends also on how desirable the properties are to Negro buyers. With more areas opening to Negroes, their attention turns to better properties in newer areas, and they bypass older areas partly settled by Negroes. Thus, pressure for Negro housing lets up, and prices drop. Some respondents claim that Negroes underpay in older areas because properties there are built better than new houses in the suburbs, constructed with green lumber and more recent, lower standards of workmanship. Some respondents reported that many Negroes will no longer buy or rent in Areas A and B because they are older.

Prices increase 10–50 per cent at the time of or just after Negro entry; the higher prices are accompanied by easier terms of payment. One respondent sums up the matter thus: "Well, you have 2 property values. One is the cash value. The other is the small down payment. The cash value is not good when Negroes enter an area. They can't pay cash, but you can sell for any price if you make the terms right. (30A)" This statement requires some qualification: Some Negroes do have cash, according to 11 respondents of Areas A, B, and CX, 4 of Area C, and 1 Area C branch office. Also, now that more housing is open to Negroes, they shop about and bargain more than before. However, according to the respondents, there are many Negroes who are not concerned about the total price so long as the monthly payment is within reach.

Houses. When Negroes are known to be approaching an area, the houses lose their desirability — that is, their *value*, in the truest sense of the word — to white people who would otherwise be prospective buyers. During the "stalemate," the "doldrums" when Negroes are coming closer but have not yet bought any property and white people are hesitating to buy — some residents are trying to sell either because Negroes may enter or for some other reason. However, these sellers do not have the usual market among white people (see p. 74 and nn. 3 and 4). Thus, prices fall. The owner who must sell and wishes to sell to a white buyer cannot obtain what the property is worth; he is often compelled to sell to a white speculator, who buys at the lowest price accepted.

The respondents maintain that property values go down in a white area when it is known that Negroes are approaching it, but the majority also believe that the major changes in value occur after entry. A few stress equally the periods before and after entry for major changes in value, but 18 respondents of Areas A, B, and CX and 5 of Area C stated that the major changes occur during the approach.

When an area is in direct line with the transition, its market becomes dormant, because you can't get white buyers interested in the district and people become anxious to sell in the white area. That will deflate your market. (17B)

When the first threat that they are approaching comes, the major change occurs. It stops almost overnight — I mean the chance to sell to white other than a speculator. (1B)

Values are depressed when there is a threat of Negroes coming in because the market thins out of people willing to buy. (58C)

During the stalemate, values go down if you're trying to sell to white. . . . I would say from the stalemate on, you can't sell at all. You can't sell to white or colored. It's almost worthless until it comes into a market of colored buyers. That's your biggest jump or difference. It's hardly worth anything. (72C)

When Negroes enter an area, white owners often hurry to sell — 14 respondents of Areas A, B, and CX and 8 of Area C spoke of owners' panicking as soon as one house in the block has been sold to a Negro. But panic-selling was the rule in the past — there are now people in Area A and in other areas who wait rather than take a loss, although they are still trying to sell. White people bring low prices upon themselves by all throwing their properties on the market at the same time — supply is greater than demand. "Suppose you take a virgin territory, a residential neighborhood of bungalows. A colored family buys one house and they have to pay a premium. As soon as they move in, the other people throw their homes on the market. With the oversupply the price goes down. Sure, the white people are doing this drop in price to themselves. In other words, they're running away. . . . The minute you start running, you cut your price. (56A)" The market is limited, as it was during the approach, but it now includes Negroes and white speculators. A number of respondents say that the limited market is a main cause of lowered prices when Negroes enter.

The limited income of many Negroes also puts a ceiling on prices. The Negro does not have so much money as the average white man for buying a house, and his cash payment frequently amounts to $1,000 or $1,500, whereas the white buyer's cash payment is often twice as large. Generally speaking, mortgage houses and credit-rating agencies consider Negro buyers poorer credit risks than white buyers. Qualification for a mortgage is determined largely by stability of employment, income, and credit standing, and Negro buyers have more often been found wanting than white buyers.

We found this: The average colored man finds it a very momentous occasion if he is buying for the first time. We find he has a very strong pride of ownership — in many cases much stronger than the white man in comparable circumstances. . . . He takes pride in meeting his payments promptly and he takes pride in maintaining his real estate. It's obvious why because the average colored man never owned real estate before — never thought he could. Only in the last few years they have been able to buy in areas where they wished to buy. They're not restricted by restrictive covenants, and mortgage money is gradually becoming more available, more available on the same terms as the white man but not yet on the same terms. If the colored man hopes to be on the same terms as the white man, he will have to prove himself as good a risk as the white man in comparable circumstances. What terms? Principally in the length of amortization. There is a feeling that property occupied by colored deteriorates much more rapidly than that occupied by white people. I think that is a fallacy that will be exploded as time goes on, although there has been a basis for that, because colored people in years gone by had to live in slum property discarded by white people. . . . Now they can go anywhere. (90A)

We pay for Dun and Bradstreet's reporting service. On our white tenants, 90 per cent will pass. Only 40 per cent of Negro tenants applying have acceptable credit. (1B)

It's a negative attitude because of the wanton destruction, the depreciation. They destroy the goddamn stuff. Even the Negro ones [lending agencies] won't take a risk on their own kind. . . . Loaning money and insuring people must be made on a basis of experience and/or past record. Fire insurance companies have left the field, the nonwhite, that is, because of a bad experience. Lenders of money have left the field because of a bad experience. It is my opinion that they are missing now a field which offers a lucrative return based on a new risk who formerly was not entitled to the benefits of credit and respect, but who now has respectful economic security and *has earned it.* I am referring to the fact that lenders, insurance companies, put all Negroes in 1 bundle. They don't know these things as I do. They don't get close to them. I got a reality. (47A)

A number of respondents recognize the economic improvement of many Negroes, as did 90A and 47A above (see also pp. 67–68). But partly because Negro buyers usually have little cash and a poor credit standing, lending agencies do not readily lend to them and do not lend at all in changing neighborhoods until some Negroes are living there (see pp. 166–172). That is why the white seller in such neighborhoods must often take a low cash price from a speculator or a small down payment from a Negro buyer with the remainder on contract (see Table 15, Appendix C). The small down payment is too small for a down payment on another house. If the owner will not sell to Negroes or needs a down payment large enough to buy another house, he will probably sell to a speculator—the total price of his property will suffer, but he will get enough cash to purchase another house.

To sum up: The two main reasons for lowered prices in an area that Negroes have entered are, according to the respondents, the oversupply that results from white owners' throwing their properties on the market and the limited market of speculators and Negro buyers brought about by the withdrawal of most white people from this market. The Negro buyers' difficulty in obtaining mortgages and their lack of cash further limit the market.

Sometimes prices of houses rise when Negroes enter. Most respondents maintain that Negroes pay a premium only for the first 1, 2, or 3 houses in a white area in order to get into the area. A few disagree, insisting that the first ones will not pay the high prices asked because they will be exposed to all the dangers of the "break-in," such as window-breaking, arson, bombing, rioting, and other violence; these respondents say those following the first buyers pay the best prices because there is no danger. Most Negroes do not want to enter a hostile area any more than white people do. Also, lending agencies will not lend when there is any risk of damage to the property, and this affects value. When the danger of rioting is over, lending agencies willing to lend to Negroes in a changing neighborhood will again make loans, and this is when better prices can be obtained.

First carries highest price, *fallacy!* Actually you find that the colored people as a whole do not want to be the first to break into an area. They're reluctant to. Usually the first will pay a little less than 2, 3, 4, 5, or 6. The first buyer, he's taking a greater risk. He's the first pioneer. He's entitled to a better deal. The men who say the first get higher are definitely wrong. The highest prices are paid by the second, third, fourth, and fifth buyers. (41A)

Since lending agencies as a rule will not make a loan for breaking a neighborhood, a number of respondents state emphatically that certain organizations supply the Negro buyer with funds to make the initial purchase in the block. The first few sales are consummated through these organizations that are interested in helping the Negro with his financing so that the first purchase can be made.

The main reason for an increase in price to the Negro buyer, say most of the respondents, is that he usually does not have enough money to make a proper down payment. The seller must finance the sale and wait longer for his money; since the seller does not have the use of his money, he is entitled to a higher price — and would be if the buyer were white or Negro. Also, the small down payment creates hardship for the white seller who needs cash with which to buy another house.

If you buy for cash you always get a better deal than if you have some financial arrangement or extended credit. The same thing applies to them as to white buyers. If they're in a position to pay cash for property I would say that in general they would get as good a deal. In those cases where they have paid too much, it's due to long term financing by the sellers who sell with a small down payment on long term contracts. Anyone who buys without a sufficient down payment to get a first mortgage loan . . . anyone, the average person, is going to pay anywhere from 10 per cent to 25 per cent more for that financing. But that doesn't mean that it's discrimination as far as the Negro is concerned because it would apply to anyone of any race who is buying on those financial arrangements. If the seller has to wait 10 or 15 years for his money, most people feel they are entitled to 10 per cent to 15 per cent more for the use of their money because they haven't the use of it during that time. The seller could make an investment in the stock market, etc. He could make a profit with that money. They're prevented from using that money because they have put it at the disposal of the buyer and tied it up for 15 years. (54C)

No, I don't think the Negro pays more. I think that a white seller in a changing neighborhood frequently takes much less than if the neighborhood hadn't changed, because, if the neighborhood hadn't changed, he could sell his property to white people at his asking price and the white buyer would have sufficient down payment and be able to get the balance financed, that is, a mortgage for the balance. In that way the seller obtains his full price, and he's able to go out and buy something else in the neighborhood he wanted to go. He has all his cash. But, in selling to a Negro, the seller might get his full asking price, but he can't get enough cash from the colored buyer, because the colored buyer will only have a small amount of cash and will have to buy on contract because he can't get a mortgage for such a big balance. So the seller doesn't get enough money out of it to go and buy other property if he sells on contract with such a small down payment. (87CX)

Prices will go up on the small down payment. It will appear to people that prices are increasing, but most of these sales are not cash sales. I question whether they are really increasing. My experience is that pricewise, property increases apparently, on the surface, when Negroes enter an area, when sales begin to be made to them. When they are on the edge, when the area is threatened, sales slow up, there is a stagnant market, prices are down. When they actually move in, prices are up some, but not nearly as much as they seem to be, because they are being bought with a small amount of cash. . . . If the white seller, if I want cash, I can't get it. If he is willing to take a small down payment, yes [the white seller will get his price]. If he has to have cash, he's going to take a licking. (13CX)

If the buyer defaults on his payments and the seller has to take his property back, it may be in worse condition than when he sold it. In addition, the loss in value may not be covered by the payments made.

Some respondents maintain that the prices paid by Negroes at present are not higher than they should be because more housing is open to them now. Also, the speculator's gain is made at the white seller's expense rather than the Negro buyer's. The speculator buys at a low price and then resells to the Negro at a price not too different from what it would have been had the area remained white.

Apartment Buildings. When Negroes approach an area, tenants as well as homeowners begin to leave, and when Negroes enter, more leave. Apartment owners try unsuccessfully to keep their white tenants with low rents. The owner who sees his building standing half empty and will not or cannot rent to Negroes wants to sell, and he may take a loss if he is eager to get rid of it. The deluxe apartment building suffers especially. Negroes are not able to pay high rents without doubling up, and Negro-occupied buildings therefore often are overcrowded, overused, and worth less. Poorer buildings may gain in value by commanding higher rents from Negro tenants than from former, white tenants. However, a Negro-occupied building receives a lower valuation than it would if occupied by white people. Also, smaller mortgages are made on Negro-occupied buildings, and this reduces their value. The property is less attractive because Negro tenants have the reputation of being generally less responsible than white tenants (although there are many exceptions), and because there is less possibility for its further development.

[A] 20 per cent [drop in value on approach and entry of Negroes] applies rather generally, but much more to the better buildings than to the mediocre buildings. There is no loss in the real poor buildings at any time. In fact, there is quite a gain. The Negro will be paying more than such property will get elsewhere in a white neighborhood, but there is a small minority of such properties. For the apartment hotels and the better hotels, it's an absolute disaster. A residence where the Negro can take in roomers don't suffer much, but the fine residences suffer sharply — more than 20 per cent, up to 40 per cent. (1B)

I've never heard of a building appreciating in value when it was colored-occupied, never. You buy a building white-occupied for 5 times the rental. You put colored in and increase the rent. If you can get 4½ times the rent, you're lucky when you want to sell. (37A)

It is also a question of the lack of liquidity in colored property. The mortgage houses won't put as much on it per room. On white property they'll put $1,000 per room. On colored property they'll put only $700 or $800 per room. The smaller mortgage depresses the potential sales price. (53A)

Without question, for the deluxe apartments of the area, values decline. They can't find many tenants who can pay high rents, $250 a month. The lowest grade building might increase in value because the white occupants will not pay as much rental as Negro occupants . . . Increased rents and therefore greater net return is not the only factor in creating values. The reason that many Negro-occupied buildings even with a greater net return are worth less than white-occupied buildings is that purchasers cannot obtain mortgages in sufficient amounts to warrant paying more or as much, in spite of increased net income. . . . In order to purchase a building, it's easier to purchase a building with white occupants, because it's easier to obtain a mortgage with white occupants. They will then have to put in less money in order to purchase a building of this kind. . . . People are more reluctant to make large investments in Negro-occupied buildings unless they can obtain greater profits from such investments. They are willing to make less money on white-occupied buildings because they feel that the investment is more secure. (73A)

Some Negro buyers are willing to pay a high price for an apartment building in order to obtain control of the block; they can then buy up the smaller properties at reduced prices. Also, the white seller may claim that the Negro buyer will raise the rents and increase the income and that therefore he is justified in asking a higher price.

Property Values in the Negro Neighborhood

The white seller is at a disadvantage when the area becomes partly Negro because, since white people no longer buy there, the Negro broker can almost dictate his price. Many respondents said that property in a largely Negro neighborhood is considered to have a lower value than if the neighborhood were white, partly because of white people's beliefs about what happens to a neighborhood when Negroes move in. As one broker said, "The history has been that Negro areas become slum areas." Some Negro owners do not have enough time or money to maintain their properties well. They often need to take in roomers to meet payments on their buildings, which are then overused and deteriorate faster. Some respondents speak of the infrequency of sales between Negro and Negro; some believe that a Negro prefers to buy a house occupied by a white man and that if he buys a house occupied or owned by Negroes, he expects to get it "for nothing." The majority of the respondents report that, although prices of homes increase during or for a while after Negro entry, the eventual outcome is a lower value than before Negro entry.

A few respondents pointed out that there are now some Negro areas, and parts of areas that are well maintained. These men believed that, with the improved economic position of many Negroes, values in Negro neighborhoods may be as well maintained in the future as in white.

Most of the respondents believe that white people will not buy property in the potential Negro neighborhood — an area approached or entered by Negroes — and proceed to act on that basis. They thereby possibly help maintain the pattern of falling prices in such areas. Robert K. Merton has called a similar process of thought and action the "self-fulfilling prophecy." [8] But a few respondents refuse to take it for granted that they cannot sell to white people in such a neighborhood and have sold property, although at low prices, to white buyers for residences. However, very few have set out deliberately to sell residences to white buyers when Negroes are approaching or entering. A number do not see why white people should run if 1, 2, or 3 Negro families move into their block and have told their clients so.

Considerably less than 10 per cent of our sales are currently to Negroes. . . . By 1951 to 1952 2 things had become obvious. The first was that the zoning laws were going to be enforced in this neighborhood [part of Area A.] This removed our fear of the neighborhood going as a whole to rooming house use. The second was that there were more white families than anyone had realized which were willing to accept and deal with the problems of an interracial community, if in exchange they received housing that normally they could not afford. . . . As we solicited more listings in the area and worked harder at finding prospects willing to accept this situation, the coracial situation of the neighborhood, we found that we were able to sell these homes to families that were acceptable to the older residents although they were of a lower economic order generally. From a sale of perhaps 1 or 2 houses a year in this neighborhood, we have gone to 12 to 14 sales per year to white families in an area where Negroes are living frequently next door, between, or across the street. My personal thought is that this situation is not as exceptional as it may seem at first sight. I think most Realtors, being after all businessmen, are too prone to take the line of least resistance, in other words, to seek only colored purchasers for properties in changing neighborhoods. It has been our experience that a significant number of white people are willing and even eager to live in a coracial neighborhood providing it remains in all other respects a pleasant place in which to live. (39A)

Summary

The following points about the effect on property values of Negro approach and entry received special stress from the respondents:

Values go down in an area that Negroes are approaching because white people will not buy in that area. After the entry of Negroes into an area, white people bring low prices on themselves by getting into a panic, throwing their houses on the market at the same time, and selling in a hurry. White people run away when Negroes enter the area. There is not so much scare-selling now in some areas — white sellers do not wish to take a loss.

When Negroes enter an area, the cash prices for houses in particular will be low. The Negro buyers generally do not have the money, except for the first few who are allegedly subsidized by agencies or may have acquired money. The high prices paid by Negroes, except for the first few, are due to the Negro buyer's usually small down payment because he does not have much cash saved. Since there are more areas opening to Negroes, they are not paying such high prices now.

The Negro's small down payment creates hardships for the white seller — the main one is that he cannot buy another house with it. In order to do this, he must sell to a speculator, who will pay less than the property is worth but will pay cash. The Negro buyer does not pay much above normal prices to the speculator; the white seller takes the loss. When Negroes enter an area, the white seller is, in most cases, limited to a market of speculators and Negroes.

Negro-occupied apartment buildings are looked upon as having a lower value than white-occupied apartment buildings of the same kind. The improvements in the economic position of many Negroes and the educational opportunities opened to them make it possible that in the future Negro-occupied areas will be better maintained and property values in such areas better preserved than in the past, or as well preserved as in comparable white areas.

A few white people have been willing to buy residential property for their own use in an area where Negroes are already living, and several respondents maintain that more such buyers could be found if the real estate men made the attempt.

According to the majority of the respondents, the pattern of effect on values of residential property when Negroes enter an area is: downward before entry, when Negroes are approaching the area; upward upon entry and/or for a period after entry; downward after entry to a lower level of value than existed in the area before Negro entry.

COMPONENT 4. BELIEFS ABOUT NEGROES' EFFECT ON NEIGHBORHOODS

An important aspect of the real estate man's thinking about the movement of the Negro population in the city is his idea of the general effect on white areas where Negroes have entered and taken up residence (see Questions 13i(3) and 14g(3), Appendix A). Respondents differ: some believe an area fares just as well with Negro occupancy as with white and see similar effects from Negro owners and tenants, whereas the majority are most impressed with some unfavorable over-all effect on the neighborhood.

A considerable number of respondents held divided opinions about Negro owners' and tenants' care of property. Most say that the Negro homeowner cares for his home as well as or better than the white homeowner, but 65 per cent of the respondents of Area A and 44 per cent of those of Area B (see p. 51) say that the Negro tenant is not so good as the white.

The few respondents who say that the effect of Negro occupancy is generally good consider Negro owners and tenants to be as satisfactory as white owners in care of property, general behavior, control of children, consideration of neighbors, interest in community welfare, and participation in projects benefiting the community.

Some respondents believe that whether the effect of either tenants or owners is good or bad depends upon the kind of building and neighborhood; the age and physical condition of the buildings in the neighborhood; the presence of taverns and other such conditions; the people's income, education, and experience in urban living; the care taken in screening; and the white and Negro owners' persistence in keeping their buildings in good repair (in good buildings one usually finds good tenants — white and Negro).

The respondents who believe the general effect of Negro occupancy is not so good as that of white occupancy include 26 out of 37 (70 per cent) in Area A, 15 out of 23 (65 per cent) in Area B, 12 out of 16 (75 per cent) in Area C, 4 out of 5 (80 per cent) in Area CX, and 2 of the 3 Area C branch offices (Table 27, Appendix C). The principal bad effects are 3: increase of crime, physical and social decline, and upsetting of communal life.

Increase of Crime

Over half the respondents in Areas A, B, and C (19/26, 10/15, 7/12 respectively) single out the increase of crime as a chief bad effect of the entering of Negroes. They refer to an increase in acts of willful destruction, stone-throwing, purse-snatching, theft, holdups, break-ins and robberies, knifings and shootings, beating with or without robbing, rape, selling and using narcotics, and murder. People cannot move about after nightfall and are held up even in broad daylight.

Negro kids ganged up and wouldn't let one of the white tenants out who was trying to go to work. We had a police guard stationed for several days to put an end to that monkey business. Knifings and shootings are a common occurrence. You get so that after a while you don't think about it. About 3 weeks ago I was sitting at my desk. I saw a gang of Negro children go in this entrance of the medical building. I went over. As I got there, they came running out. They had strong-armed a newspaper boy and taken his money from him. I grabbed one of these kids. With that one of the others came up with a broken bottle and said, "You let him go or we'll gang up on you." That kind of stuff is getting so common around here. Most of the people around here have pistols or baseball bats ready. I keep a blackjack in the drawer of a front desk. You talk about living in a jungle. This is it. These people that live in the area — a woman wouldn't think of walking alone after dark. Until such time as these people develop a sense of social responsibility, they won't be accepted by the white people, it seems to me. They're citizens, they have the same rights as anyone else. There doesn't seem to be anything one can do. (7B)

There is more rowdyism since the last 2 years than when it was all white. Now it is 90 per cent colored around X and Y [streets in Area A]. We've had complaints from storekeepers in regard to stealing. We never had that trouble from white youngsters. Before, there were only 1 or 2 robberies a year. It's pretty much every day now. We were stuck up by a colored man and had to have bullet-proof protection in our office. We have been held up several times by Negroes. (23A)

Interview the theater owners. In the theater at . . . and the theater at . . . [Area A] within 3 months after the neighborhood went colored, all the seats were torn with knives. Both theaters have been offered for sale. (69B)

In the last five years . . . as a lot of colored people began to move into Area A, a lot of disturbance was caused. For example, they snatch pocketbooks. They insult women in the street. That never happened in Area A before. I've lived around here for 50 years . . . It used to be a very high class neighborhood. (29A)

They have forced me to move out of this district. My residence, yes. Why? On account of the robberies and rapes in the immediate neighborhood [Area A]. . . . I was afraid to go out alone at night. Even the colored are afraid to go out alone at night. (31A)

[Respondent told of break-in in the real estate office itself and of hold-ups in a jewelry store and a hardware store nearby by Negroes.] These things never happened in our neighborhood [Area CX]. I am thinking of giving up my location just because of that element. I'd never stay after dark any more. (87CX)

The only experience I ever had with Negroes was being held up by them. A year ago they burglarized my home [Area C] and threatened to kill me. (82C)

Four other respondents also reported being held up by Negroes. Other descriptions of Negro crime are on pp. 63 and 79–80.

Some respondents make it clear that they are not blaming the Negro owners and tenants who have come into the area for the increase in crime, but rather a criminal element among the Negro population — the riffraff, the dregs — who not only follow law-abiding Negro people into an area but also enter nearby areas where there are no Negroes and commit crimes there.

There are very fine Negroes, but there is a tough element that follows them. If a neighborhood is white, and a Negro walks down the street, you have the right to question him on what he is doing there. But, if Negroes are living there, you can't distinguish between an owner and a prowler. White people don't want their women raped, their houses broken into, their cars stolen. (38A)

The wear and tear on the buildings is from the riffraff that comes around the buildings. The average colored family is not home at day. They are a prey for the burglaries. That's where the wear and tear comes in — mailbox robbing, the stealing of checks out of mailboxes. (56A)

I have seen it happen here in buildings that are still white with a colored fringe. The people are afraid to go out at nights. At X [Area A] in 1 month there were 6 holdups in a hallway. It caused vacancies. Eight tenants moved out. They were afraid of their lives. (67A)

Physical and Social Decline

The second over-all effect of Negro entry stressed by respondents is a general decline of the area, both social and physical. The social decline is attributed, first, to the moving away of white residents. The people who leave first can afford to buy or rent elsewhere; they are usually of high economic and social standards. It is hard to replace them with equally acceptable new families — the new families are still white, but not of the same caliber, because people who ordinarily would buy and rent there no longer find the neighborhood desirable. Eventually the hillbilly white family moves into the area.

Secondly, the social decline is attributed to the kind of Negroes that enter. A few educated Negro families may move in at first, but soon after come many uneducated ones whose way of living will make more of the white residents want to move. There is necessarily an influx of Negroes of lower social standards, since there are proportionately more uneducated people with low incomes in the Negro population than in the white. Thus, the social standards of the area generally sink lower with the entry of Negroes.

I wouldn't jeopardize any district. The first thing it does is tear down values. It does definitely tear down values. Then too, for example, I have a party right now that is in a resisting neighborhood. No colored are in there, but they are so close, they want to sell because they're afraid of colored, afraid their house won't have the value it has now. It's a good neighborhood. . . . Their homes are all worth from $20,000 to $30,000. It would wreck the neighborhood. The people would feel they have to move. When you are that type of person with an expensive home, you don't want to have colored for neighbors. We all know what they do. One family moves in, but soon you have 5 or 6 families in the same house. It's the only way they can afford to live. If you go to X [Negro area] — it used to be a lovely neighborhood. All you have to do is go down there and see what they have done to the neighborhood. The same thing applies to [part of Area A]. In other words, the colored tear down good neighborhoods once they get in. I don't know about all of them. I only know about neighborhoods. You don't find that condition in Z [area of homes and small multiple structures which has fairly recently been occupied by Negroes]. (77C)

The respondents are aware, as is 77C, of 1 or 2 well-maintained Negro areas or blocks that improved after Negro entry, but they observe that usually neighborhoods decline when Negroes enter and do so faster than comparable white areas. Fourteen respondents of Areas A and B and 2 of Area C noted that Area B and other areas were run-down before Negroes entered; but this did not excuse the increased crime, overcrowding, and littered streets that followed Negro entry. These areas have since got worse.

Illegal conversions and overcrowding are the main reasons for the physical decline of an area after Negroes enter, and they also contribute to social decline. Negro-occupied buildings are frequently overcrowded. The Negro owners charge high rents so they can meet large mortgage payments. To pay the high rent, the Negro tenant brings in another family; both Negro and white owners permit, and even encourage, this practice. An overcrowded building is overused — there is more wear and tear on its facilities and faster deterioration than there would otherwise be. A few respondents distinguished between 2 kinds of new Negro owner: one cuts up his building into small units, loads it with tenants and roomers, and milks it, even having people sleep in shifts in order to make money fast; the other must take roomers and tenants into his house or 2-flat to help pay off debt, but if he were not so hard pressed, he would observe proper standards of occupancy.

When you get Negro occupancy . . . the only way you're going to prevent blight is by some outside agency subsidizing the area, because economically I don't think they're going to be able to pay the freight themselves without crowding up. There's going to be an overcrowded condition unless there is outside help. (13CX)

The Negro in most cases is ready to pay you a higher rental. However, in most cases, he does not maintain the apartment as a single family unit; . . . he sublets part of the space and is thus able to pay the higher rental. Usually when a building changes from white to Negro occupancy, there is a 50 per cent or better increase in the occupancy. (38A)

The neighborhood cannot maintain itself with increased occupancy. It's almost a fact that when occupancy changes there is an increase in rental and the rental is being paid generally by a person in a lower income bracket than the preceding white tenant. Hence, you've got doubling up which causes a fast depreciation of the property, crowded curbs. The whole neighborhood is used by double the number of persons formerly there. It's the necessity of overuse because of high rental. I'm not saying there wouldn't be depreciation without the overcrowding, but this is the situation. The Negro owner has to make very large monthly payments. (37A)

Over half the respondents of Areas A, B, and CX considered the average Negro tenant more careless and destructive than the average white tenant (see p. 51). Because of the destruction and damage done by Negro tenants, owners make few or no repairs. Thus, the behavior of both tenant and owner adds to the deterioration of buildings. The owner's plight when Negroes enter an area is described: "There again, in general the values are affected in this fashion, that there seems to be a dropping off of maintenance because of the lack of responsibility of a great many tenants in colored buildings. I know of cases where the tenants have done so much destruction that the owners have said, 'I'm not going to spend any more money on it.' And the deterioration is reflected in the lower value. (7B)" Owing to the carelessness of Negro tenants and of others coming in, the area begins to look run-down — the streets are littered, some tenants throw garbage into yards, broken glass and empty bottles lie about.

Since the Negroes came into this area [B], it's one of the dirtiest sections in the city. I'm talking now of dumping garbage in the alleys, throwing garbage out of the windows, throwing whiskey bottles on the streets and sidewalks where they break and create a hazard to auto tires, children and so on. . . . These conditions didn't hold before this influx, certainly not to the degree that it is now. It is certainly out of hand. (7B)

Of course the colored think we shouldn't mind living among them, but it's absolutely impossible to do it, for the whites and the colored to live together happily. Their way of living is so different. Just the very fact that they can't learn, they refuse to take the trouble to put garbage in bags and to put the bags in the pail. They just throw the bag at the pail and it goes in all directions, or they just throw the garbage. We lose janitors on that account. They won't stay if there are Negroes. (33A)

Respondents pointed out that the "good" Negro will not stay in an overcrowded, littered, and noisy neighborhood, and when he leaves, he is replaced by Negroes of lower socioeconomic levels. In addition to the effects of overcrowding and carelessness, many Negro owners cannot afford to repair their buildings or to keep them repaired; they cannot afford to hire repairmen and haven't time to look after the property themselves.

Upsetting of Communal Life

Another harmful effect, and one closely related to the social decline of the area, is that the coming of Negroes upsets the life of the community generally. Their very approach causes unrest. Then, when they enter the community, they shop in the stores, their children go to the schools, they attend the movie theaters, and they go to the doctors and dentists of the area. The white residents find themselves rubbing elbows with the new Negro residents wherever they turn, and those who render essential services find themselves faced with problems of a mixed clientele. As white residents leave, churches have to decide whether to invite the new residents to become members and risk losing more old ones. Stores lose many of their old and tried customers. If the influx of Negroes has been rapid, a Negro alderman or congressman may soon represent the area, and this may come as a shock to the older residents. Problems arise in the schools. The crime rate goes up. The tax structure changes: lower assessments are made of Negro-occupied properties, and this puts a greater burden on the rest of the community and on other areas as well.

$$$$

□
□ □ V
□

The Broker's Conception of His Racial Policies and Practices, Part II

COMPONENT 5. BELIEFS ABOUT THE POSSIBILITY OF RESIDENTIAL INTEGRATION

RESPONDENTS' beliefs and convictions about the possibility of residential integration in Chicago — that is, whether an area that Negroes enter can remain integrated or whether it will inevitably go Negro — strongly affect their decisions about dealing with Negroes. I did not hold the respondents to any particular definition of "integration." However, here I shall define "racial residential integration" as the peaceable living together of white people and Negroes on the same streets in the same neighborhood, in which at least 50 per cent of the people on a street are white and from which there is no more than the ordinary amount of moving by white people over 10 years.[1] If well over 50 per cent of the people on most blocks of a street were Negro, it would be apparent that most of the white people had moved away, and the street could hardly be called integrated. If at least 50 per cent of the white people remained in most blocks, there would be some proof of racial residential integration. "Peaceable relations" means no violence or hostile acts and some evidence of normal neighborly cooperation. If this situation remained constant for 10 years, a stable situation of coracial residential living would have been achieved, I think.

The respondents' ideas and beliefs about the possibility of racial residential integration in Chicago were learned partly through Question 39 (see Appendix A). In their answers to other questions, most respondents stated that white people leave an area when Negroes enter it and that the white people who ordinarily would buy will generally not buy or rent residences when Negroes are known to be approaching or entering (see p.

102

74 and Ch. IV, nn. 3 and 4). These statements could be taken as the answer to the question about the possibility of integration, but further questions brought forth a more comprehensive answer. Question 39 was set up to obtain a spontaneous expression of the broker's beliefs about integration and segregation and was successful to a considerable extent. In the solution they offered for housing the Negroes, close to two thirds of the respondents — Area A, 19/30 (63 per cent), Area B, 12/19 (63 per cent), and Area C 11/17 (65 per cent) — revealed that residential segregation was the pattern they expected. (Table 28, Appendix C.)

When asked Question 39a, the majority of the respondents — Area A, 29/34 (85 per cent), Area B, 21/22 (95 per cent), Area C, 17/17 (100 per cent), Area CX, 5/5 (100 per cent), and Area C branch offices, 2/2 (100 per cent) — judged that racial residential integration is impossible in Chicago at present. Of these respondents, about half think that integration is not possible at all, judging from the white people's past performance, or that it will be at least a hundred years in coming because of the unwillingness of white people to live with Negroes, the school problem, white people's fear of intermarriage, the lack of control over the Negro proportion in the white area, Negroes' different way of living, people's desire to be with their own kind, racial prejudice, and lack of understanding between Negroes and white people. (Table 29, Appendix C.)

I don't think we're ready for integration yet, not within our time. I still want to go to Brazil to see how they have solved the problem. It took 300 years for them to get as far as they are in integration. (1B)

You know when there'll be integration? When Messiah will come. People got to get civilized and understand each other. . . . At present, the reason for much of this is a lack of understanding. That's right. (12B)

That never happens. White will continue to move out, to sell out, to get away. (49A)

I don't think much of it [the idea of integration] as long as white people are imbedded with their ideas which they have had for centuries. (50A)

Well, I don't think it would ever work out. I don't think so. I don't believe — 99 per cent of the white people don't want to live among the Negroes. The same thing applies to the different nationalities, the Poles, etc. You have Polish, Bohemian, Jewish sections. Any nationality you mention, they've got a section. They all want to live among their own people. (55C)

It'll never work. So far it hasn't. It's been proven. You can't get away from facts. You get right back to your school problem. That's the answer. (56A)

That wouldn't be much of a solution. You can't have a few of them moving in in each block because that can't be controlled. The colored man decides to buy where his friends are. After 3 or 4 are in the block, you can't put a stop to it. Negroes have ambitions. They'll want to be near their friends. It's something you can't control. It might be all right in theory. (51A)

You can't do it. It just doesn't work out at this time. In the future it may. Their modes of living are very different as considered by the majority of white people. When the time comes that the majority of white and colored think nothing of intermarriage, then the situation will have solved itself. (65C)

They aren't [integrating]. The Negro drives the white man out. . . . [Re continuation of exclusion policy.] My attitude hasn't changed, but I have become more firm in my conviction as to the problem which lies within. The problem is in the social and economic evaluation and understanding within and between the races. The core of the problem is biological. There's the problem. (19B)

Twelve respondents of Areas A and B and 3 of Area C listed specific improvements Negroes must make before there can be integration: better care of property; more concern about keeping and leaving a dwelling clean and tidy; better hygiene, manners, conduct, and social responsibility; and more education. White people will accept integration only when the majority of uneducated Negroes have reached a higher cultural level. These respondents speak of decades passing before Negroes reach this level.

Definitely there will come a time when there will be a mixed area. I don't believe everyone will move out of Chicago. The answer, I believe, is education of the colored people. You have to do away with the kind of situation we have now on X and Y [streets in Negro area]. It's a slum area. The people in those areas, as far as laws and morals are concerned, all would have to be improved. If you ride down Q and Z [streets in same area] you see them standing on corners and in alleys with their bottles of liquor, drinking. It's something hard to explain, but they're just not living up to the standards set by the whites, even the lowest class of whites, even on Madison Street. The colored should take steps to police their own areas and try to eliminate those conditions. A lot of whites get the idea that as soon as Negroes move into their area, that those conditions will exist in their area. (2B)

I think it is an impossibility in this decade anyhow. It'll be 2 decades or more, 50 years from now, before integration, whites and Negroes living together, could come about, because of the fact I don't see how you'll ever get this integration until the Negro children are raised in the same kind of environment as the white children. (37A)

I don't think today it's a solution. It might be accepted in 15 or 20 years. It could be longer. It's really a time question. When a colored person can come up to the level of a white person in education, financial situation, and culture, breeding, so that people won't be scared, frightened, shocked when they see colored moving in. When they won't be shocked, when they will have some respect, perhaps even a colored teacher. Of course, there are some nice ones, but they are few and far between. (72C)

I think when I got out of school I was of the opinion that Negroes were about the same as the white. I had ideas in regard to the racial problem. In my experience I found that they still need considerable education in hygiene and manners before they can be "integrated," as they say. (13CX)

Some respondents said that integration can only be gradual and that it is unwise to force it because hasty action will lead to resistance by the white people and friction between the two groups. People's ideas change slowly; little can be done until people are ready to accept a new pattern in their lives. Both white people and Negroes need to be educated to accept integration.

I mean this colored and white situation is a matter of education both for the whites and for the colored. It's like mixing flour and water together. Put in a big amount of both and they'll never mix. It's a matter of time. . . . The gradual mixing will bring faster results. (8B)

People are trying to prove you can have an interracial area. If everyone could just forget tonight the whole racial picture, because legally the Negro has the same rights, just forget trying to push the Negro into a white block. . . . Up to this time there have been so few mixed buildings with success. It'll come, but *let* it come. Don't push it down people's throats. The restrictive covenant is gone. Let it rest at that. If a Negro has been able to pay $200 for an apartment, God bless him and let him go to it, but let it come as it will. (27A)

I think it's very possible. I don't think it'll be too soon. I might not even live to see it. [Why not soon?] For the same reason that people didn't accept Edison's ideas, any inventor's ideas. . . . People get set in their ways. It's hard to change. (40A)

No, not at the present moment. In order to change anyone's views on the problem of integration where prejudice has been a factor for a long period of time, it takes just as long to reverse it. Periods of war and afterward tend to make for closer and better relations between peoples. . . .

At present in the problem of race relations, you must never grab the bull by the horns. You must go slowly, steadily, and not hurry. You must wait for the opportunity to advance. (46A)

The unlikelihood of the occurrence of integration at present was expressed by a few respondents in strong terms, such as, "I think the only way to integrate Chicago today would be at the point of a bayonet by an overwhelming government force. In the future, yes, I think so. (39A)"

Several brokers believe that integration will come in spite of the white people's wishes because of the housing situation in Chicago and the rapid growth of the Negro population.

I think it's inevitable. [Why?] Well, because they are increasing at such a rate, the white people will run out of places to run to. I don't know whether we'll see it in our time, but I think that eventually it will come to pass. In a couple of generations, probably. (15B)

I think it has to come. Well, we've got no place else to go, and we can't all live 50 miles out of town. (24B)

I think you're going to see that definitely materialize for very obvious reasons. The white tenant—the untold thousands of white tenants who rent in a borderline area can't afford to go out and purchase a home in the outlying suburbs. It's going to come to pass definitely. (61C)

A few respondents say that integration is here already and is operating satisfactorily. Others say that it is here because it could not be avoided. Many respondents are aware of the increasing size of the Negro population and its increasing political and other power; a number of respondents are worried about this.

I think they'll have to do it. Half a dozen Negroes have moved into this block. What are we to do? (29A)

Oh, absolutely. It's here now. It's *got to be* with the increase of the colored population. They have to have a place to live. (31A)

It's just as practical here as it is in Europe. It works all right. It seems to be quiet in Area A. (44A)

I think that probably might occur. In fact, it has right here in this area. Whether they're going to stay beyond the point when they can get out, I don't know. (45A)

Some brokers proposed this solution to the Negro housing problem: discourage those in the South from coming to Chicago in such numbers. This points to the flood of Negroes of a level of culture lower than that of northern Negroes as the main stumbling block for integration. For example, respondent 83C said, "The problem is these colored coming up from the bush, from Mississippi and other states. They've had no experience with society. They don't know how to conduct themselves. That's where the resistance is. They're afraid. So are the colored afraid. I know. They tell me. You've come to a real estate man, a practical businessman. They're afraid of these fellows that come from the South. Should we take care of them before they're ready for it? Should they be given the privilege of living where they please?" (See also 83C's comments on p. 64.) It appears from this that these respondents might consider integration possible if they had only city-bred, northern Negroes to deal with.

The Inevitability of Racial Succession

The respondents mentioned directly or clearly implied two beliefs about the possibility of integration, in both of which the essential element is the assumption that racial succession is inevitable. The first belief is that the expanding Negro population must find space and that its movement is inevitable and unstoppable, but also unpremeditated and unplanned.

They're moving like lava from a volcano. (22B)

No 1 broker or 10 or 100 could stem the tide. They have to have a place to live. (9B)

When the Negroes are within 2 to 3 to 4 blocks, the whites begin to flee. This creates a vacuum. It's nobody's fault. It's not a special group [selling property to Negroes]. It's the economic group, each one looking out for his economic interest. I do it, you do it. Some won't admit it, but it's the most terrific force and something no one can prevent or change. . . . The long and short of it is that when the Negro begins to get close to a neighborhood, you can no more stop it than you can stop a million tons of snow from rolling down a mountain side. . . . It was a force no one could stop. No one set out to do it. It was like a wave. You can't do anything for it or against it. It's like King Canute. The waves kept coming and coming. King Canute had very little to do with it. It's the same idea. It's a force so strong. What little the brokers could do had nothing to do with it. It's due to the expanding Negro population. (10B)

As soon as the war was over in 1945, then the avalanche came. The colored people began to pour in [area adjoining Area A]. It was just like a wave coming down X street [street running through both areas]. When they passed [the boundary of Area A], we all knew the area was doomed. I don't think there are any white residents now north of Y street [Area A]. (33A)

I can't stand there and hold the waves back. It isn't me. (47A)

The colored influx is the greatest cause of obsolescence on the South Side. I don't think the [community organizations] can stop it anyway. It has gone too far. It can't be stopped. Since the 1948 Supreme Court decision, there is no possible way to prevent these neighborhoods from turning colored, and once they have colored, there is no way to stop them from becoming slums. . . . I would predict in 10 or 15 years that the entire South Side will be colored within the city limits. There won't be anything left. (67A)

There is nothing that can stop the Negroes from continuing to find homes for themselves. (89A)

The second belief is that any area where Negroes begin to enter will become mostly or wholly Negro in time, and as soon as one Negro moves into an area, white people will move out until there are few or none left. Respondents have seen the speed with which white people of various areas moved away as Negroes entered and the unwillingness of white people who ordinarily would buy or rent to do so when Negroes have entered. They have seen, too, Negroes rapidly fill up the vacuum left by white people as they manage to buy property in white areas. The concepts "transition area" and "changing neighborhood" commonly used by the respondents express this belief in the inevitable change from white to Negro occupancy once a Negro family moves into an area; the area is understood to be in a condition of transformation from one kind of racial occupancy to the other. Thirty respondents out of 37 (81 per cent) in Area A, 19 out of 23 (83 per cent) in Area B, 20 out of 21 (95 per cent) in Area C, 5 out of 6 (83 per cent) in Area CX, and 2 of the 3 Area C branch offices revealed that they take it *for granted* that once Negroes enter an area, the white people will move out and the area will become mostly or wholly Negro.[2]

We have lost a lot of merchants that haven't catered to the colored, don't understand the colored or for some reason or other have moved, and it has affected values, because in between the time that property is fully occupied by colored tenants and the whites have moved, you have a period of time, a transition period, and during that transition period your business property values go down. (4B)

The only way you can judge that [loss of white clients because of sales to Negroes] is as the Negroes come into the area. Then the whites do go out. It will apply to business too. What was 100 per cent white business will become 100 per cent Negro. (27A)

Why kick the white people out of their neighborhoods because they

108

haven't learned to live with the colored yet? When the white move out of their own volition, all right. That is exemplified in every area that changes. When colored moves in, white moves out, and since they generally do deteriorate areas, why ruin Area C, for example? (40A)

When Property May Be Sold to a Negro

The respondents determine when they can sell property in a residential area or block to Negroes in three ways: (1) for a considerable number, when, in their judgment, the white people of the neighborhood or block have accepted the idea that it is changing to Negro occupancy and have resigned themselves to it; (2) for a considerable number, when it has become an objective situation — it is obvious to all that the area is changing to Negro occupancy; (3) for a few, when they are convinced that sales to white buyers for residential use are out of the question (see Appendix A, Question 16f). Brokers who use method (1) vary in their judgment when the people have accepted the idea of the change; some say 1 sale to a Negro is enough, others give various numbers up to 15 or about half the block (see pp. 39–42). This variation arises partly from differences in the situation between one neighborhood or block and another. The broker's own inclination may also affect his decision to sell earlier or later.

The respondents' belief in the inevitability of racial succession is tempered by some doubt in connection with the beginning of the Negroes' movement into an area. When 1 or 2 Negro families have come in, the real estate man wonders whether the white people in certain areas or blocks will panic, take it calmly and move out gradually, or perhaps not move if no more Negroes enter. Will the sales go quickly or slowly? What direction will the movement take? (As sales are made here and there, it may take a turn within the larger movement different from what he expected.) He is concerned about the trend (see pp. 33–35). He waits to see what will happen.

If there is any doubt, we stay away. All our buildings are in either 100 per cent white or 100 per cent Negro areas. (2B)

You examine the block and you know from the contiguous neighborhood or blocks that the same thing will happen to that particular block in a short time that has happened to the blocks in the immediate vicinity. That's not true in [Area A]. We will not sell to Negroes until the block is practically 50 per cent colored. [Why?] Because we feel that there is always a possibility that the people on that block will not move or sell out, but would rather hold their ground and watch to see if these Negroes who have moved in are a higher type than the average and can be absorbed without fear of the neighborhood's turning objectionable. (35A)

In Areas A and C, more respondents depend on their judgment of how the white people think and feel about the situation — method (1) — in determining when they will begin to sell to Negroes, whereas in Areas B and CX, where there has been a larger influx of Negroes, the objective situation — method (2) — is more important to the respondents (Table 30, Appendix C).

In the three methods of determining when they can sell to Negroes, there is an underlying idea by which respondents justify their particular cutoff point. Whether expressed or implied, this idea is the same for all respondents: by selling at that particular time, the respondent *cannot be blamed* for starting the change in the area or block. For example, "when the white people leave of their own accord," it was not any action of the broker's that made them leave. When the people themselves believe the block is "gone," they will not hold it against him if he begins to sell to Negroes in that block. When white people understand that other white people will not buy and ask the broker to sell to whom he can, he will be perfectly "safe" in selling to Negroes. Even at this point, one respondent assumes unless told otherwise that the seller wants to sell to white. And when the block is half Negro, the white people will certainly not hold it against the broker if he sells property in it to Negroes.

These respondents determine the cutoff according to what the white people think and feel about the situation:

Because it would be a request from the party that owns it to sell it to a Negro buyer, because white people would not buy it. (82C)

The property owners tell you very openly about it. If they come in and want to sell the property and we know there are 2 or 3 Negroes in the block, then we'll help them sell to colored. We always assume they want to sell to white until they tell us differently. We say it'll be difficult to sell to white. (87CX)

I have no measure. It's just my idea. Different blocks are different. In one block people will accept more readily than in another. One block in X street we're still staying out of. The people telephone to you, they talk to other people. This comes back to you. (9B)

After the neighborhood starts to change and the white people in it have accepted the fact that it is changing, then I'll go ahead and sell to colored because they're the ones who will buy in there, or the Japs or whoever it might be. When the other owners in the neighborhood realize that white people won't come along and buy their property. This is in regard to homes. After 2 or 3 have purchased and moved into the block. (55C)

I would in a transition area if I were called upon to do so, where there were already some in, because it's going already. I'd feel I wasn't overtly pushing something. It's going to go. It's a matter of time. My 1 sale isn't going to make much difference . . . When there are 2 or more in the block. *Above all*, if the white residents were resigned to the fact that the neighborhood is going colored. Even if there were 5 Negro families in the block, if they were fighting it, we wouldn't sell. (53A)

These determine it according to the objective situation:

At least when there's 20 per cent or 30 per cent, when the neighborhood is obviously changing, no doubt about it, when the people there have found that it's inevitable. Usually the whole block is for sale at that time. (24B)

We like to be safe. We figure if the neighborhood is 60 per cent Negro, we feel that there won't be too much resentment. There is enough friction in a neighborhood. There is no reason for us to add insult to injury. For example, Trumbull. We want to be on the safe side. We don't want to get in bad with the white or the colored. We lose a lot of sales that way, but we don't care. (23A)

These determine it according to their own convictions:

[When a street is 50 per cent sold] It wouldn't be creating any further depreciation, and also they [the Negroes] would be the only buyers you could produce for the white seller. It goes into a long explanation that depends on size of properties involved. You might sell an income property, multi-unit, to a white buyer for colored occupancy, or a single unit might be sold to a white speculator who in turn sells to a colored contract purchaser. (37A)

It is difficult to say when an area is broken — certainly considerably more than 1. If they start to come in, you have to sell to them or someone else will. White people won't buy after they have started. If they do, it is only for speculating purposes. (60BOC)

The belief of most respondents that change from white to Negro occupancy is inevitable once a Negro has entered is the basis for (1) their not selling to Negroes in an area or block because, if they did, they would be responsible for the inevitable change and all it entails, and (2) their selling to Negroes once the cutoff determined by the respondent has been reached. The real estate man speaks of that time in the process of the Negro movement into an area or block when he believes the change is bound to happen as "the inevitable trend." At that time what was reprehensible behavior — namely, selling to Negroes in a white area or block — becomes acceptable behavior because now the area or block is no longer considered white by the white residents. If he had sold before, he would have *hurt* the owners, and they would have held him responsible for the change, but after the crucial turn of the area or block from one that was or may have remained white to one that is definitely on the way to becoming a Negro one, he is *helping* the owners to sell their property, if they will not remain, so that they can buy elsewhere, and they will not hold his selling to Negroes against him.

Four brokers think that white people in Area A are adjusting to living in a coracial community and that understanding and cooperation are developing. Respondent 22B said, "A great deal of the running is stopping here — certainly in Area A. That's a matter of education too. They found they don't melt, weren't attacked, and, in not finding a place in the first 6 months, they decided to stay. They find they're not so bad." And 57A said, "Well, at first they [white people of Area A] seemed quite upset by the whole thing because of their [colored's] living conditions in other areas. They were afraid of them generally. They didn't know them, didn't understand them. Now the whites are coming around and are interested in the community program." Three other brokers spoke of good relations between white and Negro neighbors in other areas. However, the majority of the respondents in each area believe, on the basis of what they know about white people's beliefs, feelings, wishes, and actions, that racial residential integration is impossible in Chicago now and that racial succession is inevitable.

COMPONENT 6. BELIEFS ABOUT CONSEQUENCES TO OTHERS OF HIS SELLING OR RENTING PROPERTY IN WHITE AREA TO NEGROES

This component of the racial real estate ideology is directly concerned with the broker's selling or not selling/renting property to Negroes in the white area or block, and it partly summarizes the respondents' reasons for not doing so (see Appendix A, Question 16d). The respondents made it clear that their reasons for not selling to Negroes came from their experience in dealing with white people and from their observation of what happens to them when properties in their vicinity are sold to Negro purchasers. There is no doubt in the minds of many respondents that a sale to a Negro buyer in a white area or block spells suffering and hardship for the white people who move away from it and unhappiness for those who remain. Either way, the sale causes an upheaval in their lives.

The first result of the movement of Negroes toward the area is emotional upset, unrest, and concern for the residents. At their very approach, people become disturbed over the prospect of having them as neighbors and over the prospect of moving. Their planning for the future becomes difficult. They become frightened, anxious, uncertain. They worry about selling or not selling their property — they fear that there will be no market for it and, with Negroes coming close, they feel their property is devaluated. They fear for the safety of their children. They fear the decline of the neighborhood. Then, when a Negro buys a property there, the whole community becomes alarmed. Twenty-five respondents of Areas A, B, and CX and 14 of Area C stressed white people's emotional disturbance in one form or another over the approach and entry of Negroes into their area or block.

A neighborhood and someone's home means a lot to him, and unless a person lives through it, you can't realize what an upheaval that is for the people in that neighborhood. . . . When the Negroes first moved across [boundary of Area CX], I was very sympathetic to that, because of the tremendous overcrowding and because of the veterans. Now, with rent controls gone, the Negroes have moved into [respondent named 6 areas entered by Negroes in recent years]. The housing shortage for Negroes is *over*. They have their choice of apartments any place. So possibly the sympathy goes on the other foot for these people who have been living in a neighborhood for 20 years, and, although I feel there's no personal danger, morally, spiritually or physically or any way in having some Negroes living in their area, it is impossible to convince them of that until they have lived with some Negroes in their area. . . . There is no way you or I can possibly imagine the tremendous upheaval there is and heartache for people who have lived for a lifetime in a certain area. I don't agree with them. I don't say they're right, but they have this fear of neighborhood change. It's very real with them. . . . In these homes where they are half a dozen blocks away from where Negroes have already moved, the women will talk of nothing else. . . . I don't have any tolerance with them. I think they're foolish. They don't know whether to buy venetian blinds or curtains. I feel sorry for them. Some are on a pension. Some just can't pick up and move. They're afraid. (22B)

For the long established firms, I don't think you'll find that they'll take Negro prospects into a white area and disturb the peace. It disturbs the thinking, the harmony of a lot of people. It upsets their mental attitude. They say, "If Jones did it, why can't we?" Multiply that by 100 cases. (27A)

The permanency in the future planning of residents in this area was a determining angle. First those that rented would necessarily hesitate before they made expenditures. Those who owned hesitated before they made any improvements. (50A)

If they [Negroes] get one in a neighborhood, it's sufficient to cause panic in the neighborhood. They keep talking about it. All things concerning this become magnified out of its true proportion. (74CX)

In addition, 25 respondents of Areas A, B, and CX and 12 of Area C stressed suffering, hardship, and financial loss endured by white families who move from an area that Negroes are entering. The people who move do not want to move, but having the conception of Negroes which they do, they feel they must. It is a bitter experience for people who have lived in an area for many years or all their lives, or who are bringing up their children contentedly in that area. They have to give up the home they love, the neighborhood they were happy to live in, familiar sights and facilities, church affiliations, pleasant association with friends, neighbors, and tradespeople, and various other conveniences and advantages. Their children have to change schools. They have to find a house at a price they can afford in a satisfactory neighborhood and fit the furniture, drapes, and carpets of the old house into it. Then there is the anguish of the moving from the home they do not want to leave. There is the strain and heartbreak of the whole exodus. People get sick over the idea of moving, with its burden of serious difficulties. They do not comprehend or are indifferent to the total situation — the movement of the Negroes and their need for housing — and see only their own misfortune and distress. Respondents' impressions of these effects are given [3]:

There's no question about it that the owners didn't want to sell [Area B]. They were really uprooted. (12B)

By hardship I mean cases of a family being upset. You create sickness. They take it differently. They do not understand. You make them sell out and change schools. (57A)

Immediately what happens is that the people in the surrounding area become panicky and immediately are trying to find a way out of the area. The total result is the beginning of substantial losses for the people in connection with the value of their property and the necessity of giving up

114

areas which they were happy to live in. In other words, it isn't only money. It's also interest in living in a neighborhood. (73A)

Respondent 82C stated his reason for not making the first sale to a Negro as "The suffering that is created by such a sale to the other white people in the community."

The financial loss in the selling of property in an area that Negroes are entering takes various forms. As soon as a sale is made to a Negro in a white block, and even before, the residents of that block and of adjacent streets are hurt in their ability to sell their property — white owners find themselves selling in a limited market of Negro buyers and white or Negro speculators because the usual white market stopped. They need larger down payments than Negroes can usually make and are often compelled to sell at a depressed price to a speculator. People see the life's savings they had invested in their homes lost.

One makes a gain but 10 take a loss. (21B)

A lot of people have been ruined by letting Negroes come into the neighborhood. How? Well, for example, a lot of working people owned their little home, lived there for years and years, and all at once colored people begin to come into the neighborhood. Well, they possibly had to sell the home and try to find another place to live. Maybe they had to pay more than it was worth, and so on. Many things could happen. (29A)

Take an area going now like Z. In Z there were a number of bungalows. The area was built up in the 20's. A lot of hard-working, good citizens had put their life savings into their homes. It was an outstanding neighborhood from the point of view of civic pride, property appearance, and so forth. When the colored marched in, the people had to sell out at sacrifice prices with financing in some cases by contract, financing the colored purchaser their home. In some cases, they didn't get enough cash out of the initial sale to go out and buy a nice home in another area. Whether or not they were people of comfortable means, they didn't want to move. They were forced into it by the neighborhood change. (17B)

Hardship is created. They [white sellers] sell for much less. (64C)

For those who remain in the area or who cannot yet move, the prospect is not a happy one. Residents are apt to resent the "invaders," and in some areas the tension boils over into rioting and other disturbance. The Negro family and their home need police protection. The quiet, law-abiding citizens of a community are distressed. Observing the increased crime, the overcrowded and declining buildings, the broken glass and litter on sidewalks, people feel their surroundings have been spoiled, their neighborhood ruined.

The white people of the area are also hurt in their social life. Upon the coming of Negroes, their neighborhood loses its prestige for white people. They consider their social position impaired. Meanwhile, their environment changes for the worse. Although a few fine Negro families may move in, on the whole, an element of lower cultural standards has entered and surrounds the old residents. The white people are forced to have neighbors they do not want. Their children are forced to go to school with Negro children. In short, the white resident finds he is no longer living in the good, desirable neighborhood he selected. He cannot or will not associate with the newcomers, his friends are moving out, and his social life is impoverished. The Negroes' coming has spoiled the white people's enjoyment of their neighborhood.

I feel you're just intruding on the privacy of people and forcing them to live together. (8B)

If you consider the Negro owner's history, he frequently has come up from a lower-class neighborhood and sometimes introduces undesirable habits of play through his children. One white family moved out because their child couldn't understand why he couldn't be allowed to run through the back yards with his Negro friends taking empty pop or beer bottles from their positions at back doors and turning them in for spending money — just petty thievery. He also acquired a rather colorful vocabulary which his parents at any rate attributed to his Negro associates. (39A)

How are they hurt when Negroes enter their street? They are hurt by having neighbors they couldn't intermingle with socially. They would lose that neighborly feeling they had. (38A)

Suppose a fellow buys a piece of property. Along comes a change in the area. He finds that instead of his living in the neighborhood in which he bought he is living in an area which is undesirable for one reason or another. Is anyone else going to take his property off his hands at the price he paid for it? He's got to take that loss, in order to move to another area he likes, ordinarily. How does the neighborhood become undesirable? Say he has a young daughter. She can't invite people to see her in the area. There are a lot of social aspects which are even bigger than the financial ones. (45A)

In sum, the majority of the respondents are convinced that the consequences of selling property to Negroes in a white area or block are harmful to its residents in a number of ways and in some cases are disastrous.

116

COMPONENT 7. JUSTIFICATION OF RACIAL POLICY

Support for Not Selling to Negroes in the White Area or Block

The respondents strongly emphasize the ethical significance of sales to Negroes. Most stated that they would not sell to Negroes in the white area or block because of the harm that would come to other people if they did. They advanced principles and norms of conduct to which they claim they adhere, which forbid such harmful acts and thus support their racial policy. They also set forth certain values that need their racial policy to preserve them. They invoked sources of higher authority in support of their policy. Many presented more than one kind of defense.

Principles of Conduct

IT IS WRONG TO HURT PEOPLE IN ANY WAY

A considerable number of respondents — 21 of Area A, 10 of Area B, 12 of Area C, and 1 of Area CX — will not sell to Negroes in the white area or block because they do not want to hurt others, and they believe they would do so if they made such a sale. "Not hurting others" applies to feelings, financial status, social status, exposure to physical danger — not hurting other people's families and property. It is wrong, say these respondents, to make people go through unnecessary hardship, emotional crises, and an upheaval in their lives even to the point of sickness by making them sell their homes and move, and to cause unhappiness by changing for the worse the whole environment in which they were living contentedly. All this wrong can come from one broker's sale to a Negro.

Primarily, the respondents do not want to hurt the property owners living near the property that hypothetically would be sold to Negroes. They are also strongly concerned about not hurting their clients. Some spoke of the real estate broker's moral obligation not to betray his clients' trust in him and always to take into account their interests and wishes because they had put their well-being into his hands. A real estate broker is expected to be loyal to his clients. A group of respondents spoke specifically of selling to Negroes in a white block as unethical conduct. Of this group, some spoke expressly as real estate men, whereas others spoke more generally as citizens with their ideas of right and wrong — a few said their conscience would not allow them to sell to Negroes in a white block, and others held to the principle that the feelings and wishes of the people in the neighborhood should be respected (consideration for the neighbors and other property owners in the area was their first concern). Then too,

117

the respondents do not want to hurt their friends or relatives in the area. Only a few respondents — 3 of Area A, 1 of Area B, and 3 of Area C — said they do not wish to hurt either white or Negro people. The ethical view is expressed by five groups, quoted here. First, the broker does not want to hurt the neighbors:

I don't want — I wouldn't want to hurt anyone. There are lots of nice property owners on the street. . . . I'm not so anxious to get the long yellow metal in my hands as to want to hurt anyone. . . . Well, put yourself in their [neighbors'] position. How would you like it? . . . Some people don't care. They're selfish. I don't live for that. Some of them don't give a darn about the neighbors. The older established firms don't feel that way. I can live without it. As long as I don't hurt anyone, I'm happy. (25A)

I just don't like to hurt those people that's in there. I just don't think it's fair. I'm not that hungry for money. . . . We don't want to hurt anybody. How? If they want to sell. Those people who have had their homes there a long time. (28A)

Because I wouldn't want to hurt the man living next door to a property that would be sold to a Negro. I know the feeling I would have myself for a man who would sell to a Negro if he lived next door to me. (82C)

Second, he considers the wishes of the people in the community:

I wouldn't sell it to anybody, if it would make the rest of the neighborhood rightfully or wrongfully unhappy. I cannot change the world, and for a measly few dollars I certainly don't want to make people unhappy, to put people in there whom they think they don't like. I'd have made a fortune around here if I had sold to colored. (12B)

Not because of my personal feelings but because of the feelings of the people in that particular neighborhood. I would not favor 1 colored family against 50 or 100 white families living in that area and that's what I would be doing. Oh, yes, white people would be opposed and quite naturally. A community like X would be opposed to any colored coming in and I'd respect their wishes. (43A)

Third, he believes that to sell to a Negro in a white area or block is unethical:

I don't think either one of the Boards would have anything to say about that. No, that has much to do with the character of the individual. I didn't start out to be a shyster and I don't intend to start now. It's character. I always wanted to feel if I sold to people, I could go back in 5 years and sell to them again. I might err in judgment but I don't think I've made too many enemies. It's a serious business. It's not buying a dress. It's what you do once or 2 times in a life time. It must be very ethical. (27A)

I am for one that wouldn't start that kind of move. I believe an area of this type that has had white for so many years, that the people would resent the change. I believe in doing what's right, and I believe it would be the wrong thing to do. [It would hurt them?] Oh, yes, definitely. It would change the whole area. It would just make the people move out from my version of how they speak here. (49A)

It comes back to the individual and his idea of right and wrong. That would be the governing factor. If he's a part of the community, that would be a pressure point. Whether it is a doctor or lawyer or real estate man their personal integrity and moral standard has to be their governing factor. I personally believe that would be harming people there. (50A)

Fourth, he considers conduct proper to a real estate broker:

Well, we've been in the real estate business for 26 years and you respect your property owners, you respect your neighbors because they have given you business for many years and we know their desires. We are familiar with the work they have put into their homes and we know how much they love their homes and wish to keep the neighborhood the same with the same type of people, the same race. In their eyes we would fail them if we broke a block. We would in a way betray the trust that they have put in us, in our office. We wouldn't hurt them and we wouldn't want to do anything that would in any way lower the value of the property, and the market value is less when the neighborhood is changing. [How would you be betraying their trust in you?] They have given us their business. They felt that anything they put in our hands, it will be given every consideration and taken care of the way they want. . . . We won't break a block. A Realtor won't be the first one to break a block because of his responsibility and obligation to the white people. No Realtor objects to dealing with Negroes, but we have that certain obligation to the white people. The value of their property goes down. You want their faith, their good will. You have an obligation to your client, loyalty to your client. You have a moral obligation to your client not to break a block. It's an unwritten law. (87CX)

I would not because a broker is a member of a licensed profession. One of the greatest things is honesty and integrity and fair dealing. Can a man live up to the code of the profession and go into a neighborhood where he knows the Negro is not wanted as a neighbor or resident and sell property to them without violating the trust and respect that people have or should have for a member of the real estate profession? (32CX)

If the owner was willing, we would step out. We wouldn't start any trouble. In other words, we have our ethics as set up by the Chicago

Board. . . . It's just the nature of the practice in any business. Fair, you know, the nature of being fair in any business. It's not that we want to hurt the Negro. Actually, you could hurt more white people who were not expecting this kind of change, yes. (72C)

We'd just call him [any broker who sold property to Negroes in a white area] a louse and let him go at that. One who does that enters into a business relation, makes a deal for the sake of a commission. He makes deals for the money. (19B)

Fifth, he does not wish to hurt Negroes:

Well, 2 reasons, maybe several. It would help bring down the economic value of the property surrounding it. The Negro that wants to pioneer is usually of the leftist element, the Negro that pushes into a white area. Most of your Negro clients want to know if they would be acceptable in the area. . . . I won't pioneer an area as long as there is the great resentment and intolerance of the neighbors. . . . People would damn us for selling, but it's not being fearful of losing business that I won't sell in there. We're probably pioneers amongst white brokers in selling to Negroes. The Negroes we deal with are sensitive, and I don't believe it's a good policy to put him in a place of embarrassment where his feelings are hurt, and his feelings are easily hurt. I could make more money if I sold early than what I would lose by selling early. The people are more anxious to sell than we are. There are many calls from people who want to be the first to sell and to get the large bonus. The biggest reason is to keep our clients from becoming embarrassed in moving into the area. (9B)

Some respondents added that there is no Negro housing shortage now and no need for their breaking into white areas. There are plenty of areas that Negroes have already entered and where a great many more could be housed. There is no need, and hence no moral justification, they maintain, for sales to Negroes in the white area or block.

IT IS WRONG TO HURT THE COMMUNITY

Many respondents — 17, 8, 11, 3, and 2 of Areas A, B, C, CX, and C branch offices, respectively — will not sell to Negroes in the white area because it is unethical, they say, to hurt the community. This a broker may do by contributing to decline in property maintenance and values, helping to lower the cultural standard of the community, bringing about tension or even violence, contributing to increase of crime, making the neighborhood an undesirable place in which to bring up children, bringing in an unwelcome group of people unaccustomed to the level of living conditions and social standards of the community, and in other ways.

I would not advise any owner to sell a house to a Negro buyer in an area where the probability was that it would cause extreme racial conflict or tension. I'm not in business to create race riots, to create trouble. It's wrong to start trouble in any area where the people are not prepared psychologically to accept that. If you know the chances are it's going to create a riot, you don't do these things. No responsible person will create civil disturbance if he can avoid it. (54C)

I just wouldn't do it. I got to live with myself. . . . I wouldn't because it's going to reduce the value, because the other people are going to run away. A lot of people will resent that statement, particularly the Negro. . . . I think I have an absolute responsibility to the people who live in the area where I'm operating to protect and safeguard to the best of my ability rather than destroy, tear down, reduce values. After all, I have a great number of friends who live in this area. Certainly I wouldn't do anything to harm them. (45A)

We don't want to disrupt the community. You let in one colored, you do that and everything goes to pot. We have a big investment in this community. It's a shame to make everyone move. There are social values, institutions, friends, etc. We're not afraid of any effect on our business. We do pretty much what we want to do. We don't depend on the neighborhood [Area C]. (53A)

I don't want to incur the enmity of the poor whites who have to sell at depressed prices on a home they had to work for all their life to pay off the mortgage, and see the colored push them off. It only takes one in a neighborhood to ruin it. *Just one.* Then, when someone has to sell, he can't with a Negro next door. Just one, and the neighborhood is ruined. It's gone! I'll never be the one to put that first one in! (67A)

We don't encourage colored people to come in here [Area C]. It breaks the neighborhood. It starts it on a downward trend. We can't be a party to those things. If they were here, it would be a different situation. . . . The history of it is that the infiltration and influx of colored ruins properties and property values. All you have to do is go to colored neighborhoods and see if all colored people are not alike. Don't misunderstand me. Many colored people are respectable and prosperous and take care of their property, but they are few in proportion. It is unfortunate that it is like that but you can't sidestep the truth. There are many able colored people, no question about it. . . . We can't be a party to selling to colored in a white neighborhood. If you want to ruin a neighborhood, just let the colored in. We wouldn't open a neighborhood. We wouldn't harm the neighborhood. (60BOC)

Of these respondents, over half of those in Areas A and C and all those in Area CX and the branch offices spoke specifically of the broker's duty to safeguard the neighborhood and to protect property values, saying it would violate the ethical standards of the real estate business, a *service* business, to make such sales. The proper thing to do is to maintain the status quo — that is, to keep the area as it is and as the residents want it to be or to contribute to its improvement. A few respondents — 5 of A and 2 of C — stressed in particular the importance of maintaining homogeneity in a neighborhood. For harmonious community living there must be likeness in educational and economic level, ethnic background, and temperament among the residents (although a few respondents maintained that an ethnically mixed group was good for a community so long as there were no Negroes present). It is unethical to introduce people into a neighborhood who do not fit in and will therefore not be happy living there and with whom the people of the community will not be happy. Many respondents made no sharp distinction between their duties as broker and their duties as citizen or human being.

There is a Code of Ethics to which a broker is supposed to adhere, which cites that we will not submit property to any person where the purchase by that party would cause a depreciation to the *value* of the adjacent real estate. That's a published Code of Ethics, but you can see brokers not adhering to that, of course. You've got to consider too that the Negro broker would not consider that a cause of depreciation. When a broker gets a license, he gets a Code and is questioned on it. It isn't a compulsory obligation. It's a *moral* obligation. They couldn't sue you for the violation of it. (37A)

Because it would be unfair to the people that live in that neighborhood. . . . [How would it be unfair?] In the first place, the property values would depreciate, and secondly it would be abetting a possible turmoil or period of unrest or whatever you want to call it. Sometimes they border on the verge of a riot. Yes, I would want to prevent that. In other words, I look upon one of the functions of a good real estate man to safeguard and build up the neighborhood rather than tear one down. (74CX)

Well, I would say there is a certain amount of ethics in this profession. It's not ethical to do something that would be harmful to a neighborhood. You're cutting your own throat at the same time, because if you get a community down on you, you might as well pull out. [How is it harmful to the neighborhood?] Well, you introduce a foreign element into any community and you sow the seeds of change. In the case of the Negro, it is a harmful seed. It introduces an inferior culture into a neighborhood of superior culture. That doesn't apply to the individual, but it does apply to the group. (62BOC)

It's unethical when you sell out a community, when you rob a community of its pleasures of community living. It's unethical to make a situation that might be a civil commotion or disturbance factor. By community pleasures I mean good living. [How is the good living disrupted?] By putting an undesirable situation in the community as if you put a factory in the community. The white community just will not accept them as a whole. It's undesirable to the people of that community that they should have Negroes living in that community. . . . The principal function of the Realtor or a person who is an agent for the sale of real estate is not to sell property to people that would be unhappy in the living conditions that they would have to face in that situation. (65C)

Because I wouldn't embarrass the colored fellow. I wouldn't put him in where he wasn't wanted. A man buys a home for happiness. I would also have a regard for the type of people in the community, people who have things in common, to keep up the homogeneity, that's right. The colored don't assimilate as easily. I hear white people say, "I don't mind living among them, yes, but I don't want to live with them. I don't want my children to marry them." . . . When a man buys a home, he buys the neighbors, association, school, church. (42A)

Absolute Values

Apart from loyalty to clients as the duty of a real estate broker, the principle of primary loyalties is upheld by a few respondents as a reason for not selling to Negroes in the white area or block.

You know, right or wrong, a man feels that he owes allegiance to his family over and above his neighbors. If he is expected to do that, and most people do it, it must also be true that he would prefer to associate with people of his own kind socially, even in business. And there is a certain allegiance to religious faiths and to country. Therefore it can't be expected, it does not seem natural that he should treat one of a different race the same as his own race. (6B)

Whether I'm a priest, a rabbi, or a real estate man, I'm still a member of a race. What I mean is this. Naturally, anybody, if he happens to be a Jewish person, he's going to lean toward the Jewish people. Whether he wants to or not, it's his nature. Catholics will lean towards Catholics. Whites will lean toward whites. Sometimes they might despise the white person, but the same as any race or religion will act, they will always try to help their own and stick up for their own, even though in their heart they may know they're wrong in doing so. (32CX)

A larger number of respondents — 11, 4, 8, and 2 of Areas A, B, C, and CX, respectively — hold the premise that people have the right to choose their neighbors and their neighborhood and that it is wrong to force people to live with neighbors they do not want. This premise assumes another expression with some who maintain that people like to live with their own kind and that people should not go where they are not wanted. Since white neighborhoods are already established in Chicago, the implication is that Negroes should not intrude upon neighborhoods where the white people do not want them. In expressing this right to select neighbors and neighborhood, almost all the respondents make evident that they have white people in mind.

People have a right to live by themselves. . . . We don't want to go in there and do that. If people are living there and want to live by themselves, they should be able to do that. (28A)

My own thought in the matter is that I personally would not want to move into a neighborhood where I felt the majority of the neighbors wouldn't want me, and I also feel that that same condition should apply to any other race or creed or denomination. Those are my opinions, my personal opinions. (43A)

First of all, as long as it is the custom of people wanting to live among their own group, I won't pioneer in forcing them to blend with another group. I have absolutely nothing against Negroes, but I have not found any building where they, the white, are willing to blend in the same building. That has been the exception rather than the rule. . . . It isn't that I'm afraid of anything, but morally I desire to abide by their wishes. (50A)

Well, unless the people in the area themselves have thrown it open. I believe they have the right of choosing their neighbors where they have made investments. (57A)

Years ago you didn't think it wrong if you wanted to pick your own neighbors, your own friends. Today someone higher than you in political office or religious office tells me I should take him to my breast, talks about brotherhood. Let the Negro teach his own race how to live with other races. Then his problems will be simple. . . . I have a right to live where I please, to choose my own neighborhood, my own neighbors. If anyone tells me you must live with someone else, you're forced to, that gets your dander up. People like to live with their own kind. (84C)

Only 1 respondent of Area A and 1 of Area B spoke of the Negro's right to choose his neighbor and his neighborhood.

Higher Authorities

Several respondents invoked God or the Constitution of the United States as the source of authority for their restrictive policy. They argue that God did not intend the races to mingle and therefore made them distinctive. The Constitution, they point out, ensures certain rights to citizens and the right to choose neighbors is one of them.

You can't take them into your house to live. It goes so simply back to using the word, God. If it was meant we were all to be alive and associated together, mixed together, we would all have the same [color], but he didn't do that. It's something in our blood. Some people are radical enough to want to mix it, to defy the laws of God. (19B)

I firmly believe in the Constitution of the United States and the right of the freedoms that our ancestors came here to enjoy and among those rights the right to choose your neighbors and neighborhood. I would not deprive others of that right, yes. In other words, if you take X [association of Area C] or Area CY, to make 1 Negro happy and put him in there and to make thousands of people unhappy, I wouldn't do it for the mere sake of making a commission. I wouldn't do it! (69B)

Seven respondents of Areas A and B, 7 of Area C, and 1 Area C branch office referred to certain principles of "American life," as recognized by them, to justify their policy of not selling to Negroes in a white area or block. It is not democratic, says one, to force white people to live with neighbors they do not want. Another states that the settlers of this country fled from oppression in other lands and fought for freedom here. It is contrary to the freedom on which the United States of America was founded that contented people should have unwelcome neighbors forced upon them. A third points out that in this country the majority rules and that, if the majority in a neighborhood does not want Negroes to enter, the real estate man, as a good American, is bound to respect their wishes. A fourth upholds the ideal of high social standards and also the ideal of cultural pluralism to some extent. It is good Americanism, he insists, to maintain a good standard of education in your community, and equally good Americanism to retain and to protect the values of your ancestral culture and ethnic background that you treasure. It is not necessary to mix groups and to forget one's cultural heritage in order to be a good American.

Another principle of American life stressed is that people should help themselves and should not look to others to provide for them. Respondents point to "the hard-working guy," the homeowner who pays his taxes and supports his family as the man who should get chief consideration. They speak also of the immigrants who came here from Europe and worked their way up without governmental subsidy. The implication is that Negroes should build their own housing in their own areas instead of forcing themselves with police protection into white areas and forcing thrifty, self-reliant homeowners out of their homes and neighborhoods. These respondents are mindful neither of the differences which have existed between the status of Negroes and the status of European immigrants in this country, nor of the effects of these differences on opportunity.

Four respondents of Areas A, B, and CX and 3 of Area C called attention to the fact that the original builders of this country and of Chicago, the white men, struggled courageously against great odds to establish country and city. It is not just, they think, that those who made Chicago great should be driven out of their home neighborhoods. They have prior rights that should be recognized. (The respondents were apparently unaware that the first settler was a Negro trader who built his log house at the mouth of the Chicago River in 1779 and lived there for more than 16 years.[4])

The whites have gone out in this country and built up the country, financed it. What have the colored done? Isn't it just like a union going in after it is all built up? There's plenty of space in this country, in this town, for the colored man to go in and build it up. No one denies them this privilege and never has long before Mr. Roosevelt showed his face. We could have sold them property for the last 4 years at prevailing prices. (11B)

Now, there is another angle. The social workers want to elevate them. They say these poor people never had a chance. That's baloney. Take the colored people in the colored area now. They would progress faster if they would lift themselves by the bootstraps themselves in place of leaning on the more prosperous whites. No one helped me. I helped myself. I think you develop more character if you operate for yourself. The old-timers who came over here and settled our country, they helped themselves out. You get a better citizenry that way too. They — we never had a chance. Well, I made my own way. I had no money. I went to school on my own. No one gave me anything. In other words, "Help yourself." There's another angle. I find most of these people who try to do good, none of them pay taxes. They are pretty near all renters. Some one has to pay the fiddler. The man frugal enough to buy and pay taxes, he ought to have a little consideration. He's the forgotten man in my estimation. (51A)

How about these other people? How about the people who built Chicago, who built these schools? Is it all for the downtrodden? How about the hard-working guy that you never hear about, that pays his debts, his taxes, and supports his family? Let the Negro do that and he'll be all right. When I was a boy, we played with them. I never hated them, but now in the last years I'm just damned tired of push, push, pushing for the Negro.

. . . There was injustice to them in the South, yes, but consider the people who came from Europe. With their own hands they struggled and made a living and brought up their families. They had no government help, no subsidization. They're [Negroes] doing fine and they want more. The organizations that are planning for them make them resentful talking to them about discrimination. If a Negro comes in here, I'll do as much for him as for a white man, but if he takes a surly tone, I don't like it. They get every aid, medical care at the County Hospital. (84C)

Support for Selling to Negroes in the White Area or Block

Of the 7 respondents — 4 of Area A and 3 of Area B — who sell unreservedly to Negroes, 5 cite three sources of authority used by the respondents with restrictive policy, but with some difference in meaning. Two of these offer a reason which is part of the ethics of the real estate business — the duty of serving one's clients well. One looks to his conscience as his guide in his business and thinks the teachings of the Bible are not being practiced by certain people, perhaps members of the local real estate board. A fourth appeals to the law of the land, the Constitution, for his support. Like the respondents of restrictive policy, he thinks it the duty of the real estate man to protect the community, but he believes only bad character, not color, should be a reason for exclusion. These brokers express no concern over the feelings and wishes of the people of the community. They fall back on some arguments that distinguish them from the respondents holding an exclusion policy: They believe that the Negro's dollar is just as acceptable as anybody else's dollar, that people have a right to live wherever they can afford to live, and that the Negro has the same right to buy that any other citizen has. One maintains that the people of the neighborhood give the impression that it is unethical to sell without restriction to Negroes, but when it suits their purpose it is no longer unethical.

First and above all, a real estate broker's duty is toward his client who is the owner. . . . When we get listings we make sure that the people who are selling will accept them as possible buyers. We do this to avoid embarrassment. That opens up the door and whatever anybody else says in the neighborhood is not our concern, because we are acting as agents and their [owners'] desire is our command. . . . [Questions re local real estate board] We feel we're getting along just as well as anyone on the Board, and if we let our conscience be our guide, we're doing all right by all the people concerned. . . . There are people who go to church that don't practice what they are taught. For example, all men are created equal as far as the Good Book says. I think it's a matter of conscience whether they're in the Board or not — it's a matter of the personal conscience of the real estate broker. . . . I just let my conscience be my guide. (52A)

I have no objection to anybody living any place if he can afford it. (8B)

The colored man shouldn't have a right to live in a decent community? That's a lot of baloney. I say he's got a right to buy as long as we all use the same American dollar. . . . There is no question that that thinking [that it is unethical to sell property to a Negro in a white area] prevails. It becomes unethical because of the people who own the real estate affected. They charge you with being unethical. The broker has to make a living. When the area is written off, it is no longer unethical, that is, because the owners no longer by reason of their selling charge the broker with being unethical. (47A)

I wouldn't have any objection to that at all, as long as this is the law of our land. I observe the law. Why not? Their money is as good as anyone else's, isn't it? As long as the law of our land is that we should not make any discrimination [I will sell]. I wasn't born in America, but I believe in the Constitution as a part of my life. If anyone doesn't believe in the Constitution, then he doesn't believe in anything. . . . I'd be glad to sell property to anyone who has the money — U.S. money, that's all I care. I have no objection, never did have. . . . [Re community:] It's human that money comes first with a lot of people. Some people do care. Others as long as they get their money out, what do they care for the obligations of the community, of dealing in the right manner with the community. . . . It's my obligation when I sell to anyone to find out *who he is*, what character, not race or color, the morality, the moral duties of the community. (5B)

In conclusion, it can be said that, of the brokers who sell or rent with restriction, the majority — 31 out of 32 (97 per cent) in Area A, 17 out of 19 (90 per cent) in Area B, 19 out of 20 (95 per cent) in Area C, 5 out of 6 (83 per cent) in Area CX, and 2 Area C branch offices — advanced some moral principle or ideal of conduct derived from the ethics of the real estate business or some other source for not selling or renting unrestrictedly. This group considers it morally indefensible in one or more ways to sell or rent to Negroes in a white area or block and will not do so. Business and other reasons also form part of the broker's defense of his policy. There is a difference in emphasis on moral reasons and on business and other reasons among the respondents.

The Broker's Conception, Part II

COMPONENT 8. MEANING TO THE BROKER PERSONALLY OF A SALE IN A WHITE AREA TO A NEGRO

Many respondents, after setting forth principles of the real estate business or values of the national culture to justify their practice, expressed some personal value or wish underlying it. These values or wishes have to do with 3 aspects of the broker's concern over Negroes' movement into white areas: (1) his own reaction to dealing with Negroes; (2) his objection to or approval of having Negroes and white people live as neighbors in a block; and (3) his own desire to keep up the standard of the community in which he operates or to keep any neighborhood white. In a number of interviews, the broker stated that his reason for not selling property to Negroes in the white area or for not dealing with Negroes was a personal inclination.

A number of respondents (6, 3, 8, 1 of Areas A, B, C, CX, respectively, and 2 Area C branch offices) do not deal with Negroes. Of these, only 3 gave personal aversion as a reason. Of the few brokers not dealing with Negroes but willing to do so, those of Areas C and CX insisted that the area be predominantly Negro. Those of Areas A and B were less strict, the former saying, "If the area is one of transition and change is inevitable, we would do this [rent]," and the latter, "I wouldn't mind being the second one." The brokers gave the following reasons for not dealing with Negroes: (1) no Negroes live in the area(s) where broker is operating; (2) broker changed kind of property dealt in so that the occasion for dealing with Negroes does not arise; (3) broker has never been asked to serve Negroes (never had a property occupied by them); (4) Negroes give their business to Negro real estate men; (5) broker fears that such dealing will harm his business with white clients; (6) there are business disadvantages in dealing with them. One broker explained the business disadvantages thus:

I don't wish to take on such clientele. It's not that I have anything against Negroes. . . . But it's just that it's a different type of operation that does not appeal to me. First, it's extremely difficult to get a mortgage for Negroes in selling. Also, and this is secondhand information, the real estate firms that have sold to them have told me that they will say they have, say, $5,000 to put down on a piece of property, and when it comes time to close the deal, they are always $1,000, $2,000, or $3,000 short of that amount. As far as operating a building with colored in it, I've heard that the collection of rents and the job of keeping the buildings clean, neat, and in good physical condition are much more difficult. (74CX)

Thirty-one respondents of Area A, 20 of B, 13 of C, 5 of CX, and 1

129

Area C branch office deal with Negroes. A few deal with them only to help a client or when the Negro is particularly nice. Nine of Areas A and B have Negro clients because of the pressure of their situation. Several brokers are less willing than in the past to do business with Negroes as a result of their experience over the years. Most of the brokers who deal with them (19, 14, 9, 4 of Areas A, B, C, CX, respectively) expressed no particular feeling about it. A number of these have dealt with Negroes for many years, and others purposely entered Area A or B and set up offices because they saw good possibilities for financial gain when Negroes began to enter these areas in large numbers. Finally, there are a few brokers who are more willing to deal with them than in the past owing to their satisfactory experience. (Table 31, Appendix C.) For example,

The Negro people we meet out here [Area B and the areas adjacent] have a desire for a home that is unequaled in the white. I think it is because they have been in the slum areas for so long. They are so appreciative of courteous treatment that they keep sending us their friends and relatives. I have often summed it up this way. The Negroes say, "Please find a home for me." The white person says, "I dare you to find one." Their attitude is, "You're the broker. I don't like this, I don't like that. Find something to suit my needs." The Negro comes in and says, "We would be very happy if you could find us a home we could buy." . . . I enjoy selling to them, even though it's more difficult to sell to them, because they are so appreciative of what they get. . . . I didn't know I'd have this satisfaction in selling to them. (9B)

Personal Acceptance or Rejection of Integration

Apart from their judgment whether integration is a possibility in Chicago at present, many respondents stated deliberately or casually that they are for or against it. Of those who expressed their choice in the matter, two thirds (18/27) in Area A, over half (10/18) in Area B, and almost all the rest rejected the idea of integration. (Table 29, Appendix C.)

Eight of Area A and 7 of Area B were not opposed to integration. Three of Area A thought that white people and Negroes should live side by side only if they have similar educational and economic standing, cultural level, and social standards. The respondents who favor integration or are willing to consider it draw attention to the fact that the white people, by "running away" from areas which Negroes enter, contribute to the spread of segregation. They suggest that, if a few superior Negro families could take up

130

residence in the good white areas, the problem of segregation would be solved. The white people would no longer have a place to run.

A Negro in every block, that would be an ideal situation to me rather than a belt or to give them old buildings. Ten or 15 per cent in every block should be Negro. We'll get to a happy medium. That takes education on both sides. Certainly the Negroes have to get a chip off their shoulders, and certain white people have to learn they are human beings, not animals. (22B)

I think that would be ideal if it would take place. In time it should. I think it's a long way off. It'll happen where you'll have a few colored in an area — the better areas. It'll work out there. I imagine through a process of education for both groups. Both need it. *They both need it!* (41A)

I'm all for it. Try and get it. Not this year, maybe in ten years. (53A)

I feel that people should live on a social standard, not on a colored plane. They should be able to live where they choose, providing they live according to the standards of the people of that community, and more housing should be built to accommodate people of any race, color or creed, and a strong program of education should be inaugurated to prevent this flight to the suburbs — a program for white people primarily in their flight to the suburbs, but for both as areas are rehabilitated. . . . The big problem is how to stop the white people from running to the suburbs. It's like an apple with the core rotting more and more, farther and farther out. If there were 1 or 2 Negro families, carefully selected, fine professional people, in a few good residential areas, then people wouldn't run to the suburbs so much. (88A)

I'm acting according to my own convictions. I believe the Negro is entitled to just as good a home as the white person is. I believe we would have less chance for race riots if the Negroes were dispersed amongst the white people in proportion as they are to the population. I think that if the Negro professional men, of whom I have met many and found to be of the highest caliber, if a Negro doctor or lawyer would move into X [white area] where I live, and if the neighbors would not run away, they would find pleasant association with the Negro doctor or lawyer. One or 2 Negroes in every block would soon end race riots. (9B)

A number of respondents had the impression that white people would not move if they could be sure that they would not be surrounded by Negroes, that the proportion of Negroes in the block or area would remain small. However, the respondents were aware of the difficulties of controlling the proportions of Negroes and white people in the area or block (see pp. 296–301 for a discussion of benign quotas).

I wouldn't mind it at all [having Negro neighbor]. But I wouldn't want

131

90 per cent of them in a block Negro. Most people aren't concerned with their own feelings. They're concerned with their property. They're afraid to lose some money. That's why they sell out. I think it's their money primarily. Then, after there are too many colored, then anybody decides it's time to go. No one will stay. If the colored wake up to the fact, if they spread themselves more thinly, the people would stay. They say they don't want people to move, but they do so by buying block by block. I don't know how you'd fix that. The individual colored aren't big enough to say we'll go in that block. They have to take properties as they come. But if someone were big enough to put a colored family in every block, then there wouldn't be a problem. The problem would solve itself. There would be no place to go. (24B)

In two interviews, there was a conflict in the respondent's own thinking whether there should or should not be integration. Each finally decided that integration was not possible or should not be attempted now, but he was also sure that segregation is not contributing to the social good and there should be an end to it. In other interviews, the broker contradicted himself by objecting to a sale to a Negro in the white area or block at one point in the interview and by objecting to segregation at a later point, remaining unaware of the contradiction. For example, respondent 6B said he did not sell property to Negroes in a white area "because I would not like to have someone else sell my neighbor's home to a Negro family." But later he said in regard to integration, "It is a possibility. I believe that segregation is bad because it does not help the people that need the help. It does not help them to become better citizens. I have found that all of us learn many things and improve ourselves by association, so naturally it would be true with the Negro people who are segregated."

Wish to Maintain the Community Standard

Among the respondents who do not want integration (18, 10, 15, 3, 3 of Areas A, B, C, CX, and the Area C branch offices, respectively), about half of those in Areas A and C and a few in the other areas are opposed particularly because they want to keep their *own* area intact as white, stable, prospering communities; some brokers want this for *all* areas. Apart from their duty as real estate men to safeguard the neighborhood and their idea that it is unethical to hurt a neighborhood in any way, these respondents have a deep interest in the community (Areas A and C) because they feel they are members of it through long years of business operation and perhaps residence as well. They have an interest in seeing the status quo of the neighborhood maintained, regardless of the financial advantage that would accrue to them if it remained so. These respondents assume that if Negroes enter, the standard will go down. There are 2 wishes here: keep the community white and keep up its standard. Both will be accomplished by excluding Negroes. A few respondents think that, even if 1 or 2 Negroes enter the neighborhood, renewed efforts should be made to keep up the community so that no more white people will leave. To this end, they suggest enlisting the cooperation of the few Negro residents so that all would strive to uphold the standard of the community.

In our case, we simply withdrew from that market. We felt that we were offered a choice between aiding in this change which we didn't approve. We felt that this was in a sense a liquidation of the neighborhood. We felt that once the new properties were acquired by colored owners, our tasks as Realtors would become more difficult due to a natural preference on the part of the new purchasers to deal with members of their own race. . . . Our firm is traditionally an Area A firm. . . . All except 1 person in this firm lives right in Area A. Six of the personnel staff, all except 1, own their own home and have very deep roots in the neighborhood. If it were a question of money only, the whole firm could have been sold. We have roots here in considerable number. (39A)

[My main reason for not selling property to Negroes in white block is] the effect it would have upon the neighborhood. My personal feeling, yes, in regard to the area, not to break it, yes, and the millions it would depreciate in value, when they have places they can go and don't want to go, (63C)

The main reason why the real estate broker does not sell to a Negro on a street where there are no Negroes is because of his years in the area, the social and business contacts which he has created during that period, and the obligation which he feels is due to his friends who are still remaining to protect them. (45A)

[I do not sell to Negroes in white blocks] in consideration of the other owners. I would be lowering their chances of selling at a fair price, because immediately the surrounding property drops in value, and what it would be doing to the neighborhood, the very thing I've been trying to save. It isn't that I feel we're any better, but just to keep our white neighborhoods and let our children have white playmates. (33A)

I never was the first to start to sell to a Negro in any place. I have property. I wouldn't sell in any white area to a colored person, for example, in [Area C]. I *myself* wouldn't . . . no more than I would want to sell to some of these whites that don't fit into a neighborhood. You like to keep up the standard of the community, *especially if you live in the community*, and, as soon as 1 family gets in that is not nice, they bring in others of that level. I think everybody takes pride in their home, and, when they raise children, they want the community to be a fit place to raise their children. I want this for my own children and others too, surely. It seems a pity that years ago they haven't given the Negroes the right place in the country. It's more important that it would hurt the community than the business. (75C)

I believe in such areas as in [Area C and another white area] that they should *not attempt* to get in. For the other areas the better class of colored will help rather than hinder certain neighborhoods. I believe they must have a place to live, and the way they're moving in on Chicago, my God, they'll have to have a place to live or we'll have trouble. As soon as they have a place to live respectably, I believe our relations will improve. (43A)

Only one respondent, 43A above, commented on what white areas he thought Negroes should or should not enter, believing that the educated Negro of the "better class" would benefit the white areas of low social level.

Three brokers, like those not opposed to integration (see pp. 130–132), thought it should come by cultural level and in the good residential areas or else in the city as a whole at one and the same time.

The only long-term solution to this whole problem of Area A as a co-racial neighborhood is Chicago as a coracial neighborhood. When there is no place left to flee to, white people will no longer feel it is necessary for them to flee. (39A)

A mistake was made in the beginning. If the X and Y [hotels in white part of Area A and another white area] will cater to colored people, everyone will. They don't. If colored were eating and living in these hotels. It should be a mutual condition all over. If it starts, it should in the good neighborhood. (49A)

If you take the long pull, you have to have integration, but it'll be integration by culture and not by just any group of Negroes moving into any area. (62BOC)

In conclusion, few respondents have any personal aversion to dealing with Negroes. Most of those who do not deal with them have business reasons for not doing so, and most of those who do expressed no particular feeling about it. A few are less willing and a few are more willing to do business with them now than in the past, according to their experiences. Most of the brokers who expressed their stand are themselves opposed to racial residential integration; of these, some wish to see their own community of operation, and others, all communities, continue to be white areas of good standard.

COMPONENT 9. BELIEFS ABOUT CONSEQUENCES TO HIMSELF OF UNRESTRICTED SELLING IN THE WHITE AREA OR BLOCK

In the respondents' reasons for conforming to the practice of exclusion, a distinction must be made between conformity with the practice because of the broker's own identification with his community of operation, especially if the broker lives in it, and conformity because of certain pressures, actual or expected, from the community and fear of social or business consequences.

Among the respondents' reasons for not selling/renting to Negroes in a white area or block is the fear of what will happen to them if they do. A few brokers are concerned about the outcome of simply dealing with Negroes. Some manage properties with Negro tenants but hesitate to sell to Negroes because they fear this may anger white people. One respondent said, "We have never sold any to Negroes. If they came I would. I'm an American citizen. I couldn't do otherwise. I have never been interested in it. Most of the selling is in transitional areas. I don't want to go about antagonizing the white population. I can't fight with everyone. (53A)" Others sell to Negroes but will not manage property with Negro tenants because they believe it would be difficult or dangerous — "I would have to make inspection of the building occupied by them. I would fear physical harm to myself. (82C)" However, the majority are afraid of what will happen to them if they sell to Negroes in the white area or block. At least two thirds are firmly convinced that they would suffer some harmful consequence if they sold in this way. One group stressed business consequences only, and a larger group spoke only of social consequences, but most mentioned both.

The Interview Schedule contained no specific question on what the consequences to the broker would be if he sold or rented to Negroes unrestrictedly. However, if the respondent did not mention consequences to himself in answer to Question 16d (Appendix A), he was asked about them. Questions 12, 13, 14, and 15 also called forth statements on consequences of respondents' main lines of action.

A considerable number of respondents — Area A, 15/35; Area B, 10/23; Area C, 12/20; Area CX, 3/6; and 1 of 2 Area C branch offices — stressed business consequences alone or also mentioned social consequences. They fear that they will lose clients in real estate brokerage or in their insurance business; that sources of mortgage funds will dry up and financing will become difficult; that insurance companies will not give them insurance; and that property owners living near the property sold to a Negro will not give them their listings, and other white owners in the same area and in other white areas will follow suit. The broker also expects that, if he makes such a sale, he will not only be unable to sell to white people but also will find that there are not enough Negro buyers coming into the area to keep his business going. In other words, he will soon not have so good a market as he had. Respondent 13CX explained the broker's position thus: "He wants to stay in business. If he tries to sell in a white area, he'd soon be out of business. First, he wouldn't be able to find enough Negro buyers to go into this area. Secondly, white people would stop doing business with him." And Respondent 21B said, "I follow the lines of least resistance because I want to know where I'm going to be able to get a mortgage. Why try to accomplish the sale of a piece of property if you have to beat your head to get a mortgage or pay a higher premium but not from a building and loan." Respondent 72C commented about renting. "I think he'd lose all his tenants. It wouldn't be smart. I wouldn't. I would be against it from a business standpoint."

A small number of respondents are concerned about the long-range business loss they would suffer if they or other brokers sell to Negroes in a white area or block. This conviction is based on expectations of business loss to Negro brokers, decline of the neighborhood, decrease of business as property values fall in the area, and financial difficulties.

As values decrease, the broker's business is decreased accordingly, because our activity is based on the dynamics of a growing, thriving area, the availability of good real estate to buy and sell, and the demand of buyers for properties in the area. [Question about Negro entry, increase of sales:] The increase of sales is offset by the effect on the neighborhood ultimately for the broker's business. Go down to X [Negro area]. How many thriving brokers are there there? Would you care to invest in some of those properties? (17B)

Those that are doing it will burn themselves in the end when the colored control of Area A is completed. (33A)

[Main reasons for not selling to Negro in white area or block:] First, principle with a capital *P*. Secondly, the unavailability of good financing. In regard to *one*, I would be usurping a community, and in regard to *two*,

I would be more or less committing financial oblivion. We would be killing our own business — long-range business. (61C)

A larger number of respondents, except for Area C and its branch offices, are concerned more with social than with business consequences: Area A, 21/35; Area B, 15/23; Area C, 12/20; Area CX, 5/6; Area C branch offices, 1/2. The respondents expect and fear harmful consequences from adjoining property owners, people of the community, and white people in the city at large. They wish to avoid the wrath of the immediate neighbors and to keep the goodwill of the community, the respect and confidence of clients, and the good opinion of friends and the public. Some fear loss of status with business colleagues — other brokers will resent the broker's sale and will criticize him severely; they will no longer cooperate with the offender and may even ostracize him. Most of all, respondents fear damage to their reputation and their name and subsequent loss of social standing in the community. (Table 32, Appendix C.)

Thirty-one of Areas A, B, and CX, 11 of Area C, and 1 branch office maintain that the broker's position in the community will be greatly damaged if he makes such a sale. He will lose the esteem in which he was held, his company will lose its prestige, and his family will suffer. If he lives in his community of operation, the effects will be more devastating because it will apply economic and social sanctions against him and his family. The general reaction from white people will be most unfavorable to him. Many respondents spoke of more than one social consequence. There is the possible loss of the goodwill of owners, clients, friends, brokers, the public:

I wouldn't want to darken the neighborhood and make it harder for all the rest of them in there. Real estate men wouldn't make any kick, but the owners of the adjoining properties would be sore at me, and would knock me every time they had a chance. (3B)

Personally, I would consider that if I were to consummate a deal of that kind that I would lose the confidence of my clients and the public both. Personally, I just wouldn't do it. (37A)

You become a social outcast among other real estate brokers. (1B)

I don't object to selling to minority people, but there is one thing I will not do and never have done. . . . It is being the first to sell in a white neighborhood to a colored family or some race that is not wanted in the neighborhood, because you lose your prestige to start with and you lose some of your insurance business, because they get mad at you, and, to me, my goodwill is worth more to me than a few sales, and I have lost a few

137

sales that I could have made but I passed them up and let someone else be the first. (55C) [5]

There are substantial physical dangers involved such as bombing, arson, fire which jeopardize physical property as well as physical lives. There are also sanctions which are applied by the community. Yes, they are applied to the individual operator. Yes, it might be withdrawal of business. They could do anything. . . . Yes, to do this would harm the operator in his business and socially. If you lived in X [white area], and you introduced a nonwhite family and you were to remain in X, sanctions would be applied against you and your family. (34A)

There is the fear of ruining one's reputation:

Well, in the first place, you don't want to hurt your reputation to be the first to sell. No big real estate fellow, and I'm a small one, would turn around and sell a piece of property around here to a colored fellow because he wouldn't want to hurt his business, because people would really be down on him, do you understand. (75C)

We wouldn't sell to anyone if it would cause trouble in the area. That's not good business policy. For your commission it surely wouldn't pay you to ruin your name. . . . I don't think white people would want Negroes in there. (68C)

There are sometimes riots in such neighborhoods when they first move in, and if I did, my name would be implicated. . . . Say, for instance, if I sold, the neighbors would want to know who sold the house to colored. I think too much of my reputation to jeopardize it for the sake of a commission. . . . I would say it certainly isn't money. It's my reputation. I just wouldn't sell to colored where they're not supposed to be. (77C)

A small number of respondents — 8 of Areas A and B and 3 of Area C — speak of the danger of physical harm to themselves and their families and of damage to their offices if they transacted such a sale (see the statements on p. 78).

We would not be boycotted in business. The social pressure, God forbid, would be on me from personal friends in Area C or X [white part of Area A] who don't want colored to enter. That would be an additional influence. [What is the main influence?] There isn't any. I have no inclination to do it personally. Also I wouldn't want my plate glass window broken. If I moved colored in, they'd do it. (53A)

Oh, no! Absolutely no! [Re being first to sell to Negroes in a white area:] First, I'll not sleep nights for the imminent danger caused by that sale. For illustration, in this block near mine here, a building was sold to a white man who doesn't live in the neighborhood. He sold it to a colored man, and the whole 6 flats were occupied by colored within 1 day. I did not know the seller or the buyer. I did not sell the property and yet because I am in the same block my 2 windows — plate glass and wide — my 2 windows here were broken 3 times in 1 month. Just imagine if I had anything to do with it what would happen to me. (Pretest Interview A)

Some respondents themselves distinguished between the business and social consequences they expected from a sale to a Negro in a white area or block. In the case of others, a line could hardly be drawn between the two, so closely were the business and social aspects of their work intertwined in their statements. Several were not sure of their main reason for practicing exclusion. One broker finally decided that the social consequences with white people were foremost:

Maybe it's the opinion of people you come in contact with. You don't want them calling you dirty so-and-so because you did so. I don't know. It's pretty hard to state. We haven't done so and the chances are we won't. [You mentioned not hurting colored before.] It's very important not to hurt the colored but it's not primary. We live in a society where we like to feel we haven't done anything to justify the ill will of others and in that way we don't create any ill will. I don't know why it would affect our business. It might rather. Is it a social matter? I think so. If you come right down to it, it's the primary reason. We're in a position in regard to business itself where 1 or 2 individuals or even a couple dozen individuals wouldn't affect us financially. (41A)

The question of consequences of unrestricted selling to themselves is not equally important to all respondents. Many spoke of consequences to others also, but a small number spoke only of consequences to themselves. Of the large number opposed to such dealing, there are some for whom consequences to others and the principles involved in unrestricted selling and renting to Negroes are so important that they do not even mention consequences to themselves. When they were asked about such possibilities, they were unwilling to consider the question and replied, as did 81C, "I don't know. *I just wouldn't do it.*" Others, when asked, mentioned 1 or 2 possible consequences, but added that these did not apply to them or had never happened to them, or that there had not been and would not be any occasion for such consequences in their case.

The few respondents who sell unrestrictedly to Negroes do not speak of consequences either. When asked, they said there weren't any, made light of them, or said that the consequences, though considerable, do not discourage them. These brokers are unconvinced that they will be hurt

139

for unrestricted dealing, except for one who has already experienced harmful consequences but is not intimidated by them enough to desist entirely from such dealing (see pp. 162–164). In Areas A and B, the respondents at the two extremes, those who adhere to a restrictive policy and will not even consider consequences to themselves and those who are unconcerned about consequences of their unrestricted selling, are almost equal in number. One of the small group dealing without restriction described his experience, "Have there been any difficulties in regard to neighbors? Nothing to speak of. (52A)" Another said, "I would sell no matter where it's at. I've never had any results. As soon as you'd bring a colored person into an area that's white, you'd have a lot of people looking and shades going up. That's all I've had. I've never put up a sign. I usually run an ad. (78B)" Only two brokers stated that unrestricted selling would lose them the respect and the confidence of the Negro group as well.

To conclude, most respondents believe that certain dire social and business consequences are definitely in store for them if they sell or rent to a Negro in a white area or block. Some are so concerned about the harmful consequences *to others* of unrestricted dealing that they are not willing to consider what the consequences to themselves would be. Those few who sell and rent unrestrictedly are mostly unaware of serious consequences.

COMPONENT 10. BELIEFS ABOUT RESULTS OF RACIAL PRACTICES

Question 34a (Appendix A) was designed to elicit the respondent's idea of the function of his racial policies and practices and, at the same time, to check his earlier statements on the outcome of selling or renting to Negroes in the white area. The respondents' earlier answers were largely confirmed by their answers to Question 34a. There was little divergence from the stand taken before in regard to dealing with Negroes with or without restriction.

The practitioners of exclusion see as the outcome for themselves a clear conscience, peace of mind, and personal satisfaction in knowing that they are not hurting people by lowering the value of their property, giving them unwanted neighbors, or starting their neighborhood on the downgrade, and also contentment in knowing that their reputation, their status in the community, and their business itself will not be harmed. They see as the outcome for the community maintenance of standards, protection of property values and residents' equity, preservation of racial harmony without tension, residents well served and satisfied, their wishes considered, their neighborhood kept as they want it; a white area kept white. These views leave the impression that the brokers who practice exclusion are concerned with the needs of the white community, although a number expressed concern about the housing needs of Negroes.

Some of the respondents who are not opposed to unrestricted dealing also see a clear conscience and good business relations as the outcome of their racial policy and practice, whereas the others stress making money and assisting Negroes to get housing. Helping Negroes obtain housing is an outcome, but it may or may not be a primary intention.

TERMS USED BY THE BROKER

A considerable number of the respondents, in describing the movement of Negroes as they approach, enter, and take up residence in a white neighborhood, use terms that call to mind a military campaign. They speak of a "threatened area," as if an enemy were coming to devastate it or some danger were imminent. Some of the respondents who speak of planned action by Negroes to induce white people to move refer to the period when Negroes come into the neighborhood and walk up and down the street "more to be seen" as the softening-up period — an expression used at times to describe the bombardment of a place before ground forces attempt to capture it. The neighborhood that Negroes are approaching was called by several the "target neighborhood," the presumed intention of the Negroes to move into it is "planning the attack," and their action of moving in is the "attack." When Negroes are attempting to enter an area, it is "under fire." Then, when they enter, the "invasion" takes place, and the block is "broken."

The actual entering is spoken of variously as the "breaking-in period," "break a block [section, area]," "breaking into a block [neighborhood]," "the block break," and "cracking a neighborhood wide open." The broker who sells a house to a Negro in a white area is said to sell "deep," as if he were moving far into enemy territory or carrying out fifth-column action. The white people of the neighborhood "resist," say the brokers, by refusing to sell. But some person sells the first house in the block and then others follow suit. The first Negro families to enter are likened to shock troops. Finally enough Negroes have moved in so that the real estate men and the people of the area judge that the area has "turned" — that is, it is now considered a Negro block or neighborhood because it cannot be "saved" and will "go Negro." At that point, a number of the respondents say that the area or block has been "conceded" or "yielded," as if a battle has been fought over some territory and the enemy's victory has been recognized. Several respondents spoke of white people not wanting to move from "safe" areas — that is, areas that Negroes are not likely to enter for some time. The vocabulary used by many gives the impression that Negroes are committing an act of aggression by moving into a white area or block.

Other symbolism employed by respondents in describing the movement of Negroes into an area and their own role in it is that of the opening up of territory on which man has never set foot. The broker who sells to Negroes in the white area is a "pioneer" who enters "virgin" territory. "Pioneer" is used as both a noun and a verb.

TYPES OF THE RACIAL REAL ESTATE IDEOLOGY

A crucial point of inquiry of this study is the relation of the broker's racial real estate ideology to his racial policy and practice. The analysis of this relation will be made in two steps, the first in this chapter and the second in Chapter IX after the external factors affecting the broker's policy decisions have been considered.

It is necessary to distinguish the types of ideology that may appear among the respondents and to trace the distribution of these types. The ideas and beliefs underlying respondents' practices have been exposed in the ten components given in Chapters IV and V, and they will now be drawn together so that common configurations can be determined.

The three types of ideology — exclusion, intermediate, and integration — distinguished in the 40 preliminary interviews were also found in the 9 pretest interviews and the 90 interviews proper. However, to distinguish among the types a method was needed that would be as little arbitrary as possible and that would permit inclusion of new components as the study advanced. It was therefore decided to determine the type of ideology by the number of components in each ideology that were favorable, unfavorable, or balanced in judgment upon Negroes. If a majority of components 1–8 were found to be unfavorable to Negroes in their content, the ideology would be called an exclusion ideology (see pp. 57–58 about omission of components 9 and 10); if favorable, an integration ideology; and if a combination of unfavorable and favorable or balanced components in equal numbers, an intermediate ideology. Statements representative of the main ideas and beliefs of the respondents were set up as

142

guides for determining whether the components were favorable, unfavorable, or balanced. The ideological alignment of these statements was made from a preliminary analysis of the 90 interviews (see Appendix B).

When components 1–8 in each interview had been examined and labeled favorable, unfavorable, or balanced, and when the count for the ideology in each interview had been made, it was found that 30 respondents out of 37 (81 per cent) in Area A, 17 out of 23 (74 per cent) in Area B, 21 out of 21 in Area C, 5 out of 6 (83 per cent) in Area CX, and 3 out of 3 of the Area C branch offices — that is, the majority — hold the exclusion ideology. The intermediate ideology was found in 6 of Area A, 3 of Area B, and 1 of Area CX, and the integration ideology in 1 of Area A and 3 of Area B (Table 33, Appendix C).

Main Ideas of the Three Types of Ideology

The ideas in each component supported by the majority of the respondents holding each ideology were selected as the ones constituting that ideology.

THE EXCLUSION IDEOLOGY

The main ideas are: (1) There are some refined, educated Negroes, but there is a large group of uneducated Negroes who do not yet make desirable neighbors — they will improve with education. (2) Most white people do not want Negroes as neighbors because of a number of fears, the primary one being fear for the safety of their children. (3) Property values decline when Negroes enter an area. (4) Most neighborhoods decline physically and socially when Negroes enter. (5) Racial residential integration is impossible or inadvisable at present, and racial succession continues to be the rule. (6) White people are hurt in various ways when property is sold or rented to a Negro in their neighborhood. (7) Selling or renting property to a Negro in a white area is against the ethical principles of the real estate business and against the personal principles of responsible real estate brokers. (8) Some brokers are unwilling to see Negroes enter their own neighborhood or any other white neighborhood. (9) The broker who sells or rents property to a Negro in a white area or block will suffer for it in a number of ways. (10) By not selling or renting property to a Negro in a white area or block, the broker protects his business, his reputation, and the standard of his community.

The exclusion ideology has three subtypes, which can be placed on a continuum ranging from strongly negative views on all components to an almost intermediate position. The three subtypes are: (1) "unqualified" exclusion, containing unfavorable judgments for all the components to which the respondent offered answers; (2) "qualified" exclusion, containing a balanced or favorable judgment for one component; and (3) "moderate" exclusion, containing a balanced or favorable judgment for two or three components. The unqualified exclusion subtype contains some favorable ideas about Negroes, but the total answer for each component is, on the whole, unfavorable.

To almost all the respondents holding the exclusion ideology in any of the three subtypes, the following cluster of beliefs is common: white people do not want Negroes as neighbors, property values decline when Negroes enter an area, racial residential integration is not likely for a long time to come if at all, there are harmful consequences for the people of a white community when Negroes enter, and it is morally wrong or violates some principle or value of the real estate business or of the country to sell or rent to Negroes in a white area. These five points may be said to be the core of the exclusion ideology.

Disagreement among the three subtypes appears in component 1 dealing with the respondent's own beliefs about Negroes, component 4 giving his ideas about the effect of Negroes on the neighborhood, and component 8 expressing his own inclinations toward integration and dealing with Negroes. There were some disagreements in other components, but the largest number were in 1, 4, and 8.

The distinguishing point between the unqualified and qualified exclusion ideologies is in the first or the fourth component. Whereas respondents holding the unqualified exclusion ideology present a preponderance of unfavorable judgments of most Negroes as citizens, of their care of property, or of their effects upon the neighborhood, the respondents holding the qualified exclusion ideology distinguish among different socioeconomic classes in the Negro group or between the many careful Negro homeowners and the many careless Negro tenants. The latter contrast Negro homeowners' pride of ownership and community spirit with many Negro apartment owners' illegal conversions and overcrowding. The qualified exclusion group for the most part presented a balanced view in their beliefs about Negroes as citizens or Negroes' effect on the neighborhood.

The moderate exclusionists differ from the qualified ones largely in offering balanced or favorable views of Negroes both as citizens and in the

144

effect of their entry upon a neighborhood; a goodly number of moderates made favorable judgments also in other components. In Area A, 2 respondents do not believe that property values decline entirely when Negroes enter an area, 3 are not themselves opposed to racial residential integration, and 3 others believe that some white people accept Negroes as neighbors.

Area C differs from Areas A and B in the distribution of the subtypes (Area A: unqualified 10, qualified 6, moderate 14; Area B: 4, 5, 8; Area C: 7, 7, 7; Area CX: 1, 3, 1; branch offices (C): 3, 0, 0). (Table 33, Appendix C.) In Area B, fewer than a quarter of the respondents holding exclusion ideologies fall into the unqualified group, and twice as many belong to the moderate group as to the unqualified. In Area A, a third falls into the unqualified group, but the moderate group is larger than either of the other two. In Area C, a third falls into each group. Although most of the respondents hold the exclusion ideology, two thirds or more of them in each area (except for the Area C branch offices) hold the qualified or moderate subtype.

THE INTERMEDIATE IDEOLOGY

The main ideas are: (1) There are all types of both colored and white people. (2) On the whole, white people do not want Negroes as neighbors, although some don't mind. (3) Property values are maintained or increase when Negroes enter an area (4 out of 8 held this view). There is some decline, some increase (4 out of 8 held this view). (4) Negro owners have a good effect on the neighborhood, but Negro tenants usually do not. (5) Racial residential integration is impossible or inadvisable now, but it is surely coming. (6) People in the neighborhood would be hurt if someone sold or rented a property to a Negro. The community would be hurt. (7) The real estate broker does not want to hurt white or Negro people by selling or renting to Negroes in a white area or block (6 out of 9 held this view). (8) The broker himself welcomes the idea of racial residential integration. (9) The broker who sells or rents property to a Negro in a white area or block will suffer for it in some way (4 out of 8, restrictive policy). The broker has no fear of the consequences of selling or renting without restriction (4 out of 8; 2 qualified this by saying they would if neighborhood did not object). (10) By not selling or renting property to a Negro in a white area or block, the community is not hurt and people are not hurt. There is personal satisfaction, and the goal of making money is achieved. (6 out of 10.) By maintaining an unrestrictive policy, good business relations are maintained and business goals are enhanced (4 out of 10).

The chief differences between the exclusion and intermediate ideologies are in components 1, 3, and 8. In the exclusion ideology, the broker has unfavorable beliefs about the majority of Negroes and about effects on property values of Negro entry, and he rejects racial residential integration. In the intermediate ideology, the broker holds a balanced view of Negroes, has mostly favorable beliefs about effects on property values of Negro entry, and he accepts the idea of integration.

THE INTEGRATION IDEOLOGY

The main ideas are: (1) Negroes are just as good as white people. There are all types of both Negroes and white people. (2) The white people do not all leave. There are good relations between white and Negro neighbors. White people who said they were going to leave remained after they found out what fine people their Negro neighbors were. (3 out of 4.) (3) Property values do decline for various reasons at some point when Negroes enter an area, or for some types of buildings (3 out of 4). (4) Negro owners and tenants have an all-round good effect on the neighborhood (3 out of 4). (5) Racial residential integration is here, and it works well (2 out of 4). White people run away (2 out of 4). (6) Consequences to white people of selling or renting property to a Negro in a white area or block are not considered (3 out of 4). (7) There is nothing wrong in selling or renting without restriction, and there are moral principles that support such selling and renting (3 out of 4). (8) The broker himself welcomes the idea of racial residential integration (3 out of 4). (9) The broker either has not suffered any unfavorable consequences of unrestricted dealing or will not be intimidated by them. In either case he will not desist from unrestricted dealing for fear of consequences. He is unconcerned about them. (3 out of 4.) (10) Money is made, and customers and clients are satisfied. A minority group is enabled to get housing.

The most clear-cut differences between the intermediate and integration ideologies are in components 3, 5, 6, and 7. Although decline of property values is recognized by most of the respondents with integration ideologies, they do not relate this effect to consequences to others and they appear unconcerned about consequences of unrestricted dealing to others or to themselves. They and the respondents with the intermediate ideology are of one mind in their generally good and sympathetic opinion of Negroes and their welcoming of racial residential integration.

The Real Estate Ideology of the Broker

The significance of the broker's racial real estate ideology is clarified when it is seen in relation to *his ideology as a real estate man.* Then what he thinks and believes about Negroes in relation to real estate acquires its full meaning and importance as injunction for practice.

Questions 2a, 7, 33, 33a, and 34 were designed to draw out the respondents' conception of the real estate business — its functions in the society, and its goals for the real estate man himself (social function and personal goals are intertwined and, in fact, inseparable). Two main goals were revealed. The real estate business is primarily a means of livelihood for the real estate man — that is, the satisfaction of his needs of a comfortable living. "Making money" and "making profit" may refer to quite different levels of wealth, depending upon the outlook and ambition of the particular real estate man. But just making a living is not enough — the primary goal is to make a living *honestly,* without harming people. At this point, the nonmembers of the local real estate board stress making a living according to their own ethics, and the members point to the ethics of the real estate business, emphasizing its professional nature and each broker's duty to maintain such a high standard in his business practices that he will enhance his occupation and contribute to its rising to the full status of a profession.

Of course, the goal of the real estate man is to make a living for his family, but to do it in such a manner as to bring credit upon himself and the neighborhood in which he operates. I look upon the real estate business as a profession, and it should be conducted in an ethical and on as high a plane as it is possible to do, the same way as a lawyer or doctor or architect or various classes of professional people. (74CX)

I definitely think that the real estate business is becoming more and more a professional business. I think that property requires trained management, and I believe that the reputable firms are getting it on a more professional level. The amateur doesn't know how to properly manage a building — how to be properly preventive. One who is trained in the management of buildings can save the owner a lot of money, and get a better net out of the building than he can by managing it himself. In sales, I believe it takes a real estate man to sell any kind of property. I don't think the owner can sell it and get the best price on it. It takes the real estate man to know the market. He knows what similar property is selling for. He knows the financing. He knows how to show the property off to best advantage, to play off the best points. He knows what could be done with commercial properties — what changes to make to make it more attractive, to better the income. He won't be in a hurry to accept any price, like the owner. The owner is anxious to sell. When he is showing it himself, and someone makes an offer far below what the home should bring, he jumps at it, whereas the agent will hold off until the right offer is made. I think that people are becoming more and more conscious that real estate is approaching more a professional level like that of a doctor or a lawyer, that not anyone can do this work of real estate. It takes a specialist. I see the real estate business as a profession, yes. (67A)

The second goal is to provide a service to the community or communities where the real estate man is operating and, specifically, to make housing available for buying or renting. The respondents are helping to satisfy the basic need for shelter. The real estate man also deals with the use of land, "the basis of all wealth." As broker, the real estate man brings seller and buyer together, providing a market for those who want to sell and helping the buyer secure financial aid. As management agent, he sees to it that housing under his control is properly maintained and warns the owners about necessary repairs.

The respondents point out the importance of their work to the happiness and welfare of their clients, since they deal in homes, where clients will bring up their children. Hence, the real estate man has a particular moral responsibility toward his client because he can affect his client's life profoundly: People buy a home perhaps once in their lives, and all their savings are at stake. The broker learns intimate details about his client's family and financial status in order to advise him properly about a suitable house and neighborhood. He acts in a capacity of trust. Real estate transactions often arise out of calamity — death, divorce, illness, loss of job, or just a transfer to another city — although there are other reasons also, such as newlyweds needing an apartment or a growing family needing a larger home. The real estate man sees the cycle of human life in his work and grows in his acquaintance with people's ways. A few respondents told of clients' discussing problems with them as they would with a minister. The respondents are aware of the seriousness of their task and of its moral obligations.

To achieve his goal of service to the members of the community, the real estate man must help in every way he can to maintain the standard of the community and to contribute to its improvement. When the standard is upheld, property values and social benefits are protected for residents. The respondents emphasize strongly that it is their constant task to preserve the community as a desirable residential area by preventing undesirable change and by selecting tenants and buyers wisely. He must get those who will be acceptable to the people who are already living there. However, responsibility for the standard does not lie with brokers alone, but also with owners, particularly in their maintenance of property. Many respondents consider maintenance the greatest protection for the stability of a neighborhood and the property values in it. With the deterioration of buildings comes the decline of an area, because the value of a property depends not only upon its own condition but also upon that of the buildings around it and of the neighborhood in general. The real estate man of high standards will see to it that the buildings he manages are well kept up, and he will refuse to manage any that are neglected.

In speaking of the community, the respondents mean a "good" residential area. Apart from having necessary facilities and institutional structures — schools, churches, good transportation, and recreational and shopping centers — a good residential area is one inhabited by "good" people — solid, law-abiding citizens with families who own their homes, take pride in their neighborhood, and participate in community affairs. "A family unit is more important than anything," said one respondent. "They seem to be more stable. The responsibility is there." Most respondents believe that people with roots are the desirable kind for a neighborhood, and that homeowners are the best because, on the whole, they are more interested in maintaining property and standards than are tenants. The respondents speak favorably of workers' areas as well as of middle-class areas. Most important if the area is to remain desirable for residents, its homogeneity of social standard, economic level, and education must be secured. Steady employment is essential for owners and tenants so that earning is regular and property is maintained; educated people are likely to have more stable incomes than the uneducated. First and last is the *stability* of the neighborhood. In a good residential area there is a high standard of property maintenance and community living, and it is likely to be maintained. Many respondents consider the characteristics that make for stable and mutually satisfying community living to be also the characteristics most important for good citizenship and for the welfare of society as a whole. These values

149

are also among those whose maintenance helps the real estate man's business.

The Relation of the Exclusion Ideology to the Real Estate Ideology

The exclusion ideology bears a close relation to the over-all real estate ideology of the respondents. Most of them are aware of a large group of uneducated Negroes that has a lesser sense of social responsibility, a more unstable employment record, a poorer record for care of property, worse living habits, and a more unstable family life than a group of white people of comparable status. Since this large portion of the Negro population has qualities opposite to those needed for being good members of a community, the respondents cannot accept it.

The real estate man has accepted a special moral responsibility to his clients, the people of the community who give him their business. Knowing the residents of the neighborhood do not want Negroes as neighbors, he believes that to introduce them into the community would be betrayal of both property value and general welfare. Also, he would in a number of ways lower the standard of the community, the very thing he should try most to preserve. Hence, by introducing a Negro family into the community, the real estate man would be defeating his major goals: he would be violating the trust of the community instead of rendering it a service, he would be damaging the real estate profession in the eyes of the public, and he would be putting himself out of business.

In conclusion, the majority of the respondents share a set of beliefs — the ideas of the exclusion ideology — although a few hold the intermediate and the integration ideologies. The main ideas of the ideologies as analyzed in the ten components constitute the respondents' main arguments and support for their racial policies and practices, particularly in respect to selling and renting to Negroes in the white area or block. In these ideas, the first four components form the ground of argument for the remainder.

The respondents holding the exclusion ideology believe that the cultural level of most Negroes is still far beneath that of white people, that white people are opposed to having Negroes as neighbors, and that property values go down and the area declines physically and socially when Negroes enter. For these reasons, they contend that white people will continue to move away as Negroes enter, that racial succession and residential segregation will continue to be the rule, that it would bring white people hardship and suffering to put Negroes into their neighborhood, and that they, as citizens, as members of a community, and as real estate men, will not violate their principles of right conduct and bring harmful consequences upon themselves as well by introducing Negroes into an area. Their restrictive practices, they conclude, protect the community and their business and give them a clear conscience.

On the other hand, the respondents holding the integration ideology believe that Negroes are not different from white people, that many white people will not object strongly when Negroes enter their neighborhood, and that Negro tenants and owners look after their quarters as well as white tenants and owners and are just as interested in keeping up the community. For these reasons, they believe that racial residential integration is possible and already here in some areas, that selling to Negroes in the white area is no violation of moral principles, and that their unrestrictive practices benefit the Negro group in their search for housing, bring the broker business, and harm no one so long as they sell and rent to responsible people.

However, the line of argument of the respondents is not yet fully represented. The consequences which the respondents expect and fear if they should deal with Negroes without restriction can be understood only when the other factors which affect the real estate man's racial policies and practices are analyzed.

Other Factors Affecting Racial Policies and Practices

THE situational factors most important to the real estate broker in the operation of his business are the community, the lending agency, and particular sources of profit. These factors are external to him in that they represent influences other than his own outlook, but owing to them, he may have to act differently toward Negroes than he might of his own accord. They may reinforce or conflict with his racial real estate ideology.

THE COMMUNITY

Most of the respondents spoke of the community (see footnote, p. 24) in which their main business was carried on as the source of the strongest external influence upon their racial policy and the one of which they were most aware. The "community" includes clients, other real estate men, property owners (especially in a block where a property is for sale), friends, relatives, organizations, agencies, and certain conditions and events beyond control, such as the sale or rental of property by other real estate men or owners. The broker cannot control owners in a white residential area who let their properties run down and then find it hard to sell at the price they want. Such properties provide an opening for Negroes because the owner, unwilling to make the many, costly repairs necessary, welcomes an opportunity to sell to anyone who will pay reasonably well. The sale may be made to a Negro directly. If the property happens to be the first one in a block sold to a Negro, the meaning of that block for the local broker's business operations is drastically altered. Sales to white people for residential use dwindle or stop, and, if the local real estate man will not sell to Negroes in that block, it becomes for the time being a bar-

152

ren land for him. If he had property listed there for sale, he may have to relinquish it. He had no control over the first sale, but it altered his opportunities for business and set problems in his path.

In any residential area there are always people who have to sell and move. If an owner must sell in a hurry and cannot sell at his price to a white buyer, he may introduce a Negro into the block. The owner who has a grudge against his neighbors — rather common, respondents say — may take his spite out on them by selling to a Negro. And the loudest resisters may be the very ones to sell first:

People have been prone in the past to blame real estate men for selling to what they call undesirable people, where in the majority of cases it is not the real estate man but the property owner. I've had salesmen report they had canvassed a district close to Negro people and the property owners will tell them that they will never sell to Negroes. We know of instances where these same people have moved out of their homes at midnight and the next day Negroes have moved in. (6B)

In fact, you'd never break a neighborhood, if the occupants themselves would stand together. There was a fellow on X [street in Area B] who was most vociferous about not selling. One morning his neighbors saw colored in his house and learned that he had sold to them and left for the South. That was the first building in the block. (17B)

In the answers to Question 18f (Appendix A), the onus for beginning to sell to Negroes was placed completely on owners by a considerable number of the respondents. Houses and other properties are sold over the local broker's head also by speculators or other brokers, usually from outside but at times from inside the area. Properties sometimes are sold to Negroes at auctions.

The relation between the broker and the conditions and events he cannot control differs from that between him and the people of the community with whom he does or may deal. To some extent the first is a causal relationship, whereas the second is one of mutual dependence. The uncontrolled conditions and events cut across the broker's line of action and run counter to it; he is compelled to take them into account and, because of them, in all likelihood to alter his line of action. This approaches a sequence of cause and effect.

On the other hand, between the broker and the people of the community there is a two-way relationship — one of interdependence. The broker wants to retain the goodwill of his clients and other property owners. To a large extent, he depends on them for his livelihood and his standing in the community. The people in it depend on him not to introduce unwelcome neighbors. They need his expert advice in real estate matters because he knows the housing situation in neighborhood and city. To a large extent, he stands between the supply of housing and the financing available for its purchase and the consumer of housing from both dominant and minority groups. He makes crucial decisions that channel housing of all kinds in this or that direction. He is the gatekeeper, to use Lewin's term.[1]

Questions 27 and 27a (Appendix A) were set up to discover whether the broker tries to influence the residents of an area when Negroes approach or enter it. In Areas A and B, most respondents advise their clients whether they should remain in the area or sell, whereas in Areas C and CX they were almost equally divided between those who give advice and those who do not. Among those who give advice, the majority in Areas A, B, and C urge their clients *not to sell*. Of those who give no advice, most said that clients do not ask for advice; the rest that, if a client asks for advice, he is told to use his own judgment. Clients' questions in Area C differ from those in Areas A, B, and CX, since fewer Negroes have entered Area C. In Areas A, B, and CX, most respondents who give advice urge clients to stay put and hold the line, even if Negroes are already in the block.

Deliberate Pressures

Question 26 (Appendix A) was intended to find out what pressures there were on respondents from members or organizations of the community or from sources in the city as a whole. The results for Areas A, B, and CX are fairly similar; somewhat under half of the respondents (15/36, 42 per cent) in Area A, slightly over half (12/23, 52 per cent) in Area B, and half (3/6) in Area CX received requests not to sell/rent to Negroes in that area. The much smaller proportion in Area C (4/21, 19 per cent) and its branch offices (1/3) may be due to the fact that much of the area is removed from sections that Negroes had approached or entered. Hence there was less likelihood of reminders to brokers not to sell to Negroes. (Table 32, Appendix C.)

Of the respondents who answered no to Question 26, a number in Area A and particularly in Area C seemed almost to be offended at being asked. They made some statement to the effect that such a request would be unnecessary because they would not do so and the people knew that — "Just my own thinking (35A)," "Nobody has to tell me that (49A)," "I've conducted myself in such a way that there is no basis for it. I'm doing what I think is right, so what anyone else thinks is of no consequence (50A)," "No one has asked me not to burn a house down either (66C)." Respondent 30A put it more fully, "No, I have never had a direct request. Never any high pressure. I don't have to be. You know, when a man needs money, he'll do things he wouldn't do otherwise. I don't need money that badly. Any man wants all he can get. . . . No kind of pressure from anyone, never had to, never was in a position where I should."

If the respondent answered yes, he was then asked about the source of the requests. More requests had come from organizations than from individuals — in Area A, almost twice as many and in Areas B, C, and CX, three times as many (Table 32, Appendix C). In Area B, the requests had been made before Negroes had entered in considerable numbers. The largest number of requests came from a certain kind of organization — namely, the community-wide organization trying to maintain the standards of the community and, where necessary, to improve its housing and general conditions. Probably the strongest influence of such a local body was told of by respondent 38A: "If the owner says he wants to turn a building in Area A, I phone [the director of a community-wide organization] and say, 'Shall I resign that building?' If he says, 'Resign it,' I do. If he says, 'Go ahead,' then we go ahead and turn the building. We work along with [an educational institution and the community-wide organization]." "Influence" might well be called "cooperation" between the organization and a respondent who holds the exclusion ideology. However, some respondents were reticent about naming a local organization or even about specifying the kind it was — they seemed to fear some repercussion. The requests from organizations were made either by letter or by a committee calling on the real estate man. Those from individuals were made by telephone or in person. Two respondents received telephone calls from people living in the block where their firms had for-sale signs on a property. These requests were in the form of appeals, but those from the organizations were stronger.

The brokers who answered yes to Question 26 were then asked whether they had received any threats from the community. Only 3 of Area A, 1 of B, and 1 of C had received threatening letters or telephone calls from individuals and property owners' associations. Committees from the latter had also called on the brokers and made threats. Five respondents of Areas A and B had actually sold to Negroes in a white block. Those of Areas A and C who had not done so are quoted here; the others will be dealt with later as a separate group because of their unrestrictive practice.

We've received threats, anonymous ones, threatening physical harm, yes, that we should not sell certain properties to Negroes. I've one case in mind where I was threatened several times on the telephone not to sell to Negroes. I sold the property to white people, and they are now the only whites on the entire block. (38A)

You find that [influence of organizations] all over Chicago, but eventually the colored get in anyway. They usually call themselves improvement associations. The entire neighborhood gets together, forms an association, and signs an agreement not to sell to colored, and someone won't sign up. I had that experience. I was a partner in the building. The Association came to us. We had the building for sale. A party called up and wanted to see the building. One of the partners was to meet the party before the building. He was a colored man. He was standing out in front waiting for the partner. Neighbors and other homeowners saw him waiting, and saw the partner drive up and show him the outside of the building. The buyer asked the price of the building, so we had to quote him a much higher price so that the colored man wouldn't be interested. That was due to the fact that the Improvement Association brought a lot of pressure to bear on us with threats. We did not intend to sell to colored. This was in a white street and in a white area. This pressure came after the neighbors saw this colored man. We had been asked by the Association to whom we were going to sell it, because they said they didn't want any colored. We said we would cooperate. So, to get out of it, we had to state a higher price. That's why we don't want to be the first to sell. We were really threatened the windows would be broken, our arms would be broken if we would. This younger partner said, "I'll sell to whom I please." I told them I would not sell to colored. That man from the Association is dealing with me. That's why I say I don't want to spoil my reputation or goodwill. (55C)

Only 3 in Areas A and B answered yes to the question "Has there been any other type of pressure?" One was asked to vacate his office because he would not join the local improvement association, which he considers anti-Negro, and 2 spoke of ridicule from other brokers. One of these had sold to Negroes in a white area. The other, respondent 9B, said, "Pressure? Oh, yes, sure. By ridicule. I belong to a club. The brokers say, 'Here comes the biggest colored real estate broker in the city.' There has been innuendo and pressure. It has been mostly from other brokers. This pressure has been of a social nature, yes." He also said, "We do more selling to Negroes than any other office in the area."

The respondents were then asked, "Has there been pressure from any

source outside of this area to keep you from making sales to Negroes?"
A small group — 3 of Area A, 5 of B, 2 of C, and 1 of CX — answered yes.
They had received protests by telephone and letter from property owners
and community organizations in other areas where the respondent had
property listed for sale, criticism from real estate men when he began to
sell to Negroes in those areas, and anonymous threatening letters and telephone calls. Three respondents displayed letters from community-wide
organizations or property owners' associations. One told of being called in
by the director of a community-wide organization. One of Area C told of
the action of children in condemning him.

We took over a building in Area A about 6 months ago. The owner
wanted it kept white. A white woman whose husband had died recently
wanted to rent an apartment. We checked and found that what she said
was correct. She took the apartment, and a few days later an elderly,
Jewish woman in the building phoned me to say that a Negro was living in
that apartment. We investigated and found that she had married a Negro.
That has caused me a lot of trouble. [The director of community-wide
organization] called me in and said, "What do you mean by putting a
Negro in there? We want to keep this building white." I explained the situation to him, but told him that if I thought I should put a Negro in there
I would no matter what he said. However, in this case, the owner did not
want it, and I was doing all I could to get them out. It is difficult because
she has a year's lease. If the Negro members knew the real attitude of [the
community-wide organization], they would stop contributing to it. I've
had anonymous telephone calls. Years ago in [now largely Negro area].
When I first opened I was close to the top 10 per cent of the buildings sold.
I had 1 or 2 cases of anonymous calls. I ignored them. Nothing came of
it. Speculators who are first or second have been advised to get out of
town. Their reputation has been spoiled. (22B)

A tenant in a building over East that I managed went wrong and had a
colored baby. A group complained. I told them that as soon as one of
them filled out an affidavit that it was a colored baby, I would take action.
None of them did. Children wrote on the sidewalk, "X [name of 83C]
rents to niggers!" (83C)

Yes, I did once and there was colored already in the neighborhood.
Miss X [Negro television celebrity] wanted this house. I saw no reason
why she couldn't have it because there were colored right across the street.
This was in Z [area immediately north of Area A]. I got threats from the
former owner and a real estate firm. I had sold this house to another party,
a white party, and when she found colored were in the block, she turned
right around and tried to sell. She said, "Go ahead and sell to colored."

157

When I advertised, colored answered. Then the neighbors informed the former owner and complained. Then the former owner contacted me and threatened me, so I returned the money to the colored buyer. [What was the threat?] That they would take it up with the Department of Registration and would put me out of business. I didn't really have to pay any attention to them because in a year the whole block was colored. That's what I mean by neighbors and getting your name implicated. I just returned her deposit. (77C)

Yes. A circular from [the property owners' and tenants' association of nearby area] was delivered anonymously to my house, after a committee had called on me [shows circular]. It didn't worry me. They could distribute it for all I care. I do know who printed it and who was back of it. I called their attention to the fact that they had not consulted their attorney on delivering a threatening letter. Since then they have caused no trouble. . . . This [circular] is not signed. I could have hired a private agency to trace who printed it and could have brought suit. I understand you're not allowed to threaten defamation of character. (10B)

We had an ad on a building in a changing area where many colored people were living. We saw no harm in using the word "changing area" in the ad, meaning that colored could respond and immediately the next day [a community-wide organization of Area C] were on the telephone and asked us what we were trying to do and they were working so hard to preserve the area, and we told them we were not trying to turn any white area but were just offering property for sale where a good 25 per cent to 30 per cent was already colored and where the owners were willing to sell to colored. You couldn't sell to white. And this [organization] took exception and said we didn't have to advertise it as a changing area, that we should still try to sell to white, which was perfectly ridiculous and they knew it too. (87CX)

Finally, the respondents were asked whether they had complied with the requests they had received. Most respondents said that if the request was in line with their own policy, they usually complied or tried to comply. A few said that such requests had no effect on them, and a few said they were usually "ahead" of the requests in not wanting to sell to Negroes.

Two less direct questions also were framed to discover sources of pressure on the broker; respondents did not have to reveal their own experience in answering, so they were less reticent and a little more specific. Question 21b (Appendix A) followed questions about the Chicago Real Estate Board and asked what other organizations might influence brokers. The community-wide organizations were again mentioned more often than any others, and property owners' associations came next. (Table 32, Appendix C.) A few respondents pointed to connections between organizations and institutional associations and to real estate men's participation in the programs of organizations. One of Area C said that the businessmen's associations are linked with the churches in their effort to keep Negroes out. A respondent of Area CX claims that the lending agency joins with the people of the community to keep it white. Another of Area C declared that many real estate men belong to the property owners' associations in their areas.[2] Two of Areas A and B accused leaders of some neighborhood organizations of insincerity, saying they are probably real estate brokers. Such men use the bogey of "Negroes are coming — keep them out!" to exploit the white people. The respondent of Area B said,

Sales fall off, mortgage money flees, the do-gooders get together and throw bricks at the first Negro occupant, which is widely advertised in the newspapers, and it kills off all possibility of future sales to any white. Then the white organization turns a photographer loose to show the slums in the area, mentioned in order to drive away any further possibility of selling to whites. Then the real estate brokers have a field day for the next 4 years, increasing their sales percentage from 4 per cent to 25 per cent. [Brings out 2 printed circulars.] This program is the work of very sincere white people led by very insincere white brokers. Economically, the brokers can increase their sales 600 per cent. There is always a group whose economic sense exceeds their racial sense. The broker has the dollar sign as a guide post. He makes speeches every night against the colored and splits commissions with Negro brokers. (1B)

Two respondents of Areas A and C think that community organizations are showing more understanding than before. A few, they said, discourage the real estate man from selling to Negroes in their areas, but, if 1 or 2 owners sell their homes to Negroes, they urge the people to remain and to see what their new Negro neighbors will be like.

The second indirect question, 24 (Appendix A), attempts to uncover organizational pressure and especially the respondent's own approval or disapproval of the program of the organization. The respondents holding the exclusion ideology (the majority) mentioned community-wide organizations and spoke approvingly of their work; many respondents were actively cooperating with one, some in leading positions. Seven of Areas A and B thought the programs had been started too late — meaning that if they had been started earlier, they might have kept the Negroes out and the area from declining in certain ways. A few, although approving the programs, do not see how the objectives can be achieved because of the obstacles. It appears that the community-wide organizations do not need to exert much pressure on the respondents because most are already in accord with what these organizations are doing.

Only the respondents who are selling or renting with little or no restriction speak of these organizations as being, for the most part, anti-Negro and question their motives; several accused the leaders of selfish goals.

Do you want my honest opinion? I don't think any of them are doing the most to keep the area up. I think they're taking a prejudiced attitude. That's one of the main reasons that I have objections to [a community-wide organization of Area A]. If you're going to keep up an area, you don't try to get after the people because they have a different skin. I know a half dozen cases where nothing was done to improve property, but when colored moved in, inspectors came pestering them where violations had existed previously and nothing had been done about it. Inspectors of [the organization] and those sent by the city through them. It's contrary to everything we stand for in this country. (41A)

Their programs are of a prejudiced nature, very biased. They are chameleon-like. They are vicious in their programs. They are not for the betterment of the Negro or the community, but organized strictly for the purpose of being a buffer area around [an educational institution] to protect their investment. They are trying to create an impression of working for the community when in fact they are using their influence to keep Negroes out of a neighborhood by condemning sections for clearance and depopulating the sections thereof. (46A)

Several brokers told not only of requests not to sell/rent to Negroes but also of requests and threats to sell/rent to Negroes. Threats by unions were reported by two, and a race relations agency, a community-wide organization, and an educational institution made requests. Two respondents are quoted:

I had a building at X [area west of Area CX]. I was told that if I put Negroes in, they would "take care of" me. I received an anonymous letter. I also received a letter signed by the president of the [local CIO union] as to what *they* would do. It said that they'd "take care of me." They came in here — a whole organization — and tried to get me riled up to start a fight. It was a building in Z [area north of Area A]. A white tenant moved out and put a colored tenant with his wife and baby in. The owner told me to serve notice to that tenant to put him out, which I did. Then the tenant started a suit in court with the union protecting the tenant. Eighteen or 20 came to my office. He was connected with the organization and backed by it. He sent threatening orders. The police saw it in the *Daily*

Worker. They came out to see me. The letters were photostated and sent to Washington. They kept after me, but I said I rent to Negroes all over town. The tenant came in on the sly instead of applying as a colored man. The colored man stayed and is still there. The building is colored now. (23A)

I've had pressure put on me a couple of times to rent to a colored tenant where I couldn't at the moment do it. I was visited by members of [a race relations agency]. They gave me a rather rough time because I turned down a tenant and they thought it was because he was colored and they more or less insisted that we rent to these people. . . . I turned that tenant down because I didn't think he would make a good tenant. In a few months we did rent to colored tenants in that building. At that time there was 1 apartment in the building, but this tenant was not up to the mark in qualifications, that's right. The [educational institution] or factions in it, the bleeding hearts who are always out to do the impossible and hold a brief for someone or other, one small group from the [educational institution] put a little pressure on me also to rent to a particular Negro couple whom we had turned down not because of race but because of instability. (88A)

So far there has been consideration of the pressures to prevent brokers' selling or renting to Negroes in the white area or block. Now I shall record what they have experienced as a result of selling/renting to Negroes. Question 14f (Appendix A) asked whether respondents had lost any white clients because of these sales. Two said they might have lost some, but the rest had not lost any. Many were quick to point out that they "never broke into a white neighborhood" and that they were careful to deal only where many Negroes were already living. One said he had to dismiss a saleswoman for selling to Negroes in Area B too soon. Another stated that white clients would not know about the sales to Negroes, because the broker could arrange the transactions in such a way that the Negro buyer would not come to his office. He said, "Negro or white buyers don't come into the office to buy. They answer ads. They call on the telephone and the Realtor makes an appointment to take them out and show the property to them. (80C)" Another told of losing business because his firm had dealt with Negroes for many years and had the reputation of dealing with them: "The fact that we have always dealt with colored brings it about that, as soon as our sign goes up, there are fears and rumors that the colored will be put in. In 6 months this is seen to be a lie, but just the fact that we're known as dealing with colored property is enough. But the other real estate men know us too well for that. . . . I would say it does keep us from getting some white people. (67A)" One told of people's getting sore at him for not selling for them to Negroes, and a common answer was that the respondent had lost sales because he would not sell to Negroes. All in all, the number of respondents who have lost white clients because of sales to Negroes is negligible.

Of the respondents who said they would sell to Negroes in a white area either unqualifiedly or if it is the inevitable trend, if the neighborhood is willing to accept some Negroes, if there is dire necessity to sell, or if it is in an area other than the broker's home area, 2 out of 8 in Area A and 3 out of 5 in Area B spoke of unpleasant consequences. Four were threatened, insulted, to some extent ridiculed by other brokers, and ostracized socially. One respondent reported an apparently concerted effort by a community-wide organization and by savings and loan associations and insurance companies to hinder his operations. A fifth received requests from the Chicago Real Estate Board to desist from unrestricted selling (to be dealt with in the chapter on the Board).

My white clients have been no trouble at all. I still maintain all my business in [Area C and another white area]. They know, but I haven't lost a wigwam. . . . This has not hurt my position in the profession. My colleagues think I have a worm-eaten business. They think I'm in trouble. They kid me. They laugh at me, but my position is not in any way blemished. In fact, it may be enhanced. They say, "You must be a hell of a guy to sit there and take it." Actually, I have a much easier time with some of my colored-occupied buildings than I had when they were white. Can the Board do anything to me? Oh, no! For Heaven's sake, no! Institutions? Not a single instance. Social life in the community? Yes, there have been some instances but they're inconsequential. They can't cause me any trouble. The only ones caused trouble are those who don't have a red corpuscle in their veins. It's just timidity — no legal blocks. . . . I was a victim of scorn because I rented to Negroes in this area . . . I have a building on X street [in Area A, now occupied by Negroes]. An Irishwoman called me from there. She said, "Mr. X, I want to tell you, you big, fatheaded jew bastard, we won't live with those niggers!" . . . I have been called a nigger-lover, a white-hater. I have been exposed to all the attacks by both sides. I have been charged with being anti-Negro and pro-white, and with being anti-white and pro-Negro. . . . Yes, I certainly have received *a demand*, not a request, compulsory upon me. *They threatened me.* These threats have come from organizations and individuals. Clients have never asked me and never insulted me in that way. Other kind of pressure, *yes*. But they were a failure. It was worse than indirect. But they do not bother me a goddamn bit. . . . There are pressures from the unions.

. . . The pressure comes from labor unions. I will not specify. (47A; not a Jew)

The [community-wide organization of Area A] has caused me much trouble. They're not happy about this building [18B owns, manages]. They sent over a man from [real estate firm in Area A] presumably to buy the building. . . . As you know, many people wouldn't do that [sell to a Negro in a white block]. I had no qualms about doing that other than getting my head bashed in. . . . At first out of ignorance I sold this house. They set fire to it. As I get older, I haven't the stamina to stand up to the resistance. We'll buy a piece of property and then hold it until there are 1 or 2 Negroes in the block. I didn't have any objection myself and still don't have, but I got calls. They'd take me for a ride. They let air out of my tires. That house in X [area Negroes entered fairly recently], they set fire to it. We put out the fire. We had to make repairs. Then there was police protection. . . . It's nerve-racking. They threaten you. They bring pressure to bear. You get calls. All of a sudden a lot of building inspectors visit your building and find something wrong. They bring pressure on you. They get the savings and loan institutions to ride you. Insurance companies make it difficult for you to get a loan. Any destruction means an insurance problem. In the better neighborhoods, there is less trouble of a violent nature. There are still neighborhoods that no speculator will touch. They will as soon kill you as look at you. . . . Oh, I still do [sell to a Negro in a white block]. I'm showing a house right now. There's a Negro living opposite. (18B)

A lot of individuals have told me not to sell property to Negroes and have threatened me, yes. Both from organizations and individuals — from individuals in X [area into which Negroes have been moving]. I tell them I didn't break the neighborhood. They threatened to "knock your block off." They threatened to break the glass in my door. They shout at me, "Nigger-lover." It's the people themselves who break the neighborhood. . . . After 2 were in, I put 1 in at X. . . . In [an area now largely Negro], one man was standing on a ladder when I came up to him to ask him if he wished to sell his house. He shook the hammer he was holding at me. I quickly stepped back on the sidewalk. If he had hit me then, he would have been liable to prosecution. He made some nasty, threatening statements as he shook his hammer at me. I said, "All right, mister, I was just asking." As I passed along the street, a man standing near his car shouted some accusations at me, some insults. The Negro family I put in a house at X was the first in the block. No, I wouldn't do it in Area C, but here, yes, because it is the inevitable trend. (69B)

The consequences for the broker who deals unrestrictedly with Negroes are drastic in proportion to the scope of such dealing and to his position in the real estate world. Respondent 18B, a newcomer to the field, acts as a speculator, buying in areas that are opening up or that he is himself breaking and reselling to Negroes. He makes it his business to buy from the white people who want to leave such an area, and he contributes greatly to the change in racial occupancy in it. The groups opposed to such change bear down most heavily on him and on others like him. Respondent 69B, also a newcomer to the field, acts as a broker. Being more circumspect where he will introduce a Negro family, he has not experienced so much pressure as 18B, but he also makes it his business to work areas that are opening to Negroes. Both men have encountered strong hostility from the people of the neighborhoods involved. The consequences for 47A have been less drastic because he does not open up areas and work them intensively. Respondent 47A is well established and has been a member of the Chicago Real Estate Board for many years. But two respondents spoke disapprovingly of his action, and one, a Board member, had rebuked him over the telephone. Respondents 18B, 47A, and 69B live in the same, white area; none sells to Negroes in it.

Fear of Consequences in Relation to Experience of Pressure

To establish the relation between the respondent's fear of the consequences of unrestricted selling and his actual experience of pressure in the community, his answer to Question 16d was compared with his answer to Question 26 (Appendix A). The comparison yields the following results: In Area A 10 respondents fear consequences and have some experience of pressure; in Area B, 9; in Area C, 5; and in Area CX, 3. In Area A 15 respondents fear consequences without experience of pressure; in Area B, 7; in Area C, 10; in Area CX, 2; and in the Area C branch offices, 1. In Areas A and C, the number of respondents who have not previously experienced pressure far exceeds those who have, whereas in Areas B and CX those who have had such experience slightly exceed those who have not. This difference may exist partly because some respondents of Areas B and CX (which received Negroes rapidly and in relatively large numbers), wanting to maintain a white clientele, began to deal more in other areas and received requests there. Also, those who want a white and Negro clientele will seek white clients in areas nearby where the approach or entry of Negroes will make requests likely. It was also found that for those who have experienced pressure, the locus of fear of consequences often does not correspond to the source of the actual pressure — several respondents who had received requests from community organizations feared rocks through their windows, and others commonly feared the neighbors' and other owners' enmity, although most respondents who mentioned pressure spoke of community organizations as the major source.

The main point arising from the above comparison is most respondents' *fear of consequences without any experience of pressure.* They are anxious about the outcome if they sell or rent without restriction. Respondent 74CX said, "No pressure, only that I feel that if you did sell to Negroes in the neighborhood you'd certainly be ostracized. I don't know whether that's just mental or actual, but I feel that I would, but as far as anyone threatening or even requesting, it hasn't been done. It is left up to the individual's own conscience."

The explanation offered here for the respondent's fear of consequences without experience of pressure, apart from his knowledge of the pressures other brokers have undergone, is his experience in his community, with which he has dealt year after year. In the day-to-day conversations and negotiations and through this or that act or statement he hears about, he gets an impression of the people's thoughts and feelings about various topics of importance to them and he comes to know the pattern of response to having Negroes as neighbors. One respondent said, "If I work in the community, I know what the community wants." This acquaintance with the community built up over years in business enables him to feel the pulse of the community on disturbing questions of the day.

In addition to his acquaintance with the community and his impression that the unmobilized forces in it bode ill for the one who would facilitate Negro entry, the local broker learns of organizations formed within the community with avowed or hidden aim to prevent Negro entry. A distinction is made between the real estate man's *acquaintance with* the general pattern of reaction in the community and his *knowledge about* groups deliberately organized to deal with Negro entry,[8] because the unmobilized responses of individual members of the community and the conscious and planned activities of community organizations are different aspects of community reaction to Negroes. Respondents who do not mention definite pressure from the community appear to get their conviction about and fear of harmful consequences if they should sell/rent to Negroes in a white area or block from their acquaintance with the community pattern of response to racial questions. This seems to apply also to those who mention a locus for that fear other than the source of the pressure they have actually felt. Hence, the broker's fear of harmful consequences if he should deal unrestrictedly need not be a result of pressure he has experienced, but may rest solely on the conviction he has come to have about what he may expect from the community.

THE LENDING AGENCY

The lending agencies included are white ones only — savings and loan associations, savings and commercial banks, mortgage houses, and insurance companies. The respondents' answers to Question 22 (Appendix A), asking how many agencies lend to Negro buyers, bore out statements made earlier about the behavior and policy of lending agencies (see pp. 45, 88–91). Their policies are based primarily on the idea of risk and the safety of the investment. Owing to many Negro buyers' small amount of cash and at times poor credit, agencies do not lend readily to them and do not lend at all for breaking an area or for entering recently opened areas because of the risk of property damage. A few respondents knew of lending agencies that will not make loans to Negro buyers until there are at least 2 or 3 Negro families living in the block, and of others that will not lend to Negroes until a block is 50 per cent Negro. Also, every lending agency has for its portfolio a definite policy unrelated to race where it will lend and in what percentages.

Close to two thirds of the respondents in Areas A, C, and CX said that few lending agencies in Chicago make loans to Negroes. The percentage (58 per cent) in Area B may be smaller partly because its respondents have had relatively longer experience in selling to Negroes. Brokers referred to the token loans many lending agencies make — "Almost every mortgage concern will make a token amount, maybe 1 per cent or 2 per cent, as the total mortgage commitment of the loans made by a particular company (73A)"; "Many lending agencies do not lend to Negroes *in volume.* (66C)" (Table 36, Appendix C.) The greatest difficulty in obtaining a loan for a Negro buyer occurs in the older or blighted areas and in areas where Negroes are not yet present or are just entering:[4] "You try and get yourself a mortgage in this area and let the financial institutions tell you what they think about it. Let's drop it at that (16B)," and "It's very difficult, very tough. There's definite discrimination toward financing for Negroes. (22B)"

The order in which respondents place the main lending agencies for willingness to lend to Negroes is savings and loan associations, the main source; then local banks; then insurance companies, which are "slowly accepting them." These agencies often lend through correspondents in the neighborhood who are familiar with it.

A lot of insurance companics won't loan [to Negroes] at all. You see maps on the wall, shaded areas. They'll strike some areas out completely. Yes, that is writing off an area. Yes, that applies more to insurance companies than to savings and loan associations. Hardly any insurance companies will loan to colored. (28A)

There arc vcry few [lending agencies that make loans to Negroes]. At one time, the real big insurance companies wouldn't make loans to Negroes. But a couple of years ago they changed their policy because of fedcral influence. Leading insurance companies have committed themselves to making a certain proportion of Negro loans. [A large insurance company] is making a certain amount of loans in regard to new houses for Negroes. They want others to do it as well — they don't want to be the only ones. For example, in the case of [same company], for 200 homes, they said they would be willing to make a loan for 65 — that is, one third — providing they would get the rest, 135 or two thirds, from other sources. (73A)

They don't want any part of it. Some will make loans to Negro owners, but financing by insurance companies in these changing propcrties is extremely difficult. [Area A and adjoining area to the north] are pretty much out of bounds for the big insurance companies. They won't loan, in gcneral. They write off the area, yes. They won't loan. (62C)

Over half the respondents in Areas A, B, and C said a lending agency has kept them from making sales to Negroes. When asked how the agency prevented them from making a sale, most said it simply refused to make the loan. (Table 36, Appendix C.)

A number of respondents spoke also of the more difficult terms for the Negro buyer if he does get a loan: a smaller loan than a white buyer would receive, a higher rate of interest, a higher rate of commission charged by the mortgage house, a shorter term of amortization, extra expense in investigating the buyer, and larger monthly payments. One respondent explained why the loan is smaller: "When an area is in a changing neighborhood, the mortgage houses have a tendency to underappraise the value of the property. They figure the risk is greater." The rate of interest would be 5 or 5½ per cent for the white buyer and 6 or 6½ or more for the Negro buyer. The term of amortization is cut down to 10 or 12 years for the Negro buyer, whereas it may be 15 or 18 years for the white buyer. (Table 36, Appendix C.)

Some respondents are kept from making sales to white persons as well by the lending agencies' refusing to make a loan or by their making too small a loan in areas that Negroes are approaching or entering. The lending agency fears that the broker will sell the property to a white buyer who will afterwards sell it to a Negro.

Yes, it is more difficult to sell property in that area [which Negroes approach], and what you sell the lending institution and the money lenders who ordinarily finance mortgages, they cast their eyes the other way. They don't cooperate. They won't back the deal up with a mortgage. That holds for both Negro and white. (71C)

They have kept me from making a sale to a white buyer because they feared the white buyer would put Negroes in, and therefore reduced the size of the loan to such an extent and set such terms as to make the purchase unfeasible. (48A)

Either they make no loan or not enough of a loan. It's reduced. Now the [officers of a community-wide organization] are contacting loaning agencies and are helping out on that. (51A)

The interest rate may be raised even for white persons in the area which Negroes are about to enter or are entering. One respondent said, "In 1 case of a white person buying in a changing area, the lending agency raised the interest rate from 5 per cent to 5½ per cent, lowered the loan by $5,000, and shortened the term from 15 years to 12 years, after they saw Negroes near the property. That was in Area A, yes. (37A)" Several respondents were compelled to introduce the contract for a warranty deed with white buyers because lending agencies would not loan in areas Negroes were approaching or entering.

As soon as it became apparent to lending institutions, such as the larger insurance companies, most of the banks, and 90 per cent of the savings and loan that nonwhites were purchasing on the fringe of Area A these institutions then declined to make mortgages or to renew existing mortgages, which made it almost impossible to sell these properties except on contract, which meant small down payments and large monthly payments in order to accelerate the date of final payment. These sales were still to white people, yes. (35A)

A few respondents complained that the lending agency will not state the true reason for refusing to loan to the Negro buyer; it gives false reasons or uses a subterfuge.

We've tried to get financing from certain organizations, and they say, "Our quota is filled. Our funds are exhausted for loans north of X or Y [streets in area adjoining Area A]." They wouldn't make loans in certain areas. . . . If we get turned down, we quit. They won't come out and tell us it's because of the colored situation. We go to several different ones, a savings and loan or a mortgage house or a bank. (23A)

What they've done is accept an application from me and then when the applicants came in who were Negroes they turned them down for various reasons. (35A)

Some of your big lending institutions will not make any loans to colored. They say, "We have all the colored loans we can make." Yes, I couldn't make the sale. They don't come out and tell you that it's because it's a Negro, but having made similar sales for similar amounts to white persons and having had no trouble getting the loan, I assume that's why I was refused. (55C)

For example, X [a Loop bank] went up and told the Negro it was a bad buy. They killed the deal. They want his money as a depositor. They won't tell him, it's because he is a Negro. They find some other reason. (69B)

Some respondents spoke of not being able to consummate a deal because of the high commission rate and bonus charges of certain mortgage houses. Others think it is possible to get larger loans for Negro buyers in such mortgage houses if the buyer can pay the large commissions and bonuses.

I wouldn't pay the bonus. The buyer didn't feel like paying it, and I myself never did recommend it, this transaction. Some asked unreasonable bonuses. Naturally you had to put it on the price of the building. It's the same with the white. It just happened the colored man was willing to pay more. (12B)

There are quite a number of lending institutions, savings and loan, and lending agencies, mortgage brokers, downtown. They charge Negroes more interest, that means more rent, a higher price. That's how they get their properties. That's what induces some white people to deal with them. It's 1 per cent more at least, sometimes a couple of points, bonuses, commissions. The 5 per cent would be 6½ per cent or 7 per cent for Negroes including bonuses. Banks as a rule don't make loans. They used to. (29A)

I do know 1 or 2 mortgage houses that would [make loans to Negroes] but they would at 6 or 7 or 8 points on the loan or commission. That's very prohibitive. (33A)

There are a number of savings and loan that do make loans to Negroes. I do know this, if a colored institution or a white institution specializing in colored loans makes a loan, the harder the loan is for him (the colored man) to get, the more the charge is. I've known of a case of a $1,000 premium being charged for a $5,000 loan. They all charge a premium, but not that high — 1 per cent or 2 per cent, but when it comes to paying 5 per cent or 10 per cent, then you're really gouging. (55C)

Darn few [make loans to Negroes]. That's where your 4 per cent commission comes in. In some cases, it's 10 per cent. It depends on the *buyer*. Whereas in the white section, it is 1 per cent, if any. [Why?] Because they feel depreciation of the property in the section predominantly colored would be so rapid that they might not be able to get their money out of it. That's why the colored buyer has to stand up to those concerns. (63C)

One respondent distinguished between "legitimate" lending agencies that do not overcharge the Negro and those of the "underground fringe" that charge him exorbitant rates. But many respondents think the large agencies charge a Negro more than a white man for a loan, although not exorbitantly more, and offer him less advantageous terms. An Area A broker made a specific reference to FHA insurance:

You can get a loan [for a Negro] for a high rate. The fast buck man is also a mortgage man. There are good mortgage houses and fast-buck mortgage houses, especially among the building and loan. The reliable mortgage house says, "We don't loan on this section." One of the evils is that Uncle Sam guarantees the loan. The building and loan will make any kind of loan if it can get the United States to guarantee it. These building and loan take advantage of the Polish Alliance or other groups by making these loans. There are lending institutions that specialize in colored loans and others that won't make any. It's mostly those that make FHA-insured loans. Mostly the savings and loan, yes. (56A)

Because of the difficulty of obtaining mortgages for Negro buyers, a few respondents of Areas A, B, and C have either set up a mortgage department or advanced their own funds to provide a qualified buyer with a mortgage. Respondents drew attention to the increasing number of economically able buyers of homes in the Negro population of Chicago. However, in each area, most respondents consider that the land contract for a deed is more common among Negro buyers than among white, partly because of the difficulty of Negroes' obtaining loans from agencies but also because many Negroes do not have enough money to pay cash up to the point where a mortgage can be obtained. (Table 15, Appendix C.)

Because the expression "written off" has been associated with agencies' refusal to loan in areas where Negroes are entering, I asked the respondents what the expression means (Question 23, Appendix A). Two main definitions appear in the answers (Table 37, Appendix C): "going colored" or "conceded to colored" (given most frequently, with the information usually added that agencies will not lend in a changing area) and "mortgages are not written in that area" for a number of reasons, including the entry of Negroes. Most definitions stress the area's going Negro as the reason for the withholding of loans.

That's where they absolutely will not go in. Take some of these building and loan. They won't definitely go in. They won't take a chance and jeopardize your money and my money by loaning in questionable neighborhoods, and definitely not colored, and they absolutely write off those areas. (63C)

Eastern insurance companies and 3 or 4 mortgage bankers in the Loop. A good deal of those companies have written off the South Side as being out of bounds for them. They give as an excuse that they have enough of colored paper. When they do make a loan, they hold the value at exactly 60 per cent. (22B)

Question 23a (Appendix A) was intended to reveal the role of the lending agency in restriction of the Negro movement by refusing loans in areas in its path. Most respondents think the lenders have more to do with this than do real estate men.

In sum, over half the respondents have felt the "boot" of the lending agency at one time or another when trying to make a sale to a Negro buyer, especially in a nearly white area. A loan from an agency for a sale to a Negro in a white area is out of the question in the opinion of *all* respondents, and such selling would gain the broker a permanent ouster from practically all agencies. A few respondents have not been refused loans to Negroes by certain agencies, but the threat and the fear of having loans withdrawn if they sell to Negroes too soon deters such sales. Respondent 1B said, "It's like a guy carrying a club. They haven't swung it, but the fact they have it is enough. It's not the action, but the *ability* to withdraw their help that is a deterrent." Most respondents do not seem to have the idea of threat from the agency in mind, but only the "difficulty" of obtaining a loan for the Negro buyer at all or on equal terms with the white man. Only three respondents knew of agencies that loan to Negroes in "changing" areas. The many agencies who do not are also unwilling to reveal their practices with Negroes.[5] As soon as it is obvious that an area is no longer white, that white people have accepted the situation, and that the risk of damage to property is over, some lending agencies will again make loans to Negroes. The withdrawal of loans by most of them from areas Negroes are approaching or entering is in itself a restraint on the operations of the real estate man apart from their own ideas on the question. A one-way relation seems to exist between the lending agency and the real estate man with a business of moderate size; the lending agency appears to be independent of the broker.

PROFIT

Among the factors affecting racial policy and practice, the one that would most incline the real estate man toward selling/renting to Negroes without restriction is the opportunities for profit in the speculation relative to the residential movement of the Negro population. These opportunities exist primarily because of the resistance of the white people to having Negroes as neighbors.

For Outside Speculators and Brokers

The dealer or speculator is not a new phenomenon in the real estate business.[6] When the United States was being settled, speculators bought public land at public auction for resale at a profit.[7] Throughout the years, speculators in real estate have sought to buy property or land at a low price and to sell it at a high price. However, the speculator of today who buys from white people to resell to Negroes is serving a new purpose. He provides a market for the properties of the white people who wish to leave areas that Negroes may enter or are entering. He also enables the Negro to get housing by selling him a house that the white owner would not have sold him.

In answer to Question 18 (Appendix A), the respondents listed three types of real estate men who came into Areas A, B, CX, and other areas, bought property and resold it to Negroes: (1) brokers who act as brokers, (2) brokers who act as speculators, and (3) speculators or real estate dealers. The brokers are often "curbstone" brokers—that is, they have no office or operate from their home — or brokers with offices in the Loop or in other areas. The main point is that they are usually, but not always, outside brokers. The speculators and broker-speculators buy for resale, for investment, or both. In answer to Question 18a (Appendix A), most respondents stated that the speculators have to be mostly white for two reasons: the white speculator has the money to pay cash, and the white seller either does not want to sell to Negroes or can save face before his neighbors by selling to a white speculator. However, some Negro specu-

172

lators also have funds at their disposal. Some respondents think that the brokers who come into such areas are more often Negro than white, but that there are plenty of white ones too. White and Negro brokers and speculators work separately or together in all kinds of combinations – a curbstone broker may work for a speculator; two, three, or more persons may operate together as a syndicate through a broker.

White mainly, because they have the money. But Negro brokers too. They gouge the hell out of their own people. (53A)

Mostly white. They have to be white. Where their role comes in is that the white seller in the area doesn't want to introduce Negroes into the neighborhood. He [operator] gets a commission for doing that. The person sells to him. They think they are thereby fulfilling their obligation to sell to a white person. He in turn makes the introduction. He is not worried about sanctions. He is a lone operator and he works for profit only. (34A)

Both brokers and others, commonly a syndicate of several small investors operating through a broker or a lawyer representing several clients, a single investor or speculator both white and Negro and in any combination. A white broker may represent a Negro syndicate. (39A)

The speculator exemplifies how a new service may arise in a business or profession to meet certain needs within it. He does what other real estate men do not want to do, or do not think they should do, or will not admit they are doing – act as the go-between for the white seller and the Negro buyer in an area still white or nearly so. Two respondents of Area A, 3 of Area B, and 2 of Area C maintained that speculators are mostly Jewish, but one non-Jewish respondent of Area B, who does some speculating himself, of his own accord insisted that "though we hear 'the Jews are coming in and buying,' only a normal percentage are Jews. The rest are white gentiles." And a Jewish broker of his own accord brought up the matter and protested the accusation that speculators are usually Jews, pointing to his own efforts and to those of other Jewish brokers to keep the area intact. In fact, he maintained that the very ones who were accusing Jews of being block-busters had themselves more than once committed such an act surreptitiously (see comments of respondent 12B on p. 184). A small number of respondents distinguished between good and bad speculators. The good one is not trying to break neighborhoods, nor does he deceive the white seller in any way. He often works through a local broker and openly explains to the seller why the cash price he offers is below market price. If there is any subterfuge or deception, it is by the bad one.

White in all cases that I know about. The majority of our sales have been made to speculators. They have the cash. They will buy it. They are speculators and investors. There are a lot of legitimate speculators and poor speculators. [Legitimate speculators] wouldn't open a block. They'll buy, hold, and, when the block is open, sell to colored. They provide a necessary function. They come up with the cash so that the building can be sold. All these sellers want all cash. They want their money out. In other words, a white man sold a 6-flat for $30,000 all cash. It was worth $35,000 to $40,000 on a term sale. But at least he gave the man his $30,-000 cash. He was very happy to get it. But there are a few speculators who buy into a neighborhood for the sole reason of opening it up to colored. We try to stay away from them. (24B)

Mostly white. They buy for a market price. At times they are a salvation to me. Who can pay cash or pay more if the person wants to sell quickly? The seller needs cash to buy a house elsewhere. (37A)

He's just the middle man. He finances the Negro in the deal and he's entitled to some money for the gamble. As far as we are concerned, he's a legitimate buyer, a customer, a client. (72C)

There are 2 kinds of speculators. Oh, definitely. One kind is this type that will break a neighborhood or break a block, and he doesn't inform the seller that he is buying the property himself. He makes the seller think he has another buyer and the seller will sell to him completely unaware that he is selling to the speculator and that the speculator is going to sell to colored afterward. He is the speculator who breaks all real estate ethics and codes. No buyer is supposed to buy property from a seller without informing him that he himself is buying it. . . . He is the one that will come into a neighborhood and "spot" a neighborhood, that is, put a Negro in it. Then he often jumps 4 or 5 blocks and will spot some other block. He's the one that breaks the neighborhood. Generally he is a white broker. The other speculator is like [speculators mentioned previously]. After a neighborhood is broken, and they are aware of the conditions, that the colored people want to get in and they know that the colored man doesn't have too much cash and wants to buy on contract. They also know that most of the sellers in these neighborhoods want to sell, want to get out, and do not want to sell on contract because they want cash, and that type of broker does not usually solicit homes. They go to the local office like ours. He tells his story to the local agent and solicits listings from the brokers of such properties where owners want to sell and can't because they can't get cash. But he doesn't go to that property except with the local agent or some kind of introduction from the local agent to the seller. Then the local agent tells the seller all about it. If the seller is receptive, then it's arranged for this speculator to inspect the property and make an offer to the seller as to what he feels he can give as a cash price to that seller, and the seller is aware that this offer will be below market and he is also aware that this same speculator intends to resell it to colored at market value on contract with a small down payment. (87CX)

Since opportunities for gain exist in the approach and entry of Negroes, speculators, broker-speculators, and certain brokers watch the movement carefully. They buy property in its path, and they buy when an area is just beginning to change at the time everyone is trying to sell. They come in at the beginning of the doldrums and start buying.

There are brokers who follow the trend. That's their kind of business. As soon as they find it's a possibility to break in, for example, X [area on the North Side]. Some broker came in there, bought a building, and cleaned it up to sell it to a Negro on contract. That's the incentive. They're looking on the perimeter for a chance to break in. They are just real estate brokers. That's been their way of doing business. There is nothing illegal about it. You can't say what kind they are. I've known lawyers, real estate brokers, just individuals with no broker's license, who went in, bought a building and put colored in there. They're constantly alert, looking for districts where they can break in. The root of the evil is the fact that the Negro is not accepted [in the white neighborhood] and that's where he wants to get in. (35A)

In several ways the white seller plays into the hands of the buyer or broker trying to reap profits in the "Twilight Zone." There is the person in distress who must move; the more desperate his need to sell, the more willingly he listens to the speculator's offer. Speculators look for distress sales and for distressed property that has no income or not enough to maintain it but still has possibilities of rehabilitation. The man who has let his property run down to the point that no white person will buy it for his own use is easy pickings for the speculator, who will take it off his hands and remodel it for a Negro at a handsome profit. If there is a death, heirs living elsewhere and anxious to have the estate divided among them will allow an auction at which the highest bidder, whoever he is, becomes the owner of the property. Property that has fallen in arrears is also sold at auction to reimburse the municipality. At these auctions, speculators often buy to good advantage. The absentee owner who sells wants to get rid of his property at the best price and often does not care who buys it. The man with a grudge against his neighbors may sell to a speculator or to a Negro to get even with them.

The white seller plays into the hands of the speculator also because he does not want to introduce a Negro into the neighborhood, because he needs cash, and because the local brokers in many cases will not or cannot act for him if the sale is among the first to Negroes. Respondents explained in various ways people's turning to speculators and outside brokers (Question 18e, Appendix A): Some local firms will not deal with Negroes or with speculators who will sell to Negroes. Local firms are restrained by what they consider to be the wishes of the community, and furthermore, they cannot obtain a mortgage for a Negro until some Negroes are living in the area. Local men do not have clients with the financial backing that the speculator has — speculators can pay cash. Property owners are ashamed to ask a local broker to sell their house to a Negro when white people are no longer buying but Negroes have not yet entered or not yet in sufficient numbers. Sellers want the best deal and are tempted by the high prices offered by Negro or white brokers for the first 1 or 2 sales to Negroes in a block or offered by speculators who hope then to scare out the rest at low prices. People are ignorant and gullible — they believe the outside broker's promise of a high price or the speculator's promise not to sell their property to a Negro.

We had the pressure on us of the white people who frowned on us if we were selling to Negroes, and while we were trying to go along wtih them, brokers from other sections of the city, from the Loop, would come into the neighborhood and make the sales that we did not attempt to make. (6B)

Where there is money involved, people don't listen to you. In individual contacts we would talk with the owner who decided he wanted to sell and ask, "What do you think the property is worth?" We would give him a figure we thought was reasonable, and he would say, "So-and-so said he could get me X dollars more." That is the type of wedge that is used originally, putting a fantastic price on it, and they can get it for the first 1 or 2. (7B)

They're ashamed to sell to Negroes but we would sell when the area is going colored. (17B)

These fellows are equipped to make cash deals, whereas local firms are dealing with individuals who haven't the financial backing that the speculators have. These men have strong financial backing. (38A)

Because they're so hungry to make a fast buck, and most people have larceny in their heart. Good people will do foolish things to make fast money. . . . Breaking in is the work of a broker, white usually. You go into a block. You find people of different conditions, perhaps a retired man who is dying to go to Florida. He is the right prospect. He has nothing to lose and everything to gain. All you have to do is tempt him with a high price and he'll go fast. That's what happens in the residential neighbor-hoods. You have to find the weak one in the block. (56A)

A number of possibilities for profit in both selling and renting to Ne-groes were revealed in answer to Question 18c (Appendix A) and casu-ally in answer to other questions. Many respondents described other real estate men's experiences, some their own (a small number are themselves speculators to varying extent). The main source of profit in selling lies in the disparity between the low cash price the white seller is willing to ac-cept from the speculator and the high price, usually on the contract sale, the Negro buyer is willing to pay him; with this most respondents agreed —28 out of 37 (76 per cent) in Area A, 15 out of 23 (65 per cent) in Area B, 9 out of 21 (43 per cent) in Area C, 5 out of 6 (83 per cent) in Area CX, and 1 of 3 Area C branch offices. The white seller accepts a low price because he is receiving cash, but with it he can make his down payment on another house. The Negro is so eager to get housing that he will pay a high price as long as he can buy with a small down payment and on a contract, because he does not have much money. The speculator can wait for his money, but the white seller cannot do so.

The chance for profit comes in buying from the white seller at the proper time so that the lowest price can be paid. Many speculators buy at a low price as Negroes approach, and then hold and sell later to Negroes at a profit when some have entered. Some respondents do this or hold for their own investment until they can turn the property to Negro occupancy.

I buy and *hold.* I paid $15,000 for a property in [area which Negroes are approaching]. It would have cost a Negro $22,000. I have held it for 2 years now. It's occupied by white. The hammer and tongs people, the do-gooders, start yelling, "Keep the Negroes out." They're the fear-mon-gers. Then no white will buy under those conditions. I got the tip-off about this property from [a Catholic priest]. (1B)

[Answer to Question 19i:] They made it worth more. I purposely in-tended it to. I went in, bought property, waited for the change and held the property. I'm offered a profit now. I bought residential property in apart-ment house size. . . . Two years went by. The neighborhood turned. . . . We are receiving good offers, but we have kept them for investment for Negro occupancy. (22B)

If I'm selling, I'll sell at the highest price I can get, that is, immediately after they enter. We have bought in the path of Negroes for the profit, where they couldn't sell to Negroes. We'll buy it, hold it for a while, and sell to Negroes at a profit. All of our sales in [an area Negroes are approaching] now are speculative sales. Our sales in [the same area], where there are no Negroes, are distress sales, where people must sell, and we cannot sell to Negroes as yet, and there are no white buyers. Then we sell to speculators or buy it ourselves and hold it until Negroes are in the area. (9B)

A number of respondents told of sales being made to Negroes in trust, before any have entered the area, it being understood that the Negro owner will not take possession until a certain time has elapsed. Meanwhile, the ownership is not disclosed, and at times, the impression is deliberately given that a white person is buying the property. A speculator may promise the owner not to sell to Negroes for a certain time, or may himself want to wait until the first few properties have been sold to Negroes to save his own face.

They go to offices and owners direct. Don't you see how a white man can take title to white property for a colored buyer and then turn that title over to a non-disclosed trust where the colored buyer's name wouldn't be known publicly. The colored guy would be the real owner and the trust would act under his direction. (63C)

The bank officer asked for my word not to sell to colored, to wait. We waited for over 2 years. Then, when there were 3 or 4 Negroes in there, we sold. We come right out and tell him [the Negro] our position. We tell colored brokers we can't do it, if he asks and if there are none in that neighborhood. We tell him if there were 1 Negro there, or 2 or 3, we would. We don't want to be the first one to do it. We're still brokers. We have to deal with the other brokers. The other brokers would blackball us. If there was another building there, they wouldn't sell to us again. If there is no Negro there, we try to keep it. We give our word. (28A)

The bad speculator or broker, white or Negro, has certain tactics to induce the white seller to sell at a price lower than the offer he originally made. He uses the exclusive listing to advantage.

The Negro broker says to an owner, "We represent a syndicate that has lots of money. I'se a broker. You'se got no way to reach my people except through a colored broker." The difference between the Negro broker and the white speculator is this. The white speculator talks money and produces it now. He says, "I'll give you cash," and he does. The colored broker offers and produces only conversation now. He says, "I believe I can get you this and this amount." Money talks. The white speculator produces action; the colored man has an imaginary buyer and wants a commission. The white speculator is a purchaser. This is how the Negro broker operates. Suppose you have a piece of property, and you know the market value is $60,000. The colored broker says, "I'll get you $75,000 for that real estate. Don't sell to Mr. X [respondent]. He don't know." So the owner says, "Mr. X deceived me." The Negro broker says to the owner, "Give me an exclusive for 30 days," and he does and Mr. X is shut out. Sure you'll traffic with him. Then he takes the exclusive downtown and records it, and it then becomes a blemish on your title, which upon the sale to a legitimate purchaser has to be expunged, and it becomes your burden as the seller to do it. There is the opinion of title. The Negro broker can claim that you did not comply, and he can shake you down for $200 or $300. Supposing you give him an exclusive for the period, October 15 to November 30. But he records it on the sixteenth of October. If you make a deal with anyone, he collects the commission. Come November 30, he does not file statement that his rights have expired. That creates some doubt. The burden of proof is on you to cause the Title and Trust Company to believe. (47A)

For instance, on sales, they'll take listings from people at prices they know they can't sell them, but they sign them on with an exclusive. They show the building a few times to anyone, knowing they can't sell them at the price. They are employed by the seller to sell a building, but they don't disclose the fact that they know they can't sell at that price. Then they stall the man for months till he's desperate. Then they come along with a low cash price — their own. I'm talking about these changing neighborhoods — this is usually where you find the desperate man, the man who wants to sell badly. At the same time, they'll have a buyer ready to whom to resell at a much higher price with a low down payment. They don't disclose this when they pay the owner. Instead of a commission, they made a profit on the resale probably 5 times the commission. I have seen this done a lot of times. (67A)

When, as 67A described, the broker offers a price lower than he originally suggested, one perhaps lower than what the local broker had said was a possible selling price, the seller may be ashamed to go back to the local man and may not be able to do so because of the exclusive listing he gave to the outside broker. Thus he is fooled into selling at a low price.

Twenty-four cases obtained from respondents as illustrations of a purchase from a white seller and resale to a Negro buyer show relatively high profits (Table 38, Appendix C). The properties include houses and small and large multiple structures. The median percentage of profit of the 24 is 42.5, half the cases fall between 30 and 60 per cent, the lowest is 10 per cent, and there were two cases of 100 per cent profit. If the Negro buyer defaults in his payments, the speculator gets the building back, and, unless it has deteriorated much, he can sell it again at an advantageous price. A broker-speculator who has become a bit less daring in his unrestrictive selling because of consequences endured speaks with satisfaction of the white purchase–Negro sale operation:

I am an attorney. I never practiced prior to going into the service. After, I wasn't sure what I wanted to do. I called on an ex-classmate, a fellow representing a Negro real estate broker. He said, "Negroes can't get property. Look into it." They had a couple of buildings in mind they wouldn't show to Negroes. I went over and looked at them. From watching this colored broker I realized that here was a type of business that looked like it could be very profitable. I had nothing to do. I talked to this lawyer. He said I should perhaps buy a few buildings and resell them. I know nothing about real estate, but I had a feeling there was a great deal of property to be bought from white people and sell to Negroes. . . . I'm not in it as the average broker. I have a broker's license, but this is an entirely different phase. . . . As I got into this business, I began to realize there were others in the business buying properties. Negroes couldn't buy them, first because of race, and secondly because they couldn't get financing. Our purpose was to go in there because white people were having a problem selling, to buy at a cheap price and then to sell at a relatively high price with a minimum cash down payment. . . . I like the financial aspects. It makes me a comfortable living. (18B)

The speculator also makes money in a difference between the rate of interest he pays on the purchase from the white seller and the higher rate the Negro buyer pays on the purchase from him — typically, 5 per cent for the speculator and 6 per cent for the Negro. The speculator makes 1 per cent or at least ½ per cent on the difference in the interest rate. He can make still more by getting as large a mortgage on his own purchase as he can and as big a down payment as possible from the Negro buyer, so that he invests as little of his own money as possible. By keeping his equity in each investment small, he can put his ready cash to wider use. Several respondents spoke of mortgage houses where large mortgages could be obtained for proper compensation.

There are a lot of different reasons. He goes out and buys a house valued at $25,000 or $27,000 if the neighborhood were not changing or did not fear change. He would make an offer of probably 18 to 20 thousand all cash to the property owner. He would then make the biggest mortgage obtainable on the property at perhaps 4½ per cent. Then he turns around and sells that same property at approximately $27,000 on a contract basis with perhaps 3 or 4 thousand down and the balance in monthly payments with interest rates of 6 per cent. He makes on both the interest and the sale price of the property. (32CX)

Frequently these brokers go out into other neighborhoods and for cash bonuses persuade the savings and loan officers out of the neighborhood to make 70 per cent or 80 per cent loans. They'll charge 1 per cent or 2 per cent legally and 2 per cent to 5 per cent extra bonus in cash paid off to the officers of the savings and loan for making these high loans. Let's say a man or speculator buys a house for $10,000 and intends to sell it for $12,000. He goes to a savings and loan where he says he has a buyer and borrows 80 per cent of the total. Let's say he gets $9,600. This leaves him with $400 cash and $400 or $500 for banking charges. For a $1,000 investment, he makes $2,000 profit. Two months ago I bought a home from a speculator. He had paid $12,000 for it. He had a loan for $11,500 and had to put out only $500. A legitimate savings and loan will loan from 60 per cent to two thirds of the value of the property. (22B)

There is a tremendous gain. The key to it all is the financing. He gets the maximum loan that he can. Say he pays $30,000 for a 6-flat. Then he'll turn around and get a loan for $27,000 or $25,000 by paying a big commission, conniving. He has $5,000 left of his own money. He may turn around and sell for $40,000 with $6,000 to $10,000 down. He has got all his money out of it with a paper profit of about 8 or 10 thousand depending on how much time, 10 or 15 years. (24B) [8]

A few respondents spoke of the second mortgage as a source of profit and exploitation if the Negro buyer is financed by a mortgage.

The Negroes pay more for their financing. They usually pay about 1 point more interest. There are people who are making a specialty of being in contact with Negro brokers working out second mortgages with excessive discounts, which, of course, is added to the price. You can't give a percentage of how much more. They are individual cases. They work them out as best they can. The purchaser doesn't even know what he's paying to get the money. They're charging him several thousand dollars more for the property than it can be bought for. This is what someone else is doing, not I. (6B)

The outside broker at times makes 2 commissions on the same property.

After getting the listing, as a rule, they will sell the building for the particular owner, let us say a 2-flat, to Mr. X, the client, a speculator, for $15,000 with the understanding that he'll sell through them, that they will sell for him. They, as brokers, will sell to him with this understanding that they will sell it for him on contract for $20,000. Then that means they make 2 commissions, 1 from the original owner and 1 from their client. That's the incentive. In other words, it's known as a double sale, from A to B, and from B to C, and 2 commissions. (35A)

An unscrupulous broker may gain by scalping.

They do that [secure listings and sell the property to Negroes.] Fellows from . . . all over the city, when this thing got going, selling more property than we were. But these curbstone brokers have no office. They have a broker's license. They operate in a neighborhood from their house. They come in and sell like fury. They make a lot of wild promises to white people and to potential colored buyers. They even scalp sometimes. That means selling a piece of property at a certain price. They make a commission and make money selling on top of that. The seller doesn't know the law. The seller says a certain price. The broker sells at a higher price and gives the owner the price he agreed to. He sells at a higher price, and keeps the difference and the commission too. If the price the seller said was $10,000 and he sells for $12,000 or $14,000, that's legal, but to collect commission on the $10,000 is illegal. That's scalping. They do get caught. When they are caught, they take their license away. (23A)

For Local Brokers

After a few Negroes have entered an area, most of the established local firms and independent brokers sooner or later sell to them in that area. They often begin when property owners in the neighborhood come in to list property with them and say they may sell it to Negroes. When they are already selling properties to Negroes in the area, they may sell to them through speculators or outside brokers, both white and Negro, who come in to ask about listings. When the local broker sells directly to a Negro buyer, the higher total price many Negroes have been paying will result in a larger commission than he would receive from a white buyer, if there were one. (The commission stated in the Chicago Real Estate Board *Year Book* of 1957 was 5 per cent of the selling price [9]); the larger one is an inducement to the local broker to sell to Negroes. "He may get more than 5 per cent on the deal," said one respondent, and another spoke of wanting "to get in on a good thing" when he saw other brokers getting commissions of $2,000 on sales to Negro buyers.

The relation between the outside broker or speculator and the local broker presents two aspects: a legitimate one with the good speculators and brokers and a deviant one with the bad ones. After Negroes are in the area and many local firms are selling to them, some local brokers will cooperate with an outside speculator or broker on a deal. The outside men know of good Negro prospects. When the deal is consummated, the commission is split between the local broker and the outside broker. Four respondents of Area A, 2 of Area B, and 2 of Area C had cooperated on deals, but the property was in a largely or partly Negro area.

I may have a listing, and I may sell it myself or cooperate with other brokers. . . . Suppose I get a listing in [area now largely Negro]. In [same area], you couldn't sell to white. Now, I know who the legitimate brokers are. I know who the better colored brokers are, that you can give them a listing, and they'll handle the property, and if they want to show the building, I'll go over and show the building. . . . Most that I have sold [to Negroes] have been in cooperation with other brokers. . . . I get the listing for homes. Then I'll advertise. Then, as a rule, some of these colored brokers will call up, looking for a 2-flat or a 3-flat for some client and whether I'll cooperate. If they've got a buyer who has the money, I'll cooperate. I would rather make a quick half-commission than run off my feet for a month myself. (21B)

The cooperation between the local broker and the outside broker or speculator involving deviant behavior remains concealed. Long before the local firms begin to deal with Negroes in their own area, the bad speculators and brokers come in, buy property from people anxious to sell because Negroes are approaching or their entry is imminent, and begin to sell to Negroes here and there. This early selling makes the local real estate men indignant, because this is their area and they should make these sales, if any are to be made, but they cannot yet participate in these profitable transactions. A few respondents in Areas A and B sell unrestrictedly except in their own area of residence. Among the rest, according to the testimony of 7 respondents of Areas A, B, and CX, there are a few, if not more, who, being unable to make early or even later sales to Negroes but being unwilling to forego opportunities to make money, make secret deals with speculators and brokers, both white and Negro, who are ready to make such sales. The sales take place, commissions are split, and the local firm remains respectable.

[Answer to Question 18b:] Mostly through other white offices. They have a policy they won't sell directly to Negroes. That way they keep their skirts clean. Also, because we pay all cash, they'll sell to us at a pretty cheap price. [Do you deal with the established firms?] Yes, the established real estate firms, some of the biggest firms in the city, where we buy. (18B; he speculates)

[Real estate firm in Area A] and all of them sold under cover to a colored broker and took half the commission . . . They have a white man willing to sell to colored. They're managing a lot of property they can't sell to colored. They give it to a colored broker and get half a commission. On the record it says a colored broker sold to a colored owner. . . . [Another firm, Area A,] *done it right along!* (28A)

[Answer to Question 18f:] They all work together to make a dollar. They don't care how they make it. [He smiles.] Local brokers deal with colored. They'll sell to a white man for the colored man. Some firms downtown don't deal with colored. A white man comes in and asks, "Do you have a building for sale?" He buys it for the colored man. That has been done, a lot of it. The white and the colored man are working together. *Or* a white man buys a building, and then sells it to a colored man independently. (29A)

[Answer to Question 18e:]
Gullibility, and the established firms so-called, the large firms, may be the worst offenders. They will deal with these speculators themselves. That's right. [Answer to Question 18f:] It's hard to tell [who *begins* the sale of property in a white area to Negroes.] I could be an honest broker to all outward appearances. I might be the pillar of the church. I might never sell directly to a Negro, but by the same token I may know a broker who will, so, to hold my place in the community but still wish to fatten my purse-strings, I will turn the property over to another type of broker who will do anything to make a deal and a commission, and then give me part of it. But it boils down to one fact, that no one individual or group of individuals is responsible for any changing neighborhood. It is up to the individual people of that neighborhood as to whether they want to sell to anybody, be they white or colored. (32CX)

One respondent told of a sale — the *first* one in a block — to a Negro buyer in which a large local firm was involved. He said vehemently:

This block would still be white if it weren't for a large so-called ethical firm — 2 years ago a firm here the second door from here sold a 6-flat. He opened up, he did open up this block. And how! And how! Matter of fact, I tried to buy it from him, but he wanted more money. You know what these firms did? They wouldn't sell it direct. They work with every broker so as not to sell it direct, and then they blame it on the Jews. I know from my own experience. . . . Just as I told this guy who sold to the colored. I said, "Why did you sell to colored?" He said, "If you don't like the neighborhood, why don't you move out?" I said, "I live here. You moved out years ago." (12B)

Another kind of cooperation exists between local and outside brokers, especially downtown brokers. Brokers in the Loop ask the local broker to sell a property in his area for which they have a listing — they offered one respondent a full commission, and they asked another for a certain price, anything he could get beyond that was his. These are strong inducements to make the sale.

Profit from renting to Negroes is often the result of illegal operations.

184

Certain investment speculators, either as individuals or in a syndicate, buy an apartment house at the lowest price they can, get rid of the white tenants, introduce illegal conversions, load the building with Negro tenants, raise the rents at least 15 to 20 per cent, and milk or bleed the building — that is, make no repairs. They may institute weekly rents, a greater exploitation than the overly high monthly rent, and may later resell to a Negro at a good price. The owner who does not wish to deal with Negro tenants can lease the building to an investor for a certain amount, and he, in turn, will rent to Negro tenants.

The respondents agree that unrestricted selling and renting to Negroes holds great opportunities for making a profit. However, the exclusion of Negroes from white areas has also been spoken of as a source of gain for owners of substandard housing and their management agents, in that Negroes, not having access to a free housing market, must rent what they can get in the areas to which they are restricted and must pay what they are charged. Such owners, it is held, promote the exclusion of Negroes from white areas to increase and to maintain their profit, and their management agents would benefit from the large commissions (see p. 25). The respondents were asked about this in Question 36 (Appendix A). Most respondents thought the statement untrue or said they had never heard of it. Some in each area, particularly in Area C, maintained that the owners of substandard housing do not need to promote exclusion of Negroes because the white people themselves do not want Negroes as neighbors. Some pointed out that these owners could hardly exert such control over other areas. Several stated that often Negroes pay more rent to Negro than to white owners. Others said that the statement may have been true in the past, but that now Negroes have access to many areas.

These colored brokers are being diplomatic when they tell you that. They don't want to say that the whites are keeping them out, so they say the owners of slum areas want to keep them out. They put the blame on the slum owners. (12B)

I've never heard of that — of that effort. The white people in the area are not ready to accept them socially yet. Much of it is based on the pure prejudice of color, regardless of other factors, yes, the pure prejudice of color. (58C)

To me, that's a preposterous statement. That assumes on the face of it an organization which just doesn't exist. (13CX)

I have no reason to believe that's true. They [owners of slum property] seem to be living in a vacuum. They are not joiners. I don't think they'd be in a position to have this influence. Much of it is being torn down. (22B)

I think that is false in Chicago. I think I could be an authority on that from personal experience. I've dealt in both kinds of property, represented both kinds of owners. The owner of the slum property is not that for thinking. He doesn't think that far away from himself. That is a higher intellectual level than he employs. Is it profitable to the white broker? No! (Interview T; real estate lawyer, Area B)

How could they keep them out of white neighborhoods, I would like to know. For 1 man who wouldn't sell to them, there were 10 others who would. . . . Those guys that deal in and own slum properties would have very little connection with white neighborhoods, if any. So how could they keep them out from there? (29A)

That may have been true a few years ago, before 1948, the Supreme Court decision, but not now. I've never heard any owners talk about that. I don't think it's true. (2B)

No 1 broker or 10 or 100 could stem the tide. They have to have a place to live. There is no organizational method by which the Negroes could be kept from expanding. . . . I would say the owners of the property in what have been Negro areas are sad at their spreading around, because before they could get any price. When they were shut in by walls, they were exploited to a very great degree. (9B)

A few respondents thought the statement true but chiefly stressed the exploitation of Negro tenants by owners of slum properties rather than their efforts to promote exclusion. Several said that such owners benefit the real estate broker indirectly by helping to keep the area in which he operates white and thus helping to maintain normal business conditions for the white broker.

That's true because in the slum areas the owners had no scruples. They just gouge the poor Negro. (21B)

Sure, it's true. Do you want to know the reason why? Look at the *Chicago Defender*. The colored people have been trying for years to get out of the Black Belt. Now they've been succeeding, but there are so many poor ones coming up from the South and filling in those slum properties that they are still getting away with it. (56A)

Indirectly, yes, slum owners acting so were protecting the brokers. Directly I can't see any direct help. Property like that is not good to manage — more headaches than profit. (87CX)

The Real Estate Board, Part I

ACCORDING to the respondents and certain other data, the Chicago Real Estate Board exercises two kinds of influence over members and nonmembers — professional and ideological. The external, professional influence of the Board is that of the trade association. Through the services it provides to its members, the Board ties real estate men to itself and encourages conformity among them; however, in the city and country at large, the Board represents real estate interests on broad and general levels and is in this way separate and distinct from each individual real estate business. The internal, ideological aspect of the Board's control is deduced from evidence that, through NAREB and by itself, the Board acts to mold, in considerable part, the goals, values, and norms of real estate men. This appears to be partly deliberate action, and partly the latent result of Board action.

CONTROL AS TRADE ASSOCIATION

The Board informs its members of new developments in real estate, keeps them up to date in their specialties, and gives answers to trade problems ("Problems we can't solve, we can always ask the Board," said one respondent). It always carries on an educational program, with special meetings, courses, and seminars to help members and others.

The Board establishes rates of commission that are recognized by the courts and the whole field of commerce; it works to keep up the rates, since the commission is the real estate man's livelihood. It is concerned about interest rates. Delegations go to watch the assessing of property. Committees discuss zoning and watch cases on rezoning. The Board fights rent control and any other measure not beneficial to the real estate busi-

187

ness introduced in the state legislature. The Board is *the* agency which protects the interests of real estate men in the world at large.

The Board regulates real estate practice by setting standards of conduct for brokers' relations with other brokers and with the public in its Code of Ethics, by enforcing these standards, by investigating and judging complaints through its grievance committee, and, to a certain extent, by "policing immoral and improper practices in the business." In short, the Board is "the backbone of the real estate business." It has raised the status of the business and makes it more professional. Having established the Code, which members are inclined to abide by, the Board has been gaining for real estate a more favorable reputation with the public. People are learning that a Realtor* is a reputable broker. Hence, membership in the Board confers a certain prestige, dignity, and recognition. In his business stationery, window signs, and advertising a broker's membership is indicated. Many of the advantages of membership are intangible — for example, some respondents believe that people have more confidence in the broker who is a Board member.

Apart from giving the broker good standing with the public and thereby helping him in his business, membership provides business opportunities through the Board's multiple listing system in Chicago and by its bringing brokers together. Often cooperative deals result. A member of the Chicago Board is automatically a member of NAREB, which helps brokers in various parts of the country to collaborate on listings. The Board provides opportunities for fellowship and stimulation among brokers. "It's an educational process," said one respondent, "We share experience with other brokers." "You learn to know socially people with whom you will later on do business," said another. And a third said, "It's a place of interchange of information with birds of the same feather."

These are the reasons members of the Board want to be in good standing and why nonmembers do not wish to have the Board "down" on them either. The control of the Board as trade association over real estate men, and members particularly, comes partly from the brokers' willingness to conform with the Board's rulings, its Code of Ethics, and partly from the services the Board provides. It is in the brokers' interest to conform, not only because they wish to be unharmed but also because they wish to be thought well of by the Board and to benefit from its services.

The relation between the Chicago Real Estate Board and its members

* "Realtor" is the Board's term for a member. See pp. 199, 221.

and also nonmembers is partly one of interdependence. The Board directs members on matters that affect the business and require regulation, and members suggest, request, or otherwise influence the Board about changes in regulation or policy when local situations require them. Events and changes in the country at large, such as a growing stress on some new outlook, also affect the Board's policies. For example, the policy of the Chicago Real Estate Board has changed in dealings with Negroes. Respondent 66C, a former president of the Board, pointed out that formerly the Board wholly disapproved of members' selling to Negroes or even dealing with them at all. However, because of the continuing migration of Negroes into Chicago and the shifting racial occupancy in various areas of the city, real estate men were forced to accept Negro clients in order to stay in business. Federal legislation during World War II also forced them to realize that the old policy was no longer tenable. In 1945, NAREB assumed responsibility for supplying housing to Negroes (see p. 236), and accordingly, the Chicago Real Estate Board also espoused a new policy. Now high-ranking officials and members of the Board have Negro clients and tenants as well as white.

The Board, as represented by its leading officials at any one time, wants the members to be satisfied with its services so that they will remain members and wants to hold their interest for the sake of the real estate business as a whole. It does not let them forget what the Board means, bringing to their attention from time to time the value of its services. To merit the members' support, the Board has to consider and to provide for their needs and to make headway in promoting the business as a whole. It cannot function without the moral and financial support of its members — it depends upon them to put the Code of Ethics into practice in their daily operations. The Board is only as strong as the belief of its members in it and in its ideology. The members need the Board to fight their battles in the world at large, to help them in their problems and to keep them informed. There is thus a reciprocal dependence, obligation, and, hence, influence between Board and members arising from the needs of each.

There is a mutual dependence also between the Board and brokers who are not members. The nonmember respondents who hold in major part the real estate and racial real estate ideology of NAREB and the Board (pp. 191–217), as most of them do (p. 219), see themselves as part of the community of real estate men, whereas those nonmembers who do not hold this ideology see themselves as more or less outside of it. Very few nonmembers violate the Code of Ethics. All beginners in the real estate business, an established economic institution, are subject to the same license law, license examination, institutional equipment, and influence of the business; they have to operate according to its standards, accepted meanings, offices, specializations, transactional forms, and regulations. Its outlook tends to become theirs and its prescriptions to exercise a con- straint* over them. They are real estate men in thought and action before they become members of the Board. Nonmembers as well as members benefit from Board services and achievements and have a certain obliga- tion to it even if they do not belong. Some nonmember respondents aspire to become members of the Board and wish to keep in good standing with it. Nonmembers and members alike expressed fear of ostracism by fellow brokers if they sold to Negroes without restriction. Nonmembers are not independent of Board members in their business dealings, since the big- gest firms are members. A few nonmember respondents mentioned this as one reason for not selling unrestrictedly, although one quickly pointed out that the very firms that would ostracize him are themselves guilty of clan- destine selling to Negroes. However, for business reasons, he still wanted to be in good standing with these firms.

The Board, on the other hand, depends on the good behavior of non- members as well as of members for the progress of the real estate business. The Board depends largely on practicing nonmember brokers for growth in membership. A violation of the Code of Ethics by any broker affects the general standing of real estate men in the community, and in its attempts to influence nonmember brokers who are selling unrestrictedly to Negroes, the Board reveals a certain responsibility for their behavior.

IDEOLOGICAL INFLUENCE

The real estate institution becomes articulate as a unified whole through the National Association of Real Estate Boards. NAREB represents the consensus of the views of most real estate boards in the United States. In each city, the local board provides a unified outlook and standard for the real estate business, and NAREB is the unifying agent of the trade associa- tions of real estate. Since NAREB represents the real estate business and real estate men throughout the country, and since the member boards con-

---

* The term *constraint* is used here in the sense in which Durkheim used it in his later works — that is, as the moral obligation to obey a rule or the voluntary adher- ence to it as a duty (*L'Education Morale*, 1925).

tribute to and accept its views, the ideology of NAREB disclosed in this investigation will be considered to be the ideology of the real estate institution. Since the Chicago Real Estate Board took an important part in the founding of NAREB, accepts its Code of Ethics, and is, to all appearances, at one with it, the ideology of NAREB will be looked upon as being also the ideology of the Chicago Real Estate Board.

Real Estate Ideology

The ideology of the real estate institution was sought in documents of NAREB, in textbooks on real estate recommended by NAREB or written by its leading members, and in 9 interviews with high-ranking officials of the Chicago Real Estate Board. The data obtained in the 9 interviews and a reading of certain parts of the *Call Board Bulletin* of the Chicago Real Estate Board revealed values, goals, and principles largely similar to those expressed in statements of NAREB. Probably the most complete and concise expression of the main ideas and outlook of real estate men as a group is contained in the Preamble to the Code of Ethics and in the statements of policy issued at national conventions of NAREB. These statements of policy not only sum up the basic principles and goals of organized real estate but also define the basic values in American life and judge vital questions of the day relevant to these values. Although the values, goals, and principles expressed in these statements and in the Preamble to the Code may not be those of nonmembers or even of all members, they do represent the consensus of many established, active real estate men throughout the country.

The Preamble to the Code of Ethics of NAREB adopted in 1924 is as follows: [1]

Under all is the land. Upon its wise utilization and widely allocated ownership depend the survival and growth of free institutions and of our civilization. The Realtor is the instrumentality through which the land resource of the nation reaches its highest use and through which land ownership attains its widest distribution. He is a creator of homes, a builder of cities, a developer of industries and productive farms.

Such functions impose obligations beyond those of ordinary commerce; they impose grave social responsibility and a patriotic duty to which the Realtor should dedicate himself, and for which he should be diligent in preparing himself. The Realtor, therefore, is zealous to maintain and to improve the standards of his calling and shares with his fellow-Realtors a common responsibility for its integrity and honor.

191

In the interpretation of his obligations, he can take no safer guide than that which has been handed down through twenty centuries, embodied in the Golden Rule:

"Whatsoever ye would that men should do unto you, do ye also unto them."

Accepting this standard as his own, every Realtor pledges himself to observe its spirit in all his dealings and to conduct his business in accordance with the following Code of Ethics adopted by the National Association of Real Estate Boards.

The Preamble sets forth the role of the real estate man as one of great responsibility and of great importance for the well-being of the country. The real estate man has obligations surpassing those of other businessmen, but by being loyal to his calling in defined ways, he can fulfill the patriotic duty inherent in his work. To do this, he need only obey the golden rule and the Code of Ethics of NAREB. It is implied in the Preamble that the Code of Ethics is like the golden rule, or, in other words, that the ethics of the real estate business are not essentially different from the teachings of the Bible about proper human conduct.

VALUES OF THE AMERICAN WAY OF LIFE

It is necessary for the understanding of the real estate ideology to consider what is meant by "the free institutions that go to make the American way of life" in the wording of the Preamble to the Code as amended in 1955. These are revealed in the preambles to statements of policy, in books on real estate, and in the interviews with officials of the Chicago Real Estate Board. Five values were stressed particularly; the first two are essential and the last three depend on them: (1) the right to own property, (2) free enterprise and individual initiative, (3) the extension of property ownership, (4) the family, and (5) home ownership. These form a related group and may be seen as one aspect of the real estate ideology.

The right of the citizen to own property is most emphasized in the values singled out by NAREB as essential to the American way of life. Its importance and that of free enterprise and individual initiative are expressed in the Preamble of the 1945 Statement of Policy of NAREB: [2]

Preamble. As an organization speaking for the institution of property ownership, for home owners and those who properly aspire to the ownership of a piece of their country, again do we pledge our wholehearted and continuing support to our nation and its government. . . .

The mighty achievements of our fighting men give assurance that the American way of life, which we have gone to war to preserve, will not be blacked out in the world of the future.

We call for those things that distinguish free peoples. We ask that those verities which are the basis of American life be held sacred. These are the things we hold to be the foundation of the American way, and we call upon our people to preserve at all cost:

1. The right to home ownership and the enjoyment of property.

. . . . .

5. The creation on the part of government of an attitude of helpfulness to individual initiative, and a healthy relationship between federal and local government.

6. The encouragement of the American spirit of initiative, self-reliance, independence, and the virtues of individual effort, together with the responsibilities of charity, tolerance, and non-interference with our neighbors.

7. Respect for custom and tradition.

The Preamble to the 1952 Statement of Policy of the Resolutions Committee of the forty-fifth annual convention of NAREB endorses "the personal freedom and the individual enterprise that have made this nation great and powerful" and goes on to state: "We believe that the right to own property, as guaranteed by our Constitution, remains a basic human right and must today be defended and preserved because upon it depend the other human rights which we cherish. Where property rights perish, men themselves soon become the property of the state." [3] The preambles to the 1955 and the 1956 statements of policy strongly support the same rights. [4]

The Real Estate Handbook, in its dedication to the writers of the Preamble to the Code of Ethics, singles out the right to own real estate as the important belief expressed by the Preamble and as an essential part of democratic thinking. [5] The American Institute of Real Estate Appraisers, one of the institutes of NAREB, has gone on record to say: "Our system of free enterprise has meaning only because citizens have the right to own property and to utilize it as capital for personal profit. Real estate under private ownership can truly be said to constitute the keystone of capitalistic economics." [6]

The preambles to the Code of Ethics and to the statements of policy are, it would seem, the only sources of a representative statement of what

193

the organized real estate men prize most in the society. In all these documents there is the same emphasis on individual enterprise as the mainspring of the American way of life and on the right to own property as the most basic human right.

The third main value, the extension of land and property ownership, is upheld in the preambles to the Code of Ethics of 1950 and of 1955 as one of the two bulwarks upon which depend "the survival and growth of free institutions and of our civilization." The Preamble to the 1952 Statement of Policy makes it clear that widely allocated ownership of land is regarded by the organized real estate men as the best protection against political doctrines which might undermine the American way of life. In this Preamble and in that to the 1955 Statement of Policy, the importance of widespread ownership of property receives further emphasis in the stress on home ownership.[7] Also in 1955, the Build America Better Council of NAREB adopted ten principles of neighborhood conservation. Principle 7 reads: *"Widely allocated ownership is an element of health in our land economy. We should not use our attack on the evil of slums to encourage the evil of vast concentrated land ownership. . . ."* [8]

The importance of the family in the life of the country receives indirect stress in the same preambles to the Code of Ethics when the Realtor is called a "creator of homes" and also in the emphasis on home ownership in the statements of policy. In the interviews with leading officials of the Chicago Real Estate Board, the central position of the family in this society was implied when the officials pointed out how much the real estate man contributes to its welfare by providing it with a proper home in which to have its life throughout the years.

Home ownership is a central and constant theme in real estate thought and is a corollary to the right to own property. The Preamble to the 1956 Statement of Policy speaks of home ownership and security as "synonymous with our American way of life." "Widespread home ownership," it states, "brings to this great nation a stability and strength that no other country enjoys." One official of NAREB stated in an interview on September 5, 1956, "We want to encourage ownership. A homeowner is a father, a husband. He has stability. He makes a good citizen." In 1948, NAREB urged its member Boards "to undertake an aggressive campaign" to promote home ownership in the country at large on the strength of its value to national well-being and to impress on each Realtor that "when he assists an American family to become a home owner he has made an effective contribution toward the preservation of the American way of life." [9]

The advantages of home ownership and its benefits for the neighborhood and for citizenship are expressed by the chief writers on real estate in their books. Benson and North call a home a "way of life" and list twelve reasons why a man should own a home.[10] In a number of textbooks on real estate, a rather sharp distinction is made between a neighborhood occupied by homeowners and one occupied by renters. Hoagland says, "There is no question about the relative stability of an owner-occupied neighborhood." [11] May, in the examples he provides for student practice in appraisal, gives the impression that true Americans own their homes. In the best neighborhoods, he says, where there is law and order and where American values are upheld, home ownership will be found to predominate.[12]

Interviewed officials of the Chicago Real Estate Board emphasized the importance of the family, home ownership, and the extension of ownership of property in connection with the goals and functions of the real estate man. The idea stands out in the thinking of real estate leaders that people who own their homes are better citizens and are more stable than those who do not.

We're in the business of building and selling homes. The main thing is you're doing some good for humanity — you're helping them buy a home, establish residence, so that they can raise a family. I think home ownership is one of the most important things in America. I think the new generation is more conscious of this. (Interview F)

The real estate man who stays in the business develops a personal philosophy about his business. He gets satisfactions other than financial rewards. If he sells homes, he puts families into homes, and it is our feeling that families in their own homes make much better citizens than families that do not own their own homes. (Interview K)

The resistance offered to the programs of public housing by organized real estate is consistent with its chosen values basic to the American way of life. An official of NAREB said on September 5, 1956, "We're against public housing. We don't believe in a perpetual subsidy. People need help at times, during a depression, but not a perpetual subsidy. . . ."

ROLE OF THE REAL ESTATE MAN

The second aspect of the real estate ideology is the real estate man's role and duty in the realization of these values of American life. To protect these values and to bring them to fruition, the Realtor is told to follow the golden rule — that is, conduct his business in accordance with the Code of Ethics of NAREB. In the Code, the functions of the Realtor are translated into a set of precise, practical injunctions, spelled out in three parts: Part I deals with the Realtor's relations to the public at large; Part II his relations to the client; and Part III his relations to his fellow-Realtor. Part I is divided into three topics: First, his competence: the Realtor is to keep himself well informed on all matters pertaining to real estate on national, state, and local levels so as to be able to advise his clients and to guide public opinion by his sound conclusions. Second, the Realtor is to protect the public against any kind of fraud, misrepresentation, or unethical practice in real estate. Third, the Realtor is to protect property values — of particular importance because of the widespread repercussions from an act of injury to property value. Property values should be protected and held constant so that owners will not lose their equity and so that other properties in the neighborhood may not also go down in value. The Realtor is to protect the value of property as far as he is able. This is a cardinal point in the real estate outlook. This is a crucial way in which the Realtor is called upon to carry out his duty toward the public and his calling.

The emphasis on property value pervades the business of real estate. Hoagland has said, "Almost every interest in real estate is directly or indirectly related to its value." [13] Benson and North, writing of the importance of property value and of property valuation, speak of the latter as "the heart of all real estate activity." They go on, "Whether buying, selling, investing, developing, lending, exchanging, renting, assessing, or acquiring property for public use, a working knowledge of sound valuation is essential in order to put land and its improvements to the highest, best, and hence most profitable use." [14] To another authority on real estate, value of real property is "the subject matter of real estate." [15] In the interviews with leading officials of the Chicago Board, the idea was strongly expressed that it is the real estate man's task and duty to build up and create value, not to tear it down.

A whole field of specialization has grown up in the business of real estate for the proper determination of the value of property, formally represented by the American Institute of Real Estate Appraisers. Their official statement on property appraisal is contained in *The Appraisal of Real Estate*; the following quotation from it explains how, in the view of real estate men, value is created and modified: "The value of real estate is created, maintained, modified, and destroyed by the interplay of the three great forces that motivate and characterize the activities of mankind. These forces are (1) social ideals and standards, (2) economic adjustments, and (3) political or government regulations. . . . The three of them interweave, becoming one vast and ever-changing medium that surrounds and pervades every parcel of real estate on the face of the globe."[10]

The appraisers also explain how the value of a property is affected by the forces at work in the neighborhood in which it stands,[17] and to understand this explanation, one must consider their view of how neighborhoods arise and what a neighborhood is. The appraisers make it clear that residents' homogeneity of interests, traditions, social and financial standing, and even religion or race is a *natural* characteristic of residential neighborhoods. A neighborhood, they say, "includes a more or less unified area with somewhat definite boundaries and a fairly homogeneous population in which the inhabitants have a more than casual community of interests. In such an area the character of one property affects the character of all others as though they were all cogs in a machine."[18] They also find that residential neighborhoods usually grow in desirability for a while after they are established, provided they command public favor and are built up rapidly. The neighborhoods attain a peak of desirability, remain stable for a time, and then deteriorate in quality. Appraisers point out that change rather than stability characterizes cities and that the study of the value of real estate therefore involves the study of those factors that shape and influence value.

In their analysis of these factors in a residential neighborhood, appraisers state that the value levels will be influenced more by the social characteristics of the residents or prospective residents than by any other factor. Their first emphasis falls upon homogeneity. They say:

No matter how attractive a particular neigborhood may be from every other angle, it will not possess maximum desirability unless it is occupied by people who will be happy in one another's company and unless it provides the right setting for the rearing of children. Above all else, home purchasers want the best advantages they can afford for their children and this includes desirable neighbors and their children. Thus a wide tolerance or mutuality is involved in matters of race, religion, income, cultural standards, and ways of living.[19]

Since, according to the experience and observation of real estate men, residential neighborhoods tend to be homogeneous by their very nature in that they come into being through the common desires, motives, interests, and standards of people, it is to be expected that a homogeneous neighborhood will have stable desirability because it is satisfying the common desires of the people in it. Hence, to protect the homogeneity of a neighborhood — that is, to try to keep in it people who have the same standards and who are compatible neighbors — is to maintain its desirability and hence the stability of its property values. Homogeneity, the natural characteristic of neighborhoods and of residential neighborhoods in particular, comes to be looked upon as an essential characteristic of a good residential neighborhood, something to be valued and protected in a constantly changing situation because it is a guarantee of stability of property values. Home ownership is also considered a guarantee of stable property values, but there is an even greater stress on the importance of compatibility, of common interests.[20] In discussing why people want to live in neighborhoods, Atkinson makes this point: "A neighborhood, first of all, is based on mutual interests and mutual attitudes." And again, "This desire of human beings to mingle with those with whom they have something in common is fundamental to a neighborhood." [21]

One aspect of real estate men's concern with the preservation of property values is their emphasis on conservation. In objecting to public housing and the demolition of entire areas, an official of NAREB said on September 5, 1956, "We're against tearing down, clearing areas. Conserve good properties that only need rehabilitation. There's value there. Not good to waste it." The whole movement of the Build America Better Council of NAREB is based on conserving what can be conserved and rehabilitating wherever possible. NAREB proposes conservation as the basic method of overcoming neighborhood deterioration and as an alternative to public housing.

You see, I maintain that this whole situation of deterioration and blight is caused by the lack of interest of the property owner, and without the interest of the property owner to maintain his property that this blight will continue and ultimately destroy our cities, and this whole problem is a human relation and a social job of property education. I mean this continual idea that the government should place people in housing as a social obligation of the government is only destroying the fundamental right of property ownership. (Interview M; official of Chicago Board and leader in conservation movement)

The Realtor's duty in the preservation of property values may be summarized as follows: The real estate man must protect the whole neighborhood, because the value of a property depends on the condition of the neighborhood in which it is located. The stability of the neighborhood is the best guarantee of keeping its property values stable. Since cities and areas are continually changing, whatever protects stability is to be welcomed and whatever threatens it is to be eschewed. The chief contributor to stability of a neighborhood is the homogeneity of its residents, and the Realtor protects it by trying to bring into it people of the same cultural interests and social standards as those of its residents, and keeping out people who will not "fit into" it. Hence, the Realtor not only makes homes available to people and protects them from fraud and misrepresentation, but also protects residents' equity by protecting property values in their neighborhood. This cornerstone of a Realtor's duty to the public is expressed in Article 5 of Part I of the Code of Ethics (quoted on p. 201).

THE REAL ESTATE BUSINESS: A SERVICE AND A LIVELIHOOD

Although NAREB recognizes the real estate man's important function in society and his great moral obligations, it does not mention his primary need — making a living — in the various preambles to the Code of Ethics or in any statement of policy. However, this need is discussed in a number of textbooks and was brought forward by the interviewed officials of the Chicago Real Estate Board.

Local real estate boards and the Chicago Real Estate Board in particular have tried to establish for the real estate broker a dignity of status and a position of trust with the public which irresponsible and unscrupulous real estate men before the board was formed and again during depression years had taken from him. This they tried to do by raising the qualifications for admission to the business and by developing a program of education in schools and for practicing brokers. To further strengthen the real estate man's position, the term "Realtor" was adopted by NAREB to designate members, defined in the Code of Ethics: "The term Realtor has come to connote competence, fair dealing and high integrity resulting from adherence to a lofty ideal of moral conduct in business relations. No inducement of profit and no instructions from clients ever can justify departure from this ideal, or from the injunctions of this Code." [22] By making the real estate man more competent for his task and by stressing his moral obligations to society, NAREB has been trying to raise the status of the real estate business to that of a profession — an attempt explained:

When real estate men state that they are professionalizing their business, they do not mean that they are seeking to give it any fictitious dignity. They only mean that they are setting up those inhibitions upon the business conduct of those engaged in the vocation which experience has proven wise — that they are attempting to establish higher qualifications for those who desire to enter the business — that they are assembling an organized body of knowledge for the benefit of those who are now engaged in the real estate business and who will hereafter come into it — that they are conscious of a definite responsibility to society as a whole in the performance of their economic functions.[23]

Realtors look upon their business as a professional service given by competent, trustworthy experts in the field. In one of the nine interviews a former vice-president of the Chicago Real Estate Board enlarged upon the idea of service:

Our business is to house humanity properly and to give them a decent and pleasant place to live. . . . I think proper housing tends to . . . maintain family life. We have many curbstone brokers. They are licensed, but the licensing law is not rigid enough. It should admit only those qualified by proper training and experience . . . The real estate brokers are dealing . . . in a commodity which involves the welfare of the people and of the country. Their first duty is to try and secure what they want, rather than sell what they have on their listings. They should analyze the prospective real estate buyers' wants and then offer them the proper housing units that will fit their financial as well as physical needs. We are primarily in a service business — a service to properly house mankind. This view is held by the men in the business who are trying to make a profession out of it. Unfortunately, because of the ease with which they can get a license, there are those who put a fast buck ahead of service. They should not do it. (Interview L)

Most of the nine officials interviewed agreed that service cannot be separated from self-interest in the mind of the real estate man because the two are inextricably tied. Treating clients well and having an interest in the community pays dividends.

A real estate man who has no idea of civic betterment shouldn't be in the real estate business. An agent who merely takes the rent isn't doing anything. I tell the owners not to let their property run down. If new refrigerators come along, put them in. Keep the property painted outside. By keeping the property up, you protect your own investment. You keep up the neighborhood. Civic improvement means community preservation. I know from experience. You must do it. It may be self-interest, but it still helps the community, the neighborhood, and yourself. (Interview N)

Writers on real estate have stated that the most successful real estate man gives the best service. Stanley McMichael writes: "A great organization of businessmen . . . has taken as its motto, 'He profits most who serves best.' " [24]

Racial Real Estate Ideology

A prominent idea of the racial real estate ideology of the institution is that property values decline when Negroes enter and take up residence in a white area. The most important source of this idea is Article 5 of Part I of the Code of Ethics, "A Realtor should not be instrumental in introducing into a neighborhood a character of property or use which will clearly be detrimental to property values in that neighborhood." In order to appreciate the full meaning of Article 5, it is necessary to take into account that it was amended to its present wording in 1950. From 1924 to 1950, as Article 34 of Part III, "Relations to Customers and the Public," it read: "A Realtor should never be instrumental in introducing into a neighborhood a character of property or occupancy, members of any race or nationality, or any individuals whose presence will clearly be detrimental to property values in that neighborhood." In five interviews with officials of the Board and respondents, it was conceded that the meaning of Article 5 remains the same and that "a character of property or use" covers the introduction of Negroes.

The second source of this idea is the official text of the American Institute of Real Estate Appraisers. In it, the first of the factors examined "that contribute to the destruction of value" in residential neighborhoods is "The clash of nationalities with dissimilar cultures. When a new class of people of different race, color, nationality, and culture moves into a neighborhood, there is a tendency on the part of the old inhabitants to think that the neighborhood is losing desirability; and thereafter they tend to move into other districts." [25] This statement does not mention Negroes, but, since they form the largest nonwhite racial group in the United States, there is no doubt that it would apply to them. As mentioned above (pp. 196–197), the appraisers maintain that the desirability of a residential neighborhood rests primarily on its homogeneity—that is, on the residents' compatibility. When families different from the residents move in, that compatibility is lost; the neighborhood loses its desirability not only for the residents but also for all prospective buyers of the same characteristics and standards.

Racial Policies and Practices of Brokers

IN TEXTBOOKS

Like the appraisers, writers on real estate emphasize homogeneity, but they add the corollary that values in a residential area decline as a result of the introduction of Negroes. The general ideas about homogeneity developed by the appraisers are applied by the writers specifically to the Negro. Negroes are considered a different group by white people, and when they enter a residential neighborhood, the residents no longer find it desirable. As the desirability declines, the property values decline. When the residents begin to move away, people of lower income and lower social standards usually move in, and the neighborhood declines further.

A number of writers whose books are recommended by NAREB will now be considered for their ideas on how property values are affected when Negroes enter an area. The first writer of note is Frederick M. Babcock, who is credited with providing the mortgage risk rating grid for neighborhood analysis in the *Underwriting Manual* of the Federal Housing Administration. He was one of the earliest writers on real estate in the United States. In his text, *The Valuation of Real Estate* (1932), in Chapter VII, "Influence of Social and Racial Factors on Value," he proposes the idea that the development of land value depends partly on the racial heritage of the people living on it and implies that where Negroes are living land values will decline. He says, "Among the traits and characteristics of people which influence land values, racial heritage and tendencies seem to be of paramount importance. The aspirations, energies, and abilities of various groups in the composition of the population will largely determine the extent to which they develop the potential value of land." Further on he writes, "Most of the variations and differences between people are slight and value declines are, as a result, gradual. But there is one difference in people, namely, race, which can result in a very rapid decline. Usually such declines can be partially avoided by segregation and this device has always been in common usage in the South where white and negro populations have been separated." [26]

It is not surprising, then, to find in the early revisions of the *Underwriting Manual* an emphasis on race as an adverse influence on property value. In the 1936 revision, deed restrictions and natural or artificially established barriers are suggested as protection from adverse influences, including "inharmonious racial groups." [27] Homogeneity of dwellings and of residents is stressed, and one cause given for a lower rating is "the presence of incompatible racial elements." [28] In the 1947 and 1955 revi-

202

sions of the *Underwriting Manual,* there is no longer outright mention of race, but the emphasis on residents' homogeneity and compatibility remains, and "if the occupancy of the neighborhood is changing from one user group to another, or if the areas adjacent to the immediate neighborhood are occupied by a user group dissimilar to the typical occupants of the subject neighborhood or a change in occupancy is imminent or probable," any degree of risk is reflected in the rating, although additional risk may not be involved in such change.[29] Since members of NAREB and of the American Institute of Real Estate Appraisers have had a hand in the writing of the *Underwriting Manual,* their ideas are reflected here too.

Most of the writers to be considered now are those whose textbooks have been used in colleges and universities (listed in Ch. VIII, n. 85).

In *Real Estate Principles and Practices* (1954), Benson, North, and Ring define a neighborhood as "a single area in which the housing and population characteristics are qualitatively homogeneous" and recommend an analysis of it as essential in a study of residential property values.[30] They look upon large size of neighborhood as having the advantage of better protection from "infiltration of inharmonious influences . . ." As in the later revisions of the *Underwriting Manual,* there seems to be an underlying meaning in this phrase, and, although Negroes are not mentioned, the expression can be seen as a way of referring to Negroes or other racial or ethnic groups without mentioning them. In advising the prospective buyer as to where to buy a home, the authors warn him to be wary of changes in the environment, such as "dangers to welfare, health, or morality; influx or encroachment of undesirable groups" because such changes are "bound to be reflected in the desirability and value of a property."[31]

In *Principles of Real Estate Management* (1950), Downs, writing of neighborhood analysis for the appraisal of rental value, defines a neighborhood as "an area within which there are common characteristics of population and land use."[32] He also calls homogeneity the essential characteristic of a neighborhood, although the corollary about Negroes is absent.

Hoyt's study, *One Hundred Years of Land Values in Chicago* (1933), carries a section on "Expansion of racial and nationality groups," in which he points out that land values in areas occupied by certain racial and national groups are inevitably low because of the lower rents that these groups pay, their greater deteriorating effect on property, and white people's unwillingness to live near them.[33] There follows a "ranking of races and nationalities with respect to their beneficial effect upon land values," which, Hoyt says, "may be scientifically wrong from the standpoint of inherent racial characteristics," but which "registers an opinion or prejudice that is reflected in land values." It runs as follows: (1) English, Germans, Scotch, Irish, Scandinavians; (2) North Italians; (3) Bohemians or Czechoslovakian; (4) Poles; (5) Lithuanians; (6) Greeks; (7) Russian Jews of the lower class; (8) South Italians; (9) Negroes; and (10) Mexicans.[34] Hoyt explains in a footnote that the list was prepared chiefly by a real estate broker on the West Side of Chicago. But, though he was sufficiently impressed by the validity of this ranking to present it, Hoyt does not explain how the ranking was prepared.[35] However, he goes on to say, "In many cases . . . the undesirable racial factor is so merged with other unattractive features, such as proximity to factories, poor transportation, old and obsolete buildings, poor street improvements, and the presence of criminal or vice elements, that the separate effect of race cannot be disentangled." [36] Hoyt states that white people move out when Negroes and other incompatible groups enter their areas. Hoyt's conclusions about the effect of racial and national groups on land values and the ranking of races and nationalities with respect to such effect are used by Stanley McMichael to support his views in the third and fourth editions of his *Appraising Manual* (1944 and 1951).[37]

Influenced to some extent by earlier studies by Hurd and others, who noted the starlike projections of the city, in 1939 Hoyt developed the view that the pattern of residential land uses occurred largely in the form of sectors along the lines of transportation and that high-rent districts shaped the trend by pulling the growth of the entire city in their direction.[38] In 1950 Lloyd Rodwin attacked Hoyt's sector theory as tending to encourage the exclusion of certain groups, particularly Negroes, because of their "inharmonious" characteristics. Rodwin charges that Hoyt does this through his analysis of the substandard conditions characteristic of Negro neighborhoods, his comments about Negroes' effect on rents in twilight zones, his assumption of upper class attractions, and the "investment perspective perpetually chary of 'racial mixtures' " that Hoyt brings into the picture.[39]

Weimer and Hoyt's *Principles of Real Estate* first came out in 1939 as *Principles of Urban Real Estate*, with a second edition in 1948, a third in 1954, and a fourth in 1960. In 1951, according to a NAREB report, it was being used in seventeen universities and colleges.[40] In the 1939 edition, the authors, discussing new and old residential neighborhoods, speak of restrictions against the sale and occupancy of property by "persons other than of the Caucasian race" and call the clause on race in restrictive agreements a "very common" one.[41] The section in which these statements appear, "Other Forms of Private Regulation," is repeated in the next two editions with a few changes in wording.[42] In the 1948 edition under "Types of Deed Restrictions," the reference to limitation of occupancy to Caucasians only of the 1939 edition has been changed to "a restriction may prohibit certain groups of persons"; however, a footnote refers to limitation of occupancy to Caucasians, and a second footnote suggests that the Supreme Court decision about the legal unenforceability of the racial restrictive covenant can be circumvented by the device of private clubs.[43] The authors thus implicitly support racial residential segregation and the exclusion of Negroes from white areas. In the third edition of 1954, they state, "In more recent years, 'property owners' associations' or 'homes associations' have been established to enforce restrictions, administer maintenance funds if any are set up . . . and promote community activities."[44]

In their analysis of neighborhoods from the investment standpoint with reference to "the trend of real estate incomes and values," the authors point out that the concept of what is "inharmonious" may vary widely, for — and here they quote the FHA *Underwriting Manual* (rev. ed., 1952; Sec. 1309 (2)) — "Some communities reveal user group attitudes quite different from the attitudes displayed by user groups on approximately similar levels in other cities. . . . Group attitudes are therefore important in determining the location rating criteria to be applied in a given city." [45] They go on to say that, when making analyses of this kind, it is important that "current attitudes of property users and investors be reflected," because some groups are unwilling to live side by side and this "may have an important bearing on the future of the neighborhood being analysed." [46] When the authors discuss causes of change in neighborhoods, their meaning becomes clearer. They state that "the migration of families with certain readily distinguishable national, racial, or religious characteristics frequently stimulates the outmigration of previous residents in the area." [47] The authors proceed to discuss neighborhood stability: "Suburbs at a sufficient distance from the transition of uses or of inharmonious groups maintain a high character for very long periods of time, if not indefinitely. . . ." [48] In their discussion of rate of decline in a neighborhood, they consider the presence of different racial, national, or economic groups in an adjoining area to be a threat to property values in a neighborhood.[49] As far as the neighborhood itself is concerned, they maintain that there is greater stability if there is a high percentage of owner occupancy and if there is no danger of the entry of people of different race or national background.[50] However, they recognize that this statement must be modified in the light of local attitudes.

Since their book is a school text, there are questions at the end of each chapter for students to answer. At the end of Chapter VII of the second edition (1948), Question 5 asks "In which of the following neighborhoods would you prefer to invest?" and describes various differences between the two neighborhoods. For example, for Neighborhood A, "The area is zoned for single-family residences. No deed restrictions are in force." For Neighborhood B, "Deed restrictions have been established controlling the types of houses which may be built and restricting occupancy to members of the Caucasian race." [51] Restrictions on the type of house to be built makes Neighborhood B a better neighborhood, and by coupling these with racial restrictions, the authors also suggest that exclusion of nonwhite groups is a good thing for the neighborhood. Similar suggestions of non-Caucasian exclusion appear in other questions.[52]

Throughout the earlier work of Hoyt himself and in the first three editions of Weimer and Hoyt's book, there is a trend of thought that suggests loss of land value when Negroes approach or enter a residential neighborhood, decline of the residential neighborhood upon Negro entry, and the satisfactoriness of racial residential segregation.

Arthur A. May, a former dean of the American Institute of Real Estate Appraisers, in his *Valuation of Residential Real Estate* (1942), in the section on the ethnological pattern of the city, calls attention to the prevalence of racial or nationalistic neighborhoods and to the effect on real estate values of movement of these groups.[53] He points out that the foreign-born and Negroes usually occupy the older structures, and, because the supply of these units is usually insufficient, there are overflow movements into the nearby better-class districts. He refers to these groups as "inharmonious influences" for a better-class district, which declines because of their proximity. He considers "the social characteristics of city dwellers of foreign extraction and Negroes" to be "in the main, homogeneous"; they "prefer to live by themselves among their own kind." He states that residential real estate values in older districts are threatened when these districts adjoin those occupied by minority peoples. Finally, he suggests that a map be kept in the appraisal laboratory to show the location of these groups and to trace the direction of their movement.

He points out that lenders of mortgage funds look with some suspicion upon an older neighborhood that has passed the peak of desirability because the age of the structures makes long-term lending hazardous. Then he adds, "Furthermore, the impending infringement of retail, industrial, or commercial uses, or the infiltration of minority racial or nationalistic groups, accelerates the obsolescence of neighborhoods and decreases the volume of home ownership appeal." [54]

May explains that the essential criterion of the neighborhood is the residents' homogeneity in income level, race and ethnic background, and, to some extent, religion. [55] He states unequivocally that homogeneity of the neighborhood and stability of property values go hand in hand and that the mere threat of Negro entry had caused a drop of 25 per cent in an all-white neighborhood in some cities. [56]

In discussing depreciation, he defines economic obsolescence as loss in value arising from decrease in owner-occupancy appeal and consequent lack of demand. He attributes this lack to six factors, the fourth being "proximity to nuisances." It is followed immediately by "infiltration of minority racial or nationalistic groups." [57] He then develops more fully the idea that property values decline as a result of such infiltration when he says, "The encroachment of the antipathetic racial or nationalistic group brings with it, first, the threat and, ultimately, the effect of decreased values." [58]

In Chapter XVI, "Appraising the New Home," May presents four case studies for the student's practice in appraisal. In each case, the problem is to determine the market value of the property. In each case, a description of the property is followed by a solution of the problem. In Case Property I, the neighborhood is limited to occupancy by the Caucasian race (this is true of two later case studies also). [59] In Case Property II, residents are predominantly "American whites whose forebears were born here." [60]

Two texts of Hoagland are important for the recognition they receive among writers on real estate and for their use in schools. In *Real Estate Finance* (1954), in a chapter on savings and loan associations, he calls attention to the serious consideration given the neighborhood in which a property is located before an application for a loan is approved for this property, and to the careful and systematic studies to discover adverse neighborhood influences. He also states that many savings and loan operators use the FHA rating sheet for neighborhoods.[61] He does not specify to what revision of the *Underwriting Manual* he is referring, but it must precede that of 1947, in which "Protection from Adverse Influences" no longer appears among the "Rating of Location" features. The 1938 revision of the *Manual* contains the eight items to which he refers. Under the heading "Protection from Adverse Influences," Section 937 contains the following:

Quality of Neighboring Development. . . . Areas surrounding a location are investigated to determine whether incompatible racial and social groups are present, for the purpose of making a prediction regarding the probability of the location being invaded by such groups. If a neighborhood is to retain stability, it is necessary that properties shall continue to be occupied by the same social and racial classes. A change in social or racial occupancy generally contributes to instability and a decline in values.[62]

In a discussion on residential districts in his text, *Real Estate Principles*, he says: "When two or more incompatible groups of people occupy any given neighborhood, the tendency is for the group having least regard for the maintenance of real estate standards to drive out the other groups — a sort of real estate Gresham's law." [63] The new group blights the neighborhood, and property values then decline. As an example, he cites "a well-recognized fact" that some racial groups do not live harmoniously together — "One moves out as the other moves in." [64] After suggesting what the community can do to prevent or to retard blight and decline, he calls attention to the importance of home ownership and of homogeneity, racial and other, for stability in a neighborhood.

Stanley L. McMichael is prominent enough in real estate to merit an editor's note in *The Real Estate Handbook*, where he is credited with contributing "most of the text on appraising" and with holding one of the first memberships in the American Institute of Real Estate Appraisers.[65] In his and Bingham's *City Growth Essentials* (1928), in a chapter on "Racial and National Settlements and Groupings," McMichael expresses the view that "there is a natural inclination on the part of colored people to live in their own communities," but, with the increase in their numbers due to migration northward, they have swept into adjoining districts. This, says the author, has had a decidedly detrimental effect on land values, for "few white people, however inclined to be sympathetic with the problem of the colored race, care to live near them." He emphasizes his point by saying, "Property values have been greatly depreciated by having a single colored family settle on a street formerly occupied exclusively by white residents." He recommends rigid segregation as the only effective control.[66]

At the end of Chapter XXVI, three review questions are: "What effect do settlements of foreigners and negroes have on land values?" "Outline some of the problems presented in connection with the assimilation of colored people." "How did St. Louis attempt to segregate colored residents?" Questions of similar direction follow;[67] apparently McMichael meant these points to be learned. This book was endorsed on page 2 by Arthur J. Metzke, Director of the Department of Education and Research of NAREB, for its "many helpful and practical suggestions." A forerunner of this book, McMichael and Bingham's *City Growth and Values* (1923), contains almost the same passages on the Negro population in the chapter "Foreign and Racial Settlements," and these passages are followed by a paragraph on "tenderloin districts" as in the later book. The earlier book also carries an "Endorsement," signed by Herbert U. Nelson, Executive Secretary, NAREB, dated "Chicago, Ill., Oct. 15, 1923."[68]

The first edition of McMichael's *Appraising Manual*, called the bible of the appraising profession, was published in 1931, the fourth in 1951. In the first edition of the *Manual*, there are two references to race: "social or racial changes" are listed among signs of "invasion by incompatible uses" under the causes of "Twilight" zones or "Blighted" areas, and appraisers are advised to observe whether there are "undesirable racial elements in the neighborhood," and, if so, whether they are "likely to expand in a way that may injure the property."[69] He emphasizes social status in his chapter, "Appraising Homes": "Most families like to live . . . in districts in which they feel that the people who live there are on a social plane which they seek to attain."[70]

In the second edition, published in 1937, among the causes of depreciation are listed "changes in social status due to infiltration of foreign or colored elements of population."[71] For the appraisal of furnished apartment houses, he recommends investigation of "social status of neighborhood," "race infiltration," and "public opinion."[72] In the third edition, published in 1944, the chapter on blighted areas has been moved from No. 30 to No. 6, and is immediately followed by a new chapter, "Determining Value in Foreign and in Negro Neighborhoods." This chapter associates race and nationality with the value problems of the "Twilight" zones and "Blighted" areas, and states that loss of value characterizes the transitional period. The chapter also states that the "problem of obtaining loans on property occupied by colored families often affects its value." [73]

In the fourth edition, in Chapter XII, "Racial Covenants," the United States Supreme Court decision of 1948 is spoken of as the cause of "further confusion to appraising properties in foreign- and Negro-occupied districts" and as "the death knell to efforts of subdivision operators and others to restrict their properties to Caucasian occupancy." [74] After a discussion of the depressing effect of foreign-born groups on land values in which he refers to Homer Hoyt's study of land values in Chicago for support, he turns again to the effect of Negroes on property values.[75] In this respect, he writes:

Assessing authorities in Chicago, as the result of surveys, have come to the conclusion that the values in a white district are three times as high as those in an adjoining colored neighborhood. The difference is attributed to variations in levels of incomes and consequent modes of living.

It is maintained that almost always values decline when a white district is colonized by Negroes. . . .

Most large cities now have their rapidly expanding Negro neighborhoods. Heretofore, efforts have been made to retain them within restricted limits, but since the decision of the Supreme Court annulling restrictive covenants, they have spread out in all directions.[76]

In Chapter XIII, "Analyzing the Neighborhood," a qualification of the idea that property values decline when Negroes enter an area appears: "Whether rightly or wrongly, some families avoid or leave a neighborhood of mixed race or national origin. This reduces the market for homes in the area, and consequently may at first affect values adversely. As the neighborhood takes on its new character, and assuming equal maintenance of all property, value trends may reverse." [77] However, the total impression given by McMichael is that property values decline when Negroes enter a white neighborhood.

In another of his books, McMichael shows the influence of an earlier writer on real estate problems. In 1930, Knight, in discussing the causes of blighted areas, expressed an idea similar to that in Hoagland's "real estate Gresham's law." [78] He divides the causes of blighted areas into two categories and describes the first: "There are other causes of blight which can be prevented if legal sanctions can be obtained. These causes operate by *driving* people *away* and include: the ingress of undesirable racial elements into a neighborhood; heavy traffic through residence areas; the presence of nuisances; the destruction of neighborhood amenities, and other similar influences." [79] In 1945, McMichael calls attention to Knight's categories and paraphrases them in "Investment Problems in 'Blighted' Areas" in his book, *How to Make Money in Real Estate*.[80]

In his text, *How to Operate a Real Estate Business*, in Chapter XII, "Impelling Reasons for Buying and Selling," he lists these reasons, among others, for an owner's wanting to sell: "(1) Undesirable neighbors have moved next door; (2) A racial invasion has come too near for comfort; (3) Obnoxious odors, dirt, or noise have begun to make themselves felt, as the result of a factory development not too far away [conditions 4–8]." He advises that the salesman will do well to tell this promptly to a prospect or refuse to submit the property for sale because such conditions tend to depreciate the value of residential real estate and are reasons for selling promptly and moving elsewhere.[81]

In *How to Finance Real Estate*, in Chapter XXXVIII, "Influences of Racial Groups," McMichael calls attention to the fact that values "went steadily down" in city neighborhoods that changed from white to Negro. Lenders holding long-term mortgages in such areas "had to look closely to their collections of interest and principal," for "anything that affects values affects the financing of real estate." [82] He implies that investment in housing for Negro occupancy or housing near Negro-occupied property may not be sound and that the exclusion of Negroes from white areas is desirable from the mortgage lender's point of view.

In the same chapter, McMichael makes two other points: (1) The Supreme Court decision of May 3, 1948, does not make racial restrictive covenants illegal so long as they are executed voluntarily. "The court specified," he says, "that the clause in question 'erects no shield against merely private conduct, however discriminatory or wrongful.'" (2) The exclusion of Negroes can also be achieved by other devices, which he suggests.[83]

The second edition of this book has been revised drastically by McMichael and O'Keefe. Chapter XXXVIII is gone. The mortgage risk rating system of FHA is described in its more recently revised and attenuated form (1947 or later).[84] In discussing lender security, the authors draw up a list of items to be checked "in determining the desirability of a residential neighborhood." The first item, "general characteristics," includes physical attractiveness, social desirability, and homogeneity of residential properties,[85] but there is no elaboration on "social desirability." The book is devoted to the mechanics of financing.

One chapter of McMichael's *Real Estate Subdivisions* (1949) is devoted to racial restrictions in subdivisions.[86] He asks, "Can a subdivider of land so restrict sales of his lots that he can prevent, legally, the occupancy of such by non-Caucasians?" After pointing out that the entry of non-Caucasians into districts "where distinctly Caucasian residents live" tends to depress real estate values, and that a remedy is necessary to protect "the interests of subdividers, as well as the owners of property in selective sections of our great cities," he proceeds to list eight suggestions "to soften the impact of the blow that racial restrictions have received" from the Supreme Court decision of May 3, 1948. He speaks of "ethical control" by subdividers and real estate brokers and points to the Code of Ethics by which members of NAREB are governed, quoting Article 34 in full.[87] He concludes the chapter with an endorsement of racial residential segregation as a protection of neighborhood homogeneity and harmony, hence of neighborhood and property desirability, and hence of real estate value. Quoting "a student of the effects of various groups on real estate values," he continues with the assumption that "racial segregations are often advisable because persons of the same race have a tendency to possess similar tastes, traits and tendencies which encourage the harmonious relationships so important in making a neighborhood a desirable place in which to live." [88]

In his *Selling Real Estate* (1950), McMichael again deals with the subject of ethical behavior. The NAREB Code of Ethics is quoted and recommended — "This code has been in existence for a number of years and is the upright real estate man's creed. Study it and then practice it from the first to the last line." [89] In it, Article 34 still has the old wording, "members of any race or nationality." [90] Most of McMichael's books have been used widely as textbooks in real estate, and there can be little doubt that his ideas about Negroes in relation to real estate have been disseminated with the knowledge and approval of NAREB.

Husband and Anderson, in discussing causes of depreciation of property values in their textbook, *Real Estate* (1954), look upon economic depreciation as "the weathering which results from social and economic conditions." They imply that homogeneity is the essential strength of residential neighborhoods and that the entry of a different racial or economic group destroys this homogeneity and consequently depreciates real estate

212

values.[91] The authors expressed the same ideas in their *Real Estate Analysis* (1948).[92]

Ratcliff, in his well-known textbook, *Urban Land Economics* (1949), looks upon areas of greatest homogeneity as natural areas and says that "people tend to find their own social level." He also holds, as does Hoyt, that "the homes of the social leaders radiate a magnetism that attracts other families." [93] To his stress on homogeneity, he adds a number of desirable features of a residential neighborhood, among them the absence of "unwelcome social groups." He supports the use of deed restrictions to exclude such groups — since they are unspecified, the groups could include Negroes, and this interpretation seems possible in the light of a later statement about Negro families and other racial minorities "against whom artificial barriers have been built." He complements his statement about "unwelcome social groups" by including "inharmonious groups" among the forces that diminish the desirability and reduce property values of built-up areas in comparison with new areas.[94]

George L. Schmutz, a recognized authority on appraisal,[95] discusses the effect of the neighborhood on property values in it. Having established that residential neighborhoods decline in value with the passage of time, he proceeds to consider the conditions that contribute to the desirability and stability of such neighborhoods. "Congruity" (his term for homogeneity) he judges to be "the most important condition in the neighborhood." By congruity, he means not only the likeness of structures in kind, age, condition, and use, but also "the similarity of the people as regards race, color, income-earning level and social position." In addition, he sees "owner-occupancy as a condition which contributes to neighborhood stability." He observes "a tendency toward the neighborhood grouping of people of the same race, nationality, income, and social position," [96] and, like Ratcliff, he considers homogeneous areas natural areas. He then speaks of conditions preserving and destroying value. Among the latter, the first is "the presence of people of dissimilar cultures." [97]

To Harry Grant Atkinson, former executive vice-president of the American Institute of Real Estate Appraisers, the neighborhood is a homogeneous unit in the social and economic characteristics of its residents. Their interests are in one or more respects similar — "they belong to the same income group, their families are usually of about the same size, their occupations are similar, or in other ways they have the same attitude toward life." This homogeneity differentiates one neighborhood from an-

213

other and particularly from larger communities with greater variation. Neighborhoods can be classified, he says, according to the interests or attitudes of the people.

Atkinson introduces two particular ideas about neighborhoods. The first is that when racial and ethnic groups live in separate neighborhoods, they do so of their own volition, racial origin (Negroes) and custom (Germans, Jews) forming a communal interest.[98] The second idea is that neighborhoods conflict with one another, that land values are affected by adjoining neighborhoods, and that differences in race commonly play a part in this conflict. He writes, "Some neighborhoods are able to hold their balanced position for a long time and maintain stable land values . . . Sometimes the danger of decline is so apparent — as in the case of invasion by another race — that community organizations are formed to fight the deterioration of value." [99]

In *Fundamentals of Real Estate Practice* (1946) by Atkinson and Frailey, the idea that some racial and cultural groups tend to be clannish reappears, and so does the idea that "undesirable groups, races and individuals" destroy property values when they enter a neighborhood.[100] The authors make no distinction among members of the races; in addition, they couple these unnamed races with all unsavory social elements. Since they do not absolve the Negroes from detrimental behavior as they do the Germans, the reader is free to think that Negroes are included among the undesirable races.[101]

Spilker has been prominent in real estate for many years, although his *Real Estate Business as a Profession* (2nd ed., 1941) has not been widely used as a school text. Part II deals with real estate appraisal, and in Chapter VII, "Neighborhood Influence Factors Affecting Neighborhood Depreciation," his "Summary of Factors of Location Rating" is largely similar to the earlier FHA list of eight features.[102] He includes "surrounding homogeneous neighborhood" as a protection from adverse influences.[103] In Chapter VIII, he suggests that the question of race must be considered seriously among the qualifications of a city that will attract people to it.[104]

Teckemeyer in his book, *How to Value Real Estate* (1956), says that property values decline when "foreign or racial groups" enter an area, but does not explain how because "the danger of deflated values from such sources is so self-evident that it does not require heated debate or lengthy discussion." Furthermore, he looks at prices paid upon such entry not as "normal basic value, but as a bonus or premium price being paid for occupancy in a certain desirable district." [105] In other words, he does not believe there is any increase in value when such groups enter an area, only decrease.

In *Modern Real Estate Practice* (1956), Case devotes a chapter to "Analyzing the Economic Potential of Cities," in which he considers geographic, political, and social elements. In a short section on minority groups, he states that "minority racial groups" often form separate social groups within urban areas and create housing problems. "Inherent social attitudes" often bar these low-income groups from some areas in a city, and, if they succeed in entering these areas, the residents sell out and move away. He discusses only "Mexican nationals" and Negro farm workers.[106]

The books on real estate that have been examined here are not the only ones used as textbooks, but they are major ones. The position taken by these writers is that homogeneity of the residents is a basic requisite of the stable residential neighborhood and that the entry of a different racial group (Negroes are mentioned by some specifically) helps to bring about or to speed the decline of property values and of the neighborhood. Only two of the books considered give some indication of a different view. Fisher and Fisher in *Urban Real Estate* (1954) appear to accept the idea of a neighborhood where Negroes as well as white people might be living when they discuss restrictions in deeds. They point out that not all covenants are recognized by the courts, give the example of "restrictive covenants against occupancy or ownership by any persons other than members of the Caucasian race," and go on to say, "On the whole, covenants must not restrict the transfer of rights unreasonably or hinder unduly our relative freedom of social mixing and mobility." [107]

In *Real Estate Appraisal* (1956), Paul F. Wendt draws attention to recent attacks on the belief in the universality of the homogeneous neighborhood and on the belief that property values decline upon the entry of different racial or ethnic groups. He points out a weakness in the attacks on the second belief by referring to a report that prices in an area which Negroes were entering had risen principally because the sellers had been obliged to accept second and third mortgages as a part of the sales price.[108] The fact that higher prices often result from the mode of financing was revealed also in the experience of the respondents in the present study, but with the difference that the higher price resulted more frequently from a low down payment with a contract sale (see pp. 90–91). Wendt cites Babcock, the developer of the technique for the rating of residential location used by the FHA, as the source of appraisers' stress on homogeneity and calls this approach narrow in that it does not take into account "the dynamics of urban growth and district shifts." [109] Wendt has not resolved the disagreement between the empirical researchers, such as Laurenti, and the appraisers on the question of homogeneity and its significance for the stability of property values, but he has recognized some limitations in the traditional view and the existence of a view opposite to it. His view is of particular interest, as he is a Realtor, a member of the American Institute of Real Estate Appraisers, and a professor of finance in the School of Business Administration of the University of California at Berkeley, and was for two years vice-chairman of NAREB's Committee on Education.[110]

SUMMARY

According to my sources, homogeneity, particularly of people, is the basic and natural characteristic of a residential neighborhood. This means that residents have a number of characteristics in common — educational background, economic level, social standards, cultural interests, and race, and, to some extent, ethnic and religious background. When the homogeneity of a residential neighborhood is maintained, its desirability to the people of the neighborhood and to prospective buyers of similar social standard is preserved. Hence, the desirability of its properties and their value are protected. Homogeneity makes for stability.

Negroes are different racially and have different economic and social levels from white people. When Negroes enter an area, they break down its compatibility and hence its stability. White people do not want Negroes as neighbors. At the approach of Negroes to a stable residential neighborhood, its property values are threatened because the white market declines, and its desirability to residents and prospective buyers falls. Values decline from the time Negroes begin to approach the area. When they enter, and even before, the white residents sell their homes and move away. The Negro drives the white man out. After the best residents leave and people of lower economic and social standards take their place, there is overcrowding, poor maintenance of property, and other ill effects. If the area had started declining before Negroes entered it, their entry speeds its decline.

For these reasons, racial residential segregation is best for the stability of property values in white residential neighborhoods. "Natural expansion" — the moving of Negroes into street after street — is the best way for

216

them to obtain more housing. Furthermore, Negroes and other racial groups prefer to live among their own kind, and they would not be happy living where they are not wanted.

All people prefer to live with their own kind. "Birds of a feather flock together."

It is implied that the real estate man who sells property to Negroes in a white neighborhood disobeys the Code of Ethics and harms his professional group and the neighborhood. He may properly help Negroes acquire housing, but not in a white neighborhood.

The nine officials of the Chicago Real Estate Board expressed beliefs about Negroes in relation to real estate similar to those of NAREB except for one point. The view of NAREB generally and of most textbooks does not indicate recognition of different economic and social strata among Negroes, whereas the officials of the Chicago Real Estate Board distinguished between some refined Negroes and the many uneducated, low-income Negroes.

COMPARISON OF THE IDEOLOGIES OF THE RESPONDENTS AND OF THE INSTITUTION

A comparison of the ideologies of the respondents and of the institution reveals similar points in them. The real estate ideologies are alike in the following points: (1) The real estate man has to make a living, but he must do so honestly — that is, according to the Code of Ethics. In this way lies success, and in this way he is loyal to his business and helps raise it to a profession. (2) The real estate man has a particular moral responsibility to his client because of the importance of his services. (3) To achieve his goal of service, it is the real estate man's duty to protect the standard of the community so that it will remain desirable and thus stable. In this way he will protect the stability of its property values and his clients' equity. (4) To maintain the desirability of the neighborhood, he is to protect its homogeneity, so that residents will be satisfied with their neighbors of the same standards and so that there will be harmonious relations between them. (5) Home ownership contributes to the stability and desirability of an area because homeowners usually maintain their properties and are concerned about maintaining high standards in the community.

However, there are also certain differences. The institutional ideology is more systematic — it has been developed deliberately over a period of time and is therefore more logically and fully developed than that of the respondents. The institutional ideology assumes a broader, more inclusive perspective and expresses the real estate man's total function and its highest meaning. Many of the respondents are so immersed in their work that they tend to take their role of making housing available to people for granted, whereas the institution points this out. The respondents dwell on their duty to clients and to the profession, but many of them are not aware of its being a patriotic duty. The respondents do relate their work to the maintenance of certain values in American life, such as the family, home ownership, and good citizenship. However, though the higher reaches of the ideology may not be well known to the rank and file of the real estate men, the duty of maintaining and protecting property values is deeply and clearly realized and felt by all the respondents. This they have without question internalized.

The exclusion ideology of the respondents is similar to the racial real estate ideology of the institution in these main points: (1) White people do not want Negroes as neighbors. The coming of Negroes drives the white people out of their neighborhoods. People like to live with their own kind. (2) Property values decline when Negroes enter an area. (3) The neighborhood declines when Negroes enter. (4) Racial residential segregation is approved.

Again there are some differences. In the institutional ideology, no distinction is made among the nonwhite peoples, but most respondents made certain distinctions between Negroes and other nonwhite groups. In the institutional ideology, there is no recognition of different economic and social strata within other racial groups, and particularly within the Negro group, but in the respondents' ideology, the refined, educated Negroes are distinguished from the uneducated, low-income majority. The institutional ideology emphasizes the homogeneity of the residential neighborhood. This emphasis is in the respondents' ideology also, but there is in addition a consideration of the need and the possibility of maintaining the neighborhood at its standard even if one or two Negro families move in. There is also less stress on homogeneity of ethnic background. As is to be expected, the respondents' ideology is, on the whole, more specific and more personal than that of the institution. Whereas the institutional ideology emphasizes homogeneity of the neighborhood for its importance to the stability of the property values of the neighborhood *as a whole*, the respondents stress more the idea that people would be hurt if property values declined due to any action of theirs which destroyed neighborhood harmony. The respondents also pay attention to the more intimate reasons for which the residents of a neighborhood wish to move when Negroes enter it.

There is thus great likeness between the respondents' and the institutional ideologies. The question arises whether there are any marked differences among respondents between Board members and nonmembers in ideological orientation, with special reference to the exclusion ideology. A comparison of the ideologies of Board members and of nonmembers reveals the same preponderance of the exclusion ideology.

There are almost twice as many Board members as nonmembers among the respondents of Area A (24/13), and members are in the majority among the respondents of Area CX (5/1) and the Area C branch offices (3/0). In Areas B (12/11) and C (10/11), the numbers of members and nonmembers are almost equal (see Ch. VIII, n. 96).

In Area A, 20 of the 24 Board members hold the exclusion ideology, and 10 of the 13 nonmembers hold it. In Area B, all 12 Board members hold it, 5 of the 11 nonmembers do so. In Area C, all 10 Board members and 11 nonmembers hold the exclusion ideology, as do the 3 Area C branch offices (Board members). In Area CX, 4 of the 5 Board members hold it, and the 1 nonmember does so also. (Table 39, Appendix C.) Clearly, the exclusion ideology is prevalent among nonmember respondents — only in Area B are there more nonmembers who do not hold it than do (6/5). The predominance of the exclusion ideology among nonmember as well as Board member respondents would seem to indicate the ideological influence of the real estate institution, although this does not preclude other influences.

The Real Estate Board, Part II

EVIDENCE OF IDEOLOGICAL INFLUENCE

SINCE much likeness has been found to exist between the respondents' ideologies and those of the institution as represented by NAREB and the Chicago Board, I shall now present data that point to an ideological influence flowing from NAREB and the local board to the present and prospective practitioners of the real estate institution. My sources of evidence are the early history of NAREB and the rise of its Code of Ethics, acts that indicated real estate boards' approval of and insistence upon racial residential segregation, lines of communication used by NAREB and the Chicago Board to reach real estate men and those citizens interested in entering the business, and the training that respondents in this study received (to ascertain how they learned about important ideas of the real estate business).

The Code of Ethics

Real estate business in the United States can be said to have existed from 1840 on,[1] and the earliest known local real estate board in the country was formed in New York City in 1847. The New York Real Estate Exchange lasted only about a year; it was re-formed about ten years later. The second board was the eleven-member Baltimore Board of Real Estate Brokers and Property Agents, which has been in continuous existence since 1858. The first purpose of real estate organization was to protect and regulate the business of the real estate broker. The Baltimore Board stressed the obligation of broker to fellow broker in its first two rules, the second of which reads: "Expel any member who steals a sale from a fellow-member who had disclosed to him the name of the negotiating purchaser. Furthermore, announce the expulsion and its cause in one or more

220

local newspapers." To make self-discipline work, a provision was incorporated in the Board's constitution forbidding members to deal with non-member brokers or property agents. The rule was "a means of creating a controllable condition out of chaos." The Chicago Real Estate Board was formed in 1883.

The first national organization of the men in real estate was formed in 1892 and died in 1893. In 1908, the Chicago Real Estate Board, after conferring with the St. Louis Real Estate Exchange and other boards, sent out a call to the forty-five boards in the United States and Canada for a national meeting in Chicago on May 12–14, 1908.[2] The delegates organized a permanent national organization, the National Association of Real Estate Exchanges. The founders' objectives were the establishment of business practice standards, the exchange of information, and the advancement of real estate ownership.

The Code of Ethics was the Association's first project, although Herbert U. Nelson, writing of the history of NAREB, states that there were debates at first about the advisability of setting up a code.[3] Proponents pointed out that a code was necessary because, although all the members might desire to do the right thing, they could not always agree on what the right thing was. "To point out what the right thing was, the lessons of experience were assembled and formulated, and the collective conscience of the entire vocation spoke its mind with regard to the right course of conduct in the typical situations which daily confront the real estate man." [4]

The term "Realtor" was officially adopted by the Association in March, 1916, to identify persons bound by NAREB's Code (see p. 199). The first state real estate license laws were also passed about this time. In June, 1924, the Code of Ethics was completely revised at the annual convention in Washington. One revision made it compulsory for member boards to adopt the Code of Ethics.[5] Another was the Preamble, which defines the real estate man's role in the country and his obligations (pp. 191–192). The Code also contained Article 34 for the first time — thus, from 1924 on, the real estate broker was forbidden to introduce into a neighborhood "members of any race or nationality . . . whose presence will clearly be detrimental to property values in that neighborhood" (Article 34 is quoted in full on p. 201).

The fact that the Code of Ethics was to be understood as a *moral* code and not purely a business code is seen in Nelson's summary of the objectives of real estate organization in "nine phrases." The first phrase is

221

"the establishment of standards of competition in the business"; the ninth is "the evolution of ethical standards which will represent the collective conscience of the profession." In the ninth, referring to the Code of Ethics, Nelson states, "This Code is a living and growing thing, and must be changed from time to time. Our local real estate boards have not only the duty of enforcing this Code within their own ranks, but also, of developing it to fit local circumstances. The National Code is a minimum code." He also recognizes the importance of the license law, "This law is designed to protect the public against misrepresentation and fraud." [6]

As the executive secretary of NAREB, Nelson saw to it that the Code of Ethics got some publicity and became known to real estate men. In 1925, he published an article in which he practically quoted the Code, including Article 34.[7] The Code of Ethics was enlarged in 1928, and has been supplemented by the addition of specific codes for the various specialized fields, such as subdivision and appraisal.

The chief ideas of the real estate ideology in NAREB's Code of Ethics and Statements of Policy have come down from the real estate men of earlier generations — the Code adopted in 1913 had the same themes as the short-lived national organization of 1892. The Code of 1913 consisted of two parts, Duties to Clients and Duties to Other Brokers.[8] In the second Code the responsibility to the public was enlarged: Section I. Duties of the Broker to His Client; Section II. Duties of the Broker to His Prospective Buyer; Section III. Duties of the Broker to His Fellow Brokers.[9] In the third Code, adopted in 1915, the public receives further consideration still. Two more sections were added: Section IV. Suggestions to Owners and Investors, and Section V. Duty to Organize.[10] In 1924, the Preamble was added to the fourth Code, and, except for minor changes in wording, it still expresses the great responsibility which the real estate man carries toward the society — that is, utilization and distribution of ownership of the land.

The right to own land, which NAREB considers the cornerstone of American life, was established early in the United States and gave direction to the development of its way of life. The right of individuals to own land is now taken for granted, and it is generally not realized what a crucial step the establishment of this right was. In her history of real estate development in the United States, Pearl Janet Davies points out the great importance of the right to own land to the people of the United States; she also points out that the real estate business depends upon this right.[11]

222

Real estate men link the right to own land and wide distribution of land ownership with initiative in acquiring and utilizing land; they believe these are all basic to family, community, and national welfare.[12] The political significance of land ownership has also been stressed — Robert C. Givins has said, "the way to make a man a good citizen in this country is to make him part owner of it," because by doing this you further the interests of the country and convert foreigners into "Americans in loyalty, Americans in principle and Americans in land ownership."[13] The political importance of property ownership is expressed also in statements of policy by NAREB today. That the emphasis on home ownership continued over the years may be seen in a resolution passed at an annual convention of NAREB:

Own Your Own Home Campaigns

Whereas, the past work and efforts of the National Association and local boards in encouraging the Own Your Home movements have been so fruitful in results,

Therefore, be it resolved that the National Association of Real Estate Boards here assembled in San Francisco, June the 3rd, 1922, strongly urge that this work be continued and extended and we recommend that all Board members of this association put on in their respective cities Own Your Own Home Campaigns which have been so successful in their accomplishments.[14]

Acts to Protect Property Values

From the early days of real estate organization and thought, the importance of property values has been a constant theme and has led to overt acts by boards to protect real estate value. The role of the board in restrictions upon Negro residential movement has a history of fifty years, during which a basic tenet of the board has been that the restrictions are necessary to protect property values. During World War I, and even before, the moving of Negroes into northern cities created a crisis in housing.

In New York, in 1914, Frank A. Shaw, a Realtor with an office in Harlem, reported that over the preceding ten years, with the entry of Negroes, values were estimated to have shrunk "over $100,000,000" in that area and that values would shrink still more "unless something is done to control the situation." As Negroes had come into the area, white people had moved away, not wanting their children to attend the same schools as the Negro children.

Mr. Shaw included in his report a plan of action and stated that the plan had been "outlined in a letter sent to owners of property in the section affected." The plan was:

Committee of Thirty

Property Owners' Improvement Corporation
(To Be Incorporated)

. . . .

1. To arrange with the property owners to rent their properties to white tenants. This could be done section by section, thereby not causing an over supply of vacant apartments and houses at any one time. The united energetic efforts of all will facilitate the procuring of new tenants.

2. To assist owners who are unable financially to do the necessary renovating to their properties, on a proper business basis, as follows: viz., (a) Make a mortgage loan for the purpose, or (b) Take a lease of the property.

3. The Corporation to lend its assistance in arranging new and the extension of old mortgages for owners who will co-operate.

4. To co-operate in organizing a movement for the improvement of the social conditions of the negroes with the following objects: . . .

Up to this time you have suffered by reason of shrinkage in the value of your Real Estate, and a further loss is staring you in the face unless definite concerted action is taken at once.[15]

Since the article on the Negro in Harlem appeared in the official journal of the Real Estate Board of New York, the action undertaken must have had the approval of the Board. The effort, as we now know, was unsuccessful, but the attempt at restriction was made, and Board members were among the innovators.

In Chicago, in April, 1917, at a meeting of the Chicago Real Estate Board, an official "spoke at length on the invasion of white residence districts by the negroes, which was concurred in by [another official] in a most interesting and forceful manner, and at the conclusion offered a motion that a committee be appointed to go into the subject, and make an immediate report, which was duly seconded and carried . . ."[16] The president then appointed a committee to go into the matter with the first speaker as its chairman. The report of this committee to the Board contained the following:

The Committee appointed . . . to take immediate action and expedite plans to notify and assist owners of property coveted and demanded by the negro race for negro occupation beg to report as follows:

The Committee recognizes that a great immigration of negroes have arrived and are arriving in Chicago, and that some feasible, practicable and humane method must be devised to house and school them.

The old districts are overflowing and new territory must be furnished, but the committee especially wishes to call attention to and to warn owners against the methods used by some of the colored agents in soliciting property through deceit and mis-representation. The statement is commonly used, that houses or flats in a block are under contract or promise, for negro tenancy; in many cases that statement is absolutely untrue, and as a protection against such imposition the committee recommends and urges block organization of owners, without delay, as the situation is primarily in their hands, and under their control.

Neighborhood improvement associations may be employed as the nucleus to form such organizations.

The Committee is dealing with a financial business proposition and not with racial prejudice, and asks the co-operation of the influential colored citizens. Inasmuch as more territory must be provided, it is desired in the interest of all, that each block shall be filled solidly and that further expansion shall be confined to contiguous blocks, and that the present method of obtaining a single building in scattered blocks, be discontinued. Promiscuous sales and leases here and there mean an unwarranted and unjustifiable destruction of values and the loss in the majority of instances is borne by the small owner whose property represents his life savings; the loss is not only individual, but public, inasmuch as reduced values means reduced taxes.

An ordinary improved city block represents a money value of from $125,000 to $600,000 — the property invaded represents approximately 100 million dollars, for improvements exclusive of land. From thirty per cent to sixty per cent of that stupendous amount is irretrievably loss proportionally to investors, the moment the first colored family moves into a block, that sacrifice is avoidable by the use of common sense, and common justice, in the adoption of block method.

In the face of existing conditions the Committee has in an unprejudiced spirit reached the above conclusions, and hope for active co-operation from all civic bodies, and the Committee further desires to meet a representative Committee of colored citizens for the purpose of solving the problem.[17]

Seven months later, the committee had a third suggestion about segregation to make to the Board:

Mr. X, Chairman of the Committee on Negro Housing, called the attention of the members to the publication of a decision of the United States

Supreme Court, touching upon the problem of Negro Segregation, and presented the following preambles and resolution which were duly seconded and ordered published in the Bulletin:

Whereas, This Board named a Committee to investigate and deal with the colored people problem,

And whereas, Much patient attention was given the matter and a great deal of good accomplished by instructing owners,

And whereas, All negotiations, information, political, social and business aspects of the question pointed to one conclusion,

And whereas, Your Committee expressed that conclusion in a resolution adopted by this Board October 3rd, 1917, recommending Segregation under a proposed police power ordinance,

And whereas, On November 5th, 1917, the Supreme Court of the United States decided all such ordinances invalid,

And whereas, There still remains a lawful method of protecting society and property values by block organization of owners,

Now, Therefore Be It, Resolved, That this Board start a propaganda through its individual members to recommend owners societies in every white block for the purpose of mutual defense.[18]

The plan of the committee was not successful at first, but it had taken form. The idea of a property owners' organization had taken root in Chicago as in New York to keep Negroes from moving in a scattered formation, and the Board endorsed it.

In 1923, the restriction of Negroes to certain districts was approved by a Realtors' referendum in St. Louis. The adoption of the plan to establish Negro sections meant that the St. Louis Real Estate Exchange would recommend that none of its members sell or rent property to Negroes outside of the districts restricted to Negroes.[19] It was reported that 99 per cent of the 375 members of the Exchange approved of the establishment of Negro sections in certain outlined districts of the city.[20]

In the same year, it was reported that the Berkeley Realty Board in California had a ruling against any member selling, renting, or exchanging to other than the Caucasian race in restricted territory and that this ruling had never once been broken by a member of the Board to the knowledge of its officers.[21] The Board of San Bernardino, California, also in 1923, protested at one of its meetings against the selling or renting of property in communities occupied by Caucasians to persons of other races.[22] In 1924, the sale of a vacant lot to a Negro in Monrovia, California, caused an "upheaval in local realty circles." A committee appeared at the meeting of the Board and asked it to take action that would prevent the future sale of property to colored people in the sections occupied entirely by white population. By a vote of the Board, the president was directed to appoint a committee to investigate the situation as it affected that particular tract and to make recommendations that would prevent such a sale's recurring.[23] In the same year, the following resolution was adopted by the Eagle Rock Realty Board: "Therefore be it resolved . . . that we as a board and as individuals pledge ourselves against the selling, leasing, or renting of property, or being a party to any negotiation affecting anyone other than of the Caucasian race. Be it further resolved that we discourage and hold it highly unethical to sell or lease any property either by the owner or agent, to such a person or to any person of undesirable or questionable character."[24] In the same year, a Milwaukee newspaper reported, "Milwaukee will have a 'black belt' if the Real Estate Board can find ways and means to make it practicable. At the weekly luncheon of the board Tuesday noon, the advisability of restricting the Negro population in a certain area on the West side was discussed. The members say that the Negro population of the city is growing so rapidly that something will have to be done."[25] In this year also, the president of the Real Estate Board in Canton, Ohio, appointed a committee to designate sections where it would be permissible to sell to colored people, and announced that in the future when a Realtor had a Negro client, the sale had to be confirmed by an officer of the Board or by the board of directors.[26]

The New York Realtors Association, in 1924, sought to learn from the Birmingham Real Estate Board how southerners "prevent negro encroachment on white residential territory."[27] The reply stated, "things like this simply don't happen down here. If one of our white men sells a fine lot in white territory to a negro, he usually meets with serious embarrassment of one sort or another. . . . The negro understands the white man, knows what to expect, and is accustomed to the traditions that have long guided both races."[28]

In April of 1925, the following statement appeared in a newspaper about the Montebello, California, Realty Board:

It has recently come to the attention of residents of Montebello that certain individuals are buying property for Japanese in our city. Hence the following action was taken by the Montebello Realty Board: . . . resolution passed . . . at their meeting of March, 1925. . . . "Therefore be it resolved: That the Montebello Realty Board, in harmony with the laws of our state, arc not in favor of the practice of citizens of the United States holding real property for those ineligible to citizenship or for minors of such ineligibles, and that it is the sense of this meeting that all civic bodies and the City Trustees of the City of Montebello be requested to take action necessary to discourage those who attempt by technicalities or subterfuge to gain possession of real property in Montebello for those ineligible to citizenship or minors of such ineligibles. Montebello Realty Board, Chas. A. Graham, President." [29]

This action, like that of the Eagle Rock Realty Board, went far beyond simple restriction to a certain area.

In the same year, the Salt Lake City Real Estate Board asked Herbert U. Nelson, executive secretary of NAREB, whether he had any records showing official action taken by boards on the selling of a home to colored people in a locality where none reside.[30] In his reply, Mr. Nelson referred to the action taken by the boards of St. Louis, Canton, and Milwaukee, and he stated that the Detroit Board favored segregation of Negroes, that the Whittier, Monrovia, Los Angeles, and Berkeley boards of California had all passed resolutions against the sale of property to other than Caucasians in white or mostly white districts, and that the Board of Portland, Oregon, had officially adopted a measure of restriction in their Code of Ethics, "No member of the Board will directly or indirectly sell or be a party to the sale of Portland residential property to persons of the Negro or Oriental races now inhabited almost exclusively by white persons." [31] It is apparent that by 1925 real estate boards in different parts of the country had taken measures to bring about the restriction of Negroes and other racial groups to certain districts within their communities.

However, not all the restriction was initiated by real estate boards. The action of the Monrovia Real Estate Board appears to have been taken in response to an appeal by a committee. In 1925, the mayor of Tampa, Florida, proposed a Negro section to the Board.[32] In 1927, Charles O. Hooper, landscape architect and town-planning expert, told a meeting of the Salesman's Division of the New Orleans Real Estate Board about a subdivision that he planned for Negroes just outside New Orleans.[33] The newspaper article reporting his address begins, "New Orleans can easily meet the situation created by the United States Supreme Court decision knocking out the city segregation law by planning to properly provide for its very necessary Negro population." In Rockford, Illinois, the Rockford Real Estate Board, stirred by a report that property owners of Italian origin in South Rockford were ordering Negro tenants to move out of their homes, voted to have its Committee on Miscellaneous Affairs confer with Negro ministers and other Negro leaders in an effort to establish a Negro section in the city.[34]

In 1927, a survey by the California Real Estate Association concluded that the color question, though not a serious problem in the northern half of the state, was being gravely considered in all large cities and many exclusive residential communities in the southern half of the state; that Santa Monica, Pasadena, Monrovia, Riverside, Los Angeles, San Bernardino, San Francisco, Oakland, Berkeley, San Jose, and Fresno were the cities most exercised over the matter in question; and that practically all subdivisions had restrictions to protect them as far as possible from future depreciation through encroachment of a foreign race. The survey reported also that in Riverside improvement associations assisted Realtors to control foreign populations (Mexican, Japanese), that the Los Angeles Realty Board recommended that Realtors not sell property to other than Caucasian in territories occupied by them, that Santa Barbara dealers had a code of ethics restricting all property against all foreign races, which was strictly adhered to by members of the local board, and that a suggestion had come from Monrovia that a subdivision be built for Mexicans and Negroes with sanitary and street improvements with financing for those who wished to purchase. The survey found that it was the general opinion of all the boards in the state that deed and covenant restrictions were probably the only way that the matter could be controlled, and that realty boards should be interested.[35]

In 1927, Nathan W. McChesney, general counsel for NAREB, wrote in answer to an inquiry from Los Angeles about forms of restriction with reference to non-Caucasian persons as follows: "You inquire about the best forms for use in deeds and residential agreements. So far as we know, there are no such forms in use. . . . The Chicago Real Estate Board now is giving a great deal of attention to the drafting of such restrictions . . . with respect to perhaps eight or ten blocks on one of the boulevards of the city. As soon as these forms are perfected, I have no doubt they will be available for use by others." [36]

In 1934, a letter from the secretary of the Grand Rapids Real Estate Board to NAREB inquired about a Fred L. Helman, secretary of the Woodlawn Property Restriction Association of Chicago, who was offering a service to place legal restrictions on property for protection against invasion of Negroes, and ended, "Perhaps you know something of this service or of the Association which Mr. Helman represents. May we hear?" [37] The following information about Mr. Helman was given in the reply:

Mr. Helman recently came into the office and gave us some details of the work which he has been doing with neighborhood restrictions. He tells me that several years ago the Chicago Real Estate Board worked out a standard neighborhood agreement for the restriction of property against Negroes. This has been used uniformally [sic] in different sections of this city.

Mr. Helman has worked with neighborhood associations and local groups of business men, such as the Woodlawn Business Men's Association, in establishing these protected areas. We should say that he has done this work successfully in about a dozen areas in this city.

I believe that in many districts in this city property owners associations have been formed to carry on this work. [38]

The three inquiries to NAREB cited above received answers agreeing with restrictive practices, in keeping with Article 34, which appeared in the Code of Ethics in 1924 (wording given on p. 201). Article 34 may be said to be the base on which the pattern of residential restriction of Negroes and other minority groups was established, although restriction had been attempted here and there before 1924. Article 34 can also be looked upon as a unified expression of a widespread reaction to the movement of Negroes and other racial groups into areas where they had not lived before. It came from local Realtors to the National Association as a suggestion and request in consequence of their experience, and it became the norm for Realtors.

World War II brought a flood of Negro war workers into northern, eastern, and western cities, and serious Negro housing problems deepened into situations of crisis and emergency. Actions of real estate boards in a number of cities revealed their continuing pattern of restricting Negroes to certain areas or of concurring in others' actions toward this end. In 1943, the Los Angeles Real Estate Board refused to approve plans to develop new housing under the sponsorship and promotion of private builders because opposition had developed among white property owners near the proposed site, which was on the edge of the Negro district. [39] The St. Louis Real Estate Exchange continued its practice of establishing restricted and unrestricted districts for transactions with Negroes: "unrestricted districts" were blocks and neighborhoods within the city where brokers were free to sell or rent to Negroes; all other areas were "restricted" in that no transactions with Negroes should be made within them. All Realtors of the city were bound to observe these racial boundaries, shown in a map drawn in 1944 (see p. 226).[40] In Cleveland, Ohio, the Real Estate Board concurred in the action of a group of Board affiliates to block two projects by private builders to construct 400 homes for Negro workers.[41] In Atlanta, Georgia, Mayor Hartsfield approached the Atlanta Real Estate Board in 1946 and asked that something be done to reduce the number of sales that were being made to Negroes in white districts. In response to the mayor's request, the chairman of the Atlanta Board indicated that the Board was in complete agreement and explained that Negro real estate men, white property owners, and brokers unaffiliated with the Board were responsible for such sales rather than members, who were already under obligation to the Board not to sell to Negroes in predominantly white areas.[42]

In 1945 interviews with representatives of the Portland, Oregon, Realty Board and with prominent Realtors disclosed the existence of a policy of restricted sale of property to Negroes. Such restriction confined sales to Negroes by any member of the Realty Board to the segregated area, with limited sale permitted in three other areas. This policy was fully expressed in the Board's Code of Ethics, which enlarged upon Article 34.[43] A similar policy of restricted sale to Japanese and Negroes was found in Spokane, Washington, in 1946. Members of the Realty Board could sell property to Negroes and Japanese only in segregated areas arbitrarily agreed upon by the Spokane Realty Board. At the time of the study, no Japanese could buy property in Spokane unless the sale was reviewed by a special board set up by the Spokane Realty Board for that purpose. This was true for Negroes also, but if the purchase was in an area open to Negroes, the case needed no review.[44]

In Buffalo, New York, when a site had been selected within the Negro residential section for a low-rent housing project to alleviate somewhat the serious Negro housing situation in 1946, the project was opposed by politicians, the Buffalo Real Estate Board, the Buffalo Chamber of Commerce, the City Planning Association, and the Tax Payers' League.[45] In Washington, D.C., the Real Estate Board was reported in 1948 to have honored covenants consistently, to have offered assistance to property owners desiring to write agreements to bar Negroes, and to have encouraged subdivision developers to make covenants "blanketing whole areas against Negroes." It had supplemented these activities by promoting a general policy of preventing sale or rental of property in white neighborhoods to Negroes.[46]

On May 3, 1948, the Supreme Court made the restrictive covenant, the main instrument of residential restriction, legally unenforceable. The decision was accepted by real estate boards — but, it appears, with regret. One of the officials of the Chicago Board gave his opinion about this decision, revealing how he had helped develop the restrictive covenant and how the covenant as a protection of property values was in direct line with his thinking as a community-minded real estate man. He was unhappy with the decision for personal reasons also — it was hurting his business.[47]

There is some evidence that, following the Supreme Court decision, certain real estate boards, particularly some on the west coast, did not accept the decision as the Chicago Real Estate Board had. On August 12, 1948, the Los Angeles Realty Board announced that it was petitioning NAREB to "sponsor the adoption of an amendment to the Constitution of the United States to retroactively validate, and confer upon the courts of the states and the United States power to enforce conditions, covenants or provisions in deeds, contracts or other instruments restricting the ownership or occupancy of real property to Caucasians or to Negroes, respectively." The Board also took occasion to remind its members that they are subject to ouster for violating the Code of Ethics concerning the sale of property to undesirables.[48] At a meeting of the Culver City Realty Board, the president announced that the Board had approved a letter of commendation to the Los Angeles Realty Board for its constitutional amendment.[49] In a formal resolution addressed to the Los Angeles County Board of Supervisors, the San Gabriel Valley Realty Board said:

The United States Supreme Court, by ruling out the race restriction clause in real estate contracts has created chaos with persons buying in restricted districts, and is raising race problems which do not exist when each race is quartered in a restricted area. . . . We feel that our citizens are better off when allowed to congregate in districts or settlements, such as Irwindale for Mexicans. There is no reason why, in zoning, districts can't be set aside for our citizens to live and enjoy the pursuit of happiness, without upsetting the whole social structure.[50]

On August 30, 1948, the El Monte Realty Board expelled one of its members for violating Article 34 of the Code of Ethics (see p. 201). The Realtor had sold a house to a Mexican American. The mortgagee and nine neighbors petitioned the Realty Board to discipline the Realtor. In a Board hearing he was instructed "to make an earnest effort to sell the property . . . to persons acceptable" under the Code of Ethics and the Board's constitution. Failing to sell the property within the sixty days allowed to him, he was expelled from membership.[51]

A letter from NAREB in 1949 answering an inquiry from the Louisville Real Estate Board about the effect of the Supreme Court decision on the efficacy of Article 34 concluded with the following statement: "I doubt whether these opinions militate in any way against the efficacy of Article 34."[52]

A survey of Baltimore reported in January, 1950, that "the Real Estate Board of Baltimore considers it an unethical practice to sell a home to a colored family in an area occupied predominantly by whites," and that "this contributes substantially to the fact that this 20 per cent of the population occupied not more than 8 per cent of the city's residential area."[53]

Article 34 (p. 201) has been understood by Realtors to mean that Negroes and members of other minority groups are not to be introduced into white neighborhoods through sale or rental of property (the article has other meanings as well). Article 34 was revised in 1950 to read: "A Realtor should not be instrumental in introducing into a neighborhood a character of property or use which will clearly be detrimental to property values in that neighborhood." Article 34 was revised again in 1955, but only in number and position — it is now Article 5 in Part I of the Code, "Relations to the Public." The omission of the phrase "member of any race or nationality" from the revised form of Article 34 has led to the conclusion that the restriction against selling or renting property to Negroes in the white area has been removed. However, the question has been raised whether the revision of Article 34 in the Code of Ethics of NAREB has had any real effect upon the actions of the member boards, although all member boards accept the Code of Ethics and are expected to adhere to it.

A letter sent by the St. Louis County Real Estate Board to its active members on June 1, 1955, makes it clear that, although the wording of Article 34 has been changed, the original meaning is attributed to it. The letter reads:

TO ALL ACTIVE MEMBERS:

The following letter was received from Mr. Clarence Lang, Executive Secretary of the St. Louis Real Estate Board.

"Our Board of Directors wishes to call to your attention our rule, that no Member of our Board, may, directly or indirectly, sell to Negroes, or be a party to a sale to Negroes, or finance property for sale to or purchase by Negroes, in any block, unless there are three separate and distinct buildings in such block already occupied by Negroes. By a 'block is meant, both sides of the street on which the property fronts, between intersecting streets.'

"This rule is of long standing, and has our interpretation to be directly associated with Article 34 of the Code-of-Ethics of the National Association of Real Estate Boards, reading: 'A Realtor should not be instrumental in introducing into a neighborhood a character of property or use which will clearly be detrimental to property values in that neighborhood.'

. . . .

"Recently it has been observed that some Members of our Board are offering for sale to Negroes, property in the city of St. Louis in violation of our rule. In some instances thereof it is quite possible that the said offerings are made without the knowledge of the existence of our rule. Therefore, we ask that you cause a bulletin to be issued to your Members, present and future, reciting our rule and Article 34 of NAREB Code-of-Ethics, and requesting due observance thereof. . . ."

We ask that you govern yourself accordingly when dealing within property in City of St. Louis.[54]

The rule of the St. Louis Real Estate Board is, then, interpreted to be "directly associated" with the revised Article 34, and there can be no doubt that the revision is understood by the St. Louis Real Estate Board to cover the exclusion of Negroes.

There is other evidence of such an interpretation. An NAACP analysis of the Detroit riot of 1943 found the Detroit Real Estate Association a contributory factor because of its opposition to public housing.[55] A report completed in April, 1955, by William Price found that the Detroit Real Estate Board's support of racial residential segregation was one of the factors affecting the housing mobility of Negroes.[56]

In March, 1956, it was reported that the Southeast Realty Board, South Gate, California, expelled Realtor Harry Beddoe for alleged failure to comply with the Board's code.[57] Its code provides that no member of the Board shall be instrumental in transferring property for a purpose or to a buyer that would be "clearly detrimental" to property values in the neighborhood. The Realtor charged that he was expelled by the Board because he was involved in the sale of a home in Lynwood to a Mexican man and wife. In the suit for reinstatement, the Realtor's attorney said that the

Board apparently assumed that the fact that the family is Mexican is the basis on which a property devaluation would occur. He contended that it had not been and could not be shown that the nationality of this family would or could cause a property devaluation. But the real estate men believe otherwise.

One basis on which Article 34 — original and revised, and including all local variations of it — was established is the assumption that property values are lowered when Negroes and members of other minority groups enter a neighborhood; the duty of the Realtor follows from this belief. A representative of NAREB stated in an interview:

Our ideal is to create home ownership and a mortgage market among Negroes. . . . We want to encourage them to build for their own. We've been at this fifty years. We started zoning. We made it an ethical thing not to introduce any into an area. . . . Immediately after the Supreme Court decision, we met in November and it was determined to remove that article referring to race in obedience to the Supreme Court ruling, in obedience to the law of the land. It was decided there would be no reference to creed or race in the Code. All the member boards subscribe to it and accept the Code of Ethics. . . . In regard to segregation, we don't interfere with the local situation. Each community's problems are different. NAREB takes a middle of the road position in regard to racial, religious, and political questions.[58]

The essential point in the representative's statement is that NAREB "made it an ethical thing not to introduce any [Negroes] into an area." The removal of the words "race" and "nationality" from Article 34 has not changed the belief or the duty, according to the data of the five interviews referred to on page 201 and according to the overt acts of a number of boards. Although the representative of NAREB said that the National Association does not interfere at the local level, Article 34 has all along enjoined and, in its revised form, to all appearances continues to enjoin the exclusion of nonwhite persons from white areas.

There is one important difference between the present and the former role of the real estate board in regard to Negroes, at least as far as definitions of the Chicago Real Estate Board and of NAREB are concerned: formerly, any dealing with Negroes was looked upon askance, whereas now, former presidents and high-ranking members have a Negro clientele and/or a group of Negro tenants of considerable size. The outlook of the Board in Chicago may be said to have become broad enough to include dealing with Negroes, but not broad enough to be unrestrictive.

The Realtors are able to reconcile the conflict between their duty to protect property values and their duty to supply Negroes with housing. In 1926, the executive secretary of NAREB saw "no essential conflict" here and wrote in a letter: "It seems to me entirely possible therefore, for us as Realtors to develop better housing facilities for certain national or racial groups and still continue to protect in so far as we can, the real estate values in residential sections which are already established, and which rest upon the foundation of a normal wide occupancy." [59]

In 1945, NAREB itself went on record as considering the supplying of housing for Negroes and other minority groups the duty of its members. The following statement expresses this stand:

Negro Housing

This Association does not participate in any controversy or activity that has to do with social or political problems in connection with the life of any racial or minority groups in our nation. We recognize, however, that in the field of economics and business we have a definite obligation and opportunity. We believe it is our duty to seek the ways and means by which housing of Negroes and other minority groups shall be provided and that this housing shall be of such character and quality as the members of such groups can afford to buy or rent. Where such housing shall be placed in any community is a local problem to which there can be no national solution. We pledge ourselves to continue efforts begun to secure adequate mortgage funds, land development, and building activity for such housing. [60]

In taking this stand, NAREB expressly states, as did its representative above, that it leaves the placing of such housing to the community itself. However, the restrictions that are understood to be imposed upon its members by Article 5 (originally Article 34) appear to limit this policy. Nevertheless, this stand constituted an enlargement of the role of the real estate board, in policy, in the housing of Negroes and other minority groups.

Among real estate boards' overt acts with reference to racial segregation, it is relevant to mention the exclusion of Negro real estate men from white real estate boards. NAREB expressed its position on this question in the following letter:

The question you raise is, as you well know, a most tangled and difficult one. The National Association of Real Estate Boards is a federation of local boards. The local boards are self-governing, and they only perform through their national organization certain common functions with relation to national legislation and the gathering of information on which they agree. The National Association does not in any way control the conditions for admission to membership in any local real estate board. That is the business of the local board itself.

. . . .

My own feeling in this matter is that it is not possible to make a frontal attack on the prejudices and strong feelings that exist in local boards in this matter. I believe instead that the Negroes in any community who are engaged in the real estate business should organize their own real estate boards. . . .

Colored real estate dealers have their place in the real estate field and in the market, and it is to our interest that those who practice our business should be well informed and well qualified. The National Association cannot admit more than one board in a city, nor do I think it will admit to membership at this time a real estate board consisting of colored persons. On the other hand, I would personally recommend to our Board of Directors that our literature, our educational material, and, in many cases, our speakers, be made available to such colored real estate boards in every community where they exist. In this way I believe that a helpful connection could be built up in time, which would get good results.[61]

As a result of the position of individual boards and of NAREB, Negro real estate men formed their own boards and their own National Association of Real Estate Brokers.[62] The exclusion of Negro real estate brokers from white real estate boards is not complete, however. In NAREB as a whole, there were 58,744 individual members (Realtors) and 1,229 board members as of August 31, 1956.[63] George S. Harris,[64] president of the National Association of Real Estate Brokers, told me that there were in 1956 only about eight boards that had accepted Negro members. He said that there was 1 Negro member on the Pittsburgh Real Estate Board; 1 or 2 in that of Gary, Indiana; 1 in that of South Bend; 1 in that of San Diego; a few in a subsidiary board of the San Francisco Real Estate Board; and 1 in that of Pasadena. In 1951, the Negro membership of the Real Estate Board of New York, Inc., consisted of 9 broker members, 4 salesmen, and 1 owner member.[65] In the same year, the Brooklyn Real Estate Board had 4 Negro members, all real estate brokers; a fifth had died.[66] There were 1,136 active broker members of the Chicago Real Estate Board as of September 30, 1957.[67] No Negro brokers were members of the Chicago Board as of September 19, 1956.[68] Six Negro brokers applied for membership several times, but they were not accepted.[69] There are reports of rejection by other boards also. Negro members of white real estate boards are expected to observe the Code of Ethics and not to sell property to Negroes in white neighborhoods.[70]

The acts of the individual boards of NAREB can be said to contribute to the ideological influence of the real estate institution over its practitioners. These acts proclaim the belief that property values decline when Negroes enter an area and they endorse the exclusion of Negroes from white neighborhoods. They affirm the racial real estate ideology of NAREB by precedent. Such actions have been taken by boards in different parts of the country — the Middle and Far West, the South, and to some extent in the Northeast — and have been widely publicized by newspapers. They remind practicing real estate men who already know the Code of Ethics and indoctrinate those entering the business.

Lines of Communication

The many different lines of communication with acting and prospective real estate men and the public generally substantiate the impression that respondents' real estate and racial real estate ideologies have come largely from NAREB and the Chicago Board. The lines of communication are published works on the real estate business, conventions and conferences of NAREB and its member Boards, individual lectures by Realtors, and other, indirect ways.

DEPARTMENT OF EDUCATION OF NAREB

The Department of Education of NAREB is the most important transmitter of real estate thought. Almost from its beginning NAREB had an education committee which was quite active in the 1920's. In 1923, NAREB held a national conference on real estate education which mapped out books that needed to be written, secured a publisher, and "began the creation of a systematic body of real estate thought to be available to everyone of us." [71] Some books were written by Realtors, some by college faculty members, and some by both in joint authorship. A resolution was passed at the national convention of 1924 to have courses and textbooks in real estate approved by NAREB introduced into colleges and universities.[72] The ideological aim of real estate education, as expressed by the executive secretary of NAREB in 1925, included property owners as well as real estate men: real estate education was to help real estate men understand better the ethical principles involved in their social function and to help property owners understand better the economic forces and social customs controlling real estate values.[73] These and efficiency in the service itself are the deliberate aims of NAREB in its educational program.

The activities of the Education Committee were curtailed during the depression years of the 1930's and also during the war years of the 1940's. Originally, the institutes of NAREB, such as the American Institute of Real Estate Appraisers, were set up as education departments in their fields. Later, a central department was needed to gather general information on real estate and to coordinate and publicize the educational activities of NAREB, so in February, 1948, the Department of Education of NAREB was set up as a full department.[74]

One function of the Department of Education is to serve as a clearinghouse for real estate education in colleges and universities — that is, to find out from them what they are doing in real estate education, to analyze this information, and to make it available to others. A letter was sent on September 7, 1948, to all colleges and universities in the United States offering courses in business administration or commerce. The letter asked what courses were being given in real estate and whether a four-year course in real estate was planned; it explained that NAREB was interested in the establishment of such courses and wished to know what was already being done. (Several surveys have been made since 1948, and that of 1955 revealed that approximately 150 schools were offering courses in real estate.[75]) Later, other letters were sent to offer educational aids.

There are a number of ways in which the Department of Education endeavors to reach and to help instructors and students of real estate. There is the weekly newsletter, entitled *Realtor's Headlines* and described as "A weekly publication devoted to news and developments of significance to the real estate profession and allied interests." This free publication creates a tie, on the basis of news and services offered, with teachers of real estate and prospective real estate men.

An important channel of communication between Realtors and teachers of real estate is the annual conference on real estate education sponsored by NAREB's Department of Education. The chief aim of this conference is to bring together instructors of real estate, particularly full-time faculty members, and Realtors teaching, promoting, or planning educational programs for their own boards. Not all the university instructors come, but enough do to make the conference worthwhile. The two-day conference usually takes place on the campus of a university and, if possible, in or near the city where the annual convention of NAREB is being held and one or two days before it. The annual real estate educational conferences of 1954, 1955, 1956, and 1957 were held at Western Reserve University, Columbia University, Washington University, and Northwestern University (Chicago campus) respectively. Realtors and university professors were the speakers, panel members, and moderators at the conferences. The themes of these conferences and those of other years deal with real estate education in the university and point to the role of the Realtor in planning school programs in real estate. In addition, there have been various social activities for Realtors, university men, and their wives. Thus, bonds of fellowship are added to a common interest in real estate and a carefully planned program for the exchange of views — and it is likely that among them will be views of NAREB about principles, values, and goals in real estate. It is important to note that some of the university professors of real estate are themselves members of NAREB.[76]

In 1953, Ohio State University, through its College of Commerce and Administration, cooperated with the Ohio Association of Real Estate Boards in presenting on its campus the 1953 Annual Conference on Real Estate Brokerage.[77] In the same year, the South Carolina Association of Real Estate Boards and the University of South Carolina Extension Division set up a course in professional training for real estate, designed for those in the real estate business who wanted more training and for those who intended to enter it. The teachers were from the university faculty and from the real estate profession.[78] There have been cases of such cooperation at the University of Michigan, the University of California, Western Reserve University, and the University of Houston [79]; all of these programs contained 1 or more courses on the appraisal of real estate. The point is that teachers of real estate and Realtors are cooperating closely.

In some areas, Realtors are interested in the real estate offerings at the local school and work with faculty and students in real estate. They provide scholarships, part-time and summer jobs for students, and guest lecturers at classes in real estate. On the other hand, the professors of real estate also speak at Board activities. There are particularly close relations in the states of Florida and California. The Realtors in California persuaded the state legislators to turn $100,000 a year of the license funds over to the University of California for real estate education with certain stipulations as to its use. In Florida, a similar allocation was obtained for the University of Florida on a much smaller scale — $5,000. In these various ways, a close relationship in varying degree has been built up between Realtors and real estate departments and teachers of universities in Idaho, Ohio, Indiana, Illinois, and Michigan, at least.

A number of instructors in real estate are active in the real estate business. This happens particularly in the larger cities, where professors of real estate are often members of the local board and of NAREB as real estate brokers as well as in their capacity as professors. In these cases the views of NAREB are presented to students of real estate by its own members. As for speakers from NAREB itself, by 1951 a list of over two hundred speakers in over thirty states had been developed, each well prepared to speak on a particular topic.[80] There can be said to be good rapport between Realtors and university teachers of real estate.

The Department of Education of NAREB asks member boards to give some membership status to university teachers of real estate,[81] and many boards have done this. The Department asks the boards not to charge faculty members any dues to induce them to take advantage of the offer; this offer is to the advantage of the Board as well — "if you want the real estate instructor to present the views of the real estate industry to his class, you must inform him of those views."

Another instrument of communication is the *Educational Letter* issued monthly by the Committee on Education of NAREB to inform member boards and state associations about real estate educational activities throughout the country and to help them organize and promote their own educational activities. In 1956, the *Educational Letter* was being sent to approximately 300 representatives of more than 165 universities and colleges offering courses in real estate. The *Educational Letter* tells what is available and valuable among new writings, developments, and activities in real estate education. It serves to transmit ideas of the real estate ideology. This can be inferred from topics dealt with in issues of the *Letter*. For example, in 1951, some topics were: for April, "History and Ethics of the Real Estate Business"; for May, "Terminology and Definitions of Real Estate"; for June, "Neighborhood and City Growth and Change"; and for December, "What Makes Value." [82]

The Department of Education has carried on a placement service for students of real estate in the universities and colleges since 1949 by writing real estate instructors in schools offering real estate as a major field and informing them that it will list students who would like its help in its *Placement Bulletin*. This applies to real estate majors graduating that year.

From time to time students write to ask about jobs; the Department of Education will request each student to narrow his preferred locations to three cities and will then write to the Board secretaries in those cities. Through this help, NAREB is likely to enlist students' interest and favor and thus draws to itself the prospective real estate men.

The instructor in real estate is helped in several other ways by the Department of Education of NAREB: there are available over fifty outlines of lectures on real estate subjects, a *Manual for Instructors*,[83] and films on real estate topics.

Still another form of cooperation is seen in a bibliography in real estate, *The Realtor's Bookshelf*, jointly published in 1949 by the Department of Education, NAREB, and the Business Management Service, College of Commerce and Business Administration, University of Illinois. Among the books listed in the "Appraisal" and "General Real Estate Brokerage" sections are most of those described on pp. 202–216 as holding the main views of the exclusion ideology. In addition, the library of NAREB compiled a bibliography of its own, arranged by topic. Among the books recommended, those I describe as containing essential elements of the exclusion ideology are prominent on the lists, "Good Books on Real Estate Appraising," "Model Library for a Realtor's Office," "General Real Estate Textbooks," and "The Twelve Basic Books for a Realtor's Office." [84]

NAREB's Department of Education wants to know what textbooks are used in the colleges and universities for the study of real estate, as well as what courses are being given. The survey of 1955 revealed that among the textbooks used by many of the schools reporting were the ones containing elements of the exclusion ideology.[85] Some of the authors of the books that contain ideas of the exclusion ideology and that are recommended by NAREB are (or were) teachers of real estate themselves. According to the information given on the title page, this is true of Nelson L. North, Alfred A. Ring, Arthur M. Weimer, Henry E. Hoagland, Richard U. Ratcliff, John B. Spilker, and Frederick E. Case. It is to be expected that their ideas would also be expressed in their classes. The writers of textbooks disseminate one another's ideas by referring to one another; in the bibliographies, the well-known names appear again and again.

There are two other areas where Realtors take on the responsibility of instructing prospective and practicing real estate men. The first is a one-day, educational conference carried out in various locations by the state associations of real estate boards. The Department of Education of NAREB puts on a one-day conference in states where no conference is given, in the hope that the state association will start holding its own conference. In 1957, one-day conferences were held in nineteen states.

Apart from the four-year undergraduate course in real estate in universities, a Real Estate Certificate Program is offered in many state universities,[86] which consists of eight sixteen-week courses given to people who are already in the business or who are working at other jobs during the day but plan to enter the business (also, lawyers and others may take this course to get more information). Realtors take on speaking assignments in these programs, which are usually co-sponsored by the university and the state association or local boards.

THE BOARD AND OTHER SOURCES OF COMMUNICATION

All the institutes of NAREB make their publications available either to the head professor of real estate or to the university librarian upon request. In 1951, it was reported that the National Institute of Real Estate Brokers had a mailing list of 150 universities.[87]

The institutes of NAREB also cooperate with universities and colleges in putting on courses. For example, in 1953, the American Institute of Real Estate Appraisers provided twelve-day demonstration case-study courses at three universities — Stanford University, Northwestern University, and the University of Tennessee — on the subject of appraisal.[88] The teachers were all members of the American Institute of Real Estate Appraisers, and some were university professors and active in real estate appraisal or investment as well. Arthur A. May was one of the teachers at Stanford (see pp. 206–207).

The individual real estate boards also have educational programs, which may include specialized courses on sales techniques, appraisal, management, and other real estate subjects; one- or two-day sales conferences or seminars for practicing real estate men; indoctrination courses for new members; courses or seminars for prospective licensees; weekly, monthly, or semi-annual educational meetings; and occasional luncheon or dinner meetings; courses for employees in Realtor offices; and courses co-sponsored by local colleges or universities. The Chicago Real Estate Board gives its own courses, sponsors programs in real estate in several schools in Chicago, and from time to time sends out a pamphlet stressing the services rendered by it to its members and to real estate men generally.[89]

Some men interested in going into the real estate business take no courses, but study by themselves. When they are given an application for registration by the Department of Registration and Education of Illinois, they also receive a list of books recommended for use in preparation for the real estate broker examination. Five of these are general real estate texts, of which four (by Hoagland, Atkinson, Benson and North, and Weimer and Hoyt) contain elements of the exclusion ideology in their references to the importance of homogeneity and the effect of Negroes on property values and on the neighborhood. Although later, revised editions of the four texts have appeared, the list still recommends the first or earlier editions in which the exclusion ideology is clearly stressed.

The license law for brokers in Illinois, known as the Real Estate Brokers and Salesmen Law, concludes the qualifications of the three-member examining committee as follows: "In designating the Examining Committee, the Director shall give due consideration to recommendations by members and organizations of the profession. . . ." [90] It is obvious that the examining committee is likely to be composed of Realtors, and has been so. It is important to note the interlocking positions of some of the men who have been or are members of the real estate examining committee: in 1948, the chairman of the Illinois Brokers License Examining Committee was a past president of the Chicago Real Estate Board, and in 1953, the chairman of the examining committee was a Realtor and dean of the Central YMCA Real Estate Institute, and the former chairman was teaching both in the Real Estate Institute and in the Pearson School of Real Estate. It is Realtors who, through the written examination, determine what knowledge is necessary to qualify a broker to practice in Illinois. And, as we have seen, it is also they who teach courses in real estate to prepare prospective brokers for the examination.

The aim of NAREB to "secure the installation in educational institutions of courses as recommended by" its educational committee has remained constant over the years (see p. 238). At the annual convention of 1945, a resolution was passed "to establish in a number of universities of our country, schools or colleges of real estate practice and community planning." [91] In the annual convention of 1955, the resolution passed on education exhorted Realtors to make even greater efforts to bring adequate training in real estate into the universities and colleges. [92]

The *unified* nature of the effort to improve — that is, to control — real estate education is apparent in a statement of the chairman of the Real Estate Examining Committee of the Department of Registration and Edu-

244

cation of Illinois. He says, "The Department is working in close cooperation with the University of Illinois Extension Division and the educational
committees of the Illinois Association of Real Estate Boards and the National Association of Real Estate Boards. These organizations have an
established educational policy, are fostering schools and assisting in the
establishment of a curriculum which will meet with the educational requirements of the business." [93]

Through the many and varied lines of communication — from the preparation of a congenial climate for communication to the direct exposition
of the real estate point of view — the institutional ideology has been disseminated over the years among present and prospective real estate men
throughout the country. Through cooperation in courses and conferences
of common interest, the fellowship of informal gatherings, and formal
membership in real estate organizations, teachers of real estate (who may
not themselves be Realtors) and Realtors develop rapport. The real estate
man who has taken courses in real estate has encountered the real estate
ideology in them. The one who takes no courses and reads by himself, encounters it in the books. The one who has neither taken courses nor read
books encounters it in his fellow brokers, if he mingles with them, and in
their actions.

The ideology of the real estate man does not come to him entirely from
the real estate institution, as represented by NAREB. There are the influences of the environment in which he grew up and his own experiences in
the real estate business. There is a broader relation between the real estate board and the society itself. There are primarily the historical events
that gave rise to the conditions of the Negroes, of which the Chicago Real
Estate Board was aware when it took its stand for racial residential segregation in 1917 (see pp. 224–226). There were beliefs about Negroes
among the people of the country at large and among real estate men long
before real estate boards were formed. But in the real estate board, conclusions about Negroes in relation to real estate interests were crystallized
and have been stressed steadily to real estate men. The likeness between
the ideologies of the respondents and those of the institution may not be
the result of a direct influence from NAREB, but rather the result largely
of a steady presentation of the ideas of the institutional ideology by pre-
paratory, intervening, and direct lines of communication before practicing
and prospective real estate men. Through one source or another, the ideas
come to every real estate office and are transmitted to those within the

office in the daily operations. NAREB does not directly ask teachers of real estate to teach its point of view and its ideology, but it tries to bring its ideas before them and to make these ideas acceptable, so that they will be brought to its point of view.

Training

Although it is difficult to assess the relative efficacy of the various channels of communication for the ideology of NAREB and the Chicago Board, it has been possible to distinguish the chief ways the respondents got their ideas about dealing with Negroes. Questions 38 and 38a (see Appendix A) sought to discover how the respondent had learned current practice in transactions with Negroes.

Over half the respondents in each area (20/35 in Area A, 12/22 in Area B, 14/21 in Area C, 4/6 in Area CX, 2/3 of the Area C branch offices) learned mainly from their father or employer. A smaller number (6, 8, 6, 2, 1 in Areas A, B, C, CX, Area C branch offices, respectively) learned mainly from their own experience — from clients, customers, competitors, or community response. Five in Area A and 1 of Area C learned through a related business (bank mortgage department, real estate lawyer's office, maintenance work) before entering the real estate business. A few in Areas A and B learned mainly from friends in the real estate business. One respondent stated that he had learned before entering the business because these ideas are in the mores. (Table 40, Appendix C.)

Somewhat over half of the respondents in each area except CX had not taken any course in real estate. The majority of these were older men who had entered the real estate business when taking courses was not expected. Several of the respondents who had taken courses mentioned McMichael's *Appraising Manual* and several other texts with similar views as helpful. Those in Area A who had taken courses still referred to father or employer as the principal source of learning; for them, the lectures and textbooks probably corroborated the views that they had received from a more intimate source. (Table 40, Appendix C.)

Summary

A real estate ideology and a racial real estate ideology were found which are common to NAREB and the Chicago Real Estate Board. A likeness on essential points was also found between these two ideologies and those of the respondents.

Several sources of evidence were then advanced that point to the influence in part at least of NAREB and the individual board over real estate men. The first is the history of NAREB and of its Code of Ethics, the required acceptance of the Code by member boards, and the required observance of the Code by members. Records of NAREB and of the Chicago Real Estate Board were cited to show that the ideas of NAREB have been stressed over time — the real estate ideology over a period of at least seventy years, and the racial real estate ideology over fifty years. Real estate men could learn about the stands and acts of the boards through reports in newspapers or through the boards' own means of circulating news. The many lines of communication in operation in NAREB's program of education bring its ideas to school departments of real estate and to real estate offices throughout the country indirectly and directly. Through its educational aids, conferences, and courses, NAREB brings teachers and students close to itself and to the local boards. By means of the early and continuing emphasis on the main ideas of the real estate ideology in the books, lectures, and speeches of leading Realtors, there has been created a climate of thought in which real estate men think in their work. It is the real estate outlook.

In the local situation, the ideas of both ideologies pass largely by word of mouth from father to son, from employer to employee, from friend to friend, from competitor to competitor in cooperating sales. This happens at times deliberately, at times quite unwittingly.

In view of the data presented on pp. 220–246, I suggest that likeness between the respondents' ideologies and those of NAREB and the Chicago Real Estate Board arises at least partly from the pervasive influence of NAREB and of the Board. This statement is not meant to deny the possibility of a real estate man's reaching conclusions of his own that are like or unlike the ideologies of the institution, since some respondents do hold a different ideology. However, this study focuses on explaining the *exclusion* of Negroes from white residential areas by real estate brokers; the explanation of the nonrestrictive practices is important, but it would require a study in itself.

MORAL AUTHORITY

The Board's control over the broker is in part an outcome of its prerogative and its services as trade association of the business. This is the professional aspect of its control. The other aspect of its control is the ideological. A number of respondents suggested that the Chicago Board also exercises a moral influence over its members, which on the one hand is part of its professional authority, since from its beginning it has represented the sum of experience in the real estate business and hence could have the knowledge to decide what is right and wrong practice in real estate, and on the other hand is part of its ideological authority, since in its knowledge of the real estate business it has defined the real estate man's function in society and therefore can define his moral obligations. Hence, the "moral authority" of the Board is the recognition by real estate men and the public of the Board's right to determine what real estate men should or should not do in their business practice.

The men who formed the first real estate exchanges were much concerned about matters of ethical standards because of irresponsible men in the business and because of the lack of common standards and practices. Because their livelihood was at stake, competing brokers took it upon themselves to discuss and to agree upon certain standards and to organize first local real estate boards and then a national organization for the more effective control of their business. The representatives who drew up the first Code of Ethics had been empowered by their respective boards to do so. They could therefore take it upon themselves to define right and wrong real estate practice, and this they did through committee work and subsequent discussion and approval. In 1924 a later group of representatives defined the real estate man's role in society at large. Each board as representing the experience of real estate men in its locality had the right to reach conclusions about standards, and then all the boards through the cooperation of their representatives could bring the total experience of real estate men throughout the country to bear upon questions of right and wrong conduct in real estate transactions.[94] The decisions that went into the articles of the Code of Ethics of NAREB rested on the considered judgments of leading real estate men of many years' experience of their own and on the experience which they brought to the table of discussion from the work of the men in their respective boards. It is in this manner that the boards continue to determine fair practice in real estate.

The Code of Ethics is so central to the real estate business that it must be considered as primary in all aspects — professional, ideological, and moral. As the local board and NAREB created the Code, revise it, guard its observance, and proclaim its meaning, the Board was allowed and continues to have the right to interpret the real estate man's work and to define his duty. The Board has these prerogatives because it is the moral authority of the real estate business. The whole ideology of the real estate institution has been slanted by NAREB's committees in the direction of the moral significance of the real estate man's task. According to NAREB, the real estate broker's duty is more essential to the country than the duties of other businessmen; the real estate man must live up to his obligation or he will injure his clients, his profession, and the very country itself. Every trade association determines fair practices in its business, but because NAREB singles out so strongly the real estate man's moral obligation to society, the moral authority of the real estate board assumes a greater importance than the moral authority of other trade associations.

Before real estate boards came into existence, there were enough unscrupulous dealings in the business, owing to numerous opportunities for profit through fraud, to give all real estate men a bad name.[95] The men who formed the first boards struggled to establish uniform standards of conduct in order to get public respect for the real estate man. In later, depression years, confidence in the real estate man fell again. It took time for NAREB and the local boards to build up a good name for real estate men so that people would associate "Realtor" with honesty, reliability, and competence. Since the real estate business has suffered so much from its black sheep, since it has taken years of effort to establish public confidence in the real estate man, and since it appears that confidence is being gradually established, it is a particularly heinous thing in the eyes of the board for a real estate broker to commit any act that tends to destroy this hard-won confidence. Hence, the moral authority of the Real Estate Board entails a greater responsibility than that of other trade associations. The Real Estate Board is the watchdog of *all* real estate men's conduct toward the public and one another in order to protect and to increase public trust in the Realtor. Hence the broker who violates the Code by selling property in a white area to a Negro and who disregards the effect of such a sale on the value of property — the cornerstone of the real estate business — on the life of the property owner, and on the public's opinion of such a real estate man, is indeed looked upon as a traitor to the profession. These ideas underlie the statement made by a number of respondents, "No reputable broker would do it." The fact that Negroes have so much difficulty in buying into a white neighborhood attests to the effectiveness of the moral principle in the Code.

CONTROL OVER BROKERS WHO SELL TO NEGROES IN WHITE AREAS

Question 21 (Appendix A) was set up to find out how the Board looks upon a broker who sells to Negroes in the white area. Half of the member respondents in Areas B, C, and CX, and three fifths of those in Area A stated outright that the Board would disapprove of such a broker. Five Board members in Area A and a few in Areas B and C said that the Board could not take a public stand on this action because it would be against public policy, but that it has taken a private stand against it. These respondents pointed out that it is not illegal for the real estate man to sell to Negroes without restriction. This fact and the decision in 1948 of the United States Supreme Court about restrictive covenants tied the hands of the Board publicly, they said, but members of the Board could, as individuals, register disapproval. A few respondents qualified their statement about the disapproval of the Board by saying that the Board would object to a broker's unrestricted selling if it meant "breaking a neighborhood."

Some nonmembers (3, 3, 3, 1 in Areas A, B, C, CX, respectively) and one Board member spoke with some resentment of the hypocrites on the Board who disapprove of such action openly, but do the same privately; they maintained that there are just as many ethical brokers outside of the Board as in it. The Board member said that the Board "are not in favor of that type of operation," although he was sure that some members "take part in it."

Some members (8, 4, 4, 2 in Areas A, B, C, CX, respectively) stated that the Board has not taken any official position on such action, but that individual members have taken a definite stand against it. These respondents appear to be unaware of the stand which the Chicago Real Estate Board took in 1917 regarding the exclusion of Negroes from white areas in order to protect property values (see pp. 224–226). However, the fact that these respondents spoke of individual members' disapproval gives the impression that they would expect Board members to frown upon unrestricted selling.

A few members, including 2 Area C branch offices, and nonmembers said they could not speak for the Board. The 2 nonmember respondents were expecting to join the Board. The respondents of this category were the most reticent about revealing what they knew of the Board's outlook. Most of the members held a strong exclusion ideology.

A considerable proportion of the nonmembers (5, 4, 5 in Areas A, B,

C, respectively) did not know how the Board looks upon the broker who sells to Negroes in the white area, but almost all of those who gave a definitive answer thought that the Board would be against such action. There were also several members (2, 2, 1 in Areas B, C, CX, respectively) who said they did not know. (Table 41, Appendix C.)

On the whole, the answers of the Board members to Question 21 were circumspect. The members were reticent, much more so than when revealing their own stand on selling property to Negroes in a white area. Their very reticence indicates, it would seem, a recognition of the important position of the Board in relation to their own position, or some feeling of obligation to the Board not to give it away. In either case, such reticence implies a restraint emanating from the Board.

Question 21a (Appendix A) sought to find out what the respondents thought the Board can do to make the broker desist from making sales to Negroes in a white area. The answers to this question corroborated those to Question 21 and supplemented them to a considerable extent. The largest number of respondents in Area A and the largest number of Board members in Areas A, B, and C replied that the Board does not have to exert any influence because the members had this policy before they joined the Board. A smaller number of respondents repeated that the Board cannot exert any influence openly because selling to Negroes in the white area is legal and the Supreme Court's decision of 1948 supports such selling. However, members of the Board can as individuals appeal to the straying broker.

Only a small number of respondents were willing to speak more frankly about the actions and the views of the Board. These were mostly Board officials or members with long experience (other respondents may not have all the information that older members have about the Board). The informative answers fall into two categories: In the first, the main influence the Board can exert is a moral influence, in that its Code of Ethics is the highest standard of conduct for the real estate business; the Board can try to clarify to the broker what his duty is and to persuade him to act for the good of the community and the profession. In the second, the Board can introduce sanctions. (Table 41, Appendix C.) Five answers in the first category are presented below, the first four given by Board members. The fifth respondent sells to Negroes with practically no restriction. The first respondent seems not to distinguish between moral appeal and sanction.

Only by threatening to have you expelled from the Board. Moral influence is the only influence they can bring to bear. It would harm his prestige among brokers, but I doubt it would hurt him in selling. (9B)

I don't know of anything they would do. I think they would use their influence to try to *persuade* them not to make such sales. The Board would say, "You're not supporting the people of your neighborhood." A local office is not like a downtown office. Your business is more on a personal basis, and you know most of your clients personally. You have brought them and their parents into the neighborhood and there is a trust that they have in you. (87CX)

The Board uses moral control. It has no more legal power than any other trade association. But the State of Illinois has control over brokers. There should be more control of this kind. This is handled pretty loosely. However, in the 31 years that I have been in business, there has been a terrific tightening up. This has been brought about by the Real Estate Board. When I got my license, all you had to do was pay $10. Now, there is an examination. It's still pretty loose. It's up to the state. (90A)

Well, as I said before, we had a similar case. The directors of the Board got together and they would have the chairman of the X Committee write him a letter. It all depends on the seriousness of the case. If it is not too serious, we only warn him and bring it to his attention. That's embarrassing enough that the Board knows about it. If it went on, his membership would be taken from him. Actually, we try to keep things on an even keel. We're trying to keep real estate men clear of any wrong practices so that people couldn't go around saying that they're selling to colored just to make money. It's the X Committee which concerns itself regarding violations of the Code of Ethics. (72C; official of a private board not a member of NAREB although its members may be)

The only way they look upon it is this. If there were colored in there, they would never say anything. If it is in a white neighborhood, they wouldn't prefer you to rent. Many times the Board would call and say, "Are you going to rent out to colored?" They wouldn't want you to put colored in there if it is a white neighborhood. Yes, many times an official from the Board, yes, would phone. I would ask around. If there were any a block away, you could. I've did it but not where it is completely white. If there are any a block or even 2 blocks away, I would. I'd rather have a colored tenant. Every time when the neighborhood changes, the better building will turn out to be a colored building. . . . I do know the Board have called several times and asked about tenancy. (78B)

These statements reveal that the Board may take direct but inconspicuous measures to bring erring real estate men into line by appealing to them on moral grounds and by warning them. The Board watches the behavior of nonmembers as well as members and approaches the nonmember when he violates the Code of Ethics. A Board official stated in an interview on October 25, 1957, that the Board keeps an eye on some nonmember brokers who will charge less commission than the established 5 per cent in order to get the business. A former president of the Board told me in a telephone conversation on May 15, 1958, that the Board is concerned about the conduct of nonmembers: "The Board checks over them as much as they can. They have no power, you know, except through a violation of the law. If any nonmember hurts the industry, the Board would take an interest and should take an interest."

A few respondents, several of whom were also Board officials, stated that the Board can introduce certain formal and informal sanctions against the broker who violates the Code. Formal sanctions include denial of membership, suspension, or expulsion. The Board can also recommend to the Department of Registration and Education of Illinois that his license be revoked. However, none of these drastic measures have been invoked against any broker who has sold to a Negro in a white area.

The informal sanctions can include spreading unsavory rumors about him, defaming his character, and harming his business. The Board can also work through or with other agencies, such as a lending agency, to put pressure on the deviant broker.

They can bring him up before the license committee. It's very hard to prove. Very little other than they get a reputation as a louse. If the broker is with a company, a lot of pressure can be brought to bear upon the company by spreading stories showing how that office hurt the neighborhood. They can lose a lot of business and the person is usually fired. I've seen that happen many times. (22B)

I think the Board looks upon those who sell peripheral property to Negroes as being forced to do this. There is no opprobrium attached. The Board would introduce all the sanctions to the broker who engaged in a hedgehopping sale. If he did, there could be no action they could take, but insofar as the Board is the central point of the expression of sanctions — you have to get back to the club idea. It's the personal idea. You can't throw him out for doing a legal act. [What form would the sanctions take?] They might spread gossip about him. They'd spread rumors about the fellow. They'd say he's a negrophile, a red, you couldn't trust him. (34A)

Another form of informal sanction is the epithets that both members and nonmembers use for brokers who break a block and for speculators who pay a high price for a property, put a large Negro family into it, "scare" out the other white owners at depressed prices, and resell to Negroes at high prices. These epithets are: shrewd connivers, crooks, sharpies, scavengers, locusts, a prostitute, jackal, scalpers, fast buck men, buzzards, specie of vermin, and shysters. Several epithets convey the idea that such dealers are like birds of prey.

Despite its restraints, the Board has not kept nonconformists from unrestricted selling. However, such brokers are relatively few, which indicates the high degree of conformity with the Code among both members and nonmembers in the city. A former president of the Board stated that there are very few violations of the Code among members and nonmembers. The conformity of nonmembers is impressive when it is remembered that most real estate brokers are not members of the Board.[96] The former president also called attention to the fact that real estate boards of Chicago which are not members of NAREB accept the Code of the Chicago Real Estate Board, saying "They don't have to follow the Code, but they do." [97] Many of the members of these boards belong to the Board, speakers from the Board go to them, and the relations between them and the Board are good. These boards provide a common meeting ground for Board members and nonmembers and a forum for the ideas and values of the Board.

That Negroes have been moving into white areas in Chicago is an observable fact. Not all the first sales to them are made by brokers, but some are. The question raised here is, How is it that the Chicago Real Estate Board cannot keep certain brokers from making such sales? The reasons for its failure appear to be certain loopholes in its system of control.[98]

The first loophole is that restriction cannot be enforced legally and openly. When a real estate broker sells a property to a Negro in a white area, the Board considers his act a violation of Article 5 of the Code because in their eyes it introduces a use detrimental to property values in that area. Ordinarily, the Board can take a broker to task for violating an article of its Code. If there is an act of misrepresentation or fraud, he can be brought before its Reference and Arbitration Committee and also before the Department of Registration and Education of Illinois, because such an act would violate both the Code of Ethics of the Board and the Illinois Real Estate Brokers and Salesmen Law. Difficulty arises, however, when the violation of Article 5 has particular reference to selling property in the white area to Negroes, because, although the belief that introducing Negroes lowers property values is shared by real estate men and the act indirectly barred by the Code, racial restrictions do not enter into the Illinois

Real Estate Brokers and Salesmen Law. "The protection of property values cannot be legislated," a past president of the Illinois Association of Real Estate Boards said in a telephone conversation on February 6, 1958. It is not illegal for a broker to sell to Negroes in a white area or block, and this fact is the first loophole in the system of control of the Board. The most the Board can do is to expel the broker if he is a member, but usually he is not and cannot be controlled by formal sanctions.

A second loophole in the Board's control is the financial rewards of deviant operations. The attractive opportunities for moneymaking by unrestricted sales to Negroes are beyond control and outweigh appeals by the Board to the broker to consider the welfare of the community and the good name of real estate men if the deviant broker has a different point of view.

A third loophole lies in the deviant broker's manner of operation — he is mobile, has unusual clients, and does not depend on one community, other brokers, or the conventional lending agencies. When the Board tries to appeal to the deviant nonmember broker on ideological-moral grounds or to introduce informal sanctions against him, it encounters difficulties. It cannot easily reach him through regular financing channels because such brokers often have sources for large loans by under-the-table operations. Only one of the few deviant respondents mentioned pressure on him from lending and insurance agencies, a community organization, and city departments to desist from making first sales to Negroes. The pressure did make him a bit more wary, although he said that he still does make such sales (see pp. 162–164). The brokers who participate in unrestricted selling are not usually dependent on any one area but move from one to another, anticipating the movement of the Negro population. They work an area that Negroes have entered until there is little left there to sell profitably and then move on to another area. Furthermore, they are not dealing with ordinary clients but often with white owners in a hurry to sell who may want to sell clandestinely when the sale is being made to a Negro and there are not yet any in the block. Members of the Board would hardly be able to influence such clients against dealing with deviant brokers, if they tried to do so; such sellers need the deviant broker, since the conforming real estate man will not start selling to Negroes until there are some in the block.

The deviant broker usually does not live in any of the areas where he is making unrestricted sales. Hence, he depends neither on the real estate men in the area nor on its residents, except for owners who require his services.

The only ones that sell for breaking into districts to people not desired by the community are usually fly-by-nights who are not established, with no roots in the living standards of any society as a whole — who have no background, no business standards, who don't belong to civic, fraternal or other type of organization. They operate almost like a crook. (65C)

They're like scavengers. They are out strictly for their own personal gain regardless of whom they hurt. They come from outside. They are strangers to the community. They would be ashamed to do this in their own community, to pull these tricks. It's very common. (90A)

There are about 15 or 20 white brokers that specialize in doing just that, being first. They have no responsibility. A lot of brokers are not in an office. They operate out of "their pocket" or "their hat," as we call it. They specialize in being first. There is always a buck to be made in being first. By first I mean first, second, third, fourth, or fifth when the police have to be there. They live North or East near the lake. They're in a position where they can't be touched. Many offices on the South Side have been threatened and windows broken. Some operate in conjunction with Negro offices, in going out, getting a listing and selling it to Negro offices, telling the people they have a white buyer or he buys it himself. He takes his wife along and says he's buying a home for himself. Then 2 weeks later he sold to a Negro buyer and he makes $3,000. (22B)

Many other respondents stated that the deviant broker and speculator are strangers to the communities in which they operate and have no feeling of responsibility toward them. Several deviant respondents said they would not sell to Negroes in the community where they are living. Hence, there would be hardly any way in which the Board could reach the deviant broker through his home community.

Even if the Board can approach the deviant broker, it must do so covertly. The fourth loophole is the discrepancy between the judgment of NAREB on unrestricted selling and the judgment which would be in accord with the official American democratic stand on questions of race. Real estate men as an organized group look upon the selling of property to a Negro in a white area as a harmful act with reference to the white people in the area, an unethical act in regard to the real estate man's duty to his clients, and an act of disloyalty toward other brokers and the profession in that he destroys public confidence in the real estate man. But in the light of national policy regarding the status of Negroes as American citizens, unrestricted selling conforms with democratic principles and the law. It is an act of "nondiscrimination," whereas deliberately refusing to sell property to Negroes in the white area or block is an act of "discrimination" — that is, unequal treatment.

There has been a growing emphasis in this country on full equality for Negro citizens and on the elimination of restrictive practices from every area of living, owing largely to the events of World War II, the increased employment opportunities for Negroes, the elimination of segregation in the armed forces, the telling political power of Negroes in many states and cities, the growing influence of the NAACP and its white allies, the internal and international political situation, and the efforts of intergroup relations agencies to improve the lot of the Negro group and other minority groups. This goal has received reinforcement and a label of correctness from recent Supreme Court decisions, particularly the ones on the unenforceability of restrictive covenants and the inequality inherent in the doctrine of separate but equal public education. The protests in various parts of the world against racial discrimination in the United States have also helped put restrictive action in a bad light. Thus, for the Board to condemn a man openly for selling property to a Negro would be against public policy and undemocratic, as some respondents said themselves. The Board could hardly punish a broker publicly for acting without racial discrimination, and it therefore has to introduce indirect pressure so that the democratic creed will not appear to have been violated.

This fourth and main loophole has two aspects. First, there is the discrepancy between, on one hand, the national ideology with its democratic principles and its emphasis on equal opportunity, equal legal protection, and equal rights for all, and, on the other hand, the real estate ideology with its primary emphasis on the right of private property ownership and the importance of protecting property value. In the real estate ideology, the right to own property is looked upon as the fundamental, basic right upon which all other rights depend, whereas in the national ideology there is no such hierarchy distinctly formulated among the rights (see pp. 193 and 284). Secondly, the official point of view concerning the rights of Negroes to purchase real property as revealed in the Supreme Court decision of 1948 is opposed by many white people in American cities generally, and in Chicago in particular, when applied to selling property to Negroes in their own neighborhoods. Gunnar Myrdal even sees the Negro problem as a moral dilemma for white people; in several of the respondents, such a dilemma appeared to be present.[99]

There is evidence that many white people do not want Negroes as neighbors, the most weighty of which is the actual movement of white people from areas which Negroes have entered. Most respondents' statements about white people's beliefs, wishes, and feelings about Negroes reveal white people's unfavorable conception of Negroes and their unwillingness to have Negroes as neighbors. Two studies made in Chicago [100] corroborate such attitudes and actions on the part of white people. In the Duncans' study, racial residential succession in Chicago was found to occur rather constantly over the ten-year period of 1940–1950. It seems true that there is a discrepancy between the national ideology as it pertains to race relations and the actual beliefs and feelings of many white people that underlie their reactions to Negroes' choices of residence.

An apparent contradiction within the national ideology itself lies in a conflict between a citizen's right to equal opportunity in residence and an owner's right to dispose of his property as he wishes (see pp. 283–287). This problem also enters into the fourth loophole in the system of control of the Board.

The situation of race relations in the country at large and national policy concerning such relations provide the deviant broker with an opportunity to make high profits and to violate with impunity the Code of Ethics of NAREB and the Chicago Board. The hands of the Board are tied: it can neither control his profitable prices and commissions nor easily hinder him in his transactions nor publicly condemn him. Whatever it tries to do must be undercover. The study indicates that there is a discrepancy between the outlooks, with reference to race relations, of two social systems — that of the total social system, that is, of the society as a whole as expressed in public pronouncements at the government level, and that of a system within it, that is, the real estate group as represented by NAREB and in Chicago by the Chicago Real Estate Board. There appears to be a conflict of ideas and of values between the subsystem and the total system, and the broker who is deviant in the Board's view is correct in the view of official national policy. This discrepancy is suggested as the main loophole in the system of social control of the Chicago Real Estate Board.

Importance of Ideological Control

The primary influence which the Board exercises over member and nonmember, according to the data of this study, is the ideological — the more important partly because it is subtle. The respondents seem unaware that their real estate thought has been fashioned in part at least in the mold of real estate thought as expressed by NAREB and the Chicago Board. The respondents whose views differ from the traditional ones are aware of this difference in thinking and do not look upon themselves as belonging to the fraternity of real estate men, whereas the respondents who hold the traditional views, whether they are members of the Board or not, see themselves as being a part of the body of real estate men. The respondents are not aware of the influence which the Board has through far-reaching channels and over many years exercised over them and their predecessors in the business. The likeness between most respondents' ideologies and the institutional ideologies points to the conclusion that in part at least the system of communication from the Board and NAREB to members and nonmembers has been effective enough to result in most respondents' holding the essential points of the ideologies; very few respondents violate the Code openly or at all by selling or renting to Negroes in a white area or block. (See Tables 42 and 43.)

It may be thought that too great an influence on real estate men has been attributed to the Board and NAREB and that a greater stress should be put upon the social environment, where similar beliefs may prevail. From its early days American society has emphasized individual enterprise, the right to own property, and a minimum of government intervention, as Williams has summarized it.[101] These values at least are common to the ideologies of the nation and of NAREB, and there has possibly been a circular influence between the greater society and NAREB with its member boards with regard to these values. However, it is important to note the fact that NAREB and the Chicago Board have carried and do carry on a definite program whereby the real estate ideology and the racial real estate ideology are steadily brought to the attention of people in or entering the real estate business. There has been a racial ideology taught both in the South[102] and in the North, but NAREB incorporated its racial real estate ideology within its very Code of Ethics, making the introduction of Negroes into a white neighborhood *an unethical act*. (See pp. 235–236).

NAREB and the individual boards are not imposing from above a point of view foreign to real estate men. The Code of Ethics represents the collective experience of many real estate men throughout the country and their judgment on essential points in the business, including the question of unrestricted selling to Negroes and its relation to the stability of property values. In its position of representative of and authority on the real estate business, the Board acts (1) to formulate this judgment as a moral imperative under a collective sanction, (2) to make known to real estate men the importance of protecting property values, and (3) to watch over their business conduct as far as it can to see that its judgment is observed. The conformity in thought and practice with the Board's judgments that appears to be present among most respondents in each area, member and nonmember, is impressive.

When the respondents, except the few deviant brokers, were asked why they would not sell or rent to Negroes in a white area, few mentioned the Board or the Code of Ethics, but most answers revealed a group of ideas and beliefs in keeping with those of the Board and a conformity with the Code which was to the respondent a matter of doing what he himself thought right and proper. The fact that the American national ideology contains the democratic creed whereas Article 5 of the Code runs counter to the creed and the fact that most respondents observe Article 5 although they know that it is against official public policy reveal the completeness of the internalization of the Code of Ethics.

There is another reason for the Board's ideological control's being more important than its professional control involving positive and negative sanctions. The second kind is a *moral* control implanted in the minds of real estate men. Emile Durkheim stressed this kind as basic to social life. Parsons supports Durkheim in his view that the primary source of constraint lies in the moral authority of a system of rules and the citizen's internalization of and attachment to those rules. Sanctions form a secondary mode of enforcement of the rules, because the sanctions depend themselves on moral authority for their enforcement.[103] The primary source of social control is, then, the attachment of citizens to their rules because they have internalized them, have grown up to consider them as right, and observe them voluntarily out of a sense of moral obligation.

In the interviews, respondents of long experience maintained that the chief strength of the Board's control lies in its moral influence — that is, in the degree to which its rules are observed by its members from motives of moral obligation. Even those whose observation of the rules is only lip service recognize proper real estate practice — no selling to Negroes in a white area — in their very concealment of deviant action. There is no contradiction between respondents' statements about the moral influence of the Board and their answers that reveal that (1) most respondents will not be the first to sell or rent to a Negro in a white neighborhood or block, in keeping with Article 5, and (2) most respondents in each area advanced primary reasons of moral principle for not doing so. Thus, the data of the interviews point to the conclusion that the Board exercises a moral-ideological influence.

A number of the respondents would not make a first sale or rental out of varying degrees of self-interest, but in most cases the primary motive was a moral one. There are respondents who conform primarily because of the advantage of obedience and the disadvantages of disobedience. And lastly, there are those who do not conform to Article 5 partly because of monetary interest and partly because of ideas different from those of the institution. For the majority of the respondents, however, the Code of Ethics is their own standard of conduct (although not necessarily mentioned by them) and is elaborated and explained by them beyond its official formulation. A number of the respondents introduced ideas of their own, but the moral justification for the exclusion of Negroes from white areas is present in the majority of the interviews in each area.

The reciprocal relation between Board and members could be said to pave the way for internalization of institutional values, although the internalization does not depend on this relation and may take place without it. However, the better the reciprocal relation is, the better the situation for internalization, and conversely, the more internalization, the more support the members give to the institution and the less the purely instrumental character of the institution. For the member in whom the internalization is complete or fairly so, the reciprocal relation gives way to identification with the Board. He feels himself to be a part of it, and there is no longer an interlocking of interests alone. For some members, the Board will remain on the lower level of an instrument for immediate and for personal advantages. However, "interest" is not to be understood too narrowly, for it includes enjoying fellowship with other men in the same occupation. It could be said that the reciprocal relation and the internalization of institutional values are complementary, although without the internalization, the reciprocal relation would be tenuous at best.

It appears, on the basis of the data of the study, that the Chicago Real Estate Board in its Code of Ethics, in its various activities as trade association, in its program of education, and in its watchfulness over the business conduct of member and nonmember, has contributed and is contributing in large measure to the exclusion ideology, policy, and practice of the majority of the respondents. This finding is significant in two respects: it confirms empirically the role of institutions in socializing their members and the Board's socialization process also affects nonmembers (a large proportion of whom, particularly those in Areas A and C, hold ideologies essentially similar to those of the Board). From whatever source they have received the institutional ideologies, the nonmembers have internalized them. They think with the real estate group and feel themselves to be a part of it. It is recognized that most people who grow up in the cities of the United States and enter the real estate business will have some ideas about Negroes and real estate before they enter the business, and it is true also that their own experience in the business will contribute to these ideas, but the fact that a large number of nonmember respondents hold the institutional ideologies indicates that the Board's influence has reached them indirectly.

The Relation of Ideology and of Other Factors to Practice

STATISTICAL tests revealed it highly improbable that the relation between the exclusion ideology and the practice of exclusion has arisen from chance,[1] and it seems reasonable to conclude that there is a relation of dependence between the two. The first eight of the ten components discussed in Chapters IV and V were selected as the racial real estate ideology proper because these eight express the broker's own convictions about what is right racial policy for the world around him. It was then decided that if five out of the eight were unfavorable to Negroes, a respondent's ideology would be considered an exclusion ideology (pp. 142–143).[2]

The further analysis of the relation between ideology and practice involves two parts: Ordering of Main Reasons for Practice and Typology of Real Estate Men.

ORDERING OF MAIN REASONS FOR PRACTICE

The ordering of respondents' main reasons for the practice of exclusion will indicate differences in emphasis; main reasons for practice other than exclusion will be dealt with separately. Question 16, the crucial question on whether the respondent would sell or rent property to a Negro in the white area, was followed by a question (see Appendix A) to elicit his reasons for his yes or no answer to Question 16. Toward the end of the interview, two more questions, 34a and 35, were set up to act as checks on the respondent's first answer about his reasons. It was expected that the respondent, if he had been reserved in his answers to earlier questions, would be encouraged in his answer to Question 35 to state his own reason without having to admit that it was his own. Some respondents' answers only reinforced the earlier answers, whereas other respondents gave restrained answers about reasons to Question 16d and freer answers to Questions 34a and 35, in which deeper values and wishes were revealed. Or some respondents came out strongly, spontaneously, and bluntly in their answers to the early question, but by the time they reached the later questions, they seemed to withdraw a bit, as if they thought they had revealed too much already. Sometimes reasons of status or business were given in the first answer and reasons of moral principle in the last, and vice versa. Those respondents who gave business reasons first disclosed their personal sentiments and their principles and ideas concerning consequences to others only after probing — perhaps they judged their true reasons undemocratic and business reasons safe.

Many respondents offered several reasons for their policy and practice with respect to restriction or the lack of it. For each respondent, the answers to all other questions were examined for statements bearing on such reasons. The following criteria were used to determine the principal reason if a respondent offered more than one category of reason: (1) amount of attention devoted to the reason (number of sentences and amount of repetition); (2) vocabulary used for the reasons; (3) observable feeling accompaniment (deprecatory gestures, grimaces, anger or other emotion in tone of voice, noises of disgust or other feeling); and (4) the consistency of the total interview.

The respondents in each area could be ranged along a five-point continuum with those stressing moral or other ideological reasons at one end, and those stressing business reasons at the other; between these extremes were combinations of reasons — ideological beliefs, status and/or business, and physical danger — in which combinations the main emphasis shifts from ideological principle to status reason to business reason as one moves along the continuum. At the middle of the continuum (point 3), ideological principles and status or business reasons received equal stress.

The percentage of respondents who gave entirely or mainly ideological principles as the reasons for not selling to Negroes in a white area is 72 in Area A (23/32), 55 in Area B (11/20), 70 in Area C (14/20), and 83 in Area CX (5/6). Thus, most respondents placed *sole* or *primary* stress on ideological reasons for not being willing to make a "first" sale to a Negro in a white area. (Table 45, Appendix C.) Ideological reasons were, in most interviews, of a moral character and largely of ideological principles of real estate, but religious, political, and other principles were also present. A number of respondents advanced several reasons of ideological nature; of these, 6 of Area A, 6 of Area C, 2 of Area CX, and 1 Area C branch office also revealed strong identification with the community of their present or former residence or of their business operation for many years, and expressed their concern about preserving the neighborhood and keeping it white (this was one of their reasons for not introducing Negroes into the area or block). A number of this entire group had lost "a lot of sales" because they did not "open up an area." On the basis of the respondents' *own* answers, it seems indicated that reasons of ideological principle lead to their practice of exclusion for the majority in each area, although the percentage is less in Area B than in the other areas.

The 7 respondents who stated they would sell freely to Negroes gave ideological reasons less often than those who sell with restriction. Of these 7 (Area A, 4; Area B, 3), 1 of Area B stressed ideological reasons solely, 2 stressed such reasons primarily, and 4 stressed other reasons equally or primarily.

The exclusion ideologies in which moral, ideological principle is the main reason and in which consequences are not even discussed are the most complete. These ideologies contain the most ideas, the fullest development of their meaning, and the most systematic exposition of the relation between them and the practice of exclusion. At the other end of the continuum, the ideologies are, on the whole, less well thought out, there are fewer ideas, and statements show the least abstractness of thought.

TYPOLOGY OF REAL ESTATE MEN

The second step to clarify the relation of ideology and other factors to practice is arranging the respondents in paradigm form in a manner similar to Merton's classification of discriminators.[3] Two almost pure types and two mixed types (with subtypes) were distinguished among the real estate brokers: (1) consistent, wholehearted exclusionists, (2) inconsistent, halfhearted exclusionists, (3) inconsistent, halfhearted integrationists, and (4) consistent, wholehearted integrationists. The noun in each type's name ("exclusionist," "integrationist") refers to *practice*. These four types are distributed as follows: Area A, 22, 11, 1, 3; Area B, 10, 8, 1, 4; Area C, 19, 2, 0, 0; Area CX, 2, 3, 1, 0; Area C branch offices, 3, 0, 0, 0. The typology is based on the presence or absence of conflict between ideology and other factors with reference to racial policy and is designed to disclose as far as possible the dominance of any one factor in relation to the racial practice of the respondent. In the ordering of main reasons (pp. 263–265), distinctions of emphasis appear between inner principles involved in the consideration of consequences to others of unrestricted selling and fear of consequences to the broker himself from outer situational elements. Now these distinctions will be brought into sharper focus to reveal conflict, if any, among factors, the dominance of any one factor, where possible, and conflict within ideology (although this conflict does not affect the final relation between ideology and practice in any crucial way). (Table 46, Appendix C.)

The consistent, wholehearted exclusionists have held the exclusion ideology in its more extreme forms and have practiced exclusion of Negroes from white areas from the beginning of their business. The Real Estate Board, the lending agency, and the community — clients, fellow brokers, friends, neighborhood institutions and organizations, and other community aspects — reinforce his stand with their approval and support of his exclusion practice. There is no conflict between his ideology and any other factor, except financial gain from deviant behavior which he says he will forego. The consistent exclusionists can be divided into three subtypes — moral-minded, status-minded, and business-minded exclusionists.

The moral-minded exclusionists have a strong sense of moral obligation not to introduce a Negro family into a white area or block, for the sake of both the neighbors and the community. They are much concerned about the harmful consequences to others resulting from such an action. They do not doubt that they are doing the right thing — they would rather lose sales than make money by hurting people. Moral obligation wins out over any other consideration. For these respondents, ideology is dominant. The majority of the consistent exclusionist type fall into this first subtype (Area A, 17/22; Area B, 5/10; Area C, 13/19; Area CX, 1/2; Area C branch offices, 2/3).

The status-minded exclusionists are concerned either equally with inner principles and status consideration or else primarily with status considerations — their standing in the community, the esteem of clients, fellow brokers, and friends, public opinion. Moral considerations are present, but these men want equally or mainly to maintain their reputation, not to endanger their good name, not to antagonize people, to keep the community's goodwill, cooperation, confidence, and respect, and to avoid physical danger.

The business-minded exclusionists stress such reasons as keeping mortgage sources open. Although they mention ethical or status reasons, the business reasons are foremost.

All consistent exclusionists appear at peace with themselves, and their thought and action are consistent. Some even said that they are unwilling to deal with Negroes or to see them enter white areas. But all have a conflict between their exclusion ideology and the possible financial gain from deviant behavior. However, among the moral-minded, the conflict is solely or principally between ideology and sources of gain in deviant behavior, one of the important "outer" factors. Among the status-minded, the conflict is between ideology/community pressure and possible gain from deviant behavior, or between community pressure mainly and such gain. Among the business-minded, the conflict is between business pressures such as losing mortgage sources, insurance business, listings, and so forth, with other types of reasons and gain from deviant behavior. In the second and third subtypes, the conflict is among outer, situational factors, as well as between ideology and the outer factor of gain from deviant behavior. In the first subtype, the conflict is resolved by the dominance of the ideology over the outer factor of sources of gain in deviant behavior. In the second subtype, status considerations mainly or equally with ideological principles are dominant over such sources of gain. In the third subtype, business considerations of long-term or large-scale significance are dominant over immediate sources of gain in deviant behavior. In the second and third subtypes, the conflict is resolved by the dominance of one outer factor principally, or in conjunction with ideology, over another outer factor. Among the respondents of the first main type, there seems to be no conflict within their thinking itself on the exclusion of Negroes from white areas. They are the consistent, wholehearted exclusionists.

The inconsistent, halfhearted exclusionists can also be divided into three subtypes — the sympathetic, the expedient, and a combination of both. Respondents in this group mostly hold the moderate exclusion ideology or the intermediate ideology. They have a better opinion of Negroes generally and are more sympathetic to them than consistent exclusionists, although many of the latter appreciate certain Negroes and evince some concern about problems that Negroes have to face.

The sympathetic exclusionists realize well the conditions with which Negroes have to struggle and would like to see them get a fair deal, but they also sympathize with white people and understand their suffering when

Negroes enter their neighborhood. They have decided that their duty lies in not harming the white people, and out of moral principle, they adhere more or less strictly to a policy and practice of exclusion. Three respondents in Area A will consider selling or renting to a Negro even "in an advanced position" if they think the neighbors will accept him. Others say the shortage in housing for Negroes is over and they do not need to break into new areas. Several in each area pointed out that exclusion is safest for the Negro family as well and spares it embarrassment or danger.

For respondents of the sympathetic group, there appears to be no conflict between ideology and external factors, but there is conflict *within* their ideology in two forms: First, out of sympathy for Negroes and understanding of them, the respondent does not wish to restrict their movement in their attempt to improve their living conditions, but for the sake of the white people and the safety of the Negro family, he thinks he should restrict sales. Second, he disapproves of racial residential segregation and may favor integration, but he believes it impossible or undesirable at present. These respondents resolve their conflict by adhering to the ideology and practice of exclusion, but their action is not entirely consistent with their outlook. They are not quite at peace with themselves. What they are doing is not fully satisfactory in their eyes, but for the time being they see no other way. Their heart is not in their exclusion practice, but they think it is the best thing as long as white people think and feel as they do. These respondents are like the moral-minded consistent exclusionists in that moral principles are the sole or principal reason for their exclusion practice. Ideology is dominant for both.

The expedient group of the inconsistent exclusionists also hold the mildest exclusion ideology or the intermediate ideology. They adhere to the practice of exclusion partly or principally for status reasons, but in most cases they are ready to sell to Negroes after the first house in a block has been sold to one. These respondents are not opposed to integration, but they do not want to go against the wishes of the white people and to antagonize them, to be censured by the community, to have the prestige of the community hurt, or to be attacked physically. There is a direct conflict between inner convictions and outer factors (specifically, community pressures), but their need of community approval is greater than the strength of their liberal views. At times they speak of doing the right thing by the community, but status considerations are dominant. For the sake of expediency mostly they maintain a policy and practice of exclusion.

Ideology and Practice

A third subtype among the inconsistent exclusionists combines the characteristics of the first and second. These respondents sympathize with the Negro and largely favor integration, but at the same time they recognize that white people are opposed to having Negroes enter their neighborhoods and get upset over this prospect, and that the people in a neighborhood have certain rights regarding who should enter it. They do not want to go against white people's wishes, to lose status with their clients or to be ostracized, to cause riots or civil disturbances, or to endanger the Negro family and themselves. In their case, there is a double conflict: one within their ideology in that they are concerned over the welfare of Negroes and over unfairness to them, but they are also aware of unfairness to white people and their suffering when Negroes enter their neighborhood; and a second conflict between their ideological approval of integration and the outer factor of community pressure. However, unfairness to the white community, fear of loss of status and business, and fear of physical danger take precedence. Among these respondents, ideology is dominant for some, and considerations of status, business, or physical danger are dominant for others.

A third type of real estate man distinguished among the respondents is the inconsistent, halfhearted "integrationist." The respondents in this category are *not* integrationists in the full sense of the word, but their selling or renting property to a Negro in a white area or block leads to the situation necessary for the coming about of integration. They are uninterested in racial residential integration, or do not think it can happen, or do not want it to happen. Only in the sense of helping unwillingly or unwittingly to bring about integration are these respondents integrationists. Two distinct subtypes appear, both quite small — the sympathetic and the expedient integrationists.

The sympathetic integrationist holds the qualified exclusion ideology but is not particularly sympathetic toward Negroes. He sympathizes with the white owner who has to sell and finds it difficult to do so at a proper cash price when Negroes are approaching or entering his neighborhood, and he sympathizes with white owners who feel forced to sell as soon as a Negro has moved into their block. He frowns on selling to Negroes in a white area or block and avoids it if he can, but under extenuating circumstances, where a Negro is the only buyer, he will make such a sale. He will also manage property and rent apartments to Negroes if there are vacant apartments and no white, properly qualified tenants can be had, even

269

though the apartment house is in a white block. There is a conflict within his ideology: He believes that white owners resent being crowded out of their own neighborhoods by Negroes and that racial residential integration is unlikely to come for some time, and should not be forced. Yet, he thinks he should help where the need is greatest, and judges that the desperate seller is the one to be considered. He is satisfying a humanitarian principle, but he is not acting consistently with the exclusion ideology that he has clearly and strongly expressed. He is helping to bring about the very situation which he says emphatically should not be forced. He does not seem to encounter opposition from the other factors bearing on his situation, and he does not admit profit as a motive for his deviant action. To some extent he resembles the sympathetic exclusionists, since they also have an ideological conflict.

The expedient integrationist holds an exclusion ideology, but sells almost without restriction because of the profit. And he admits it! He is "the hungry wolf" type of real estate man who is concerned about his own pocket and little else. He is helping to bring about integration, but he himself either does not want it or does not think it possible. He believes that white people do not want to live near Negroes and will keep moving away from them; he maintains that white people have a right to choose their neighbors (but advises them to move because "this particular area is going anyway"); he says that property values go down when Negroes enter an area (but does not associate this decline with his own action). At the same time, he is unconcerned about the effect of his unrestricted sales on the people of the neighborhood where he is operating for the time being. He is not eager to deal with Negroes and has a bad opinion of most of them, but he wants to get in on the ground floor with them because he expects them to be a good source of profit for some time to come. He does refrain from hedge-hopping sales * and keeps within a block or two in advanced selling, but he is still acting inconsistently with his ideology. He encounters some opposition from the community, but generally evades restraint from the real estate group or other groups or individuals. Still, he has a little concern about reputation. In his case, the conflict is between his exclusion ideology and the factor of gain in deviant behavior, and his interest in monetary gain is an easy winner over ideology.

* To make hedge-hopping sales is the same as to spot — that is, to sell a house to a Negro in a block in a white area and then to skip several blocks and again sell a house to a Negro.

The consistent, wholehearted integrationists are genuine integrationists. These brokers hold the intermediate or the integration ideology and sell or rent to Negroes wherever they can afford to buy or rent, on the whole. They are as willing to deal with Negroes as with white people. They recognize the differences among Negroes, give each his due, and have a friendly approach toward them. They think that racial residential integration is good, that it already exists in certain areas, and that they are doing the "right thing" in selling and renting freely to Negroes. They see no particular harm to white people from such action and take the view that white people will become accustomed to interracial living. There is little or no conflict within their ideology, and they manage to keep pressures from without from weighing too heavily upon their minds or their actions. They see no community turmoil as an outcome of their unrestrictive practice, and they are doing good business. Most important, they are at peace with themselves. Among these respondents, ideology is dominant with some and profit is uppermost with others, or both are equally important.

CHANGES IN IDEOLOGY AND PRACTICE

Respondents revealed certain changes in racial real estate ideology or practice, one aspect of which supports the hypothesis that ideology contributes to policy and practice. The changes to be considered here are largely those which took place in the respondent's views about race or his practice *after* he began to deal with Negroes. Changes were stated directly in answer to Question 37 (see Appendix A) and were also revealed in other answers. In the analysis of these changes, attention was given to type of change and the factors to which the change was due.

Slightly over half the respondents in Areas A and C and over two thirds of those in Area B underwent no change in ideology or practice.[4] Of those whose ideology changed, two thirds or more (Area A, 10/23, Area B, 4/6, Area C, 6/9) became more favorable toward Negroes. Of those whose practice changed, 6 out of 10 in Area A and 2 out of 3 in Area C reported more dealing with Negroes, and 3 of the 6 in Area A reported less strict practices. In Area CX, 5 out of 6, the largest proportion in any of the areas, changed in ideology and practice, and 4 out of 5 changed favorably. (Table 47, Appendix C.)

The ideological changes favorable to Negroes had to do with learning their ways of thinking and habits and distinguishing differences among them in education, cultural attainment, occupational level, economic

271

standing, and social standards. After getting to know Negroes better, a respondent often learned that they and white people are "pretty much alike" and that there are many Negro people worthy of respect and admiration. However, although some respondents had attained more favorable views of Negroes, their reasons for not selling freely to Negroes in a white area or block stood — that is, effects of unrestricted selling, ideological principles, and consequences for themselves. In short, their beliefs about the consequences of unrestricted dealing were not altered by their new knowledge of Negroes or by more favorable ideas of them.

Those few respondents who became less favorable toward Negroes as a result of their experience (Area A, 3, Area B, 2, Area C, 3, Area CX, 1) spoke of Negroes' aggressiveness and arrogance and of their demands for rights they have not earned by responsible behavior.

Favorable changes in practice included withdrawal of the security deposit as Negro tenants proved reliable in rent payment and care of property, more dealings with Negro clients and customers, and willingness to sell or rent to them in "transition" areas (see p. 108) rather than solely in largely Negro districts.[5] Unfavorable changes in practice included fewer dealings and setting up of certain restrictions in payment of deposits for apartments or in making appointments. In no cases did ideology and practice change in opposite directions.

For most respondents who reported change in ideology, such change was due largely to more experience with Negroes and to observation of Negroes' advances in many fields. They spoke also of changes in governmental housing policies and changes in the world at large — in particular, the struggles for freedom in Asia and Africa. One spoke of a change in his thinking on segregation after getting acquainted with students from all over the world at college. Some spoke of the Charter of the United Nations, and some referred to the Supreme Court decision on restrictive covenants and "separate but equal" schools. Following the lead of the federal government, these respondents resigned themselves to dealing with Negroes; they accepted Negroes as citizens, but not as neighbors. Most respondents' ideological changes were relatively small.

Changes in practice came from business experience with Negroes, business pressures, and the Supreme Court decisions. For five respondents in Areas A and B, change in practice preceded change in ideology. Four of them did not wish to sell or rent to Negroes in their own area or even to deal with Negroes, but since Negroes were moving in, business was needed, and the Supreme Court decisions were in the Negroes' favor, these brokers began to deal with them. In time, their ideology changed from rejection of Negroes to recognition of their rights.

Two points stand out: over half the respondents in Areas A, B, and C showed no change in ideology or practice, and favorable changes in ideology were accompanied by some favorable changes in practice, but did not affect the practice of exclusion. Such changes in ideology did not weaken the close link between the respondent's main exclusionist beliefs and his practice of exclusion, nor did they drive any wedge between the ideology and practice of exclusion. The respondent's practice of excluding Negroes from white areas remained the same.

IDEOLOGY AS A DETERMINANT OF RACIAL PRACTICE

Primarily, ideology enters into the determination of racial practice [6] by supplying the beliefs on the basis of which the respondent judges his actions toward Negroes. In the light of the exclusion ideology, first sales are directly and simply reprehensible, provided that the respondent has internalized these beliefs — and the ordering of respondents' main reasons for their actions (see pp. 263–265) indicates that the majority in each area have done so.

However, the ideology proper also underlies component 9, the respondent's beliefs about consequences to himself of unrestricted dealing and particularly beliefs about community pressures. Integrationists do not fear consequences to themselves, but the exclusionists fear the resentment of white people and harm to themselves if they make first sales — such consequences are predicated, at least partly, on the basis of their ideology.

Ideology is also related to racial practice with reference to the *total role* of the real estate man. All the respondents want primarily to make a good living, but they want to do so in a way that satisfies clients, benefits the community, and is honest and ethical according to the Code. The real estate ideology, including its racial aspect, and the Code of Ethics set out how a real estate man is to perform his task *vis-à-vis* client, fellow broker, and the public with reference to transactions and the protection of property values in a neighborhood. The situation in a white area which Negroes are approaching and may enter and the effect which Negroes will have if they enter is defined in the ideology and the Code, indirectly if not directly, in such a way that the broker would be violating his duty to protect property values if he sold a property to a Negro in a white area.

Thus, if he has internalized the principles of the real estate ideology and the injunctions of the Code, the real estate man cannot sell property to a Negro in a white area or block and reach his total goal of making a satisfactory living and having the respect of his clients and colleagues. The determining effect of ideology upon racial practice appears in the respondents' acceptance of the definitions supplied by the institutional ideology: the internalization of real estate tenets underlies their belief about consequences of unrestricted selling both to others and to themselves. It is possible — and they may believe — that their idea of consequences has arisen directly from experience. However, the real estate body itself puts a stamp of improper behavior upon unrestricted selling that can hardly fail to reach any real estate man who has had the experience of acquiring a license and has carried on a real estate business.

It is not possible to "prove," as in an experiment in physics or chemistry, that ideology enters into the determination of racial policy and practice; it is possible only to point to certain evidence supporting this conclusion. The evidence suggests that ideology, particularly the exclusion ideology, is a determining factor and, it appears, of first importance for most respondents, though to a greater extent in Areas A, C, and CX than in Area B. At the very least, it can be said that the exclusion ideology accompanies the exclusion policy and practice of the majority of the respondents in each area.

FINDINGS

The main findings of the study for the respondents' practices and ideology are: Most respondents deal with Negroes in sales and/or management but will not sell or rent to them in a wholly white area or block. They will sell or rent to them only after certain conditions have been satisfied — from "when the residents of the area are prepared to accept them," "after one Negro is in the block," "after one Negro is in the block and some are in the vicinity," to the condition that the area should be predominantly Negro.

Some respondents treat their Negro tenants differently from their white tenants in screening procedures, amount of rent, and some other respects. Negro prospective home buyers and applicants for apartments are treated differently from their white counterparts in how property is shown and in the use of techniques to avoid selling or renting to them in a white area or block. In the majority of cases in each area, the owner made the change

274

from white to Negro occupancy in an apartment building on the advice of his real estate agent.

Although respondents think well of Negroes as homeowners, this does not lessen their unwillingness to sell to them in the white area or block. This unwillingness rests upon certain convictions: The majority of the respondents firmly believe that the sale of property to Negroes in a white area or block has consequences for property values, the condition of the neighborhood, and the experience of families that are harmful to the white owners and residents of that area or block, and believe that such an act on the part of a real estate man is therefore unethical. Some respondents are unwilling to sell or rent unrestrictedly also because of the harmful consequences of such transactions for the Negro buyer or renter. Most respondents believe that white people will continue to move away as Negroes enter their neighborhoods, and they act accordingly, making sales to Negroes and not trying to sell to white people. This belief is based on the respondent's acquaintance with the feelings, wishes, and beliefs of the white people about Negroes as a result of his experience in dealing with them and on other learning. These convictions, including the respondent's own judgments of Negroes, constitute the exclusion ideology which most respondents hold.

The majority of the respondents speak of the community in which their main business operation is carried on as the source of the strongest external influence exerted upon their racial policy. This pressure has different sources and takes different forms. Most respondents firmly believe they will suffer harmful business and/or social consequences if they sell or rent to Negroes in the white area or block. Less than half have received requests from white residents not to sell property to Negroes. The others fear harmful consequences on the basis of what they know the people of the community feel about having Negroes as neighbors.

Many respondents advise their clients when asked whether they should sell or not when Negroes are approaching or entering their area; most of these advise their clients not to sell.

Other influences besides the community affect the real estate man's racial policies and practices: the lending agency, sources of profit in unrestricted selling, and the real estate board. Over half the respondents have been kept from making sales to Negroes by a lending agency in a number of ways. Various opportunities for profit exist for the real estate man in the "changing neighborhood" owing to white people's resistance to having

Negro neighbors. White people bring financial loss upon themselves through their own actions. They deal with good and bad speculators. The fast-buck or hungry-wolf real estate man and certain long-established firms are alleged to have cooperated on hidden unrestricted sales. The hungry wolf is the bad speculator or broker, the blockbuster, who has no sense of responsibility for any neighborhood and who is concerned solely with moneymaking. Certain firms are accused of making advantageous deals secretly with such men while proclaiming outwardly the tenets of the exclusion ideology and accusing other real estate men of the unethical acts of which they are themselves guilty. These firms remain respectable.

The real estate board exercises a professional and ideological influence upon real estate men. The ideological influence is carried out directly through its Code of Ethics and indirectly by interpersonal influence. The respondents' exclusion ideology was found to be essentially the same as the ideology of the Chicago Board and of NAREB. The real estate broker who sells to a Negro in the white area is looked upon in the light of the Code as being a traitor to the profession and as acting unethically. The ideology of the Real Estate Board supports what most of the real estate men interviewed in this study have learned of the wishes, feelings, and beliefs of white people about Negroes. However, the respondents are not so aware of the influence of the Board as they are of the influence of the community.

Four types were distinguished among the respondents on the basis of the relation between the factors affecting their racial policies and practices and the practices themselves: consistent exclusionists, inconsistent exclusionists, inconsistent integrationists, and consistent integrationists.

The main cog in the exclusion practice of the respondents seems to be their ideology, centered on the belief that unrestricted selling or renting is *unethical.* Such selling or renting constitutes an unethical act because, according to their way of thinking, it runs counter to the white people's wishes, hurts them financially and socially, and creates a dangerous situation for the family, especially the children.

Current Practices of Exclusion

THE question may be asked whether the racial practices of real estate brokers in the study are still as restrictive as they were in 1955–1956 when the interviews were held. A less extensive study was made during 1964–1965 to ascertain whether there have been any significant changes from the findings of the original study in either ideology or practice. It appears that restrictive practices are still the rule among real estate brokers in Chicago and other cities of the United States, and that real estate boards are still insisting upon such practices. In addition, the boards have taken on an additional task — warding off fair housing (open occupancy) legislation [1]

REAL ESTATE BOARDS

The Chicago Real Estate Board has not publicly stated that the original policy of block-by-block settlement of Negroes has been changed (see pp. 224–226), and the conclusion follows that this policy still stands. The Board has taken active steps to eliminate some fair housing legislation in Chicago and has worked to prevent the passing of such legislation in Illinois.

In June, 1962, after releasing its study, *Selling and Buying Real Estate in a Racially Changing Neighborhood*, the Chicago Commission on Human Relations invited the general public to a hearing and asked witnesses to offer recommendations for the correction of abuses uncovered in the study. In their testimony, twenty-nine witnesses repeatedly emphasized the existence of a "dual housing market" — one white, the other Negro — and the need for legislation on fair housing practices. One witness recommended that "such legislation should also eliminate racially restrictive practices in the real estate industry and housing industry." [2] Proposed legislation that would have given all citizens the legal right to buy, sell, or rent housing in any neighborhood or area of their choice was defeated by the Illinois General Assembly in 1961.

In January, 1963, a Real Estate Brokers Ordinance and, in July, 1963, an Open Occupancy Ordinance were introduced in the City Council of Chicago, and two public hearings were held for the ordinances. At the hearing for opponents, held on August 6, 1963, Alderman Despres, sponsor of the ordinances, filed for the record a list of dwellings denied to Negroes.[3] The first witness was the Chicago Real Estate Board. Alderman Despres asked the president of the Board, "what is the policy of the Chicago Real Estate Board? In favor of, or against the two ordinances we are considering today . . ." The president answered, "It is against." Alderman Despres asked, "And why is it against?" The president answered,

It is unthinkable that by law, the right of property as a civil liberty could be destroyed in a democracy that is founded by seven centuries of progress in human freedom. Property rights are a basic human right within the concept of civil liberty. Property ownership should be nourished as a part of human dignity. To restrict the right of choice in property sale or occupancy is a restriction on human rights. . . . The Constitution of the United States did not originally create civil liberties. The Bill of Rights, as an amendment, created the legal protection of the citizen in his civil liberties. The Bill of Rights has, as its predecessor, the Magna Charta, the Statute of Westminster, the Petition of Right, Trial by Jury, the Habeas Corpus Act, and the English Bill of Rights.[4]

The opposition of the Board to open occupancy had also been expressed publicly before this hearing. In an article dealing with the meaning of "Realtor" in a Chicago daily newspaper of wide circulation, a Realtor had said, "You also have to mention the position the board has taken for preservation of property rights in opposing the 'open occupancy' housing bill and in fighting the danger of rising real estate taxes." [5]

Despite the Board's opposition, on September 11, 1963, the City Council of Chicago passed a Fair Housing Ordinance forbidding real estate brokers to discriminate in any way against any person on the basis of race, color, religion, national origin, or ancestry.[6] The ordinance also forbids any form of "panic peddling." The Open Occupancy Ordinance, if passed, would have restrained property owners from discrimination.

In the late summer of 1963, when the two ordinances were still being discussed, the Property Owners Coordinating Committee (POCC) was established. It is a federation of 175 local property owners, improvement, and taxpayer associations with a total of over 250,000 participating members, "dedicated to fight against inequitable real estate taxes and those forms of legislation which would erode the rights of private property ownership." [7] An account of POCC states: "When the issue of Forced Housing (Open Occupancy) became a 'hot' one, many of these organizations became truly alarmed. They felt that Open Occupancy posed a threat to the rights of private property ownership far beyond anything which had been contemplated previously." [8] When the City of Chicago passed its Fair Housing Ordinance seriously restricting real estate brokers' rights in doing business, the Chicago Real Estate Board and 26 Chicago Realtors initiated a lawsuit to test the constitutionality of the ordinance in the courts. Specifically, the Board sought to enjoin the city from enforcing the ordinance on the ground that the city lacks "home rule power" to pass such an ordinance. The suit challenged the city ordinance on three major questions:

1. IS THE City of Chicago empowered by the State of Illinois to enact a fair housing law?

2. EVEN if such enabling legislation exists, can the state give municipalities the power to make fair housing laws without violating the Illinois Constitution's provisions regarding enabling legislation and the individual's right to due process of law?

3. DOES the Chicago Ordinance violate the individual's right to due process of law as specified in the 14th Amendment to the United States Constitution? [9]

After the Chicago Real Estate Board had taken up the legal fight against the ordinance, the POCC asked the Board for help with their organizational problems, since the issue of open occupancy vitally concerned both groups. The Board agreed to provide its own offices for use as headquarters for the POCC, to handle the dissemination of all information, to act as custodian of funds raised by the POCC, and to make available to the POCC the services of the secretary of its Property Owners Council in an advisory and coordinating capacity.[10]

At the end of January, 1964, the POCC started a campaign to obtain enough signatures on a petition for a referendum on open occupancy in the November, 1964, elections in Illinois. The purpose of the referendum was to forestall state legislation on open occupancy and to prevent any legislation enabling municipalities to create such statutes. The petition carried the following question to be submitted to the voters on November 3, 1964: "Shall the State Legislature pass or amend statutes, so as to force owners of real property or their agents, to sell, lease, or rent any real property to anyone not of their choosing, and; should the statutes permit the State or any County or Municipal Corporation to force owners or their agents to sell, lease, or rent any real property to anyone not of their choosing, by instituting regulatory practices on the licensing of Real Estate Brokers, Agents, or salesmen, or by any other means whatsoever?" [11] The directors of the Chicago Real Estate Board resolved to "work with any and all civic groups" in getting the necessary 510,000 signatures.[12] Funds were raised to carry on both the trial and the referendum. Both efforts were considered necessary by the Board and the POCC for the following purposes: "(1) The litigation to make clear through the judicial process that cities do not have the right to pass Forced Housing Legislation; and (2) The Petition-Referendum Campaign to make sure that the Legislature does not enact such laws or give this right to the cities." [13]

Meanwhile, Governor Otto Kerner of Illinois denounced the drive for a statewide advisory public policy referendum on open occupancy; he accused the real estate groups spearheading the campaign of misrepresentation in depicting freedom-of-residence proposals as "unAmerican forced housing schemes" that violate constitutional property rights.[14] The referendum fell through. The Illinois Electoral Board ruled that the proposition urged by 545,000 voters could not appear on the ballot because it improperly posed two unrelated questions.[15]

On December 22, 1965, Judge John J. Lupe of the Circuit Court in Chicago declared that the city had the statutory power to pass the ordinance, that the ordinance is reasonable, and that it does not violate the Illinois State Constitution or the Constitution of the United States. On January 20, 1966, the Chicago Real Estate Board and the other plaintiffs filed a notice of appeal from Judge Lupe's decree in the Supreme Court of Illinois.[16]

On March 27, 1967, a rehearing was denied to the Board by the Supreme Court of Illinois, and the Court ruled that the city had authority to adopt the ordinance prohibiting brokers from discriminating on account of race, color, religion, national origin, or ancestry in sale, rental, or financing of residential property and that the application of the ordinance to real estate brokers only was not a denial of equal protection of the law.[17]

Another instance of opposition by a real estate organization to open occupancy arose in California, where the Rumford Act was passed in 1963 after months of angry debate. It forbade discrimination on the basis of race, color, religion, national origin, or ancestry in the sale or rental of 70 per cent of California's housing, including 25–30 per cent of the single-family residences. The California Real Estate Association started a campaign to get the statute off the books, and it was the prime mover in getting Proposition 14 on the November 3, 1964, ballot, by collecting more than half a million signatures to initiative petitions.[18] Proposition 14 became an amendment by a ratio approaching 2 to 1 and gave a property owner "absolute discretion" in the sale and rental of his property. It not only negated the Rumford Act, the earlier Unruh Act, and other legislation in the civil rights field, but also prevented such legislation from being passed in the future. It restored to the private property owner the absolute right to discriminate among applicants for the tenancy or purchase of his property.[19] There was immediate reaction to the amendment. The National Committee against Discrimination in Housing charged the California Real Estate Association with misleading the public "into believing they are protecting absolute property rights, which are non-existent."[20] Legal action challenging the constitutionality of Proposition 14 was filed on December 14, 1964, by an attorney of the NAACP.[21] W. Byron Rumford, author of the Rumford Act, predicted that the amendment would be carried to the Supreme Court of the United States to test its constitutionality,[22] and he was right. On June 8, 1966, in a case in which the defendants refused to rent unoccupied apartments to the plaintiffs solely on the ground that they were Negroes, the Supreme Court of California held

that article of California constitution prohibiting state from denying right of any person to decline to sell, lease or rent his real property to such persons as he in his absolute discretion, chooses constituted affirmative action on part of state to change its existing laws from situation where discrimination was legally restricted to one wherein it was encouraged and thus denied plaintiffs and those similarly situated equal protection of laws as guaranteed by Fourteenth Amendment to federal constitution and article was void in its general application.[23]

On December 5, 1966, the Supreme Court of the United States granted a petition for writ of certiorari to the Supreme Court of California, and on May 29, 1967, affirmed the judgment of the California Supreme Court.[24]

A statement by a citizens' association in support of the Illinois Fair Housing Act proposed in 1961 listed "typical practices existing in practically every city and village in Illinois." One of them reads: "No colored broker is a member of the community's Real Estate Board . . . Members of this Board are forbidden from participating in the sale of homes on an all-white block to a colored person, or a house on an 'all-Christian block' to a Jewish person. Such brokers have stated openly — 'I would be blackballed and lose my membership if I showed you a house.' 'It would be a kiss of death to me if I even attended a Human Relations Council meeting to discuss the housing needs for Negroes.' " [25]

In Sarasota, Florida, in 1963 the Board of Realtors expelled a broker for selling a house to a Negro doctor in a white neighborhood. [26]

In 1963, the executive director of the Chicago Commission on Human Relations charged local real estate boards with being "the major social engineers of the dual housing market." [27]

In February, 1964, the first vice-president of the Ohio Association of Realtors promised the Toledo Board of Realtors that the Ohio Association would continue to fight any legislative attempt anywhere to pass new open occupancy laws. He said that "forced housing legislation presently being passed throughout the country is taking our rights away. . . . We don't want any ordinances passed that will affect our way of making a living or deprive a citizen of his basic constitutional right — the right to sell to whom he chooses." He declared that the Ohio Association is against open occupancy legislation because there "is no legislation humanly possible that can tell me to like you." [28]

After two fair housing bills were introduced in the Ohio legislature in 1965, the president of the Ohio Association of Real Estate Boards stated that he would start a campaign to get enough signatures to put the proposition of fair housing before the voters in a referendum as had been done successfully in Detroit and Akron. [29] In the measure he advocated, he followed the California pattern of making open occupancy legislation an impossibility in the future. In the hearings before an Ohio Senate committee in March, 1965, Realtors from Cincinnati, Dayton, and Cleveland spoke against the fair housing bills. [30] The executive secretary of the Columbus Board of Realtors stated that financial inability — not discrimination — accounts for Negroes failing to achieve desired homes in Columbus. [31] Petitions seeking public support against passage of fair housing legislation, printed by the Ohio Association of Real Estate Boards, were distributed in Toledo to about 150 Realtors and 900 real estate salesmen by the Toledo Board of Realtors. [32] The Board of Realtors of Ann Arbor, Michigan, expressed its opposition to open occupancy in a statement published in a local newspaper which is similar to the position taken by NAREB.[33]

Real estate boards that are not members of NAREB also took a stand against fair housing legislation. In Chicago, telegrams and letters were received by Mayor Daley and Alderman Despres from the West Side Real Estate Board, the Beverly Suburban Real Estate Board, the South Side Renting Men's Association, and the Northwest Real Estate Board stating their opposition to the Fair Housing Ordinance when it was being considered.[34]

There is noticeable unity in the stand of NAREB, the state associations, and the local boards against open occupancy legislation. In 1963, NAREB set up and distributed among its member boards a *Property Owners' Bill of Rights* which spells out in detail the power of "absolute discretion" of the owner in regard to his property and draws attention to the early recognition of property rights in the development of political rights in the United States, referring particularly to the first ten amendments and the Fourteenth Amendment of the United States Constitution.[35] In a statement of policy on minority housing issued at the same time, NAREB expressed its opposition to open occupancy legislation that would restrict the rights of the owner in regard to his property: *"Realtors may properly oppose any attempt by force of law to withdraw from property owners the right freely to determine with whom they will deal with respect to their property, irrespective of the reason therefor, and any law or regulation which would operate to prevent a real estate broker from representing any property owner or faithfully abiding by the terms and conditions of any agency stipulated by the property owner."* [36] A similar emphasis was placed on the importance of property rights by the president of the Chicago Real Estate Board (see p. 278), and a spokesman for the Property Owners' Coordinating Committee expressed similar ideas at the beginning of the campaign to put the issue of open occupancy on the ballot in November, 1964. The spokesman, stressing the fundamental nature of property rights, said:

This campaign has nothing to do with civil rights. It is a matter of protecting our basic fundamental rights as owners of private property. These rights have been sacred since the days of the Magna Charta in England and are a part of the American way of life. When you tell a man he no longer has the right of choice as to whom he may sell, lease or rent his property, you take away this age old fundamental right. Fair Housing ordinances, Open Occupancy or Forced Housing legislation constitute a serious threat to these basic rights of ours as private property owners.

We believe that all people have a right to live wherever they choose if they can afford to do so, but we believe very strongly that to attempt to legislate this right through Open Occupancy legislation is to deprive other people of a basic right. Laws of this kind have not remedied the situation they sought to correct. In fact, they have created many other problems. They also set a very dangerous precedent which would inevitably lead to even more restrictive legislation.

We believe the only way the job of Open Occupancy can be successfully accomplished is through a program of education.[37]

The Chicago Real Estate Board and the California Real Estate Association also took the position that housing integration can come about only through education and persuasion, the California Association contending that legal action to bring about mixed neighborhoods will fail because it is coercive. The Association prepared a voluntary fair housing code which suggests that each local real estate board "subscribe to the policy that a favorable public attitude for equal opportunity in the acquisition of housing can best be accomplished through leadership, example, education and the mutual cooperation of the real estate industry and the public." The code is based on the responsibilities of real estate brokers to "offer equal service to all clients without regard to color, religion, or national origin in the sale, purchase, exchange, rental or lease of real property." [38] The voluntary code promises much.

The president of NAREB, in his keynote address at the fifty-seventh annual convention in Los Angeles on November 10, 1964, declared that private property rights are more basic to human liberty than the civil rights of minority groups. He said, "Those who voted against 'forced housing' [re Proposition 14] consider the right of decision in private property a liberty essential to the preservation of their most basic human right — separate and apart from civil rights. . . . If the freedom to hold and dispose of private property is abridged, the foundation upon which all rights rest is weakened, if not destroyed." [39] The president was here stressing a major point in NAREB ideology: the importance of the right to own property. The Preamble to the 1952 Statement of Policy of the Resolutions Committee of the forty-fifth annual convention contained the same idea (quoted on p. 193). In the Preamble, property rights are made fundamental, basic to all other rights in American life. Civil rights are looked upon as secondary to property rights. In this stand, the Realtors are sure that they act morally, according to the basic value of American life.

284

Since another point of view about the relative importance of property and civil rights has also been seriously supported, it is presented here. Richard R. B. Powell reviews some twenty aspects of the law in which the absoluteness of property rights has been rejected because of the basic proposition that "one cannot use what he owns in a fashion harmful to the community of which he is a part." [40] In each of the twenty areas — such as soil conservation, timber control, zoning, blight prevention — the criterion has been, "Is the claimed exercise of property rights one which is consistent with the public welfare?" If not, the claim is found not to be right. The history of the law of private ownership, says Powell, has witnessed simultaneously a playing-down of absolute rights and a playing-up of social concern as to the use of property. Property rights have been "redefined in response to a swelling demand that ownership be responsible and responsive to the needs of the social whole." Property rights cannot be used "as a shibboleth to cloak conduct which adversely affects the health, the safety, the morals, or the welfare of others." [41]

Judge Lupe in his decree on the Chicago ordinance expressed a similar thought when he ruled: "Neither property rights nor contract rights are absolute, for government cannot exist if the citizen may at will use his property to the detriment of his fellows, or exercise his freedom of contract to work them harm. The Constitution does not secure to anyone liberty to conduct his business in such fashion as to inflict injury upon the public at large, or upon any substantial group of the people." [42]

Only one mortgage banker in the Chicago real estate group favored open occupancy "from a strictly business point of view." He believes that open occupancy "if applied intelligently and received intelligently . . . will create a more stable and productive real estate market which can and will have better financial benefits for all concerned." [43]

On the basis of the evidence cited, the conclusion is reached here that NAREB and its member Boards hold intrinsically the same ideology and position toward restriction as in the study of 1955–1956.

Objections may be raised to this conclusion on the ground that two pronouncements by NAREB give a different impression. In 1963, for the first time, NAREB distributed to local Boards a book interpreting the Code of Ethics. In its second (1964) edition is an illustration of the application of Article 5 (p. 201 above): A Realtor sold a home to a nonwhite buyer in a block with no other nonwhite occupants. A neighbor complained to the Board that this Realtor had violated Article 5 of the Code. When the complaint was reviewed before the Board's committee on professional standards, the Realtor contended that, since the words "occupancy" and "race" were stricken out many years ago, the intent to exclude any such considerations from the Article was thereby demonstrated. The Board found the Realtor not guilty of unethical conduct.[44]

In its *Policy on Minority Housing* (1963), NAREB sets forth the rights and duties of members in real estate transactions pertaining in particular to the housing of racial, creedal, and ethnic groups. In this statement, NAREB opposes open occupancy (n. 1, this chapter), but makes explicit certain duties for the broker that tend to protect the minority group in its rights, or at least to lessen the possibility of discrimination. However, intended protection of minority rights is not to be inferred from the statement of policy itself, which is about "the Realtor-client relationship in our free market regardless of any racial, creedal, or ethnic group problems, whether existent or not." NAREB states that the Realtor has "no right or responsibility to determine the racial, creedal, or ethnic composition of any area or neighborhood or any part thereof," that "no Realtor should assume to determine the suitability or eligibility on racial, creedal, or ethnic grounds of any prospective mortgagor, tenant, or purchaser," but that he should "invariably submit to the client all written offers made by any prospect in connection with the transaction at hand," and, upon acceptance by his client of any offer, the Realtor should "exert his best efforts to conclude the transaction irrespective of the race, creed, or nationality of the offeror." The Realtor should also feel free to enter into a broker-client relationship "with persons of any race, creed, or ethnic group." Also, if "a Realtor's counsel is sought by a client with respect to property situated in an area or neighborhood which is undergoing or which is about to undergo transition in terms of occupancy by members of racial, creedal, or ethnic groups, the Realtor should take particular care to render objective advice . . ." The policy statement makes it very clear that the attitude of the owner is the determining factor in any real estate transaction and that the real estate broker should not be expected to inhibit or promote open occupancy. The broker is only the marketing intermediary. The last section of the statement reads:

Realtors should endeavor to inform the public, religious, and civic groups that enhanced opportunity for the acquisition of private housing by minority groups must of necessity depend upon the attitudes of private property owners and not upon real estate brokers, who are the marketing media; that the right of property owners freely to determine with whom they will deal is a right fundamental in the American tradition; that the real estate broker cannot fairly be utilized in his agency function as a means for accomplishing the withdrawal of the right of free decision from the property owner; that the broker fully performs his legal and social responsibilities when he faithfully engages to find a purchaser acceptable to his principal; and that real estate brokers should not be expected to inhibit or promote "open occupancy" housing, this being a matter to be resolved between prospective buyers and sellers of private residential real property and not by real estate brokers functioning as the marketing intermediary.

The policy statement is silent on the question of restriction except for the encouragement for Realtors' opposing fair housing legislation, the aim of which is to outlaw restriction. NAREB's policy statement and its Property Owners' Bill of Rights give the owner complete freedom to determine with whom he will deal with respect to his property, "irrespective of the reason therefor." Freedom of choice or "absolute discretion" includes freedom to restrict. And there is evidence, in spite of the interpretation of Article 5 of the Code (pp. 285–286, 301), that in the local situation the Board expects the broker *not* to sell to a Negro in the white area or block.

The policy of real estate boards not to accept Negro brokers as members or to accept them on a token basis continues (pp. 236–238). A survey made in 1962 of the extent of Negro membership in the Boards of NAREB found that in 42 cities of the United States only 18 had 1 or more Negro members (see tabulation).[45]

City	Negro Members
Baltimore	6
Berkeley	Several
Boston	2
Buffalo	7
Chicago	4 (admitted 2-18-63)
Denver	1
Detroit	3
Gary	2
Los Angeles	1
Minneapolis	1
New York	Indefinite
Philadelphia	7
Pittsburgh	2
Portland, Ore.	2
Providence	1
San Francisco	Several
Seattle	1
Toledo	2

REAL ESTATE BROKERS

The fact that a fair housing ordinance was passed in Chicago demonstrates that respondents and other brokers are still excluding Negroes from white neighborhoods. It is significant too that a number of organizations made a persistent effort which resulted in an alderman's sponsoring two ordinances and that the city council passed the one dealing with restriction by brokers rather than the one concerning owners.

Statements by spokesmen of intergroup relations agencies also indicate the continuing exclusion of Negroes from white areas by real estate brokers and their refusal to sell to Negroes until the area is clearly no longer white. One statement refers particularly to Realtors: "In a neighborhood or suburb where a Negro family has bought a home for the first time, the dual housing market usually creates a realty vacuum which draws panic peddlers. Realtors who sell to whites in such a block pull out temporarily to see whether the neighborhood 'will go colored.' When enough Negro families move in so that the block can be written off as Negro, some Realtors may return to deal with Negroes, only to find that speculators have skimmed the cream off the market." [46]

Five months after the Real Estate Brokers Ordinance was passed in Chicago, the following statement appeared in the Negro *Daily Defender*:[47]

If a real estate broker refuses to show you a listing — don't wave your fist and shout "We Shall Overcome." Call the Chicago Commission on Human Relations . . .

An eager-eyed, bushy-tailed staff is sitting by the telephone just pining away for citizens to complain of real estate broker discrimination.

"People shouldn't worry about proof," declared Commission Coordinator Hal M. Freeman earnestly. "Let us worry about that."

He ticked off the "can'ts" for brokers since the City Council passed the fair housing ordinance last spring.

This statement further indicates that real estate brokers in Chicago have been refusing to show certain listings to Negroes.

That brokers in Chicago are still carrying on restrictive practices is apparent also from the 28 complaints filed by July, 1964, under the Fair Housing Ordinance with the Chicago Commission on Human Relations, charged with the implementation of the ordinance. Nineteen of the 28 complainants were Negro; 10 of the 28 alleged ordinance violations occurred in Area A and 8 in Area C,[48] pointing to respondents' continued restrictive practices. By December 31, 1964, the Chicago Commission had received 77 complaints, 57 from Negroes; the complaints were refusal to rent, 53 cases; refusal to sell, 6; eviction, 5; "panic peddling," 7; exploitation, 6.[49] In 1967, three brokers' licenses were suspended under the ordinance. The brokers were charged with refusing to show homes to Negroes. Peter Fitzpatrick, chairman of the Chicago Commission, said, "We urged suspensions to the Mayor after investigation, hearings and efforts at conciliation" ("Three Brokers' Licenses Suspended under cfho," *Human Relations News of Chicago,* IX, No. 5 (September, 1967), 2 — published by the Chicago Commission on Human Relations). However, George S. Harris, former president of the National Association of Real Estate Brokers (Negro), when telephoned in Chicago on November 16, 1967, and questioned by me about the efficacy of the ordinance, said, "The Ordinance isn't doing the job because the authorities don't feel they can always make a case. People can't afford the time, to testify, to be away from work. For those three brokers who lost their licenses, there are many cases where they are getting away with it." He considered a public law at the federal level on a nationwide basis with the acceptance of the public as the only solution. This has happened in public accommodations, he said.

A community area association on the North Side of Chicago, in an effort to promote stability in its area, set up a rental referral service to try to "match up" owners with renters so as to bring qualified persons of any race into the community. When this work became too time-consuming, a committee went to Realtors in the area and asked them whether they would help place good Negro families in the area if any applied. Some Realtors refused, and others were evasive. Some gave a qualified yes, reserving the right to use their own judgment about the situation in certain buildings when renting to Negroes. The president of the association stated that real estate brokers are still conservative and afraid. "They are not ready to make a first sale in our area; they are afraid to start it," he said. "They might be stigmatized as bad operators by the people of the community who would not want to deal with them any more." In the western section of the area, where there is more hostility to Negroes, the real estate brokers refused to sell to Negroes, saying that stones would be thrown at their windows and that the neighborhood was not ready for the introduction of Negroes; they pointed out that they are businessmen making their living there and they do not want the whole block angry at them. In the last two years, about fifteen Negro families have moved into this general area. The brokers who gave a qualified yes answer said they would sell to Negroes, provided it was in keeping with the wishes of the owner and the people in the block; the brokers had been in the area a long time and thought they knew the wishes of the people. These answers are similar to those of the respondents of the present study.[50] Most of the cooperative real estate men offered another reason for not being too willing to comply with the request of the committee: "We ran into telephone calls from Negro students and families. They seemed to expect us to hand them an apartment on a silver platter." These brokers said they did not want their office flooded by people expecting to have their apartment-hunting done for them.[51]

There is evidence that real estate brokers in the Chicago suburbs also practice restriction. An organization comprising at least 50 suburbs on the southern periphery of Chicago (35 all white, 4 all Negro, and the rest have Negroes on a segregated basis) planned to develop a Fair Housing Committee which would act as a go-between. The organization was to ask people with houses for sale in all-white communities (beginning with a selected 4) whether they would sell to a Negro; if they were willing, the organization would give this information to Housing Opportunities Made Equal so that buyer and seller could be brought together. "This gets into the area of dealings with real estate people," said the informant, and then continued:

We are going to write to them, the white real estate people in the South suburbs, about 1,200 of them, and tell them we're doing this because they are not doing their job properly. We want them to service people regardless of their race. Because if you are a Negro and if you come into one of these communities and say you want to buy a house, the Realtors won't talk to you. They won't handle Negroes who want to move into an all-white community. We are not saying that all Realtors are like that. Some are more liberal, but as an industry in general they are not doing the job they should be doing. I am referring to all the practicing real estate brokers in all these communities.

Then our next step is to get the Realtors together at a meeting and to urge them to change their practices and show houses to Negroes.

There is no problem if the white person doesn't want to sell to Negroes. No one has to sell to a person he doesn't want to sell to at the present time. But this is not a function for the Realtor to decide. This is something the seller should decide. The Realtor shouldn't take it for granted that the seller won't. We feel that if a Negro shows an interest in a house in a community that he should be treated the same as a white family. That real estate man should present the Negro prospect to the white seller.[52]

In Evanston, Illinois, 38 men and women, white and Negro, picketed four real estate firms in a peaceful demonstration to demand open housing in that city. The demonstration was conducted by members of the Evanston Nonviolent Action Council. A leader of the group said that his organization planned to continue demonstrations until all Evanston real estate firms "provide fair housing for all." [53] In April, 1966, an ordinance was proposed to the Evanston City Council, aimed at "preventing brokers from bias in sale, leasing and rental of properties." [54]

A comprehensive report made by the Illinois Commission on Human Relations in December, 1960, revealed that minority housing throughout the state was "crowded . . . limited and (almost entirely) segregated. . . ." [55]

The Ohio Civil Rights Commission in its study of discrimination in housing found that real estate brokers and salesmen refuse outright to show members of minority groups, especially Negroes, houses in all-white areas and consistently discourage them from making purchase offers, except in specified neighborhoods.[56] In Toledo, Ohio, more than 30,000 of the city's 42,000 Negroes have been compelled to live in the "Old West End Ghetto," the president of the NAACP local chapter said. He believes that the housing problem in Toledo can be solved if "Realtors and bankers really want to solve it." [57] In Akron, Ohio, the NAACP filed a suit against twenty-eight Akron real estate firms along with the Akron Real Estate Board itself, accusing them of violating federal antitrust laws through alleged housing discrimination. The suit charged that the defendants have conspired as an "unlawful combination" in restraint of trade by practices allegedly aimed at preventing Negroes from owning property in parts of Akron "occupied solely or primarily by white persons." This was to be a test lawsuit and similar suits were to be brought in other cities, an NAACP lawyer said. A fair housing law was approved by Akron's council in June, 1964. In a referendum in November of the same year this law was repealed, and Akron Realtors were reported by a councilman to have presented the strongest opposition to it.[58]

In Pittsburgh, Pennsylvania, a property owner in a good white residential neighborhood who needed to sell her home and could not find a proper white prospect soon enough was willing to sell it to a qualified Ne-

291

gro buyer, but several real estate firms to which she applied said they would not sell the property to a Negro because if they did they would get no more business from the community.[59]

In Teaneck, New Jersey, the Fair Housing Committee filed 33 complaints against nine Bergen County real estate brokers. It charged that they had discriminated against Negroes by refusing to show houses in white neighborhoods.[60]

In the 1961 report on housing of the United States Commission on Civil Rights, discriminatory practices by real estate brokers and realty boards were found to be "often the rule rather than the exception." [61] In San Francisco, a white homeowner was told by her real estate agent that "she must be psychotic for even thinking of selling to a nonwhite family in her neighborhood." In the Palo Alto area, the Commission learned, only 3 of the 600 real estate brokers and salesmen show property on a nondiscriminatory basis. In the Detroit hearing, the Commission was informed that many Realtors "maintain separate listings of properties which may be shown to Negroes and which may be shown to white home owners." [62] In the 1963 report of the Commission, real estate brokers are again considered to be "a source of discrimination." [63] Although Newark real estate brokers are prohibited from engaging in discriminatory practices in housing covered by New Jersey's fair housing law, the Commission heard testimony about the letters "PATO" (Purchaser Acceptable to Owner) appearing on certain listing agreements of the Newark, Irvington, and Hillside Real Estate Board. The New Jersey Division on Civil Rights investigated the use of PATO, and one broker told them that it was used "to keep out nonwhites and Jews." [64]

As of April 1, 1963, 3 cities, 12 states, and 1 territory had enacted legislation on fair housing practices, applicable to private housing with varying coverage.[65] As of September, 1964, 24 cities and 14 states had fair housing practices laws.[66] The passing of these laws is evidence of continuing restrictive practices.

It seems possible to conclude that the practices of real estate brokers in the areas of the study, in other parts of Chicago, and in other cities of the United States in 1969 are not markedly different from what they were in 1955 and 1956. They are still largely restrictive, with certain but not significant variations. In other words, it appears that the findings of this study are valid.

Current Practices of Exclusion

BOARD DISTINGUISHED FROM BROKER

The unitary stand of NAREB and the local board is to be distinguished from the varied views and practices of the member and nonmember brokers. As discussed in Chapter II, writers on the problem of discrimination in housing tend to put brokers' views and practices in the same category with those of the high-level policy makers in the real estate field (see p. 15). However, the study of 1955–1956 revealed a wide range of belief and practice among the respondents, although the majority share the five core beliefs of the exclusion ideology and will not sell or rent to a Negro in a white area or block (see p. 144). The Board as represented by the leading spokesmen for real estate expresses a composite opinion, but the real estate brokers, members and nonmembers, vary with it at points. Members and nonmembers follow the Code on the whole and the wishes of the community, but many are ready to sell without restriction if the community and the Board will allow them to do so. Although most of the respondents hold the exclusion ideology and practice exclusion, the majority of these hold a moderate form of the exclusion ideology and vary in their practice of it in their conditions for sale or rental to Negroes.

Most respondents believe that white people do not want Negro neighbors and that an area will "go Negro" after one or two Negro families have entered. However, a few succeed in selling residential property in the mixed area to white people for their own use (although different motives may be present), and many respondents consider it better to have a few Negroes in each block. Most respondents are keenly aware of deterioration in largely Negro areas, but many also recognize that Negroes, when not too over-burdened with debt, make good homeowners and that in some Negro areas, given their present upkeep, property values are not likely to decline any faster than in comparable white areas.

Most respondents believe that it is unethical to sell or rent property in the white area or block to a Negro, because it will hurt the white client; in this they voice NAREB's judgment as to the duty of broker to client. However, many are willing to sell if the community will permit it, and most do so. If the community and the local Board were not saying no to such sales, the respondents would not have to say no to the Negro. There are, to be sure, some respondents who themselves want to keep an area white and some who wish to keep their community of operation white in order to protect their long-range business.

There is also a greater awareness of the plight of many Negroes and of the differences among Negroes among the respondents than appears in the official statements of the Board.

A respondent who was a former president of the Chicago Real Estate Board told how it had been at one time improper for a real estate broker to deal with Negroes, but when Negroes started entering various neighborhoods the Realtors in those areas told the Board they were hard pressed and would have to begin to deal with them. Then the Board listened to the needs of its members and in time it became "respectable" for Realtors, even board presidents, to have Negro clients, especially after 1945 when NAREB itself undertook to supply housing for Negroes (see p. 236). The institution does not alone influence the participants. They also influence the institution. This idea seems to underlie an open letter sent to the real estate industry by the Chicago Conference on Religion and Race.[67] The letter states in part:

Surely it is time that members of the real estate industry faced the issue of a single housing market for all residents of our community . . . Surely it is time for the real estate industry to acquire spokesmen who are aware of the moral and economic imperative of housing for all, regardless of their race or religion.

We know that many people within the real estate industry are concerned about the moral implications of housing segregation and dissatisfied with the public posture of spokesmen for their professional organizations.

This statement supports the findings of the present study both in regard to the brokers' restrictive practices and the differences of view between many of them and the "spokesmen for their professional organizations."

PROPERTY OWNERS

NAREB's Code of Ethics is fashioned from the experience of real estate men. The primary emphasis is service to the client and the public — the property owner's satisfaction and the protection of his property and neighborhood are the focal points, although the tenant's satisfaction is also included. NAREB and the lending agencies have stated that as long as white people think and feel the way they do about Negroes, real estate men must respect their wishes and serve them loyally, protecting equity, property value, and neighborhood by not selling to Negroes in the white area or block.

A conclusion arising out of the present study is that not the broker but the property owner or tenant — that is, the white American citizen and his conception of Negroes — is the basic problem in housing discrimination. White people's unfavorable conception of Negroes is learned partly from parents and others and is constantly fed by observation of the way of life of the poor, underprivileged, culturally impoverished portion of the Negro population — a large portion, in spite of the growing Negro middle class.

It has been said that the real estate board and real estate men exercise great influence over property owners, and several studies have attested to the strength of this influence,[68] but, according to the data of the present study, neither the Board nor the "legitimate" real estate broker urges white people to move when Negroes enter their area. The panic peddlers, the block-busters frighten them into moving, whereas most respondents insisted that, when asked, they advise their clients to stay. Furthermore, neither the Board nor the broker needs to tell the white people to move. White people acquired their prejudiced attitudes and their unfavorable conception of Negroes long before they came to deal with the broker.

There are two crucial points in the question of housing discrimination against Negroes — the resistance of white people to Negroes' entering their areas, and the moving of white people from areas Negroes have entered. It is hypothesized here that the resistance and the moving of white people are due, in part at least, to white people's unfavorable conception of Negroes, and that, if this conception were changed for the better, white people would not move away and produce a segregated neighborhood. Racial residential integration would require, at the least, a change in white people's conception of and attitudes toward Negroes. Research is necessary also, to refine our knowledge about differences in white people's reactions to Negroes as neighbors.

NAREB's statement on policy on minority housing makes it clear that the Realtor is only the marketing intermediary and that the property owner has the right to determine the terms and conditions of the sale.[69] In other words, the property owner and not the Realtor is the determining factor in the whole real estate transaction. Now, if, with better earning power and higher educational level, more Negroes were able to keep their property in good repair, and if white people began to have favorable attitudes toward Negroes, two main reasons for the Board's insistence upon restriction would be removed. Throughout the country there are now many integrated buildings, blocks, and developments, but the moving of white people as Negroes enter their areas has so far occurred much more frequently and on a larger scale than has integration. If in many parts of the country many white people stopped moving away, real estate boards would have to change ideology and practice. However, right now many real estate men are convinced of white people's opposition to Negro neighbors and of the adverse effects on property conditions and values when Negroes enter, and they tend in their business relations with clients to reinforce white people's prejudice against Negroes.

WHITE-NEGRO RATIOS

Even now, with white people's attitudes as they are, a considerable number of the respondents believe that white people would remain in their neighborhoods when Negroes enter if they were sure that they would not be surrounded by Negroes, that they would not be "inundated," that the neighborhood would not "go all Negro," that they would not be "the only white family." The respondents thought a neighborhood could become 15 to 25 per cent Negro before the white people would judge that the neighborhood was going Negro. They thought a white neighborhood could absorb up to 25 per cent without becoming disturbed. Morton Grodzins calls the limit of tolerance the "tip point":

Once the proportion of non-white exceeds the limits of the neighborhood's tolerance for interracial living (this is the "tip point"), the whites move out. The proportion of Negroes who will be accepted before the tip point is reached *varies from city to city and from neighborhood to neighborhood* [italics added]. . . . This is to say that tipping may come slowly and does not necessarily indicate any immediate downgrading of the given neighborhood. What it signifies is the unwillingness of white groups to live in proximity to large numbers of Negroes.[70]

To reduce housing segregation and its many harmful effects, the crucial requisites are acceptance of some Negroes in white areas and white people's remaining. If the hypothesis is true that many or most white people would stay if they could be sure that the area would be mostly white, then two crucial questions arise, How is the proper proportion for a particular area to be determined? How is the proper proportion to be maintained? As long as "proportion" or "balanced population" is used, no one seems to be disturbed, but as soon as "quota" is used, it calls forth the accusation "undemocratic." Several students of minority problems have pointed out that this quota would be benevolent or benign in that it would facilitate integration and prevent further segregation. Charles Abrams, former director of the New York State Anti-Discrimination Commission, opined that such a quota is desirable and described the need for "a workable balance" in housing projects, meaning inclusion, not exclusion of people.[71] Maintaining racial proportions in a neighborhood or in a block is a part of the whole program necessary to break down segregation, but the hope is that it would in time become unnecessary. Abrams recognizes this when he says about interracial housing projects, "There would be no need to maintain a balance in any project if adequate housing were available for all, and there were no barriers. Until that has been attained, the maintenance of workable communities during the development process is essential." [72]

Oscar Cohen, national program director of the Anti-Defamation League, discussed the pros and cons of the "benign quota" in 1959 and drew attention to Morris Milgram's quota policy in his large-scale interracial housing developments, notably Concord Park and Greenbelt Knolls near Philadelphia, 55 per cent white, 45 per cent Negro and "two thirds white, one third Negro" respectively. Milgram, in common with other professional builders, had found that there is a tipping point in integrated housing — that is, whites will move out when the Negro percentage exceeds a certain figure because they conclude that the integrated development is becoming an all-Negro one and that the school system will be affected. Hence Milgram accepted the need for a benign quota so that the white people will feel secure and will remain; his experience showed that the quota system worked.[73]

Testifying before the United States Commission on Civil Rights in 1959, Saul Alinsky recommended a benign quota as the only means of keeping the white people from moving. During a race riot some years ago he asked some rioters whether they would allow Negroes to live among them if they were sure that only 5 per cent of the population would be Negro. The leader answered, "Mister, if we could have 5 per cent or even a little bit more, but we knew for sure, and I mean for sure, that that was all there was going to be — you have no idea how we would jump at it!" But the man knew "that when Negroes start coming into a neighborhood, that means the neighborhood's gone." [74] James C. Downs, chairman of the Real Estate Research Corporation in Chicago, expressed a similar view, "The real problem comes when a white is convinced that his entire neighborhood will become nonwhite. He thinks so, and he is right — that is exactly what is happening in central cities. So the white man moves. . . . The exception, housing experts say, is where there is an 'element of management' in housing patterns." [75] Those convinced of the harm in residential segregation and the benefits of integrated housing need to face this essential issue. Designating the same fact by a different name does not alter the basic question of the need for maintaining a certain proportion. As Alinsky said, "Whether we call it ratio, percentage, balance, proportion or stabilization, it all comes to the same; a quota by any other name spells the same."

The question is, How can a certain racial proportion be maintained in a block? A housing authority can maintain a certain proportion in a project, a developer can in his development, or a cooperative group can in their own apartment building or new community in some outlying area, but an ordinary city block is not subject to a unitary control.

The question of how the minority group looks upon integrated housing seems to have been overlooked in research and intergroup relations programs. If Negroes are interested in maintaining an integrated area or block, the task of maintaining a certain racial proportion will be one of cooperation between the white and Negro residents. Such an effort could hardly be called undemocratic if the minority group itself recommended it, even though it might interfere with people's freedom of choice. In several cases on record, Negroes have made it known that they want the area they have entered to remain a mixed area and have taken steps to achieve this. In Lakeview, Long Island, Negro residents of an integrated section of the community urged other Negroes not to buy homes there in order to keep the area from eventually becoming predominantly Negro. Lincoln Lynch, a Negro leader in the community organization seeking to stabilize the Negro-white proportions said, "This campaign was designed to stop the panic-selling which has developed in the neighborhood and to alert the Negro that if he continues to buy in this neighborhood or in any other neighborhood where the percentage of Negroes has reached a high level he runs the risk of creating a segregated situation for himself." Part of the campaign to discourage Negroes from buying in the area was carried out by means of signs. Signs appeared on lawns and in the picture windows of about twenty-five Negro homes specifically addressed to potential Negro buyers. Typical signs read: "Negroes: Your purchase of a home in this neighborhood is your contribution to segregation" and "Negroes: This is an integrated neighborhood. Help integrate Massapequa, Bellmore and others." When asked what he considered the proper Negro-white ratio in an integrated area, Mr. Lynch said he did not know the exact point, but they were trying to use the national percentage as a yardstick — about 10 per cent Negro. He also said that about forty white residents in this community of 150–200 homes had offered their homes for sale because of the increase in Negro residents. The houses were in the $17,000 to $25,000 class as of 1961.[76]

In Teaneck, New Jersey, there was also panic selling due to an influx of Negroes into one section of the township that started in 1954. In 1961, for-sale signs were to be seen in the section, but so were placards of the Fair Housing Committee. Some of the latter, said to have been displayed by Negroes, read: "Has your agent shown you homes in *other* areas?" The underlined "other" referred to a move to have Negroes buy homes in other parts of the township to avoid a concentration in any one section. Other placards, said to have been posted by white people, read: "We welcome integration. Our house is not for sale." [77]

In the Winneconna Lakes area in Chicago, the Negro president of the interracial neighborhood improvement association expressed a strong interest in seeing the area remain mixed: "Yes, there are many Negroes in the neighborhood who do not want it to become a slum. Those of us who have a stake in the neighborhood and have invested in it feel that we could have a better community and better protection if the neighborhood remained at a mixed level, because so many of us have seen what has happened when a neighborhood has completely changed to Negro. We have an idea it is beneficial to the neighborhood to keep it mixed." [78]

Similarly, Andrew Adair, the Negro president of the Dorr-Secor Community Association in Toledo, Ohio, pointed out in an interview on March 21, 1965, that from a practical, economic point of view it is better for Negroes when the area remains mixed, because then lending agencies will assess property higher, better services will be provided by the city, and schools will have better conditions.

Thus it can be said that some white and Negro people seriously concerned about housing segregation see the maintenance of a white-Negro ratio as a way of ending segregation. Other people maintain that segregation can be broken down by another method — open occupancy, under which any citizen is free to buy whatever and wherever he can afford to buy. Detroit has been developing community councils in the northwest section of the city to prevent the creation of new segregated areas. Of five new councils, the Bagley Community Council is the most organized, the most active, and the best financed; according to its president, it deserves much of the credit for persuading the white residents "to stay put." Between June, 1960, when the first Negro bought in Bagley, and March, 1962, 137 homes changed hands; white buyers outnumbered Negroes by 9 to 1 and have continued to come in. By contrast, when Negroes entered the Russell Woods area, the white residents panicked and within a comparable two-year period the area became predominantly Negro. In Bagley, council members pointed out to residents the losses in moving elsewhere and the merits of their own neighborhood, with the result that the residents kept their heads and the neighborhood remained stable. In 1962, 765 of the approximately 4,000 families in the Bagley area were members of the council. The average value of the homes in 1962 was $15,000 to $16,000.

Detroit's community relations commission came out for open occupancy rather than stabilization (maintenance of a white-Negro ratio or quota), which they considered impossible. The Bagley council's president agreed, saying that Bagley does not try to keep Negroes out or establish quotas, but simply tries to hold real estate turnovers to the normal volume by preventing panic selling.[79] Open occupancy and the work of council members with the residents of Bagley seems to have maintained Bagley as a mixed area. But there are other areas in Detroit where the people are not so receptive, where they want "a decent place to live," and where they demonstrate with statistics that crime and vice are higher in Negro residential areas. The methods of Detroit's community relations commission may be successful in Bagley, but the question arises whether similar measures in other communities would produce comparable results. An answer requires thorough investigation of the methods used by community councils in this area of interracial relations.

It is necessary to clear up some confusion about the significance of open occupancy or fair housing, which means equal opportunity to obtain housing. Open occupancy and integrated housing are separate questions, each of which requires careful study. Open occupancy or fair housing legislation does not guarantee that segregated housing will end. If properly implemented, it will give Negroes and other minority groups equal opportunity to obtain housing — a great boon. If that is all they want, then legislation is enough. But open occupancy does not ensure that white people will remain and that the area will be integrated. If Negroes want integrated housing as well as equal opportunity in obtaining housing, then attention must be given to the conception which many white people have of Negroes and a program of very wide scope is necessary if more favorable attitudes between white people and Negroes are to be developed. It is assumed that when each group's conception of the other has changed, segregation will diminish (much difficult research, over time, will be necessary to confirm or negate this assumption). In the 1963 report of the United States Commission on Civil Rights, the state advisory committees came to similar conclusions. All of them noted "a continuing pattern of housing segregation, resulting in the larger cities in crowded, unsanitary ghettos in which housing is substandard and overpriced." Although some progress has been made, they say, it is negligible when compared to the magnitude of the problem. The statement on housing of the state advisory committees ends with the sentence: "It would appear from these inquiries that housing discrimination is perhaps the most ubiquitous and deeply rooted civil rights problem in America." [80] Whether the housing provisions of the 1968 Civil Rights Act will result in true amelioration of this problem is a debatable question.[81]

APPENDIXES, NOTES,
BIBLIOGRAPHY, AND INDEX

Appendixes

1. When did you go into the real estate business? *a.* How did you happen to go into it? *b.* Have you remained in it continuously since you went into it?

2. Do you plan to remain in the real estate business? *a.* If yes: What is it that you like about it? *b.* If no: Why do you plan to leave the real estate business?

3. When did you establish this business? *a.* Are you the sole owner? If not owner: *b.* When was this firm established? *c.* What is your position in the firm?

4. What are the main functions of your business? (Probe re change in function.) *a.* In what kind of property does your firm deal mostly?

5. In what areas of the city is your business carried on at present? (Main area) *a.* Was your business carried on there in the past also? (If no, probe re change in area.) *b.* Has your business been located here from the beginning? (If no, probe re reason for moving.)

6. How many salesmen do you have? *a.* Approximately how many sales has your office made a year in the last few years? *b.* How many persons do you require to handle your management business? *c.* How many buildings does your office manage? Residential only? *d.* How many units does that make? *e.* How many management clients do you have?

7. What would you say is the chief factor that makes for a good residential area, a good neighborhood?

8. When Negroes began to come closer to [name of area], how did this affect your sales and rentals?

9. When Negroes entered and took up residence in this area, how did this affect your business? *a.* What adjustments did you make? (Probe re change in function or type of property.)

10. What is the present situation in this area with reference to conditions affecting the neighborhood and your business?

11. What do you call this area in regard to its racial composition? (Probe re conception of other kinds of areas.)

12. Do you manage any properties for Negro owners?

If yes: *a.* How many of such clients do you have? *b.* How many of such buildings do you manage? *c.* When did you first take them on? *d.* How did you happen to do so at that time? *e.* How many of these properties contain (1) Negro tenants only? (2) white tenants only? (3) white and Negro tenants? *f.* In what areas are these properties located? *g.* How many Negro tenants do you have in these properties? *h.* Have you lost the management of any properties that were sold to Negro buyers?

If no: *i.* Have you ever managed such properties? *j.* If yes: How is it that you gave up managing them? *k.* If no: Why do you not manage such property? (Probe re fear of loss of clients.)

13. Do you manage any properties owned by white persons but occupied partly or wholly by Negroes?

If yes: *a.* How many of such clients do you have? *b.* How many of such buildings do you manage? *c.* When did you first take these properties on? *d.* When did Negroes begin to move into these properties? *e.* Did the owners make the change in occupancy on your advice? *f.* How many of these properties contain (1) Negro tenants only? (2) white and Negro tenants? *g.* In what areas are these properties located? *h.* How many Negro tenants are there in these properties? *i.* How do the Negro tenants with whom you have come to deal compare with white tenants of similar properties in regard to (1) payment of rent (rent difference, contract terms)? (2) care of property? (3) effect on the neighborhood? (4) Do Negro tenants pay more rent than white tenants for the same kind of apartment? (5) Do you require a security deposit from white and Negro tenants? (6) Is the cost of maintenance the same for white-occupied and Negro-occupied buildings of similar type? (7) Is your method of rent collection the same for white and Negro tenants? (8) Are your screening procedures the same for white and Negro tenants?

If no: *j.* Have you ever managed such properties? *k.* If yes: How is it that you gave up managing them? *l.* If no: Why do you not manage such property?

14. Are you selling properties to Negroes? (In Area C: Do you sell property to Negroes?)

If yes: *a.* When did you begin to make such sales? *b.* How did you happen to do so at that time? *c.* About how many sales to Negroes have you been making a year for the last few years? *d.* In what areas are these properties located? *e.* Are there any differences for white and Negro clients in regard to (1) your procedures in showing the property? (2) the price? (3) the financing of the sale? (Probe re inducement, hindrance to Negro practice.) *f.* Have you lost any white clients on account of these sales? *g.* How do Negro owners of property compare with white owners of similar properties in regard to (1) upkeep of payments? (2) care of property? (3) effect on the neighborhood?

If no: *h.* Why do you not sell property to Negroes? (Probe re fear of loss of clients.)

15. If broker does not deal with Negroes: Have you ever had Negro clients? *a.* If yes: How is it that you do not have any now? *b.* If no: Why do you not have Negro clients?

16. Would you sell (or rent) property to Negroes in an area where there are no Negroes? If not owner: Would the firm . . .?

If yes: *a.* Why would you do so? *b.* When would you do so? *c.* Have you ever had occasion to do so?

If no: *d.* Why would you not do so? (Probe re reactions from brokers, clients, community.) *e. When* would you consider you *could* sell property on a street to Negroes? *f.* How do you determine that you could do so *then*? *g.* Has this been your policy since the beginning of your business? (Probe re change.) *h.* Would you adhere to this policy when considering the management of property owned by Negroes or property occupied by Negroes?

17. How do you handle the matter of refusing to sell a piece of property to a Negro? (Probe re change in practice.)

18. Have any brokers come into this area to buy up property and to resell it to Negroes? If yes: *a.* Are they white or Negro? *b.* How do they go about buying in the area and reselling? *c.* What are the sources of gain in these transactions? *d.* Do you take any steps to warn owners in the area about the situation? *e.* How is it that the people of the community will deal with these brokers instead of the local, established real estate firm? *f.* In most cases, who *begins* the sale of property in a white area to a Negro buyer? *g.* What obstacles may the broker encounter in the process of selling property to Negroes in a white or nearly white area? (Probe re how he copes with

them.) *h.* What circumstances would make it easier for a broker to sell to Negroes in a white area?

19. In your experience, have you found that property values are affected in any way when Negroes enter an area? If yes: *a.* In what way? *b.* How does this come about?

Add *c–i* if necessary: *c.* When do the major changes in value occur — *before* Negroes approach an area, *when* they are approaching an area, or *after* they have entered it? *d.* How much of a change in price is there? *e.* Does this trend apply to all kinds of property? *f.* Is the white seller likely to get a fair price from a Negro buyer, if he sells through a reliable broker? *g.* As Negroes begin to move into an area, *at what time* during this shift do sellers get the *highest* price and the *lowest* price for their property? *h.* How do these changes in value affect your business? *i.* How do these changes affect your own ownership of property, if any, in this area? (Probe re Negro tenants.)

20. Are you a member of the Chicago Real Estate Board?

If yes: *a.* Are you active in the Board? (attendance, positions) *b.* How long have you been a member? *c.* What does it mean to you and your business to be a member?

If no: *d.* Why do you not become a member?

21. How does the Board look upon a broker who sells property in a white area to a Negro buyer? *a.* What influence can the Board bring to bear upon a broker to discourage him from making such sales? (Probe re Code of Ethics, nonmembers.) *b.* What other organizations can influence the broker in this respect, either directly or through the Board? (Probe in what ways.)

22. How many banks and how many savings and loan associations in Chicago make loans to Negro buyers of residential property, as far as you know? *a.* Has the action of a lending institution ever kept you from making sales to Negroes? *b.* If yes: *How* has it kept you from doing so? (Probe re terms, other ways.)

23. What does it mean when real estate brokers and lenders say that an area is "written off"? *a.* Would the lenders have more to do with determining this than the real estate men? *b.* Do you know of any white families that have bought property for residential purposes in an area where there are Negroes living? *c.* If yes: Did they buy from Negroes?

24. What organizations in [name of area] are, in your opinion, doing the most to protect the neighborhood? (Probe re program, participation.)

25. What do the white people of this community say about having Negroes as neighbors? (Probe re children playing together, attempt to drive white people out.)

26. Have you received any requests from within the community not to sell or rent property to Negroes in [name of area]?

If yes: *a.* From whom did these requests come (clients, organizations, businessmen, etc.)? *b.* Have you received any threats (withdrawal of business, physical)? *c.* Has there been any other kind of pressure? (Any social pressure?)

d. Has there been any pressure from any source outside of this area to keep you from making sales to Negroes? *e.* Did you comply with the requests which you received?

27. What do you advise the people of the community to do when Negroes are moving closer to the area? *a.* When they are already in the area?

28. Have any Negro brokers come into this area? If yes: Could you tell me something about their procedures and influence in the area in regard to change?

29. Do you live in [name of area]? *a.* If yes: How long have you lived here? *b.* If no: Did you ever live in [name of area]? If yes: *c.* How long? *d.* When, why moved?

Group A: Brokers living in area of business operation:

30. Do you participate in the community life of [name of area] — I mean belonging to a local organization or church or taking part in some community work or program?

31. Where does most of your social visiting take place — in [name of area] or outside of it?

32. Do you plan to remain living in [name of area]? If yes: Why do you plan to remain here? If no: Why do you plan to leave the area?

Group B: Brokers living outside area of business operation:

30. Do you participate in the community life of [name of area] — I mean belonging to a local organization or taking part in some community work or program?

31. Where does most of your social visiting take place — in your area of residence, in this area, or elsewhere?

32. Do you plan to continue your business in [name of area]? If yes: Why do you plan to continue your business here? If no: Why do you plan to leave the area?

33. What would you say is the goal of the real estate business? *a.* What do you consider to be *success* in your business?

34. What do you achieve by your present policy? (For his business, the community.) *a.* What purpose do you serve by selling/not selling property in a white area to Negro persons?

35. For a broker to whom his work means a good deal, what would you say is the main deterrent, the main thing, that keeps him from selling property to Negroes in a white area?

36. If owners of slum properties promote exclusion of Negroes from white areas, is that policy profitable to the white broker?

37. Has there been any change in your thinking in regard to the Negro population in relation to real estate?

If yes: *a.* What change? *b.* What contributed to this change? *c.* Did your practices change when your ideas changed? *d.* If yes: How did your practices change? *e.* If no: How is it that your practices did not change when your ideas changed?

If no: *f.* Has there been any change in your practices with Negroes since you have been dealing with them?

38. When you first entered the real estate business, from whom or from what source did you learn what was current practice in regard to selling or renting property to Negroes? *a.* Have you had any courses in real estate?

39. What would be your solution to the problem of housing the increasing Negro population in Chicago? *a.* What is your opinion on the possibility of integration? *b.* How do you yourself feel about having a Negro neighbor? *c.* How do you feel about white and Negro children playing and going to school together, growing up together, perhaps marrying later?

40. Where did you grow up?

41. What were your experiences with Negroes as you grew up?

42. In what religion were you brought up?

43. What is the last school you attended?

Appendix B. Criteria to Determine Direction of Components 1–8

Components	Respondents' Statements Favorable toward Negroes	Respondents' Statements with Balance of Favorable and Unfavorable Views of Negroes	Respondents' Statements Unfavorable toward Negroes
1.	Negroes are like white people or better; judgments in general involving praise with no comparison with white people.	Some judgments containing praise, some blame.	Negroes are below white people in various ways; adverse criticism of all or majority of Negroes.
2.	Expressing acceptance of Negroes by white people.	Some expressing acceptance of Negroes by white people, others rejection or both acceptance and rejection.	Expressing rejection of all or of majority of Negroes by white people.
3.	No drop in property value occurs when Negroes approach or enter area, or after; increase of value.	Drop in property value and also increase in value with different kinds of property and/or different time periods during approach and entry.	Any drop in property value occurs because of Negroes' approach and entry into area.
4.	Negro owners and tenants have beneficial effect on neighborhood.	Negro owners have beneficial effect on neighborhood but Negro tenants do not; both good and bad Negro areas.	Negro owners and tenants generally have harmful effect on neighborhood; some over-all effect(s) of Negroes' entry are harmful.
5.	Racial residential integration is here or possible now and racial succession not inevitable.	Racial residential integration not possible now but may come in this generation.	Integration impossible or inadvisable now and racial succession inevitable for present at least and likely for long time to come.
6.	No harmful consequences to others as result of Negroes' entry into area.	Beneficial or harmful consequences to others depending on caliber of the Negroes entering area.	Harmful consequences to others as result of Negroes' entry into area.
7.	Principles, values, and/or higher authorities supporting sale or rental to Negroes in white area or block.	Principles supporting sale or rental to Negroes in white area or block where community known not to object or where Negro movement would not be advanced thereby.	Principles, values, and/or higher authorities justifying refusal to sell or rent to Negroes in white area or block, with or without specific reference to component 6.
8.	Approval of racial residential integration and/or a personal wish for it.	Personal disapproval of segregation and approval of racial residential integration, but doubt advisability of promoting integration now.	Personal rejection of racial residential integration and wish for continued segregation.

Appendix C. Tables 1–47

The total number of respondents in each area, unless otherwise noted, is 37 in Area A, 23 in Area B, 21 in Area C, 6 in Area CX, and 3 in the Area C branch offices. DNA refers throughout to *does not apply.*

Table 1. Age of Business in 1956, by 5-Year Periods[a]

Starting Period	Respondents in Area				
	A	B	C	CX	C, Branch Offices
1951–1955	4	1	2		
1946–1950	5	6	4	2	
1941–1945	2	2	2	1	
1936–1940	4		3	1	
1931–1935	4	4	1	1	1
1926–1930	1	2			1
1921–1925	7	2	4		
1916–1920	4	1		1	1
1911–1915	1	1	2		
1906–1910	1	2			
Before 1906	4	2	3		

[a] Question 3, Appendix A.

Table 2. Respondents' Main Business Functions[a]

Main Functions	Respondents in Area				
	A	B	C	CX	C, Branch Offices
Sales	2	2	3		
Management	1	4			
Sales, management ...	10	6	1	3	2
Sales, management, insurance	11	4	10	3	1
Sales, management, insurance, mortgages	2	3	2		
Sales, management, insurance, mortgages, appraisal	8	2	1		
Sales or management, other[b]	3	2	4		

[a] Question 4, Appendix A.
[b] Insurance, mortgages, appraisal, consulting, building.

Table 3. Time of First Dealing by Respondents
with Negroes, by 5-year Periods, as of 1956[a]

Starting Period	Respondents in Area				
	A	B	C	CX	C, Branch Offices
1951–1955	10	10	10	4	1
1946–1950	4	5	2		
1941–1945	4	1	1		
1936–1940	3			1	
1931–1935	1	2			
1926–1930	3	1			
1921–1925	1				
1916–1920	4				
1911–1915		1			
1906–1910	1				
In the past, not now ...	3	1	1		
No dealings yet	3	2	7	1	2

[a] Questions 12c, 13c, and 14a, Appendix A.

Table 4. Distribution of Respondents by Time in Their
Business When Dealings with Negroes Began and
by Area Where They Began

Area	At Start	After Start	No Dealings Now	No Data
A	12	18	6	1
Home	7	7		
Other	5	11		
B	8	12	3	
Home	2	8		
Other	6	4		
C	2	11	8	
Home				
Other	2	11		
CX		4	1	1
Home		1		
Other		3		
C, branch offices		1	2	
Home				
Other		1		

Table 5. IIow the Respondents Happened to Begin to Sell to Negroes
and to Manage Negro-Occupied Buildings

	Respondents in Area				
Circumstances	A	B	C	CX	C, Branch Offices
Selling to Negroes					
Negroes entered, couldn't sell to anyone else ..	14	9	2[a]	3	
Negro neighborhood, people listed property ..	3	4[b]	4		
Policy from start in Negro areas	3	2	2		
Set up office where Negroes entering, to make money	5	3	1		
To help white client leave	2		4	1	1
No sales yet but willing	1	2	3	2	
No dealings	2	1	5		2
Manage property with Negro tenants but no sales	6				
DNA[c]	1	2			
Managing Negro-Occupied Buildings					
Vacancies, couldn't rent to white people	14	10	1	4	
Policy from start	4[d]	2			
Took over Negro-occupied buildings	4	1	1		
Acquired buildings where Negroes entering area	2		1		
Made sale, hence got management	4	3	1	1	
No data	3				
DNA	6	7	17	1	3

[a] Refers to dealings in some area other than Area C.

[b] In 1 case, a Negro owner listed his property.

[c] DNA here refers to management firms.

[d] One respondent in Area A took over a business already managing Negro-occupied buildings and continued the policy.

Table 6. Respondents' Reactions and Adjustments to Negroes'
Entering Their Area of Operation

	Respondents in Area		
Reactions and Adjustments	A	B	CX
No dealings with Negroes	6	3	1
Manage buildings in white part of area	5[a]		
Manage buildings in other areas		1	
Changed business function and area	1[a]	1[a]	
Extended operation city-wide			1
Began operation in subdivision		1	
Tried to avoid dealing with Negroes by making adjustments, finally had to begin, still maintain adjustments	3	2	2
Extended operation into other areas			1
Extended operation city-wide	1	1	1
Concentrated on finding white purchasers	1		
Opened branch office in suburb	1[b]	1	
Began to deal with Negroes when no choice, but without adjustment	9	10	3
Began to deal with Negroes, but not too dependent on them	3	1	
Manage own buildings in other areas	1	1	
Manage others' buildings in other areas	1		
Have clients elsewhere	1		
Dealt with Negroes elsewhere, began in home area	7	3	
Established office when Negroes entered to deal with them	9	4	

[a] 3 in Area A and 1 in Area B dealt with Negroes in the past.
[b] Branch office proved unsuccessful and was closed.

Table 7. Properties Managed by Respondents for Negro Owners[a] and for White
Owners with Negro Tenants[b] and the Ratio of Negro Owners
to the Total Number of Owners of Property Managed

Properties Managed	Respondents in Area				
	A	B	C	CX	C, Branch Offices
Negro-owned					
Yes	16	8	2	1	
No	18	11	13	5	3
DNA	3	4	6		
White-owned, Negro-occupied					
Yes	23	12	2	4	
No	7	3	13	2	3
Self-owned, Negro-occupied	4	4			
DNA	3	4	6		
Ratio of Negro owners to all owners					
1–9.99%	5	5	1	1	
10–24.99%	5	2			
25–49.99%	4	1	1		
No data	2				

[a] Question 12, Appendix A.
[b] Question 13, Appendix A.

Table 8. Respondents' Loss of Management of Buildings Sold to Negroes [a]

Loss of Management	Respondents in Area				
	A	B	C	CX	C, Branch Offices
Yes	18	4	4	2	1
No	11	11	11	4	1
Did not wish to retain	3	1			
No data	2	1			1
DNA	3	6	6		

[a] Question 12h, Appendix A.

Table 9. Respondents' Dealings with Negroes at First and in 1955–1956,
by Business Function

Business Function in Dealings with Negroes	Respondents in Area				
	A	B	C	CX	C, Branch Offices
First Dealings					
Sold	12[ab]	11[ab]	11[ab]	2	1
Managed	16[c]	6[c]	1	1	
Sold and managed	6	4	2	2	
None yet	3	2	1	1	2
Dealings in 1955–1956					
Sell and manage	21	12	3	4	
Sell only	3[d]	4	9[d]		1[d]
Do not sell	8	3[e]	6		2
Do not sell, but willing	4[f]	2[e]	3[g]	2	
DNA (re selling)	1	2			
Manage only	7	4	1	1	
Negotiate mortgages [h]	11	5	7	1	
Sell insurance [h]	8	4	5	2	
Make appraisals [h]	4	1	3	1	
Build houses [h]		1			
Give free advice [h]	2		2		
None	6	3	8	1	2

[a] Respondent still dealt with Negroes in sales only. In Area A, 1 case, in Area B, 2, and in Area C, 1.

[b] Firm dealt with Negroes in past but not in 1955–1956. In Area A, 3 cases, in Area B, 1, and in Area C, 1.

[c] Respondent still dealt with Negroes in management only. In Area A, 6 cases, in Area B, 3, including 3 in Area A and 2 in Area B who partly or wholly owned the Negro-occupied property they managed.

[d] Of these, 1 respondent of Area A, 2 of Area C, and the Area C branch office sell only to help a client.

[e] 1 sold to Negroes in the past.

[f] Of these 4, 3 sold to Negroes in the past, and 1 of the 3 was selling Negro-owned lots in an outlying subdivision to white buyers. The fourth man had just taken over another man's business and expected many future sales to Negroes.

[g] 1 had sold to Negroes in the past, but in 1956 was selling houses in a new development in an area where there were no Negroes.

[h] There was no question in the Interview Schedule about services other than sales and management, but some respondents volunteered the information. Hence, these data do not represent the result of a complete canvas of the respondents.

Table 10. Sales to Negroes as a Percentage of
Respondents' Total Sales for 1951–1955[a]

			Respondents in Area		
Percentage	A	B	C	CX	C, Branch Offices
<1	1	1	2		
1–9.99	4	2	4	1	1
10–24.99	5	4	3	1	
25–49.99	4	3	2	2	
50–74.99	2	3			
75–89.99	5	1			
90 and over....	3	2	1		

[a] Questions 6a and 14c, Appendix A.

Table 11. Negro-Occupied Units as a Percentage of
the Total Number of Units Managed by
Respondents in 1955[a]

		Respondents in Area		
Percentage	A	B	C	CX
<1	1			1
1–9.99	4	2	2[b]	3
10–24.99	5	2		1
25–49.99	5	4	1[b]	
50–74.99	5	3	1	
75–89.99	3	2		
90 and over ...	4	3		
No data	1			

[a] Questions 6d, 12g, and 13h, Appendix A.
[b] In Area C, 2 of the 4 brokers were managing co-operative apartments with tenant-owners.

Table 12. Respondents' Restrictions in Dealings with Negroes

	Respondents in Area				
Restrictions	A	B	C	CX	C, Branch Offices
No dealings with Negroes	6	3	8	1	2
Partially restricted sales and/or management	27	17	13	5	1
No restriction	4	3			
Willing to sell property in white area to Negroes [a]					
Yes	4	3			
Qualified yes	4	2	1	1	
No	27	17	20[c]	5	3
DNA	2[b]	1			
Willing to rent property in white area to Negroes					
Yes	3	4		1	
Qualified yes	3	1	1		
No	29	15	11	5	3
Unwilling to manage property with Negro tenants	1	2	4		
DNA	1	1	5		

[a] See Question 16, Appendix A. It was understood that the white owner was willing to sell to a Negro.

[b] One said that Question 16 did not apply to him and refused to take a stand. He spoke of selling only very large properties which Negroes do not usually buy.

[c] The owner of one firm was not required to answer Question 16 but said, "I haven't been confronted with it and I don't know. I wouldn't want to take a stand on it. That's the ultimate of controversy. I would just as soon not arrive at any conclusions in that respect at all." However, in another answer he revealed his willingness to sell to Negroes — but not in an area where there are no Negroes.

Table 13. When Respondents Consider They *Could* Sell to Negroes, According to Emphasis on Neighborhood or Area, Neighborhood and Block, and Block [a]

When Respondent Believes He Could Sell to Negroes	Respondents in Area				
	A	B	C	CX	C, Branch Offices
Any time	4	3			
Neighborhood or area	8	5	10	2	
Residents of area prepared to accept them	3	1	3		
Some Negroes in neighborhood, no trouble	2	1	3		
5 or 6 Negroes in area and properties for sale to any desirable family	1				
Neighborhood 1/4 Negro and owners ask him to sell			1		
Neighborhood 1/2 Negro	1	1	2	1	
Neighborhood at least 3/5 Negro	1				
Neighborhood 3/4 Negro			1		
Neighborhood all Negro		1		1	
Negroes in area and Catholic Church accepts them		1			
Neighborhood and block	3	3	1		1
1 building sold to Negroes, other Negro owners in the vicinity, police protection, trend inevitable ..		1	1		
Neighborhood partly Negro, residents resigned to neighborhood's going colored, and 2 or more Negro families in block	1				1
3 or 4 Negro families in block, tenants give notice, and enough in area to indicate trend	1				
4 or 5 Negroes in the block, neighborhood obviously changing, people know it's inevitable and list properties		2			
No longer possible to sell to white [b]	1				
Block	17	10	7	4	1
1 Negro in block	5	2	1		
2 buildings Negro		1			
2 or 3 Negro families in block ..	5	2	2	2	
3 Negro families in block	2	1			
3 or 4 Negro families in block ..	1	1		1	
4 or 5 Negro families in block ..		1	1		1
Block 1/2 Negro	2	2		1	
Block >1/2 Negro	2	1	2		
Not under any circumstances	1	1	2		
Has not thought about it	1		1		
Would not take a stand	1				
"That would not enter our work" ..	1				1
DNA	1	1			

[a] Question 16e, Appendix A.   [b] Applies only to home area.

318

Table 14. Respondents' Techniques of Refusal to
Sell Properties to Negroes

	Respondents in Area				
Technique of Refusal	A	B	C	CX	C, Branch Offices
No misrepresenting	15	10	11	4	2
Direct no	1	1	1		1
Owner doesn't want to sell to colored	6	2	3	2	
Send him to owner, let owner tell him			2		
"It's in a white area. We can't sell."	4	3	1		
Don't want to be first one to sell, explain our position	2	1	2	1	
Nothing in this section I can sell to colored	1	1	1		1
Property not yet available for Negro purchase	1	2		1	
Don't have homes for sale to Negroes			1		
Warning	1		1	1	
Don't think they would be happy in there (with explanation)			1	1	
Mention danger to property	1				
Misrepresenting or evading	7	6	5		
Don't submit it to him	3	2			
Building not for sale	1	1			
Building sold (or, we have deposit)	1		1		
Don't have a thing in this block for sale	2	3	2		
Don't have what they want — or if we find it, we'll call back			1		
Get name over the telephone and judge whether they're colored or not — then say you already have a contract, it's sold			1		
Other	4	3	2	1	1
Never had occasion to refuse	3	3			
Don't take listings where those things exist	1				
Don't know, never had the experience				1	
They don't ask us			2		1
No data	1	1			
DNA	9	3	2		

Table 15. Differences in Showing Property to White and Negro
Prospective Buyers and in Financing the Sale [a]

Differences	Respondents in Area				
	A	B	C	CX	C, Branch Offices
Showing property					
Yes	4	4	2	3	
No	16	11	9	1	1
No data	4		1		
DNA	13	8	9	2	2
Financing sale					
Land contract for deed more common among Negro buyers than white	20	11	9	2	
First mortgage as common among Negro buyers as among white ...	4	6	4	1	1
Purchase money mortgage more common among Negro buyers than white [b]	1			1	
No data	3	1			
DNA	9	5	8	2	2

[a] Question 14e(1),(3), Appendix A.

[b] Benson, North, and Ring, *Real Estate Principles and Practices*, p. 157: *"Purchase money mortgage.* In many sales of realty the purchaser does not wish to pay the full price in cash. Under such circumstances it is stipulated in the contract between the parties that the purchaser shall give to the seller his bond (or note) and a mortgage on the property to secure part of the price. This is known as a 'purchase money mortgage.' "

Appendixes

Table 16. Respondents' Techniques of Refusal to Rent Apartments to Negroes

	Respondents in Area				
Technique of Refusal	A	B	C	CX	C, Branch Offices
No misrepresenting	19	9	7	4	
Direct no	1				
Owner not considering renting to colored at present	6	1	1	3	
Owner won't mix occupancy		1	2		
Submit application to owner, who turns it down; or call owner	3				
It's in a white area; nothing we can do about it	1	1			
Nothing in this section I can rent to colored			1		
Don't want to be first ones to rent to nonwhite				1	
Building hasn't changed over yet	3	1	1		
Building not eligible for Negro occupancy	1	2			
Not a neighborhood for colored	1	2	1		
Don't have apartments for rent to Negroes			1		
Explain danger of our position, public relations problem	3	1			
Warning	1		1	1	
Don't think they would be happy in there (with explanation)			1	1	
Mention danger of damage to property	1				
Misrepresenting or evading	7	3	1		
Don't offer it to them, no addresses in ads	1	2			
Don't have any apartments			1		
Apartment not for rent		1			
Apartment rented	1				
Offer him location among colored	1				
We find excuses	4				
Other	4	4			
Never had occasion to refuse ...	2	4			
Never been asked that	1				
Don't handle such properties ...	1				
No data	2		1	1	
DNA	4	7	11		3

321

Table 17. Respondents' Role in Change from White Tenants to Negro[a]

Owner Changed Occupancy	Respondents in Area			
	A	B	C	CX
On respondent's advice	9	10	2	3
Of his own accord	5	1		
Because of trend (joint decision) ...	3		1	1
Respondent's property	6	4		
No data	1			
DNA	13	8	18	2

[a] Question 13e, Appendix A.

Table 18. Treatment of White and Negro Tenants in Screening Procedures, Security Deposit, and Amount of Rent

Treatment	Respondents in Area			
	A	B	C	CX
Screening procedures [a]				
Same for white and Negro applicants	10	6	2	2
More careful for Negroes	13	7	2	2
Less careful for Negroes	1			
No data	4	3		
DNA	9	7	17	2
Security deposit required [b]				
From all white and Negro tenants	9	5		4
From neither white nor Negro tenants	7	3	2	
From all Negro tenants, some white	3			
From Negroes only	5	6	1	
Wage garnishment for Negroes		2		
No data	4			
DNA	9	7	18	2
Amount of rent [c]				
Negro tenants pay more than white	9	9	2	2
Negro tenants pay same as white	15	6	1	1
Negro tenants pay less than white	2	1		
No data	4			1
DNA	7	7	18	2

[a] Question 13i(8), Appendix A.
[b] Question 13i(5), Appendix A.
[c] Question 13i(4), Appendix A.

Table 19. Comparison of Negro and White Tenants' Payment of Rent [a]

Negro Tenants' Payment of Rent	Respondents in Area			
	A	B	C	CX
More prompt than white	1		1	
As prompt as white	15	10	2	2
Better than hillbillies, not so good as white ...	1	1		
Not so prompt as white	14	5	1[b]	1
DNA	6	7	17	3[c]

[a] Question 13i(1), Appendix A.
[b] These are the tenant-owners of cooperative apartments.
[c] One respondent said that he had started converting a building from white to Negro occupancy not long before, and it was too early to say.

Table 20. Comparison of Negroes and White People as Owners and Tenants in Care of Property and as Tenants in Cost of Building Maintenance[a]

Comparison	Respondents in Area				
	A	B	C	CX	C, Branch Offices
Negro owner's care with white					
Better	8	5	3	1	1
Just as good	15	7	7	4	
Not so good	3	5	1		
Don't know		1	1		
No data	1	1			
DNA	10	4	9	1	2
Negro tenant's care with white					
Better	1	1	1		
Just as good	10	8	3	2	
Not so good	19	5			
Very bad	1	2		1	
DNA	6	7	17	3	3
Cost of maintenance in Negro-tenanted buildings with white tenanted					
Same cost	9	6	3	2	
Higher cost	18	11		1	
No data	2				
DNA	8	6	18	3	3

[a] Questions 13i(2),(6) and 14g(2), Appendix A.

Table 21. Direction of Respondents' Policy on Dealing with Negroes

Direction of Policy on Dealing with Negroes	Respondents in Area				
	A	B	C	CX	C, Branch Offices
Will avoid it as long as possible ..	2	1	4[a]		2
Have not done so yet, but will in a predominantly Negro area, or if they enter area of operation	1	1	3	1	
Did in the past, not at present, but willing to do so	3		1		
Do in areas largely Negro, but contemplate moving offices to white area	1[b]	2		2	
Toward *less*	4	2	4		1
Do by necessity	2	4		1	
Old policy of dealing with them continued	7	4	1		
Policy of dealing begun, will be continued	5	3	6		
Forced to begin, but more and more satisfied to do so		3		1	
Toward *more*	4		2	1	
Began with purpose of doing so and continuing	8	3			

[a] One of the 4 maintains that if "there has been a penetration of one or two colored families, . . . the white residential property owners, instead of headlong panic, should hold fast and maintain the fine little community in which they live . . ."

[b] This broker plans to do some building in a southern state and to spend only part of the time in the office in Area A.

Table 22. Respondents' Distinctions among Negroes [a]

Distinctions among Negroes	Respondents in Area				
	A	B	C	CX	C, Branch Offices
Believe all types of colored and white — good and bad in both — should be treated as individuals	11	9	4	2	
Distinguish lower, middle, and upper class	4	2	1		
Distinguish "high and low" or "good and bad" classes	6	2	3	1	
Regard some as fine, educated, but majority not	15	7	10	3	2
Observe caste system among Negroes	1	1			
No distinctions made		2	3		1

[a] Question 37, Appendix A, elicited many of the answers in this table. The questions on payment of rent, care of property, and property values contributed as well.

Table 23. Respondents' Reports of White People's Responses
to Having Negroes as Neighbors [a]

White People's Responses	Respondents in Area				
	A	B	C	CX	C, Branch Offices
Do not want Negro neighbors, sell and get out	16	9	17	4	1
Before Negroes enter, say, "I don't mind," but when Negroes enter, move	4	1			
Some who remain say Negroes are good neighbors, but majority don't want them, want to leave as soon as they come in	5	5	2	1	1
Some willing to accept a few nice Negroes	1	3			
Some say Negroes good neighbors, some say opposite	3	2	2		
Reaction from one extreme to the other	3	1			
Don't object so much as before....	1	1			
Good relations between white and Negro neighbors	2	1		1	
Question has not come up	1				1
No data	1				

[a] Question 25, Appendix A.

Table 24. Respondents' Reports of White People's Purchases of Residential Property in Negro Areas for Their Own Use[a]

White People's Purchases in Negro Area[b]	Respondents in Area				
	A	B	C	CX	C, Branch Offices
Yes	17	4	7		2
Heard of it	3	2	2	1	
No	12	16	12	5	1
No data	5	1			

[a] Question 23b, Appendix A. Such purchases are the exception, but they are occasionally made.
[b] Limited to those purchases known to respondents.

Table 25. Effects of Negro Entry on Property Values

Effects on Property Values	Respondents in Area				
	A	B	C	CX	C, Branch Offices
Values change[a]					
Yes	35	19	18	6	2
No	1	1	1		
No experience		3	2		1
No data	1				
Timing of major changes[b]					
Before entry, Negroes approaching	11	4	5	3	
From entry on	22	13	10	3	2
Before and after entry equally		2	2		
DNA	4	4	4		1

[a] Question 19, Appendix A.
[b] Question 19c, Appendix A.

Table 26. General Patterns of the Effect of Negro Entry on Residential Property Values, by Direction and Time of Effect

Patterns	Respondents									
	Area A			Area B			Area C		Area CX, Homes and Apt. Bldgs.[a]	Area C, Branch Offices, Homes and Apt. Bldgs.[a]
	Homes and Apt. Bldgs.[a]	Homes[b]	Apt. Bldgs.[b]	Homes and Apt. Bldgs.[a]	Homes[b]	Apt. Bldgs.[b]	Homes and Apt. Bldgs.[a]	Homes[b]		
Ultimate Decrease										
Downward from approach on	3	1		6	2	1	2	1		
Downward before entry, upward upon entry,[c] downward after entry	3	3	1	2			9		4	2
Upward upon entry,[c] downward after entry	6	1	2	2	1		3		1	
Downward after entry	5	3	5	1		2	1			
Ultimate Increase										
Downward before entry, upward after entry	1	1			1					
Upward upon[c] and after entry	2	2	3	2		1			1	
Other										
Downward before entry, upward or downward after depending on various factors	1	1	1							
No effect	1					2	2			
Not enough experience to answer						1	1			
No data	1		3	3	2		2			1
DNA	4	4	1	1	1	1	1[d]			

ᵃ Respondents who see a similar effect on homes and apartment buildings. According to the statements of the real estate brokers, the effects on the smaller multiple dwellings, the 2- and 3-flat structures, follow closely the effects on homes. A number of the respondents stressed the demand for these smaller buildings that provide income as well as most of the advantages of the single dwelling. Although they are income-producing properties, the respondents coupled them with the single dwellings.

ᵇ Respondents who see a different effect on homes and apartment buildings.

ᶜ "Upon entry" includes first entry and the period immediately following.

ᵈ The respondent managed an apartment building. The column for "Apt. Bldgs." for Area C was omitted for lack of space. The table appears in its entirety in Rose Helper, "The Racial Practices of Real Estate Institutions in Selected Areas of Chicago," Ph.D. thesis, Department of Sociology, University of Chicago, 1958, pp. 235–236.

NOTE: Table 26 presents the general patterns of effect on values of homes (including the smaller multiple dwellings) and apartment buildings of the movement of Negroes into an area. Although a number of patterns could be distinguished, there are enough similarities among them to permit a less detailed summarization. One such similarity is present in the outcome of Negro entry. In the first 4 patterns, the entry of Negroes into an area results in a decrease in the value of residential property, whereas in the fifth and sixth patterns it results in an increase in value of such property. A percentage for the number of respondents in each of Areas A, B, and C who saw decrease in value as the outcome was obtained in the following manner. The numbers of column 1 in each area were doubled to give representation to the respondent's 2 judgments, one for homes and the other for apartment buildings. The numbers of the first 4 patterns in the 3 columns of each area were added, and a subtraction was then made. Several answers among the first 4 patterns estimated a final effect of neither increase nor decrease, but a return to the market prices before Negro entry — that is, normal prices. There were 2 such answers in Area A for homes and 2-flats, 1 in Area B for all kinds of residential property, 1 in Area C for homes, and 1 of the Area C branch offices for homes and apartment buildings. These were subtracted from the totals of the 4 patterns in the columns to which they belonged. Before the percentages were calculated, the numbers of the last 3 categories were subtracted from the totals of their respective columns.

For Area CX and Area C, Branch Offices, the columns for "Homes" and "Apt. Bldgs." were omitted because none of these respondents saw a different effect on homes and apartment buildings, and there was no room for these columns on the page.

Table 27. Respondents' Opinions about the Effect
of Negroes' Entry on a Neighborhood[a]

Effect	Respondents in Area				
	A	B	C	CX	C, Branch Offices
All-round good, as good as or better than white	1	1		1	
Good and bad, as with white people	4	3	2		
Not so good as white people's for 1 or more reasons	26	15	12	4	2
Divided judgment: Negro owners, good; Negro tenants, not good	4	2			
Incomplete answer: Negro owner only, like white; Negro tenant only, not so good	2[b]	2[c]	2[c]		
Not enough experience to answer ..			4	1	1
No data			1		

[a] Questions 13i(3) and 14g(3), Appendix A.

[b] These respondents do not sell to Negroes. They only manage buildings with Negro tenants.

[c] These respondents either do not manage buildings at all or do not manage buildings with Negro tenants. They do sell buildings to Negroes.

Table 28. Respondents' Proposed Solutions to the Problem of Housing More Negroes in Chicago[a]

Proposal	Respondents in Area				
	A	B	C	CX	C, Branch Offices
Continued conversions of white areas into colored, since white people leave as Negroes enter	12	4[b]	3	1	1
Separate district where homes could be built	2			1	
First build on vacant land, then tear down old buildings they occupy	2[c]	2			
Build in colored areas	1	1[d]	3		
Build in communities where they are already accepted			1		
Let Negroes provide housing for themselves		3[e]	2		
Colored should buy where Negroes already are			1[d]		
Public housing	2[f]	2	1		
Rebuild slum areas			1		
Build more apartment buildings and houses	1[d]	1	1		
Provide better mortgage financing for private owners	1[d]				
Start admitting Negroes in good neighborhoods	1				
Stop influx from South by various means	3		2	1	1
No shortage now	5	6	2		
Don't know	4	3	4	3	1[g]
No data	3	1			

[a] Question 39, Appendix A.

[b] One respondent said, "I would house them in apartment buildings — private — by buying apartment buildings and converting them."

[c] Only 1 was opposed to public housing. One suggested that Negroes go to a farm or buy a farm.

[d] These respondents were opposed to public housing for various reasons.

[e] One suggested that the federal government guarantee construction loans.

[f] One suggested public and private projects.

[g] "That is certainly not my business."

Appendixes

Table 29. Respondents' Views of Integration and of the Possibility
of Integration in Chicago

	Respondents in Area				
View of Integration	A	B	C	CX	C, Branch Offices
Personal stand					
Accept or willing to consider ...	8	7			
Conflict of values concerning integration and segregation	1	1		2	
Reject	18	10	15	3	3
Unexpressed	10	5	6	1	
As possibility in Chicago[a]					
Won't work, white people won't live with Negroes	15	9	8	3	1
Will come if certain conditions satisfied	8	4	3		1
Will come gradually, don't force .	4	3	5	2	
Will come in future	2	3			
Must come, no place for white people to run to		2	1		
It's here, must live with it	2				
It's here, works all right	3	1			
Don't know whether it will work or not	1	1	4	1	1
No data	2				

[a] Question 39a, Appendix A.

Table 30. How Respondents Determine When They Could Sell to Negroes[a]

Criteria	Respondents in Area				
	A	B	C	CX	C, Branch Offices
What white people think and feel ..	16	6	13	2	1
White owners ask broker to sell property to Negroes because they know white people won't buy it .			6	1	
White residents prepared to accept them	3	1	1		
White people in block have accepted change and understand situation (no white buyers, etc.) ..	1		2		
People in block resigned to change	2		1[b]		
People consider that when 2 sold, block is gone, and they won't hold it against broker	1			1	
White people begin to flee of own accord	1	1[c]			
Colored there and no difficulty for them	2	1	1		
After 1 Negro in block, no censure — people begin to think of moving	3	2	1		
Feeling in area	3	1	1		1
Broker's own convictions	2	1		1	1
Can't sell to anyone but colored .	2	1			
No alternative — if you don't sell, someone else will				1	1
Objective situation	10	11	5	3	
Block ½ gone, broker's reputation safe		3[d]			
Block ½ gone, whites get out ...	1				
Block predominantly colored (no demand from white, area already colored, etc.)	2	1	3	2	
No doubt area is going to change	3[e]	5	2	1[e]	
Area of transition, change inevitable	4[c]	2			
Sells to Negroes anytime, anywhere	4	3			
Will not sell to Negroes anytime, anywhere	3	2	2		
Did not know what he would do if Negroes entered his area			1		
Would not discuss	1				1
DNA	1				

[a] Question 16f, Appendix A.

[b] He said, "After 3 are in, the neighbors won't resist."

[c] The respondent in Area B and 1 in Area A do not sell at all, and their answers referred to the renting of property. The answers about renting property were largely similar to those about selling.

Appendixes

[d] One respondent considered that if 4 or 5 buildings in the block had been sold to Negroes, "we would be justified in offering property in the block to Negroes."
[e] One respondent in Area A and the respondent in Area CX considered 3 or 4 sales sufficient.

Table 31. Respondents' Willingness to Deal with Negroes,
by Business Relation with Negroes

Willingness	Respondents in Area				
	A	B	C	CX	C, Branch Offices
Not dealing with Negroes					
Never did, will not do so	2	1	3[a]		1
Never did, will if necessary			1		1
Never did, but will if they are in area	1	1	2	1	
Did, will again if opportunity arises	3	1[b]	2		
Dealing with Negroes					
As little as possible, to help client or with a particularly nice Negro	2		4		1
Do by necessity	5	4			
Less willing than in past	3				
Neither for nor against	19	14	9	4	
More willing than in past	2	2		1	

[a] 2 said they would deal with Negroes to help a client.
[b] Not too willing to deal with them again.

Table 32. Pressures on Respondents Not to Sell or Rent to Negroes
in a White Area or Block

Pressures	Respondents in Area				
	A	B	C	CX	C, Branch Offices
Types of consequences feared on basis of acquaintance with community[a]					
Business and social	11	9	9	3	1
Social only	10	6	3	2	
Business only	4	1	3		
No statement even when asked (opposed to such selling)	5	4	5	1	1
No concern (sell freely or with some qualifications)	5	3			
No data	1		1		
DNA	1				1
Experience of pressure — requests received not to sell or rent to Negroes in a white area or block[b]					
Yes	15	12	4	3	1
No	21	11	17	3	2
No data	1				
Sources of requests[c]					
Property owners, local improvement associations	2	2	1	1	
Community-wide organizations (commissions, councils)	9	9	2	2	1
Educational, religious institutions	3	1			
Members of community (clients, property owners, neighbors, friends)	8	4	1	1	1
Other sources of influence[d]					
Community-wide organizations	13	7	5	3	1
Business associations	1	2	3		
Property owners' associations	5	4	4	3	1
Educational, religious institutions	3	1	2		
Lending agencies	3	4	1	1	
None	7	4	5	1	
Don't know	6		3		

[a] Question 16d, Appendix A. Answers about the consequences of renting property to Negroes in a white area or block were largely similar to those of selling.

[b] Question 26, Appendix A.

[c] Question 26a, Appendix A. Some respondents mentioned more than 1 source.

[d] Question 21b, Appendix A. The number from each area that answered Question 21b was: Area A, 17; Area B, 16; Area C, 10; Area CX, 6; Area C branch offices, 2. Some gave more than one answer.

Appendixes

Table 33. Types of Ideologies Held by Respondents

Type of Ideology	Respondents in Area				
	A	B	C	CX	C. Branch Offices
Exclusion	30	17	21	5	3
Unqualified	10	4	7	1	3
Qualified	6	5	7	3	
Moderate	14	8	7	1	
Intermediate	6	3		1	
Integration	1	3			

Table 34. Relation between Respondents' Residence in Area of Their Business Operations and Their Holding of the Exclusion Ideology

Respondents	Area				
	A	B[a]	C	CX	C, Branch Offices
Resident					
Exclusion ideology	15	3	16		1
Other ideology		1			
Nonresident					
Exclusion ideology	15	14	5	5	2
Other ideology	7	5		1	
χ^2	3.995				
n	1				
P	.05				

[a] No significance according to Mainland's Tables (Mainland, Herrera, and Sutcliffe, *Tables for Use with Binomial Samples*, pp. 15–22, Table IV).

Table 35. Relation between Respondents' Residence in Area of Their
Business Operations and Their Practice of Exclusion[a]

Respondents	Area				
	A	B[b]	C[b]	CX	C, Branch Offices
Resident					
Practice of exclusion	13	3	15		1
Other practice	2[c]	1	1		
Nonresident					
Practice of exclusion	16	15	5	5	2
Other practice	6	4		1	
χ^2	.5578				
n	1				
P	<.50				

[a] The preliminary tests made in Tables 34 and 35 reveal that there is a relation of statistical significance only between residence and ideology among the respondents of Area A. In the test for the respondents of this area where $N > 30$, Yates's correction for continuity was applied to check the result. (Fisher, *Statistical Methods for Research Workers*, pp. 92–96. See also Walker and Lev, *Statistical Inference*, pp. 105–106.) The lack of significance in the other tests is taken to mean that, in the final analysis, no matter where the broker lives, he will probably hold the exclusion ideology and practice exclusion in his area of operation.

[b] No significance according to Mainland's Tables (Mainland, Herrera, and Sutcliffe, *Tables for Use with Binomial Samples*, pp. 15–22, Table IV).

[c] Including respondents who gave a qualified yes to Question 16, Appendix A. See Table 12.

Table 36. Influence of Banks and Savings and Loan Associations
on Respondents' Sales of Residential Property to Negroes

	Respondents in Area				
Actions of Lending Agencies	A	B	C	CX	C, Branch Offices
Loan to Negroes[a]					
Few or very few (<10%) ...	19	11	12	4	1
Quite a number (many, 50%, all)	11	8	5	2	1
Don't know	2		2		
No data	1				
DNA	4	4	2		1
Prevent sales to Negroes[b]					
Yes	15	10	5	2	
By not extending loan[c]	11	10	5	2	
By making too small a loan[c] ..	7	4	2	1	
No	11	7	4	2	1
No data	1	1			
DNA	10	6	11	2	2

[a] Question 22, Appendix A.
[b] Question 22a, Appendix A.
[c] Question 22b, Appendix A. Some respondents mentioned more than 1 method.

Table 37. Respondents' Definitions of an Area That Is "Written Off"[a]

	Respondents in Area				
Definition	A	B	C	CX	C, Branch Offices
Lending agencies will not make loans, afraid area is going to go colored		2	5	1	
Lending agencies will not make loans in changing area (going colored, conceded to colored)	16	6	8	3	2
Lending agencies will not make loans in an area when it has become colored (area gone, turned over to colored)		5	1	1	
Mortgages not written in area for number of reasons, including entry of Negroes	12	5	2		
Don't know	2	2	5	1	1
No data	6	1			
DNA	1	2			

[a] Question 23, Appendix A.

Table 38. Array of Buying and Selling Prices with Differences
in Amount and Percentage of Gain[a]

Interview No.	Buying Price	Selling Price	Amount of Difference	Percentage of Gain
69 ....$	8,000–9,000 (house)	$ 16,000–18,000	$ 8,000–9,000	100
34	9,000 (house)	11,000	2,000	22.2
23	10,000	12,000–14,000	2,000–4,000	30.0
37	10,000	16,000	6,000	60.0
78[b]	11,000 (2-flat)	19,000–20,000	8,000–9,000	77.3
21	12,000 (2-flat)	15,000–18,000	3,000–6,000	37.5
13	13,000	17,500	4,500	34.6
35	15,000	20,000	5,000	33.3
1	15,000	22,000	7,000	46.7
1	16,000	18,000	2,000	12.5
32	18,000–20,000 (house)	27,000	9,000–7,000	42.5
29	25,000	35,000–50,000	10,000–25,000	70.0
24	30,000 (6-flat)	35,000–40,000	5,000–10,000	24.9
36	30,000	40,000	10,000	33.3
4	40,000 (6-flat)	55,000–60,000	15,000–20,000	43.8
53	45,000 (6-flat)	55,000–57,000	10,000–12,000	24.4
15	45,000	50,000–70,000	5,000–25,000	33.3
61	52,000	75,000	23,000	44.2
75	140,000	240,000	100,000	71.4
63				10.0+
25				50.0 (house)
5				50.0
83				70.0
74				100

[a] There was no question in the Interview Schedule about gains in prices but some respondents volunteered these examples of sales known to them but mostly not made by them. Some gave less information about the property than others, but I did not question them further, since I was interested chiefly in the amount of gain.

[b] The respondent was referring to a 2-flat which would have to be converted to a 4-flat in order to yield a profit, and the cost of remodeling would have to be taken into account. He said, "It would cost them maybe $5,000 to remodel."

Table 39. Respondents' Holding of the Exclusion Ideology by Membership
in Chicago Real Estate Board [a]

Member of Board	Respondents in Area				
	A	B	C	CX	C, Branch Offices
Yes	24	12	10	5	3
Hold exclusion ideology	20	12	10	4	3
No	13	11	11	1	
Hold exclusion ideology	10	5	11	1	

[a] Question 20, Appendix A. See also Table 33.

Table 40. Respondents' Training in Real Estate and in Selling
and Renting Practices with Regard to Negroes

Training	Respondents in Area				
	A	B	C	CX	C, Branch Offices
Formal courses[a]					
At Chicago Real Estate Board ..	5	1			
At YMCA Real Estate Institute ..	1	3	3		
At Northwestern University	1	4		1	
At Kent School of Law				1	
Taken, school not named	6		2		
None, read on own	2	2	1	1	
None	16	12	13	1	2
No data	6	1	2	2	1
Current practice of selling or renting to Negroes learned[b]					
From own experience	6	8	6	2	1
From employer or associates, experience in employer's office	8	5	10	2	1
From father or other members of family	12	7	4	2	1
From friends in the business	3	2			
Through experience in related businesses[c]	6		1		
No data	2	1			

[a] Question 38a, Appendix A.
[b] Question 38, Appendix A.
[c] Bank mortgage department, real estate lawyer's office, maintenance work.

Table 41. Pressures from the Board to Discourage Brokers from Selling to Negroes in a White Area

Forms of Pressure	Area A Members	Area A Non-members	Area B Members	Area B Non-members	Area C Members	Area C Non-members	Area CX Members	Area CX Non-members	Area C, Branch Offices, Members
Board's attitude[a]									
Disapproval	7	4	4	1	3	1	1		
Disapproval, but cannot take stand—against public policy; members can disapprove	5			2	1				
Members disapprove openly but do same privately—a matter of conscience		3		3		3	1	1	
No official position, members can take stand	8		4		4	1	2		
Couldn't speak for Board	2		1	1		1			
Don't know		5	2	4	2	5	1		2
No data	2	1	1					1	1
Board's Action[b]									
No influence, none needed, members had these policies before joining	12	6	4	1	3	3	1		
Cannot exert influence openly (no right, not illegal); members can appeal to broker	4	2	3	2	2				
Can exert moral influence; attempts to persuade privately	1		2	1	1		1		
Can introduce formal and informal sanctions	3		1	1	1		1		
Don't know	2	4	2	6	2	6	1	1	2
No data	2	1	1	1	1	2	1		1

[a] Question 21, Appendix A.
[b] Question 21a, Appendix A.

Table 42. Relation between Respondents' Membership in Chicago Real
Estate Board and Their Holding of the Exclusion Ideology

	Area				
Respondents	A[a]	B	C	CX	C, Branch Offices
Member					
Exclusion ideology	20	12	10	4	3
Other ideology	4			1	
Nonmember					
Exclusion ideology	10	5	11	1	
Other ideology	3	6			
χ^2	.22588	6.83399			
n	1	1			
P	>.50	.01			

[a] In Tables 42, 43, and 44, in the tests for the respondents of Area A, Yates's correction for small samples was applied to check the result. In Table 44, Yates's correction and Mainland's Tables were applied in the test for the respondents of Area B. (See Table 35 for references.)

Table 43. Relation between Respondents' Membership in Chicago Real
Estate Board and Their Practice of Exclusion[a]

	Area				
Respondents	A	B	C[b]	CX	C, Branch Offices
Member					
Practice of exclusion	21	12	10	4	3
Other practice	3			1	
Nonmember					
Practice of exclusion	8	6	10	1	
Other practice	5	5	1		
χ^2	1.9967	4.5540			
n	1	1			
P	.10–.20	.05			

[a] The test results of Tables 42 and 43 suggest that in the largely Negro area are to be found a greater proportion of nonmember respondents who do not hold the exclusion ideology or practice exclusion, whereas in the white or partly white area the nonmember respondents think and act largely as do the members. Except for Area B, it appears that the respondent will hold the exclusion ideology and practice exclusion whether he is a Board member or not, except that in Area A the result might be looked upon as being "on the line" with reference to practice.

[b] No significance according to Mainland's Tables (Mainland, Herrera, and Sutcliffe, *Statistical Tables for Use with Binomial Samples*, p. 15, Table IV).

Table 44. Relation between Respondents' Holding of the Exclusion Ideology
and Their Practice of Exclusion

Respondents	Area				
	A	B	C	CX	C, Branch Offices
Hold exclusion ideology					
Practice exclusion	27	16	20	4	3
Practice other	3	1	1	1	
Hold other ideology					
Practice exclusion	2	2		1	
Practice other	5	4			
χ^2	9.4416	6.3895			
n	1	1			
P	.01	.05			

Table 45. Respondents' Reasons for Not Selling to Negroes in a White Area
by Type of Reason Receiving Main Stress[a]

Type of Reason Receiving Main Stress	Respondents in Area				
	A[b]	B[b]	C	CX	C, Branch Offices
Ideological[c]	11	7	5	3	1
Primarily ideological; then status and/or business; physical danger[d]..	12	4	9	2	
Equal stress on ideological, status, and/or business; physical danger ..	5	3	5		1
Primarily status and/or business; then ideological; physical danger...	4	5	1		
Business solely or principally, with ideological and/or status; physical danger		1		1	
Inadequate data	1		1		1

[a] Questions 16d (answers to 16h were largely similar), 34a, and 35, Appendix A.

[b] 2 respondents in Area A and 1 in Area B who only manage property were included.

[c] Moral principles, ethical principles of the real estate ideology, beliefs about race, human rights, loyalties, invocation of higher authorities.

[d] Possible physical danger was mentioned by some respondents in each category. See pp. 77–78, 138–139.

Table 46. Types of Respondents, by Consistency of Ideology and Other Factors
in Relation to Practice

Type of Respondent	Respondents in Area				
	A	B	C	CX	C, Branch Offices
The consistent, wholehearted exclusionist[a]	22	10	19	2	3
The moral-minded	17	5	13	1	2
The status-minded	5	3	6		1
The business-minded		2		1	
The inconsistent, half-hearted exclusionist	11	8	2	3	
The sympathetic	6	5	1	3	
The expedient	2	1			
The sympathetic-expedient	3	2	1		
The inconsistent, half-hearted integrationist	1	1		1	
The sympathetic				1	
The expedient	1	1			
The consistent, wholehearted integrationist	3	4			
The moral-minded	1	2[b]			
The status-minded	1				
The business-minded	1	2			

[a] "Exclusionist" and "integrationist" refer to practice. Consistency refers to the extent of correspondence between ideology and practice. Subgroupings refer to the relative prominence of the ideological-moral, status, and business reasons respondents gave in their explanations of policy and practice.

[b] Interview 14 was included here. This respondent is a wholehearted integrationist in renting property; he does not sell property.

Table 47. Changes in Respondents' Ideology
and/or Practice Concerning Negroes [a]

Direction of Change in Ideology and Practice	Respondents in Area				
	A	B	C	CX	C, Branch Offices
No change in either	18[b]	15	11	1	3
In ideology to more favorable, none in practice	4	4[c]	4	2	
In ideology to more favorable, in practice to more dealing and/or less strict [d]	6[c]		2	2	
In ideology to less favorable, none in practice	2		2		
In ideology to less favorable, in practice to less dealing and/or stricter	1	2	1	1	
None in ideology, in practice to less or no dealing	3	1			
No data	3	1	1		

[a] Question 37, Appendix A.

[b] 2 said that their views had not changed but had been formed.

[c] 2 in Area B and 1 in Area A also gave some less favorable views that they had come to have.

[d] "Strict" as used here does not refer to the practice of exclusion but mostly to regulations in selling or renting.

Notes

CHAPTER I. THE PROBLEM IN NATIONAL PERSPECTIVE

NOTE: Refer to Bibliography, pp. 368–380, for information about publication of works cited herein. NAREB is used throughout for "National Association of Real Estate Boards."

1. Minutes of regular monthly meeting of the Chicago Real Estate Board, April 4, 1917, contained in the *Chicago Real Estate Board Bulletin*, XXV (April, 1917), 313–317. See also pp. 224–226 above.

2. U.S. Housing and Home Finance Agency, "Special Problems and Approaches in Housing of Minorities and the Role of the Racial Relations Service," in *Sixth Annual Report 1952*, p. 91.

3. U.S. Housing and Home Finance Agency, *Our Nonwhite Population and Its Housing*, p. iii. "While the nonwhite population is comprised of a number of racial groups including the Chinese, Japanese, and American Indians, Negroes accounted for 92 percent of the group in 1960," pp. 1–2.

4. *Ibid.*, p. 13.

5. *Ibid.*, pp. 11–12.

6. *Ibid.*, p. 12.

7. Robinson, "Relationship between Condition of Dwellings and Rentals, by Race."

8. U.S. Housing and Home Finance Agency, *Our Nonwhite Population and Its Housing*, p. 14.

9. Duncan and Duncan, *The Negro Population of Chicago*, p. 81.

10. Duncan and Hauser, *Housing a Metropolis — Chicago*, p. 190.

11. *Ibid.*, p. 200.

12. *Ibid.*, p. 193.

13. Wallace, "Residential Concentration of Negroes in Chicago" (Ph.D. thesis).

14. Taeuber and Taeuber, *Negroes in Cities*, pp. 32–35.

15. *Ibid.*, p. 32.

16. Johnson, *Patterns of Negro Segregation*, p. 8; Myrdal, *An American Dilemma*, Vol. I, p. 618; Williams, "Factors Affecting Reactions to Public School Desegregation in American Communities" (paper).

17. Grodzins, *The Metropolitan Area as a Racial Problem*, p. 11.

18. Sengstacke, "Our Segregated Schools," p. 13.

19. Buder, "Boycott Cripples City Schools; Absences 360,000 above Normal; Negroes and Puerto Ricans Unite," p. 1; Buder, "School Boycott Is Half as Large as the First One," p. 1; Berquist, "Willis: 224,770 Out; How Big Was the Boycott?" p. 1; Gilbreth, "Leaders of Boycott Call It Big Success," p. 1; Fenton, "20,571 Pupils Out

in Boston Boycott," p. 23; Abbey, "63% of Negroes Participate in Boycott of Schools Here," p. 1; Pomfret, "Milwaukee Poles in Johnson Camp," p. 22.

20. *Chicago Sun-Times*, "White Parents in N.Y. Planning School Boycott," August 11, 1964, p. 4; Dunbar, "Board Unit OKs S. Side High School Cluster Plan," p. 1; Banas, "Willis' New School Plan Offers 93 Proposals to Improve Education: Acts to Carry Out Report by Hauser," p. 1.

21. Newman et al., "Teachers' Tale of Terror," pp. 1, 61.

22. *Chicago Tribune*, "Boycotts Seen as Cause of Class Attacks," March 5, 1964, Sec. 1, p. 16.

23. "Schools Boycotted," p. 19.

24. Powledge, "New White Group Asks Integration — Seeks Common Front with Negro and Puerto Rican Rights Leaders Here," p. 1.

25. Lewis, "Civil Rights Suit over Imbalance in Schools Fails," pp. 1, 27.

26. Loftus, "Chester Attacks Racial Problems," p. 59.

27. Silberman, "Give Slum Children a Chance: A Radical Proposal," pp. 37–42. U.S. Department of Health, Education, and Welfare, Office of Education, *School-Home Partnership in Depressed Urban Neighborhoods*.

28. Wilner et al., *The Housing Environment and Family Life*, p. 243.

29. *Ibid.*, p. 252.

30. *Ibid.*, p. 243.

31. Nathanson et al., "Surveillance of Poliomyelitis in the United States in 1956," p. 390.

32. *Ibid.*

33. *Ibid.*

34. Chicago Community Inventory, University of Chicago, *Population Growth in the Chicago Standard Metropolitan Area 1950–1957*, Table 6, p. 10.

35. Lichtenstein, *M.T.S. Annual Medical Report — 1961*, p. 2.

36. U.S. Department of Health, Education, and Welfare, Public Health Service, *Tuberculosis in the United States*, Tables 5 and 6, p. 11.

37. Letter from M. R. Lichtenstein, Medical Director of City of Chicago Municipal Tuberculosis Sanitarium, dated July 7, 1964.

38. Myrdal, *An American Dilemma*, Vol. I, p. 335.

39. *Ibid.*, p. 643.

40. *Ibid.*, pp. 346–347.

41. Chicago Commission on Human Relations, *Mortgage Availability for Non-Whites in the Chicago Area*, p. 17.

42. Frazier, *The Negro Family in the United States*, pp. 634–636.

43. Brown v. Board of Education of Topeka. Summaries of the findings of the Mid-century White House Conference on Children and Youth and of other studies on the effects of prejudice, discrimination, and segregation on the personality development of children are given in Witmer and Kolinsky, eds., *Personality in the Making*, Ch. 6; Clark, *Prejudice and Your Child*, pp. 166–178; and Grossack, ed., *Mental Health and Segregation*.

44. Grodzins, *The Metropolitan Area as a Racial Problem*, p. 11; McEntire, *Residence and Race*, pp. 95–96.

45. Deutscher and Chein, "The Psychological Effects of Enforced Segregation: A Survey of Social Science Opinion," pp. 259–287.

46. Myrdal, *An American Dilemma*, Vol. I, p. xliii.

47. *Ibid.*, pp. 567–568; Lee and Humphrey, *Race Riot*; Rudwick, *Race Riot at East St. Louis*.

48. *Chicago Tribune*, "9 Attacked by Mob; Seize 18 — Teen-Agers on Rampage on North Side," June 27, 1964, p. 1.

49. "New York City in Trouble: Story of a Rising Fear," pp. 72–77; "New York City in Trouble — Another Chapter," pp. 43–45.

Notes

50. *Ann Arbor News,* August 11, 1964, p. 11.

51. *Buffalo Evening News,* July 19–22, 1964; Miller, "Race Strife: A Tale of Two Cities: Rochester and Chicago," pp. 1, 4; *Chicago Tribune,* "2 New Jersey Cities Racked by Race Riots," August 13, 1964, p. 7; *Buffalo Evening News,* "Riot in Chicago Suburb Quelled after 50 Are Hurt," August 17, 1964, p. 18; *Daily News* (New York), "Philly Keeps Riot Curfew on for Week," August 31, 1964, p. 2; *Blade* (Toledo), "School Boycott Mob Routed," February 20, 1965, p. 12. In this case, the boycott turned into a riot. Police quelled a demonstration by 200 teen-aged Negro school boycotters after 2 days of street riots in Brooklyn; 28 youngsters and 27 adult leaders were arrested.

52. Clark, director, *Youth in the Ghetto,* pp. xi, 1–21.

53. "Rent Strike in Harlem — Fed-up Tenants Declare War on Slum Landlords and Rats," pp. 112–120.

54. Ford, "NAACP Aide Says Harlem, Cleveland East Side Alike — Peace Corps Volunteers Given Report on Status of Race Relations in U.S.," p. 4.

55. *Ibid.*

56. "Race Friction — Now a Crime Problem?" pp. 21–24, 58–62.

57. *Chicago Sun-Times,* "4 Killed in L.A. Rioting; National Guard Sent In, 24 Injured, 90 Arrested Here," August 14, 1965, pp. 1, 5.

58. *Chicago Tribune,* "Tampa Places Riot Damage at 1.5 Million," June 17, 1967, 2nd sec., p. 10; *Blade* (Toledo), "Guard Keeps Shaky Peace in Cincinnati," June 17, 1967, p. 20; *Blade* (Toledo), "Second Night of Rioting Hits Boston," June 4, 1967, A sec., p. 14; *Toledo Times,* "1 Dead, Two Are Wounded in Atlanta Incidents," June 21, 1967, p. 5; *Toledo Times,* "7 Are Shot in Buffalo as Police Fight Rioters; Roving Gangs Tip Cars," June 29, 1967, p. 1; *Blade* (Toledo), "Negro Riot Broken Up in Iowa," July 10, 1967, p. 6; "N.J. Governor Orders Guard to Stem Rioting in 'Rebellious' Newark," *Blade* (Toledo), July 14, 1967, pp. 1, 4; "More Rioting Hits Newark; 20 Now Dead," *Chicago Tribune,* July 16, 1967, pp. 1, 2; WSPD Radio Broadcast, Toledo, July 17, 20, and 26; "Newark Calm Broken by Gun Battle, Death," *Blade* (Toledo), July 18, 1967, p. 6; "New Jersey Solidifies Shaky Truce; Newark Riot Toll Reaches $15 Million," *Toledo Times,* July 19, 1967, p. 2; "Race Rioting Rages in Detroit," *Toledo Times,* July 24, 1967, pp. 1, 4; "U.S. Troops Moved into Detroit," *Toledo Times,* July 24, 1967, pp. 1, 4; "Spanish Harlem Riots Rock 10-Block Stretch," *Toledo Times,* July 25, 1967, p. 1, WJBK TV, Channel 2, Detroit, July 25, 1967, "Noon Report"; "Toledo Police Are Defied by Crowds as Disturbances Become Serious," *Toledo Times,* July 26, 1967, pp. 1, 4; "FBI Seeking Race-Group Head in Maryland Riots," *Toledo Times,* July 26, 1967, p. 1; WSPD Radio Broadcast, Toledo, July 28, 1967; *Blade* (Toledo), July 29, 1967, p. 4, and July 30, 1967, Sec. A., p. 2; "Tight Lid Is Clamped on Milwaukee District; 4,000 Guardsmen Due," *Toledo Times,* August 1, 1967, p. 1; "Fourth Milwaukee Death: Negro Student Shot by Police," *Montreal Star,* August 3, 1967, p. 1.

59. Grodzins, *The Metropolitan Area as a Racial Problem,* pp. 12–15; "Hauser Discusses Negro," p. 1; Weaver, "Class, Race, and Urban Renewal," p. 239.

60. Kramer, "Residential Contact as a Determinant of Attitudes toward Negroes" (Ph.D. thesis); Star, "Interracial Tension in Two Areas of Chicago" (Ph.D. thesis); Winder, "White Attitudes towards Negro-White Interaction in an Area of Changing Racial Composition" (Ph.D. thesis); Rose et al., "Neighborhood Reactions to Isolated Negro Residents: An Alternative to Invasion and Succession," pp. 497–507; Fulton, "Russell Woods: A Study of a Neighborhood's Initial Response to Negro Invasion" (Ph.D. thesis); Wolf, "Changing Neighborhood: A Study of Racial Transition" (Ph.D. thesis).

61. Duncan and Duncan, *The Negro Population of Chicago.*

62. "Housing Segregation Called Worst Problem," pp. 1, 4.

347

CHAPTER II. PURPOSE AND METHOD OF THE STUDY

1. Long and Johnson, *People vs. Property*, pp. 56–58; Weaver, *The Negro Ghetto*, pp. ix, 215; Abrams, *Forbidden Neighbors*, p. 158.

2. Frazier, "Race Contacts and the Social Structure," p. 11; Lohman and Reitzes, "Note on Race Relations in Mass Society," p. 240; Simpson and Yinger, *Racial and Cultural Minorities*, Pt. II, "Minorities in the Social Structure: The Institutional Patterns of Intergroup Relations"; Francis, "Multiple Intergroup Relations in the Upper Rio Grande Region," pp. 85, 87; Roucek, "Minority-Majority Relations in Their Power Aspects," pp. 24–30; King, "The Minority Course," p. 82; Williams, *Strangers Next Door*.

3. Mannheim, *Ideology and Utopia*, pp. 49–50.

4. Parsons, *The Social System*, p. 349.

5. Mead, *Mind, Self and Society*, Pt. III, "The Self"; Blumer, "Psychological Import of the Human Group," pp. 196–197; Blumer, "Attitudes and the Social Act," pp. 61–63.

6. Marx and Engels, *The German Ideology*, pp. 39–40; Marx, "The Eighteenth Brumaire of Louis Bonaparte," p. 126.

7. Weber, *Die protestantische Ethik und der Geist des Kapitalismus*, p. 202.

8. Dewey, *Logic*, p. 7.

9. Parsons, *The Social System*, p. 349.

10. *Ibid.*, pp. 356–357.

11. Copeland, "The Negro as a Contrast Conception," pp. 178–179.

12. Johnson, *Patterns of Negro Segregation*, p. 194.

13. Myrdal, *An American Dilemma*, Vol. I, pp. 101–102.

14. *Ibid.*, Vol. I, pp. 110–111; Vol. II, p. 1197.

15. Thomas and Znaniecki, *The Polish Peasant in Europe and America*, Vol. II, p. 1852.

16. There were 1,669 members of the Chicago Real Estate Board as of June, 1964, according to information given by Sally Reid, Membership Secretary, on August 7, 1964. The number of registered brokers in Cook County (slightly larger than Chicago) in 1963 was approximately 11,403, according to the Department of Registration and Education, State of Illinois, *Registered Real Estate Brokers — 1963*.

17. Survey made by the National Opinion Research Center, Spring–Summer, 1956. The difference in the 2 nonwhite totals, 27,502 and 27,420, is due to the fact that several blocks, parts of blocks, and particular buildings were excluded from the survey area but were included in the estimation of total population so that a comparison could be made with the census total of 1950.

18. Kitagawa and Taeuber, *Local Community Fact Book 1960*.

19. *Ibid.*

20. *Ibid.*

21. *Ibid.*

22. Hauser and Kitagawa, eds., *Local Community Fact Book for Chicago 1950*. The northern boundary of Area A is 4 blocks further north than that of the area in the 1950 survey.

23. The 121 interviews I carried out included: 12 exploratory, 9 pretest, 90 of the study proper, 5 in Areas A and B which were useful but could not be included in the distributions of the study because the respondents lacked certain characteristics required for inclusion in the universe, and 5 interviews contributing data on the real estate board and lending agencies.

CHAPTER III. RACIAL POLICIES AND PRACTICES

1. Only one of the branch firms deals with Negroes, and it began to do so in another area some time after the beginning of its business.

2. Certain pertinent events occurred before or just at the beginning of the interviewing period. In Area A, a real estate agent who had vacancies in a building he was managing and who did not wish to handle Negro tenants turned the management of the building over to a local real estate company (a respondent) and left the area. In Area B, a broker left the real estate business completely because he had had an unsatisfactory experience in trying to sell property to Negroes. Still another changed from dealing in apartment buildings to business properties and finally moved his office to another area because he had lost some prospective clients who assumed that he was a Negro from his address in Area B.

3. One broker who would sell to Negroes when the block is 50 per cent Negro would do so only in his own area, Area A. In other areas, he would sell after the first 2 or 3 houses or 1 large building had been sold.

4. One respondent said that his firm would sell to Negroes only when sales at a fair price to white purchasers were no longer possible. However, this would hold only for his home area, Area A. In others, except Area C, the firm would have no compunctions about selling to Negroes where there were none. The reason for this difference was that so many white people had run from Area A to other areas that "we don't think we have to consider them."

5. In a study in Chicago, the installment contract was found to be the principal means of purchase by Negro homebuyers. Chicago Commission on Human Relations, *Selling and Buying Real Estate in a Racially Changing Neighborhood*, pp.8–9.

6. Of the respondents who gave a qualified yes, 3 had a managing policy somewhat different from their selling policy. One, of Area A, was willing to sell property to Negroes if there were 2 or 3 Negro families in the block, but would consider location before agreeing to manage a property. Another in Area A was willing to sell to Negroes after there was 1 Negro family in the block, but he would manage a property only if the owner was taking Negro tenants because of vacancies. A respondent in Area B was willing to sell property to Negroes if there were 2 Negro buildings in the block, but he would manage a property with Negro tenants in an area where there are no Negroes only "if we wouldn't offend or be unfair to our clients who held immediate or adjoining property."

Of those who answered no, 3 of Area B and 1 of Area CX said that if a building had already turned Negro, they would manage it, but if it were still white, they would not take it to turn it. Two of Area A, 2 of Area B, and 1 of Area C would manage a building for a Negro owner in an area with no Negroes if the tenancy remained white. A respondent of Area B, owner of the property he manages, said he would not deliberately put Negro tenants into a white building, but he would do so when the white tenants began to flee. One of Area A was willing to sell property to Negroes after there are 2 or 3 Negro families in the block, but he would not rent apartments to them until the area was predominantly Negro. He said, "We have always been the last one to turn a building colored. We rent to whites as long as we can. Our building is usually the last apartment building in the area to turn." A broker of Area C was also willing to sell to Negroes if there were 2 or 3 Negro families in the block, but the conditions he set for renting to Negroes were "if it's on the fringe or surrounded by colored."

7. Duncan and Hauser, *Housing a Metropolis — Chicago*, p. 200. See p. 6 above for their and others' mention of rent differences.

8. In addition to the studies named in Chapter II (p. 16 and n. 1), other studies reveal restrictive practices of real estate men in cities other than Chicago.

A survey of intergroup relations in 1946 in San Diego, California, called a certain area, Logan Heights, an interracial community, but real estate dealers considered it a Negro district and prevented the movement of Negroes from it into other sections of San Diego (Hewes, *Intergroup Relations in San Diego*, pp. 14–15).

In a community audit of Montclair, New Jersey, in 1947, interviews with about a dozen real estate brokers and agents revealed that in both sales and rentals there were certain areas in Montclair in which houses could not be sold or rented to Negroes, Jews, or Italians, under a gentlemen's agreement among real estate operators (*Montclair Civil Rights Audit*, report at Montclair Forum, p. 7).

A survey of sales, rentals, and financing in Minneapolis stated that in 1947 70–80 per cent of the firms extended rental services to Negroes, Jews, and Orientals, but only in areas in which these minorities were located; 50–75 per cent of the agencies exercised similar proscriptions for sales; and 54–75 per cent restricted financing of housing for minority groups. On the other hand, in dealing with Negroes 26 per cent of the firms, with Jews 44 per cent, and with Orientals 36 per cent of the firms negotiated sales, provided rental service, or financed housing in any section of the city, provided that the client was of the same social and economic class as other persons of the area in question. (American Missionary Association, *Minneapolis Community Self-Survey on Human Relations, Racial Problems in Housing*, pp. 15–20.)

In 1950 in Cleveland, Ohio, Negroes, other nonwhite minorities, and Jews experienced great difficulty in living where they liked. Real estate brokers and home builders resorted to various devices to restrict the sale of homes in certain sections to these groups and also to certain non-Jewish whites. (Letter from Roosevelt S. Dickey, Assistant Executive Director, City of Cleveland Community Relations Board, July 3, 1950.)

According to the 1950 census, nonwhite families were living in 60 of 61 census tracts in Portland, Oregon, and in 1952 a survey of Portland revealed both favorable and unfavorable sides to the housing situation for nonwhite groups. Private owners and some real estate brokers made a number of homes available to minority families in previously restricted areas. Approximately half of the Negro population lived outside the Albina area, usually considered the Negro section. However, among the many homes offered for sale in Portland, only a few were available to Negroes, Orientals, or Indians. Many real estate brokers, builders, and homeowners discouraged or turned away non-Caucasian buyers. Thus, in many cases, members of these minority groups were forced to accept old, inadequate houses in the least desirable areas of the city. (Urban League of Portland, "Portland Balance Sheet on Race Relations," p. 3.)

In 1955 the Urban League in Seattle, Washington, reported that 7 firms refused to sell a house to Negroes. Two of the firms would not deal with Negroes at all; 3 refused to sell because they would not introduce Negroes where only white people were living; one refused because he believed property values would go down if Negroes moved into the area; and one mistook the light-skinned wife of one Negro couple for a white person and would not sell to a mixed couple. (Urban League of Seattle, "Investigation of Discrimination in Housing 1955.")

In 1955 Negro buyers encountered much difficulty in purchasing good housing in Denver, Colorado. Realtists (members of the Negro organization, the National Association of Real Estate Brokers) complained that not only did the lending firms refuse to certify their loans, but that the Realtors (members of the National Association of Real Estate Boards) had an unwritten agreement not to deal with Negroes who wanted to move into white neighborhoods. (Brown, "Much Difficulty Faced by Negroes as They Try to Buy Decent Homes.")

In 1955 in Syracuse, New York, a high degree of community acceptance of Negroes was offset by the resistance Realtors and builders offered to their trying to find homes in desirable neighborhoods (Weaver, "The Effect of Anti-Discrimination Legislation upon the FHA- and VA-Insured Housing Market in New York State," pp. 303–313).

In Manhattan, New York City, from 1953 to 1955 a survey was made of real estate brokers, selected from the 1951 Manual of the Real Estate Board of New York, to investigate exclusion of Negroes from apartments in predominantly white neighborhoods. In 22 of the 27 cases surveyed (over 81 per cent) a difference in treatment of Negro and of white would-be renters was distinguished. The Negro tester in the survey would be told that the broker had no apartment anywhere near his rent range, whereas the white tester, approaching the broker not more than half an hour later with the same apartment specifications as the Negro, would be offered one or more apartments. In similar tests carried out in May, 1954, for apartments listed in the Sunday *Times*, differences in treatment were found in 10 out of 17 apartments visited. (Committee on Civil Rights in East Manhattan, "Survey of Apartment Rentals through Applications to Brokers.")

In another, somewhat similar study in 1955, techniques used by real estate men in discouraging sales to Negroes were investigated in a suburb. Two teams of sociologists, each composed of 2 Caucasians and 1 Negro, visited 12 Realtors. The Negro, acting as the follow-up, requested housing comparable to that requested by the Caucasian couple. At the end of the survey, 46 reasons or techniques to exclude Negroes were distinguished, among them some fairly similar to ones I found: Realtors won't sell to Negroes; there is no Negro living in X area; harm may come to the Negro family; a Negro sale would be tantamount to putting him out of business; a Negro would not be satisfied or happy in X area; nothing is available in X area for colored people; overpricing for comparable listings given white couple; and refusal to give listings in the X area. (Kirk and Spano, *Private Housing Boom — For Whites Only.*)

In White Plains, New York, in 1956 Negroes encountered difficulties when they tried to move from the downtown slums into modern apartments or private homes in the hills. They were told "we never have vacancies," "the neighbors would object," or "our mortgages would be canceled." Real estate brokers "invariably feel they would lose all their business if they dealt once with Negroes." (Folsom, "White Plains Big Problem," p. 24.) According to the *New York Times* in 1956, in Buffalo's suburbs developers just didn't sell to Negroes, in Detroit real estate interests tried to "hold the line" against the advance of Negroes into white areas, and in Boston Negroes cited occasional, token acceptance by private Realtors of a professional Negro family (*New York Times*, "Housing in North Sets Bias Picture," April 25, 1956, p. 28). On the basis of a complaint, in 1956 the Connecticut Commission on Civil Rights advised real estate agents in the state that they are required to serve all persons as clients, regardless of race, creed, or color (*New York Times*, "Connecticut Lifts Real Estate Bars," February 26, 1956, p. 58). In Pittsburgh, Pennsylvania, an investigation of the racial practices of real estate brokers resulted in a campaign for fair housing legislation and in a fair housing law (National Urban League, *Building for Equal Opportunity*, p. 16; U.S. Housing and Home Finance Agency, *State Statutes, and Local Ordinances and Resolutions Prohibiting Discrimination in Housing and Urban Renewal Operations*, pp. 101–106). The 1957 annual report of the NAACP stated that "the West Coast regional office sponsored a survey of real estate practices in the peninsula area which substantiated allegations by the NAACP that the real estate industry was the controlling and throttling factor in preventing integrated housing in that area" (NAACP, *Civil Rights Crisis of 1957*, p. 62. For other cases of restrictive practices by real estate brokers see also Youngstown Interracial Clinic, "Report of the Sub-Committee on Negro Residence and Property Values"; American Jewish Congress, *Northtown Survey on Human Relations*, pp. 37, 39; National Conference of Christians and Jews, "Human Relations in New York City, Assets — Liabilities — Balance," p. 3; Poston, "This Happened in New York," p. 56; Goldblatt, *Westchester Real Estate Brokers, Builders, Bankers and Negro Home-Buyers*, pp. 15–17; *New York Times*, "Gains by Negroes in West Reported," February 26, 1956, p. 51. For a summary statement see Black, *Who's My Neighbor?* pp. 5–6, and Toledo Board of Community Relations, *Program for Progress 1956–1960*, p. 20.). In 1959 Donald S. Frey discussed the practices of real estate brokers in Illinois — statewide restrictions, block-busting methods, and refusal to show properties: "Equally dangerous to a community are the actions of realtors [sic] who refuse to show homes to otherwise qualified Negro buyers in other than prescribed areas of the community. This action creates the conditions already described that inevitably destroy community values" (Frey, " 'Freedom of Residence' in Illinois," p. 16).

CHAPTER IV. THE BROKER'S CONCEPTION OF HIS
RACIAL POLICIES AND PRACTICES

1. Riesman et al., *The Lonely Crowd*, pp. 15, 25.
2. *Ibid.*, pp. 22–23, 25–26.
3. Thirty-three respondents out of 37 (89 per cent) in Area A, 22 out of 23 (96 per cent) in Area B, and all those of Area C, CX, and C branch offices maintained this.
4. Thirty-two respondents (87 per cent) of Area A, 20 (87 per cent) of Area B, 20 (95 per cent) of Area C, all those of Area CX, and 2 Area C branch offices stressed this point.
5. U.S. Federal Housing Administration, *Underwriting Manual* (rev. March 15, 1955), par. 1005(1).
6. American Institute of Real Estate Appraisers, *The Appraisal of Real Estate*, p. 38.
7. Scott, "Residential Value," p. 347.
8. Merton, *Social Theory and Social Structure*, Ch. 11, "The Self-Fulfilling Prophecy," pp. 421–436.

CHAPTER V. THE BROKER'S CONCEPTION OF HIS
RACIAL POLICIES AND PRACTICES, PART II

1. There is no one definition for racial residential integration. Duncan and Duncan look upon census tracts with nonwhite proportions of 25–75 per cent as tracts with "mixed" population (*The Negro Population of Chicago*, p. 120).
2. Cf. Helper, "Neighborhood Association 'Diary' Records History of Citizen Effort to Adapt to Racial Change," pp. 137–138.
3. A similar impression was given by Norris Vitchek, a real estate man who sells without restriction: "Actually, block-busting probably is tougher on the whites than the Negroes. Nobody who has lived in a neighborhood for years, seen his children grow up there, remodeled his home exactly to his liking and become accustomed to nearby school, church, and shopping facilities likes to be uprooted. This is particularly true if it happens so suddenly that he has no new neighborhood in mind, if he has to accept less living space and a higher interest mortgage than he previously had and if he must sell his property at a loss. Several elderly persons have died because of the anguish and upheaval involved." ("Confessions of a Block-Buster," p. 18.)
4. Bontemps and Conroy, *They Seek a City*, pp. 1–8. The respondents also overlook the important work of many Negroes in the development of the United States.
5. Respondent 55C and several others stated, before they were asked Question 16, that they would not be the first to sell a piece of property in a white neighborhood to a Negro.

CHAPTER VI. OTHER FACTORS AFFECTING RACIAL POLICIES AND PRACTICES

1. Lewin, "Frontiers in Group Dynamics," p. 145.
2. Mikva, "The Neighborhood Improvement Association: A Counterforce to the Expansion of Chicago's Negro Population" (M.A. thesis), pp. 72, 105–108.

Notes

3. See Park, "News as a Form of Knowledge: A Chapter in the Sociology of Knowledge," pp. 669–675.

4. This finding is corroborated in a recent study, although it found more lending agencies willing to lend to Negroes than did the correspondents in the present study. The study referred to is *Mortgage Availability for Non-Whites in the Chicago Area*, issued by the Chicago Commission on Human Relations, pp. 6, 10.

5. Similar finding in *ibid.*, pp. 9, 17.

6. Cadwallader, *How to Deal in Real Estate*, p. 1, "The simple definition of a real estate dealer, as I use the term, is: *one who buys and sells real estate.*"

7. Davies, "Real Estate Achievement in the United States," p. 20.

8. A pretest respondent gave this example: A speculator buys a house for $12,000. He obtains an inflated mortgage of $10,000 through questionable arrangements at 5 per cent interest. He sells the house for $15,500 to a Negro with a cash down payment of $500 and the rest in monthly payments at 6 per cent interest. With the $500 down payment and his mortgage, he has himself had to invest only $1,500. He makes a profit of $3,500, and the 1 per cent difference in interest rate will pay at least part of his office expenses.

9. Chicago Real Estate Board, *1957 Year Book of the Chicago Real Estate Board*, pp. 210–233. "Customary Real Estate Brokerage Charges in the Chicago Area," p. 224: "Section 2 — Residential Property Sub-Section E — Charges for Making Sales. Item 1. Improved Property. In selling improved residential property the commission is 5 per cent on the first $250,000 of the sale price and 3 per cent on the excess selling price over $250,000. The minimum charge is $100.00." In 1965, the commission for selling improved residential property was 6 per cent on the first $50,000 and 5 per cent on the selling price over $50,000; the minimum charge was $300.00. Chicago Real Estate Board, *1965 Year Book of the Chicago Real Estate Board*, p. 232.

CHAPTER VII. THE REAL ESTATE BOARD, PART I

1. This is the wording of 1924–1950. The Code, first adopted in 1913, has been amended a number of times. The Preamble first appeared in the 1924 Code and remained unchanged until 1950. The wording of it was then altered somewhat, but the intrinsic meaning remained the same. The 1961 wording was again that of 1924.

2. NAREB, "Statement of Policies," approved by the Resolutions Committee and adopted by the Board of Directors of NAREB at its meeting in Chicago on January 27, 1945; contained in NAREB, *Policy Handbook*, Vol. III.

3. NAREB, *Statement of Policy of the Resolutions Committee*, Miami Beach, Florida, 1952, p. 1.

4. NAREB, *Report of the Resolutions Committee: Statement of Policy*, New York, 1955, p. 1; NAREB, *Statement of Policy*, submitted by the Resolutions Committee, St. Louis, Missouri, November 14, 1956, p. 1.

5. Holmes and Jones, *The Real Estate Handbook*, p. vii.

6. American Institute of Real Estate Appraisers, *The Appraisal of Real Estate*, pp. 22–23.

7. NAREB, *Report of the Resolutions Committee: Statement of Policy*, New York, 1955, p. 1.

8. NAREB, Build America Better Council, "Ten Principles of Neighborhood Conservation," p. 2.

9. NAREB, "Statement of Policy of the National Association of Real Estate Boards," submitted by the Resolutions Committee, New York, 1948, contained in *Policy Handbook*, Vol. I, p. 1.

10. Benson et al., *Real Estate Principles and Practices*, 4th ed., pp. 428–430.

11. Hoagland, *Real Estate Principles*, 3rd ed., pp. 65–66.

12. May, *The Valuation of Residential Real Estate*, 1st ed., pp. 224, 228, 233.

13. Hoagland, *Real Estate Principles*, p. 214.

14. Benson et al., *Real Estate Principles and Practices*, 4th ed., p. 337.

15. Atkinson, *Modern Real Estate Practice*, Vol. I, Preface, p. 3.

16. American Institute of Real Estate Appraisers, *The Appraisal of Real Estate*, p. 1.

17. *Ibid.*, p. 101.

18. *Ibid.*, pp. 101–103.

19. *Ibid.*, pp. 105–106.

20. Holmes and Jones, *The Real Estate Handbook*, p. 222; Unger, *Real Estate*, p. 366; Case, *Modern Real Estate Practice*, p. 69; Spilker, *Real Estate Business as a Profession*, p. 369.

21. Atkinson, *Modern Real Estate Practice*, p. 172.

22. NAREB, *Code of Ethics* (1962 rev.), p. 2, Conclusion. See pp. 221–222.

23. Nelson, *The Administration of Real Estate Boards*, p. 2. A more recent statement indicating the effort toward professionalization of the occupation appears in Van Buren, *Real Estate Brokerage and Commissions*, p. 3.

24. McMichael, *Selling Real Estate*, 3rd ed., p. 367.

25. American Institute of Real Estate Appraisers, *The Appraisal of Real Estate*, p. 115.

26. Babcock, *The Valuation of Real Estate*, pp. 86, 91.

27. U.S. Federal Housing Administration, *Underwriting Manual*, rev. April 1, 1936, FHA Form No. 2049, Pt. II, Sec. 2, Arts. 228, 229.

28. *Ibid.*, Art. 252.

29. U.S. Federal Housing Administration, Housing and Home Finance Agency, *Underwriting Manual*, rev. March 15, 1955, FHA Form 2049, Pt. III, Sec. 13, Arts. 1301 (1,2), 1320 (1,2).

30. Benson et al., *Real Estate Principles and Practices*, 4th ed., p. 344.

31. *Ibid.*, p. 436.

32. Downs, *Principles of Real Estate Management*, p. 61.

33. Hoyt, *One Hundred Years of Land Values in Chicago*, p. 314.

34. *Ibid.*, p. 316.

35. *Ibid.* The ordering is similar in some respects but dissimilar in others to results obtained by Bogardus in *Immigration and Race Attitudes*, p. 25.

36. *Ibid.*, p. 317.

37. *McMichael's Appraising Manual*, 3rd ed., pp. 48–49.

38. Hoyt, *The Structure and Growth of Residential Neighborhoods in American Cities*, Pt. I, Ch. 6; Pt. II, Ch. 4.

39. Rodwin, "The Theory of Residential Growth and Structure," pp. 295–317.

40. NAREB, Department of Education, report on use of real estate textbooks in universities and colleges, November 1, 1951.

41. Weimer and Hoyt, *Principles of Urban Real Estate*, 1st ed., p. 285.

42. *Ibid.*, pp. 286–287; 2nd ed., p. 198; 3rd ed., p. 315.

43. *Ibid.*, 2nd ed., pp. 196–197.

44. *Ibid.*, 3rd ed., pp. 314–315.

45. *Ibid.*, p. 362.

46. *Ibid.*

47. *Ibid.*, p. 370.

48. *Ibid.*, p. 371.

49. *Ibid.*, p. 373.

50. *Ibid.*, p. 375.

51. *Ibid.*, 2nd ed., p. 140.

52. *Ibid.*, 3rd ed., pp. 316, 590, 385, 602.

53. May, *The Valuation of Residential Real Estate*, pp. 73–74; 2nd ed., pp. 73–74.

54. *Ibid.*, 1st ed., p. 81.

55. *Ibid.*, p. 89; 2nd ed., p. 86.
56. *Ibid.*, 1st ed., p. 90.
57. *Ibid.*, pp. 145–146.
58. *Ibid.*, p. 147.
59. *Ibid.*, pp. 219, 240, 251.
60. *Ibid.*, p. 224.
61. Hoagland, *Real Estate Finance*, pp. 198–199.
62. U.S. Federal Housing Administration, *Underwriting Manual*, February, 1938, Pt. II, Sec. 9, "The Rating of Location."
63. Hoagland, *Real Estate Principles*, 3rd ed., p. 65.
64. *Ibid.*
65. Holmes and Jones, *The Real Estate Handbook*, p. 82.
66. McMichael and Bingham, *City Growth Essentials*, pp. 342–343.
67. *Ibid.*, pp. 348–349.
68. McMichael and Bingham, *City Growth and Values*, pp. 179–183.
69. McMichael, *Appraising Manual*, 1st ed., pp. 272, 278.
70. *Ibid.*, p. 249.
71. *McMichael's Appraising Manual*, 2nd ed., p. 53.
72. *Ibid.*, p. 151.
73. *Ibid.*, 3rd ed., p. 55.
74. *Ibid.*, 4th ed., p. 156.
75. *Ibid.*, pp. 159–160, reference to Hoyt, *One Hundred Years of Land Values in Chicago*. See above, pp. 203–204.
76. *McMichael's Appraising Manual*, 4th ed., pp. 161–162.
77. *Ibid.*, p. 169.
78. Knight, "Blighted Areas and Their Effects upon Urban Land Utilization," pp. 135–136.
79. *Ibid.*, p. 138.
80. McMichael, *How to Make Money in Real Estate*, pp. 37–38.
81. McMichael, *How to Operate a Real Estate Business*, pp. 101–102.
82. McMichael, *How to Finance Real Estate*, pp. 318–321.
83. *Ibid.*, pp. 321–323.
84. McMichael and O'Keefe, *How to Finance Real Estate*, 2nd ed., pp. 105–107. See above, pp. 202–203.
85. *Ibid.*, p. 181.
86. McMichael, *Real Estate Subdivisions*, Ch. 22, pp. 201–209.
87. *Ibid.*, p. 208. See above, p. 201.
88. McMichael, *Real Estate Subdivisions*, p. 209.
89. McMichael, *Selling Real Estate*, 3rd ed., p. 367.
90. *Ibid.*, p. 371. See above, p. 201.
91. Husband and Anderson, *Real Estate*, rev. ed. (1954), p. 298.
92. Husband and Anderson, *Real Estate Analysis* (1948), p. 279.
93. Ratcliff, *Urban Land Economics*, p. 113.
94. *Ibid.*, pp. 114, 334, 402–403.
95. Stanley L. McMichael dedicated the 4th ed. of his *Appraising Manual* to Schmutz, calling him the "Dean of American Real Estate Appraisers."
96. Schmutz, *The Appraisal Process*, pp. 168–169.
97. *Ibid.*, p. 175.
98. Atkinson, *Modern Real Estate Practice*, Vol. V, pp. 169–171.
99. *Ibid.*, pp. 171–172.
100. Atkinson and Frailey, *Fundamentals of Real Estate Practice*, p. 34.
101. *Ibid.*
102. U.S. Federal Housing Administration, *Underwriting Manual*, 1938, pars. 901–902.

103. Spilker, *Real Estate Business as a Profession*, p. 370.

104. *Ibid.*, p. 373.

105. Teckemeyer, *How to Value Real Estate*, pp. 77–78.

106. Case, *Modern Real Estate Practice*, p. 61.

107. Fisher and Fisher, *Urban Real Estate*, p. 119.

108. Wendt, *Real Estate Appraisal*, pp. 132–133.

109. *Ibid.*, p. 139.

110. Wendt, "Real Estate Education at Colleges and Universities," p. 226.

CHAPTER VIII. THE REAL ESTATE BOARD, PART II

1. Data on the early history of NAREB are drawn from Davies, "Real Estate Achievement in the United States," Chs. I and II, used by courtesy of Janice B. Babb, Librarian, NAREB, Chicago. Unless otherwise stated, documents on the history of NAREB were obtained in the vertical files of the library, NAREB, Chicago.

2. "Some Main Dates and Circumstances of NAREB's Founding and Early Development."

3. Nelson, "A History of the National Association of Real Estate Boards as a Factor in Modern Business Advance," p. 6.

4. *Ibid.*, p. 7.

5. Ennis, Kansas City, "Annual Report of the President," January 16, 1925, pp. 6–7.

6. Nelson, "The Objectives of Real Estate Organization."

7. Nelson, "The Real Estate Code of Ethics," pp. 273–274.

8. National Association of Real Estate Exchanges, *Ethics of the Real Estate Profession*, 1913.

9. National Association of Real Estate Exchanges, *Ethics of the Real Estate Profession*, Second Code.

10. NAREB, *Code of Ethics*, Third Code, 1915.

11. Davies, "Real Estate Achievement in the United States," pp. 1–2.

12. Doolittle, "Homestead Exemption from Taxation," pp. 39–41.

13. Givins, "Ownership *vs.* Communism," p. 51.

14. Report of the Committee on Resolutions, NAREB, to the annual convention, San Francisco, June 3, 1922, quoted in NAREB, *Policy Handbook*, Vol. I, p. 7.

15. Shaw, "The Negro in Harlem," pp. 21–23. I obtained the following information about Frank A. Shaw from Frank E. McKeown, Executive Vice-President of the Real Estate Board of New York, in a letter dated May 19, 1958: "We have referred to the February 1914 issue of our Board's Monthly Real Estate Bulletin of that era and located the article you refer to by Frank A. Shaw. Our records indicate that Frank A. Shaw was an active member of this Board, with a real estate office in the Harlem area at the time he wrote that article, so it would appear that he had a first-hand familiarity with the neighborhood of which he wrote. It does not appear that Mr. Shaw was an Officer of this Board at any time, and from the addresses of the others of the Committee of Thirty, it appears that many of them were Harlem area real estate men, members of this Board, while the others were property owners and clergymen."

The following quotation is from "The Negro in Harlem": "Doubtless very few have considered deeply the actual condition of the Harlem Real Estate situation and its problem which must be solved. That is, the negro problem. This is one of the most difficult social and economic questions which the active minds of men, of both the white and negro race, have been trying to solve for many years. It is because of its economic relation to Real Estate that this article is written; but in considering means of overcoming its adverse effect on Real Estate, it becomes necessary to take into consideration the social question. In some sections of this country many unsuccessful attempts have been made to handle this problem. Perhaps they were unsuccessful because they were antagonistic to the negro. Perhaps if the negro had been considered and not antagonized, the problem could have been worked out.

"This is the day of co-operation, the day of give and take, the day of uplift, — that is as it should be. Therefore, in the plan for solving the problem in Harlem, it is intended to consider the negro.

"Harlem, up to a few years ago, was acknowledged to be an ideal residential section. . . .

"The population today is approximately 300,000 and property was assessed by the city in 1913 for $260,000,000. The same basic conditions exist today that made property values in the past, and in addition the Subway has added to transit facilities which were always good.

"There were at the time of the last census about 24,000 negroes, while at the present time it has been stated that there are from 30,000 to 40,000 of them. Some are desirable citizens and some most undesirable.

"This is Harlem's problem, and it is the purpose of the Real Estate interests to solve it, and considering the enormous amount of money invested, this seems quite worth while.

"In the past ten years values are estimated to have shrunk over $100,000,000, and furthermore, unless something is done to control the situation, values will shrink still more. This same plight may befall other sections of the city if some method of controlling such situations is not put into practice.

"The beginning of the present conditions was in 1899, and was caused by the small practice of an owner who wanted to sell a flat house, and who thought that by renting to negro tenants the purchase of the property could be forced upon other owners in the neighborhood. Unfortunately for other Harlem owners, the neighbors were not as neighborly as had been expected. As a consequence of this act, other houses in the block lost their white tenants, and owners had no alternative but to rent their properties to negroes.

"The situation might have been controlled very easily at that time, but no one could forsee what the future had in store. Very naturally the negro children attended the public schools in the vicinity, and the white people were forced to move to other sections so that their children would not be compelled to attend the same schools. This caused more vacant apartments and dwellings, and more negroes were brought to the section to fill the vacancies, until today the negroes occupy flats, private dwellings and elevator apartments in streets which formerly were most desirable.

"Everyone knows what effect this has had on values. Mortgages have been called, many foreclosed, and investments which represented in many cases the life savings of the unfortunate owners, some of whom were widows whose husbands had thought to leave them a comfortable home or an investment for their support, were lost.

"Taking all of these facts into consideration, and also the fact that the negro is entitled to adequate housing in a neighborhood which will afford proper environment, a plan has been evolved with the double object of conserving Real Estate values and providing for the negro. . . .

"Following is the plan of action as outlined in a letter sent to owners of property in the section affected."

16. *Chicago Real Estate Board Bulletin*, XXV, No. 4 (April, 1917), 313.

17. *Ibid.*, pp. 315–317.

18. *Ibid.*, No. 11 (November, 1917), 623–624.

19. *St. Louis Real Estate Bulletin*, "Segregation of Negro Districts Approved by Realtors' Referendum," September 1, 1923. All data on real estate boards, unless otherwise stated, were obtained in the vertical files of the library, NAREB, Chicago.

20. *Nashville Banner* (Tennessee), "St. Louis Exchange Favors Segregation," October 21, 1923.

21. *Glendale California News*, November 3, 1923.

22. *San Bernardino California Telegram*, August 15, 1923.

23. *Monrovia California News*, June 13, 1924.

24. *Glendale California News*, February 8, 1924.

25. *Milwaukee Journal*, September 16, 1924.

26. *Canton, Ohio, Real Estate Bulletin*, November 20, 1924.

27. *Birmingham Age-Herald* (Alabama), "New York Has Color Line Idea," January 19, 1924.

28. *Ibid.* Letter of reply by S. C. Starke, Executive Secretary, Birmingham Real Estate Board to F. A. Werthman of Utica, New York, an official of the New York Realtors Association, quoted in newspaper article.

29. *Terra Della News* (Montebello, California), April 10, 1925.

30. Letter from A. H. Parsons, Secretary-Treasurer, Salt Lake City Real Estate Board, to Herbert U. Nelson, Executive Secretary, NAREB, November 28, 1925. He raises the question with reference to Chinese and Japanese in cities on the Pacific Coast.

31. Letter from Herbert U. Nelson to A. H. Parsons, December 5, 1925.

32. *Tampa Tribune*, April 18, 1925.

33. *New Orleans Picayune*, March 20, 1927.

34. *Rockford Morning Star*, "Realty Men Ask Separate Negro District in City," March 23, 1927, pp. 1, 2. Article confirmed in letter from Louise Johnson, reference librarian, Rockford Public Library, Rockford, Illinois, October 8, 1956.

35. Preusser, "Color Question in California Reveals Many Problems," p. 35. The article was compiled from data furnished by various real estate boards to Serena B. Preusser, private secretary to Harry B. Allen, President, California Real Estate Association. The survey by questionnaire and accompanying letter was made in 1927 to assist Professor Eliot G. Mears of Stanford University in preparing a report for the conference to be held in Honolulu.

36. Letter from Nathan W. McChesney to Farnsworth Bros. of Los Angeles, May 4, 1927.

37. Letter from Louise A. Hunsinger, Executive Secretary, Grand Rapids Real Estate Board, to NAREB, January 4, 1934.

38. Letter to Louise Hunsinger from NAREB, January 23, 1934 (unsigned).

39. Long and Johnson, *People vs. Property?* pp. 61–62, quoting Special Report by National Committee on the Housing Emergency.

40. *Ibid.*, p. 61.

41. *Ibid.*

42. *A Monthly Summary of Events and Trends in Race Relations*, III, No. 10 (May, 1946), 304.

43. *Portland City Club Bulletin*, XXVI, No. 12 (July 20, 1945). In this issue: "The Negro in Portland," a report by the Committee on Race Relations authorized under the Section on Social Welfare, p. 62.

44. Kennedy, "Racial Survey of the Intermountain Northwest," p. 174.

45. Evans, *Race Fear and Housing in a Typical American Community*, pp. 10–11.

46. National Committee on Segregation in the Nation's Capital, "Residential Segregation: Discriminatory Housing in the Nation's Capital," p. 49. The director of research was Joseph D. Lohman. (Unpublished MS., 1948; 80 typewritten pp.)

47. Interview N, with an official of the Chicago Real Estate Board in 1955, partly quoted here: "I recognized as a youngster when I went into real estate that, to run a successful real estate office, you had to back it up. If you were going to progress, you had to do more than just run your own business, buying, selling and managing property. You couldn't do that alone. I have always insisted that a good real estate man ought to be a good community man. Following that line of thought, while our major business was real estate, we found that in the local areas even in those early

days, and it still prevails, the municipal authorities didn't cover many facilities, and that the local business ought to be active in community interests. To illustrate, as a youngster . . . some others and we organized the [Area A] Improvement Association. That was for the purpose of keeping the streets clean. The city departments have to be supplemented by local community effort. Street cleaning and the sewer system are frequently neglected. I was [an officer] of this [Area A] Improvement Association. Then we would get the property owners to become members and make subscriptions each year. That membership subscription hooked them into the community interest. We gathered up enough money to hire people to keep the streets sprinkled in the summer and to shovel snow in the winter, and to see that the sidewalks were kept clean and repaired, and that nobody should open little stores in a residential street. In those days, zoning ordinances were not enforced. I early found out that in a nice residential street someone wanted to open a little grocery store in a basement. My idea was keep business on business streets and do not break down residential streets with grocery stores and other little businesses that hurt the good residential streets that shouldn't be broken down with business. Later, I was very active organizing the [Area A] Property Owners Association. It expanded the activities of the other in regard to street cleaning, sprinkling, properties being kept up, garbage being properly collected, and many facilities for the good of the community.

"About the character of people, I was always alert to that in handling people. In renting, I was always very particular about the class of people I sold and rented to. . . . There's something besides being able to pay the rent. Where there are 10 or 12 people living in a building, I want them to be of the same standard. Do you know the trait in human nature known as selectivity? That runs all the way through human nature, the animal world and people. Birds of a feather flock together. I can't emphasize that point too much. . . . I always emphasized, in talking with real estate brethren, the idea of keeping your neighborhood up by keeping the class of people of the same standard that would be applicable to that neighborhood. For example, there was a woman in an apartment who caused complaints. I got her to move. *The social standing of the people that exists in a neighborhood must be kept up, maintained, to keep up a neighborhood.* I don't mean to be snooty. People that work in overalls are good people.

"It [approach of Negroes] did affect our business and very materially. We recognized many years ago that there was a large area on the South Side that was occupied by colored. . . . Well, in those days [street in area now occupied by Negroes and west of Area A] was a very wonderful street. There were mansions and beautiful homes of $50,000 and $60,000. They weren't very far from the colored area and pretty soon, it was a kind of slow process, but some of the colored became successful and a colored banker bought a home on [street mentioned above]. From that time on they began to integrate into [area mentioned above], and, as they began to come in, gradually white people began to sell out and they sold their houses at a discount in order to get out. Well, we recognized that very early. We saw the trend coming, so, knowing what had happened, and subsequently it developed that when they integrated more and more on some of those good streets, a very important thing happened. The tax structure was affected. Properties are assessed every 4 years and the taxes are based on that value. Nobody paid much attention, but, as our taxes began to go up, we found out that in the good territories while our taxes were going up, in the colored area they were going down. There was one factor about the colored area. They couldn't get the taxes from that particular area because the rental values were low, and the value of properties is based on their rental value, their income value. So the good white territories were carrying the tax load. It turned out that values in the colored area fell. Rents fell. So value went down and assessment went down. So many taxes are necessary for taxes, and we in the white territories were helping to carry a good deal of the load. The colored area was not the only factor in the increase in taxes. That carried itself to such an extent that it was really quite alarming, and the same kind of city service had to be furnished there as elsewhere, but they didn't get the taxes to warrant them.

"Then the next step was in [part of Area A]. . . . The trend was coming that way. We conceived the idea — the Chicago Real Estate Board and members especially of the South Side had meetings — we conceived the idea and got our attorneys to draw a restrictive agreement. The purpose of it was not to hurt anybody. It said property owners have a right to join together as a body and to agree to do what they wish with their own properties in unison as an organization, providing, however, that nothing they do would be unconstitutional. So this restrictive agreement was very carefully drawn up and organizations were set up to get the signatures of property owners and to put it into effect. . . . A couple of community people in [Area A] including myself took on the burden to carry out this agreement in [Area A]. I spent a lot of time without compensation. We got donations. We signed it up in blocks and then consolidated all the blocks. We were careful before we started that to get the O.K. of the [title and trust company] on that agreement. We said, 'Will you recognize it in your titles? This agreement will be a legal, recorded instrument.' They investigated it and said yes, and that it would appear on all transfers of property. This recorded legal instrument was called a restrictive agreement. Then [Area A and Area B] signed up. We never got 100 per cent in every block. The preamble was that it didn't require 100 per cent in every block. In some blocks we took 75 per cent, in some 80 per cent. Then we recorded the instrument and it was effective. We had to have a secretary, and office, someone to do the footwork. This was accomplished on voluntary contribution from individuals and organizations.

"There was no prejudice in my set-up. I had this theory. I don't want to hurt the colored people. They're humans the same as we are and some are better than us, but I recognize, you see, if you had a little home that you bought on [street in Area A]. You paid off the mortgage. You had saved and now you had it clear. This I recognized early in colored infiltration — 75 per cent of it was for exploitation purposes, not to help the colored. If your neighbor hadn't signed the agreement, he would get hold of a colored person right next to you. How does that affect you? Right now your property value is depreciated. No question about it. Perhaps it is a high-class colored person. But it's just the idea about selectivity. I'd want to sell my property too and get out. For practical purposes that is what happened. [People sold out?] Definitely. They're doing it today, following the same pattern. Human nature doesn't change much. That person probably sold at a depreciated value in order to get out, because he was not used to living next to colored. With the restrictive agreement we were able to control this, but there was a little opening, but very little of that was done.

"There was a case on this restrictive agreement some 10 years ago in [western extremity of Area B]. . . . We won completely. He [judge of the Lower Court] ordered the property transferred back to the original owner and ordered the colored man to move out. . . . They appealed the case to the Appellate Court from the Lower Court. . . . They upheld the Lower Court's decision. Then they appealed to the Illinois Supreme Court. They upheld it. So that colored fellow had to restore the property back to the original owner. They upheld the restrictive agreement as constitutional, legal, enforceable.

"After World War II, the United Nations was organized. It made certain decisions. There was the question, do they contravene the Constitution of the United States? The colored people about that time brought the case to the Supreme Court. We didn't have any opposition. They — the Supreme Court decided that there was nothing unconstitutional about that restrictive agreement, but they added, we will not enforce it. That opened the door. From that time on, the colored began to pile in in great numbers. After that we found we couldn't legally prevent them. They could buy any place. They began to crowd in here. . . . It has affected our business very materially. We're taking plenty of punishment."

48. Senn, "Report on Efforts in the Los Angeles Area to Circumvent the United States Supreme Court Decisions on Restrictive Covenants," p. 1.

49. *Ibid.*, p. 2.

50. *Ibid.*, p. 3.

51. *Ibid.*

52. Letter to Ruth E. Dillon, Louisville Real Estate Board, from an official of NAREB, August 3, 1949.

53. Baltimore Urban League, *Civil Rights in Baltimore*, p. 11.

54. Photostatic copy of letter sent by St. Louis County Real Estate Board to all active members, June 1, 1955; it was supplied to me by George S. Harris, President, National Association of Real Estate Brokers, September 27, 1956.

55. White and Marshall, *What Caused the Detroit Riot?*

56. Price, *Factors Influencing and Restraining the Housing Mobility of Negroes in Metropolitan Detroit*. The research was conducted between November 1, 1954, and April 1, 1955.

57. *South Gate Press*, "Mexican Family Suit against Realty Unit Charges Discrimination," March 4, 1956; *South Gate Press*, "Suit against Realty Board," June 21, 1956.

58. Interview with NAREB official, September 5, 1956.

59. Letter sent to L. E. Alderdyce, Battle Creek, Michigan, by the Executive Secretary of NAREB, July 3, 1926. (At that time, Herbert U. Nelson was Executive Secretary.) Mr. Alderdyce had written his letter to Mr. Jemison, President, NAREB, on June 29, 1926, according to vertical files, NAREB.

60. NAREB, "Statement of Policies," approved January 27, 1945, contained in *Policy Handbook*, Vol. III.

61. Letter from Executive Vice-President, NAREB, to R. P. Van Pelt, Memphis, Tennessee, on July 12, 1945, in vertical files, NAREB.

62. National Association of Real Estate Brokers, *Your Future and the N.A.R.E.B.*

63. NAREB, "Realtors Membership Progress Report," Report No. 8, August 31, 1956, p. 3.

64. Interview, September 20, 1956.

65. Telephone conversation with Evelyn M. Tauber, Membership Department, Real Estate Board of New York, November 14, 1951. Negro membership in 1958: brokers, 12; salesmen, 6; owners, 1. Letter from Louis W. Shaw, Membership Secretary, November 5, 1958.

66. Telephone conversation with Secretary, Brooklyn Real Estate Board, November 14, 1951.

67. Information supplied over the telephone by Nancy McWilliams, Membership Secretary, Chicago Real Estate Board, October 14, 1957.

68. *Ibid.*, September 19, 1956.

69. Telephone conversation with Albert Johnston, Secretary, Dearborn Real Estate Board, September 19, 1956. See below, p. 287.

70. Interview with George S. Harris, President, National Association of Real Estate Brokers, September 20, 1956.

71. Herbert U. Nelson, "The Objectives and Content of Real Estate Courses," in NAREB, *Annals of Real Estate Practice*, Vol. I, pp. 195–197; "Our Literature of Real Estate Thought: Real Estate Education," in "Address to Be Given on Presentation of Charter to Board of Realtors," p. 5.

72. Report of the Committee on Resolutions, NAREB, to the annual convention, Washington, D.C., 1924, quoted in NAREB, *Policy Handbook*, Vol. I, p. 31.

73. Nelson, *The Administration of Real Estate Boards*, pp. 199–200.

74. Data on Department of Education were obtained largely from Kathryn Neary, Director, Department of Education, NAREB, in an interview on October 18, 1957.

75. NAREB, Department of Education, *Study of Real Estate Courses Offered for College Credit at Universities and Colleges throughout the U.S.*; National University Extension Association, *Guide to Correspondence Study*.

76. At the 10th Annual Real Estate Conference held at Northwestern University, the speaker representing the university in the theme of the conference was Wallace S. Schall, Realtor and Chairman, Department of Real Estate, Northwestern University. Reported in NAREB, *Educational Letter*, IX, No. 6 (October, 1957), 2.

77. NAREB, *Educational Letter*, V, No. 1 (January, 1953), 2.

78. *Ibid.*, p. 4.

79. *Ibid.*, IX, No. 3 (March–April, 1957), 4–6.

80. NAREB, Committee on Education, "Highlights in Activities of NAREB Department of Education, 1951," report to Executive Council of NAREB Committee on Education at meeting, November 12, 1951, Cincinnati, p. 2.

81. *Ibid.*, p. 11.

82. *Ibid.*, pp. 3–4.

83. *Ibid.*, p. 9.

84. Copy of the bibliography was supplied by Janice B. Babb, Librarian, NAREB, October 15, 1957.

85. NAREB, Department of Education, *Study of Real Estate Courses Offered for College Credit at Universities and Colleges throughout the U.S.*

Author and name of textbook and number of schools reporting its use: Benson et al., *Real Estate Principles and Practices*, 43; American Institute of Real Estate Appraisers, *The Appraisal of Real Estate*, 33; Weimer and Hoyt, *Principles of Urban Real Estate*, 24; May, *The Valuation of Residential Real Estate*, 21; Hoagland, *Real Estate Finance*, 20; Husband and Anderson, *Real Estate* or *Real Estate Analysis*, 16; McMichael, *McMichael's Appraising Manual*, 12; Hoagland, *Real Estate Principles*, 12; Ratcliff, *Urban Land Economics*, 11; McMichael and O'Keefe, *How to Finance Real Estate*, 9; Schmutz, *The Appraisal Process*, 7; McMichael, *How to Operate A Real Estate Business*, 6; Atkinson and Frailey, *Fundamentals of Real Estate Practice*, 5. Twenty-six schools reported using Downs's *Principles of Real Estate Management*, which contains the idea of homogeneity of the neighborhood.

86. Information on the certificate program was given by Kathryn Neary, Director, Department of Education, NAREB, October 18, 1957.

87. Minutes of meeting of Executive Council, NAREB Committee on Education, May 9, 1951, Chicago, p. 3. Also report to Executive Council of NAREB Committee on Education at meeting, November 12, 1951, Cincinnati, "Highlights in Activities of NAREB Department of Education," p. 10.

88. "American Institute of Real Estate Appraisers Announces Its 1953 Demonstration Case-Study Courses."

89. Chicago Real Estate Board, *1800 of Us Invite You*. Information given by John H. Campbell, Manager, Advertising and Purchasing, Chicago Real Estate Board, October 25, 1957.

90. Illinois, Department of Registration and Education, *Real Estate Brokers and Salesmen Law*, p. 8.

91. NAREB, "Statement of Policies," approved by the Resolutions Committee and adopted by the Board of Directors of NAREB at meeting, Chicago, January 27, 1945, contained in NAREB, *Policy Handbook*, Vol. III.

92. NAREB, *Report of the Resolutions Committee: Statement of Policy*, 1955.

93. Illinois, Department of Registration and Education, *Registered Real Estate Brokers*, 1957, p. 6.

94. Nelson, "A History of the National Association of Real Estate Boards as a Factor in Modern Business Advance," p. 7.

95. Spilker, *Real Estate Business as a Profession*, p. 7.

96. In the Chicago area as a whole, there were somewhat over 8,000 registered real estate brokers in 1956 (Illinois, Department of Registration and Education, *Registered Real Estate Brokers*, 1957, calculated from lists given for Cook County, pp. 17–195). Of this number, about 14 per cent were members of the Board. In 1963, there were approximately 11,400 registered real estate brokers in the Chicago area (Illinois, Department of Registration and Education, *Registered Real Estate Brokers — 1963*, calculated from lists given for Cook County, 475 pp.). The membership of the Chicago Real Estate Board in December, 1963, was 1,672, according to Josephine Rizzo, Membership Secretary, on April 27, 1965. In 1963, somewhat over 14 per cent of the brokers in the Chicago area were members of the Board. In the country as a whole in 1954, "less than one-third of all active real estate brokers" were members of boards affiliated with NAREB (Benson et al., *Real Estate Principles and Practices*, p. 20). As of June 30, 1964, there were 1,482 member boards of NAREB and 77,725 members (NAREB, "Realtors Membership Progress Report 1964, Report No. 6, June 30, 1964," p. 2). In 1964, there were in the United States as a whole approximately 316,097 licensed real estate brokers (National Association of License Law Officials, 1963–1964 Summary on License Law Statistics. Totals for 48 states and the District of Columbia were given. There is some overlapping because some states grant licenses to out-of-state brokers.). Thus, in 1964, not quite 25 per cent of the active real estate brokers in the country were members of NAREB.

97. Telephone conversation, May 15, 1958. NAREB charters a real estate board by area, whereas the state of Illinois charters a board only by name. When NAREB charters a board, it outlines its area and charters no other board from that area.

98. In discussing deviant behavior and social control, Parsons states that "the tendency to deviance is finally also conditioned by the objective opportunities provided in the social system, in the structuring of which the 'loopholes' in the system of social control are particularly important" (*The Social System*, p. 321).

99. Myrdal, *An American Dilemma*, p. xliii.

100. Star, "Interracial Tension in Two Areas of Chicago" (Ph.D. thesis), pp. 153–154; Duncan and Duncan, *The Negro Population of Chicago*, p. 120. See also the studies mentioned on p. 347, n. 60, above.

101. Williams, *American Society*, p. 143.

102. Johnson, *Patterns of Negro Segregation*, Ch. 10, "The Ideology of the Color Line."

103. Parsons, *The Structure of Social Action*, pp. 399–408, "The Role of Institutions."

CHAPTER IX. THE RELATION OF IDEOLOGY AND OF OTHER
FACTORS TO PRACTICE

1. The tests, χ^2 and other, used in the testing of the hypothesis indicated that there is a relation of statistical significance between the holding of the exclusion ideology and the practice of exclusion at the .01 level in Area A and at the .05 level in Area B. No test was made in Area C, but 20 out of 21 respondents of this area both held the exclusion ideology and stated that they would not make a "first" sale to a Negro in a white area. In Area CX 4 of 6 respondents and the 3 Area C branch offices both hold the exclusion ideology and practice exclusion. In the test for the respondents of Area A, where N is over 30, Yates's correction for continuity was applied to check the significant result (Fisher, *Statistical Methods for Research Workers*, pp. 92–95). In the test for the respondents of Area B, both Yates's correction and Mainland's tables were applied (Mainland et al., *Statistical Tables for Use with Binomial Samples*, pp. 15–22, Table 4). See Appendix C, Table 44.

2. When the exclusion ideologies were examined according to a second criterion,

6 out of 8 components, 5 of Area A, 3 of Area B, and 2 of Area C fell out of the exclusion type. When a test was made of the exclusion ideology/practice hypothesis with the new totals, the result was still statistically significant in Area A, but now only at the .05 level. In Area B, the probability rose from the .05 level to slightly below the .10 level — in other words, the result was no longer clearly significant but could be looked upon as being on the line. In Area C, 19 out of 21 still were found to hold the exclusion ideology and to practice exclusion, according to their statements. There was no change in Area CX or among the branch offices of Area C. There are perhaps two more reasons for accepting the first criterion (5/3). Since the first criterion constitutes a simple majority, it can be looked upon as being less arbitrary than the second (6/2). Also, it is possible to conclude on the basis of the test made with the second criterion that, beyond a certain point on the integration-exclusion continuum, the association between ideology and practice decreases. In other words, beyond a certain point, ideology may be less or more strictly exclusionist, but practice remains exclusionist.

3. Merton, "Discrimination and the American Creed," p. 103.

4. In Area B there are some of the oldest and most restrictive firms and some of the most recent and least restrictive firms of the three areas. However, no correlation was established between age of firm and degree of restriction in practice.

5. Only 1 respondent in Area A admitted that he had begun to sell property to Negroes in what was "deemed" a white area after he had been dealing with Negroes for a number of years. Business needs compelled him to make this change in practice; he had come to have less favorable views.

6. There is no idea of mechanistic causation here. "Determination" is used in the sense in which Mead's "generalized other" enters into and determines or influences the thought, the decisions, and presumably the actions of the individual (Mead, *Mind, Self and Society*, pp. 152–164). Mills has described the nature of this "determination" in "Language, Logic, and Culture," pp. 672–673.

CHAPTER X. CURRENT PRACTICES OF EXCLUSION

1. The terms "fair housing" and "open occupancy" are both used to refer to equal opportunity in obtaining housing. They refer to the absence of discrimination on the basis of race, color, religion, national origin, or ancestry in housing. "Fair housing legislation" and "open occupancy legislation" ensure equality of opportunity in the obtaining of housing. Such legislation makes illegal the restrictive practices required of brokers by real estate boards. A distinction between "fair housing" and "open occupancy" appears in some statements on discrimination in housing and in some titles of legislation, where "fair housing" refers to elimination of discrimination by real estate brokers, and "open occupancy" refers to elimination of discrimination by property owners. But in other statements, the two terms appear to have the same meaning.

2. Summary of the testimony heard at the public hearing conducted by the Chicago Commission on Human Relations, August 9, 1962, pp. 1–2.

3. Minutes of the Committee on Judiciary, City Council, Chicago, August 6, 1963, A.M. Session, p. 4.

4. *Ibid.*, p. 81.

5. Jedlicka, "The Realtor: Real Estate Dealer, Plus," p. 19.

6. Chicago Fair Housing Ordinance, Ch. 198.7-B, *Journal of the Proceedings of the City Council of the City of Chicago, Illinois*, September 11, 1963, pp. 977–980.

7. *Chicagoland's Real Estate Advertiser*, "An Introduction to POCC," February 7, 1964, p. 10.

8. *Ibid.*

9. McClure, "Realtors Loom as Strongest Open Housing Foe," p. 5.

Notes

10. *Chicagoland's Real Estate Advertiser*, "An Introduction to POCC," February 7, 1964, p. 10.

11. Property Owners Coordinating Committee, "Petition to the Secretary of State, Springfield, Illinois, to place the question of 'Open Occupancy' before the voters of the State in a statewide referendum at the General Election to be held on the third day of November, A.D., 1964."

12. Geyer, "Realtors Hire Lawyers to Fight City Housing Law," p. 11.

13. Property Owners Coordinating Committee, *Bulletin — the Chicago Forced Housing Lawsuit and the Petition-Referendum Campaign*, p. 2.

14. Littlewood, "Kerner Defends Open Occupancy," p. 3.

15. *Chicagoland's Real Estate Advertiser*, "Housing Referendum Dead — NAREB Will Not Go to Court," September 11, 1964.

16. "Court Upholds Validity of City's Housing Law," p. 1.

17. Chicago Real Estate Board v. City of Chicago, 36 Ill. 2d 530, 224 N.E. 2d 793 (1967). The Court further held that the device of "panic-peddling" whereby owners were induced to part with their property by implanting or inflaming fears that property values would diminish because Negroes were or might become residents was a handmaiden of discriminatory practices prohibited by the ordinance and was not entitled to constitutional protection; so that the ordinance provision prohibiting distribution by brokers of any written material designed to induce the owner to sell or lease his property for such a reason was not a violation of freedom of speech guarantees.

18. *New York Times*, "Anti-Rights Plan Winning on Coast," November 4, 1964, p. 34.

19. Committee for Yes on Proposition 14 to Abolish Rumford Forced Housing Act, *Some Questions and Answers*, p. 2; *New York Times*, "Coast Rights Chiefs Map Plan to Void Fair Housing Setback," November 5, 1964, p. 18; Krock, "Proposition 14's Chances of Survival in the Courts," p. 36.

20. Fowler, "President of Realtors Puts Property Rights First," p. 30.

21. *Toledo Times*, "Proposition 14 Challenged in California Suit," December 15, 1964, p. 2.

22. *New York Times*, "Coast Rights Chiefs Map Plan to Void Fair Housing Setback," November 5, 1964, p. 18.

23. Mulkey v. Reitman, 50 Cal. Rptr. 881, 413 P. 2d 825 (1966), cert. granted, 87 S. Ct. 500, 17 L. Ed. 2d 431 (1966). Reitman v. Mulkey, 385 U. S. 967, 87 S. Ct. 1627, 18 L. Ed. 2d 830 (May 29, 1967) 35 U. S. L. Week 4473.

24. *Ibid.*

25. United Citizens Committee for Freedom of Residence in Illinois, *About Fair Housing*, p. 2.

26. Moore, "I Sold a House to a Negro," pp. 92–100.

27. Marciniak, "Breaking the Housing Barrier," p. 588.

28. *Blade* (Toledo), "Open Occupancy Fight Vowed by Realtor Group," February 28, 1964, 2nd news sec., p. 21.

29. News broadcast by Jim Uebelhart, News Director, WSPD Radio Station, Toledo, March 24, 1965.

30. *Blade* (Toledo), " 'Forced Housing' Claims Voiced in Senate Hearing — Realtors, Builders State Opposition to Proposed Law Aimed at Discrimination," March 24, 1965, p. 3.

31. *Toledo Times*, "Loan Official Hits Items in Fair-Housing Plans," March 25, 1965, 2nd sec., p. 17.

32. *Blade* (Toledo), "Petitions Oppose Fair-Housing Bill — Board of Realtors Seeks Signatures," March 27, 1965, 2nd news sec., p. 13.

33. *Ann Arbor News*, "Local Realtors Outline Position on Integration," September 22, 1962, p. 8.

34. Telegram from the West Side Real Estate Board to Alderman Leon M. Despres, September 10, 1963; telegram from the Beverly Suburban Real Estate Board to Alderman Despres, September 10, 1963; letter from the South Side Renting Men's Association to the Honorable Richard J. Daley, August 30, 1963; letter from the Northwest Real Estate Board to the Mayor and Aldermen of Chicago, September 10, 1963. This information was obtained from the office files of Alderman Despres on January 31, 1964, in Chicago.

35. NAREB, *Property Owners' Bill of Rights*, June 4, 1963.

36. NAREB, *NAREB Policy on Minority Housing*, June 4, 1963.

37. Remarks of James W. Thezan, Chairman Pro Tem, Property Owners Coordinating Committee, at the Official opening of POCC Open Occupancy Petition-Referendum Campaign, February 10, 1964, Chicago.

38. Fowler, "President of Realtors Puts Property Rights First," p. 30.

39. *Ibid.*

40. Powell, "The Relationship between Property Rights and Civil Rights," p. 148.

41. *Ibid.*, pp. 149–150.

42. "Court Upholds Validity of City's Housing Law," p. 4.

43. *Chicagoland's Real Estate Advertiser*, "Open Housing and Stability," March 13, 1964, p. 11; *Chicago Sun-Times*, "Erwin A. Salk Assails Realty Racial Barrier," March 11, 1964, p. 9.

44. NAREB, *Interpretations of the Code of Ethics*, pp. 40–41.

45. Survey by the Chicago Commission on Human Relations to determine the extent of Negro membership on local boards of NAREB, completed November, 1962.

46. Marciniak, "Breaking the Housing Barrier," p. 589.

47. Calhoun, "Here's What You Do If You're Turned Down Because of Race in Buying or Renting," p. 8.

48. Chicago Commission on Human Relations, "Report on Complaints Received under the Fair Housing Ordinance for the Period Ending June 30, 1964."

49. Chicago Commission on Human Relations, "First Annual Report of Complaints Received under the Chicago Fair Housing Ordinance."

50. *Supra*, pp. 39–42, 135–139. In a survey of real estate brokers in downstate Illinois, the brokers stressed the caution they exercise "to place Negro purchasers in areas where a minimum of opposition would arise therefrom" ("The Negro Housing Market from a Real Estate Broker's Point of View: An Illinois Survey," p. 262.)

51. Information obtained from William G. Friedlander, Executive Director, Lincoln Park Conservation Association, Dorena Mitchell, Chairman, Human Relations Committee of Lincoln Central Association, and Ben Canaday, Lincoln Central Association, February 13, 1965, Chicago.

52. Information obtained from Herbert F. Schwarz, member of the Executive Committee, South Suburbs Human Relations Council, February 13, 1965, Chicago.

53. *Chicago Sun-Times*, "4 Evanston Realty Firms Are Picketed," June 14, 1964, p. 66.

54. *Chicago Daily News*, "Evanston Weighs Realty Law," April 12, 1966, p. 17.

55. Illinois Commission on Human Relations, *Tenth Biennial Report*, May, 1963, p. 20.

56. Ohio Civil Rights Commission, *A Survey of Discrimination in Housing in Ohio*, January, 1963, pp. 21–23.

57. Conconi, "Toledo NAACP Stresses Legal Integration Efforts," p. 3.

58. *Toledo Times*, "Housing Test Filed in Akron by NAACP," April 8, 1965, p. 4; *Blade* (Toledo), "Akron Housing Mistakes Told," June 4, 1967, A sec., p. 14.

59. Information obtained from Judith Salgaller, September 7, 1964, Pittsburgh.

60. Slocum, "Teaneck Unit Files Complaints Charging Race Bias in Housing," p. 6.

61. U.S. Commission on Civil Rights, *Housing*, 1961, p. 123.

62. *Ibid.*

63. U.S. Commission on Civil Rights, *Civil Rights '63*, p. 162.

64. *Ibid.*

65. Campbell and Marciniak, *A Report to the Mayor and the City Council of Chicago on the Present Status and Effectiveness of Existing Fair Housing Practices Legislation in the United States as of April 1, 1963*, p. 5.

66. "Twenty Cities Adopt Fair Housing Laws in Past 17 Months," p. 3.

67. "Realty Brokers Asked to Back Fair Housing," p. 2.

68. Mikva, "The Neighborhood Improvement Association" (M.A. thesis), pp. 72–92, 105–108; Bouma, *Why Kalamazoo Voted No* and *The Social Power Position of a Real Estate Board*; National Committee on Segregation in the Nation's Capital, *Segregation in Washington*, pp. 30–47; *Southtown Economist*, "POCC Asks Housing Fight Funds," February 2, 1964.

69. NAREB, *NAREB's Policy on Minority Housing*, Sec. 4.

70. Grodzins, *The Metropolitan Area as a Racial Problem*, p. 6.

71. Abrams, *Forbidden Neighbors*, pp. 311–312.

72. *Ibid.*, p. 312.

73. Cohen, "The Benign Quota in Housing: The Case For — and Against."

74. U.S. Commission on Civil Rights, *Report of the United States Commission on Civil Rights, 1959*, p. 444.

75. "Chicago: A Big City Meets Its Problems," p. 75.

76. Silver, "L.I. Negroes Fight Panic Home Sales," p. 35.

77. Slocum, "Teaneck Revives Anti-Bias Board," p. 148.

78. Helper, "Neighborhood Association 'Diary' Records History of Citizen Effort to Adapt to Racial Change," p. 138.

79. Ford, "Neighborhoods Guide Own Integration in Detroit," pp. 1, 9.

80. U.S. Commission on Civil Rights, *Civil Rights '63*, p. 237.

81. Public Law 90-284, 90th Congress, H.R. 2516, April 11, 1968, An Act. Title VIII — Fair Housing, pp. 9–17. See Sec. 803–807. Note also *Digest of Public General Bills and Resolutions*, cumulative issue, No. 4, 1968; 90th Congress, 2nd Session; Legislative Reference Service, Library of Congress, E169 (H.R. 17234): "Mr. Brown (Ohio): 5/13/68 (Jud.) Revises the provisions of Public Law 90-284 relating to the sale or rental of single family houses so as to exempt from the Act the sale or rental of such houses (now exempted only if sold or rented without the use of real estate brokers, agents, or salesmen)."

Bibliography

BOOKS

Abrams, Charles. *Forbidden Neighbors — A Study of Prejudice in Housing*. New York: Harper, 1955.

American Institute of Real Estate Appraisers. *The Appraisal of Real Estate*, 2nd ed. Chicago: the author, 1952.

Atkinson, Harry Grant. *Modern Real Estate Practice*. Chicago: Lane, 1944.

———, and L. E. Frailey. *Fundamentals of Real Estate Practice*. New York: Prentice-Hall, 1946.

Babcock, Frederick M. *The Valuation of Real Estate*. New York: McGraw, 1932.

Benson, Philip A., Nelson L. North, and Alfred A. Ring. *Real Estate Principles and Practices*, 4th ed. New York: Prentice-Hall, 1954.

Bogardus, Emory S. *Immigration and Race Attitudes*. Boston: Heath, 1928.

Bontemps, Arna, and Jack Conroy. *They Seek a City*. Garden City, N.Y.: Doubleday, 1945.

Bouma, Donald H. *The Social Power Position of a Real Estate Board*. Kalamazoo: Western Michigan University, 1961.

———. *Why Kalamazoo Voted No: The Defeat of a Housing Proposal*. Kalamazoo: W. E. Upjohn Institute for Employment Research, June, 1962.

Cadwallader, Clyde T. *How to Deal in Real Estate*. New York: Prentice-Hall, 1955.

Case, Frederick E. *Modern Real Estate Practice*. New York: Allyn, 1956.

Chicago Real Estate Board. *1957 Year Book of the Chicago Real Estate Board*. Chicago: the author, 1957.

———. *1958 Year Book of the Chicago Real Estate Board*. Chicago: the author, 1958.

———. *1965 Year Book of the Chicago Real Estate Board*. Chicago: the author, 1965.

Clark, Dennis. *The Ghetto Game*. New York: Sheed and Ward, 1962.

Clark, Kenneth B. *Prejudice and Your Child*, 2nd ed. Boston: Beacon Press, 1963.

———, dir. *Youth in the Ghetto: A Study of the Consequences of Powerlessness and a Blueprint for Change*. New York: Harlem Youth Opportunities Unlimited, 1964.

Cooley, Charles H. *Social Organization*. New York: Scribner, 1929 (c. 1909).

Dewey, John. *Logic: The Theory of Inquiry*. New York: Holt, 1938.

Downs, James C., Jr. *Principles of Real Estate Management*. Chicago: Institute of Real Estate Management, 1950.

Duncan, Beverly, and Philip M. Hauser. *Housing a Metropolis — Chicago*. Glencoe, Ill.: Free Press, 1960.

Duncan, Otis Dudley, and Beverly Duncan. *The Negro Population of Chicago: A Study of Residential Succession*. Chicago: University of Chicago Press, 1957.

368

Bibliography

Durkheim, Emile. *De la Division du Travail Social.* Paris: Félix Alcan, 1893. Also, Preface to 2nd ed., "Quelques remarques sur les groupements professionnels," in 6th ed., 1932.

———. *L'Education Morale.* (Bibliothèque de Philosophie Contemporaine, publication directed by M. Marcel Mauss; founder, Emile Durkheim.) Paris: Félix Alcan, 1925.

Ely, Richard T., and Edward W. Morehouse. *Elements of Land Economics.* New York: Macmillan, 1924.

Ely, Richard T., and George S. Wehrwein. *Land Economics.* New York: Macmillan, 1940.

Fisher, Ernest M. *Urban Real Estate Markets: Characteristics and Financing.* New York: National Bureau of Economic Research, 1951.

———, and Robert M. Fisher. *Urban Real Estate.* New York: Holt, 1954.

Fisher, Sir Ronald A. *Statistical Methods for Research Workers,* 13th ed., rev. New York: Hafner, 1958.

Frazier, E. Franklin. *The Negro Family in the United States,* rev. ed. New York: Macmillan, 1957.

Grodzins, Morton. *The Metropolitan Area as a Racial Problem.* Pittsburgh: University of Pittsburgh Press, 1958.

Grossack, Martin M., ed. *Mental Health and Segregation.* New York: Springer, 1963.

Hauser, Philip M., and Evelyn M. Kitagawa, eds. *Local Community Fact Book for Chicago 1950.* Chicago: Chicago Community Inventory, 1953.

Hertzler, J. O. *Social Institutions.* Lincoln: University of Nebraska Press, 1946.

Hetherington, H. J., and J. H. Muirhead. *Social Purpose.* London: Allen, 1918.

Hoagland, Henry E. *Real Estate Finance.* Homewood, Ill.: Irwin, 1954.

———. *Real Estate Principles,* 3rd ed. New York: McGraw, 1955.

Holmes, Lawrence G., and Carrie Maude Jones, eds. *The Real Estate Handbook.* New York: Prentice-Hall, 1948.

Homans, George C. *The Human Group.* New York: Harcourt, 1950.

Hoyt, Homer. *One Hundred Years of Land Values in Chicago.* Chicago: University of Chicago Press, 1933.

———. *The Structure and Growth of Residential Neighborhoods in American Cities.* Washington, D.C.: U.S. Federal Housing Administration, 1939.

Husband, William H., and Frank Ray Anderson. *Real Estate Analysis.* Chicago: Irwin, 1948; rev. ed., *Real Estate,* Homewood, Ill.: Irwin, 1954.

Johnson, Charles S. *Patterns of Negro Segregation.* New York: Harper, 1943.

Kitagawa, Evelyn M., and Karl E. Taeuber. *Local Community Fact Book 1960.* Chicago: Chicago Community Inventory, University of Chicago, 1963, Philip M. Hauser, Director.

Laurenti, Luigi. *Property Values and Race.* Berkeley and Los Angeles: University of California Press, 1960.

Lee, A. McClung, and Norman D. Humphrey. *Race Riot.* New York: Holt, 1943.

Long, Herman H., and Charles S. Johnson. *People vs. Property: Race Restrictive Covenants in Housing.* Nashville, Tenn.: Fisk University Press, 1947.

McEntire, Davis. *Residence and Race.* Berkeley: University of California Press, 1960.

MacIver, R. M. *Community.* London: Macmillan, 1917.

McMichael, Stanley L. *Appraising Manual.* New York: Prentice-Hall, 1931; 2nd ed., *McMichael's Appraising Manual,* 1937; 3rd ed., 1944; 4th ed., 1951.

———. *How to Finance Real Estate.* New York: Prentice-Hall, 1949.

———. *How to Make Money in Real Estate,* rev. ed. New York: Prentice-Hall, 1945.

———. *How to Operate a Real Estate Business.* New York: Prentice-Hall, 1947.

———. *Real Estate Subdivisions*. New York: Prentice-Hall, 1949.

———. *Selling Real Estate*, 3rd ed. New York: Prentice-Hall, 1950.

———, and Robert F. Bingham. *City Growth and Values*. Cleveland, Ohio: Stanley McMichael Publishing Organization, 1923.

———. *City Growth Essentials*. Cleveland, Ohio: Stanley McMichael Publishing Organization, 1928.

McMichael, Stanley L., and Paul T. O'Keefe. *How to Finance Real Estate*, 2nd ed. Englewood Cliffs, N.J.: Prentice-Hall, 1953.

Mainland, Donald, Lee Herrera, and Marion I. Sutcliffe. *Statistical Tables for Use with Binomial Samples — Contingency Tests, Confidence Limits, and Sample Size Estimates*. New York: New York University College of Medicine, Department of Medical Statistics, 1956.

Malinowski, Bronislaw. *Crime and Custom in Savage Society*. New York: Humanities Press, 1951.

Mannheim, Karl. *Ideology and Utopia*, trans. by Louis Wirth and Edward Shils. New York: Harcourt, 1936.

Marx, Karl, and Friedrich Engels. *The German Ideology*, Pts. I and III, ed. with an intro. by R. Pascal. New York: International Publishers, 1947.

May, Arthur A. *The Valuation of Residential Real Estate*. New York: Prentice-Hall, 1942; 2nd ed., 1953.

Mead, George H. *Mind, Self and Society*. Chicago: University of Chicago Press, 1934.

Merton, Robert K. *Social Theory and Social Structure*. Glencoe, Ill.: Free Press, 1949, 1957.

———, Marjorie Fiske, and Patricia Kendall. *The Focused Interview: A Manual*, 2nd ed. New York: Columbia University, Bureau of Applied Social Research, 1952.

Myrdal, Gunnar. *An American Dilemma: The Negro Problem and Modern Democracy*. New York: Harper, 1944.

National Association of Real Estate Boards (NAREB). *Interpretations of the Code of Ethics*, prepared by the Committee on Professional Standards, 2nd ed. Chicago: the author, April, 1964.

———. *Policy Handbook*, Vols. I–III.

National Committee on Segregation in the Nation's Capital. *Segregation in Washington*. Chicago: the author, 1948. Joseph D. Lohman was director of research.

Nelson, Herbert U. *The Administration of Real Estate Boards*. New York: Macmillan, 1925. (Author was secretary of NAREB.)

Park, Robert E. *Race and Culture*. Glencoe, Ill.: Free Press, 1950.

Parsons, Talcott. *Essays in Sociological Theory*, rev. ed. Glencoe, Ill.: Free Press, 1954.

———. *The Social System*. Glencoe, Ill.: Free Press, 1951.

———. *The Structure of Social Action*, 2nd ed. Glencoe, Ill.: Free Press, 1949.

———, and Edward A. Shils, eds. *Toward a General Theory of Action*. Cambridge, Mass.: Harvard University Press, 1951.

Ratcliff, Richard U. *Urban Land Economics*. New York: McGraw, 1949.

Riesman, David, with Reuel Denney and Nathan Glazer. *The Lonely Crowd: A Study of the Changing American Character*. New Haven, Conn.: Yale University Press, 1950.

Rudwick, Elliott M. *Race Riot at East St. Louis*. Carbondale: Southern Illinois University Press, 1964.

Schmutz, George L. *The Appraisal Process*, rev. ed. North Hollywood, Calif.: the author, 1951.

Simpson, George E., and J. Milton Yinger. *Racial and Cultural Minorities: An Analysis of Prejudice and Discrimination*, 3rd ed. New York: Harper, 1965.

Bibliography

Spilker, John B. *Real Estate Business as a Profession,* 2nd ed., rev. Cincinnati, Ohio: John G. Kidd, 1941.

Sumner, William G. *Folkways.* Boston: Ginn, 1940.

Taeuber, Karl E., and Alma F. Taeuber. *Negroes in Cities: Residential Segregation and Neighborhood Change.* Chicago: Aldine, 1965.

Teckemeyer, Earl B. *How to Value Real Estate.* Englewood Cliffs, N.J.: Prentice-Hall, 1956.

Thomas, William I., and Florian Znaniecki. *The Polish Peasant in Europe and America,* Vol. II. New York: Knopf, 1927.

Unger, Maurice A. *Real Estate: Principles and Practices.* Cincinnati, Ohio: Southwestern, 1954.

Van Buren, DeWitt. *Real Estate Brokerage and Commissions: Law and Practice.* New York: Prentice-Hall, 1948.

Weaver, Robert C. *The Negro Ghetto.* New York: Harcourt, 1948.

Weber, Max. *Die protestantische Ethik und der Geist des Kapitalismus.* Tübingen: J. C. B. Mohr (Paul Siebeck), 1934.

————. *The Theory of Social and Economic Organization,* trans. by A. M. Henderson and Talcott Parsons. New York: Oxford University Press, 1947.

Weimer, Arthur M., and Homer Hoyt. *Principles of Urban Real Estate.* New York: Ronald Press, 1939; 2nd ed., 1948; 3rd ed., 1954.

Wendt, Paul F. *Real Estate Appraisal: A Critical Analysis of Theory and Practice.* New York: Holt, 1956.

Williams, Robin M., Jr. *American Society.* New York: Knopf, 1951.

————. *Strangers Next Door: Ethnic Relations in American Communities.* Englewood Cliffs, N.J.: Prentice-Hall, 1964.

Wilner, Daniel M., Rosabelle P. Walkley, Thomas C. Pinkerton, and Matthew Tayback. *The Housing Environment and Family Life: A Longitudinal Study of the Effects of Housing on Morbidity and Mental Health.* Baltimore: Johns Hopkins Press, 1962.

Witmer, Helen L., and Ruth Kolinsky, eds. *Personality in the Making.* New York: Harper, 1952.

ARTICLES

Abbey, Harlan. "63% of Negroes Participate in Boycott of Schools Here," *Buffalo Courier Express,* May 19, 1964.

"American Institute of Real Estate Appraisers Announces Its 1953 Demonstration Case-Study Courses," *Headlines,* XX, No. 10 (March, 1953).

Banas, Casey. "Willis' New School Plan Offers 93 Proposals to Improve Education: Acts to Carry Out Report by Hauser," *Chicago Tribune,* August 13, 1964.

Berquist, Ronald. "Willis: 224,770 Out; How Big Was the Boycott?" *Chicago Sun-Times,* October 23, 1963.

Blumer, Herbert. "Attitudes and the Social Act," *Social Problems,* III, No. 2 (October, 1955), 59–65.

————. "Psychological Import of the Human Group," in Musafer Sherif and M. O. Wilson, eds., *Group Relations at the Crossroads.* New York: Harper, 1953.

Brown, James C. "Much Difficulty Faced by Negroes as They Try to Buy Decent Homes," *Call* (Kansas City, Mo.), November 4, 1955.

Buder, Leonard. "Boycott Cripples City Schools; Absences 360,000 above Normal; Negroes and Puerto Ricans Unite," *New York Times,* February 4, 1964.

————. "School Boycott Is Half as Large as the First One," *New York Times,* March 17, 1964.

Calhoun, Lillian S. "Here's What You Do If You're Turned Down Because of Race in Buying or Renting," *Chicago Daily Defender,* January 29, 1964.

371

"Chicago: A Big City Meets Its Problems," *U.S. News and World Report,* LX, No. 13 (March 28, 1966), 74–78.

Chicago Real Estate Board. *Chicago Real Estate Board Bulletin* (or *Call Board Bulletin*), Vols. I, XXV.

Cohen, Oscar. "The Benign Quota in Housing: The Case For — and Against," *ADL Bulletin* (pub. by Anti-Defamation League of B'nai B'rith), XVI, No. 1 (January, 1959), 3, 7.

Colean, Miles L. "The Factual Findings," in *American Housing: Problems and Prospects.* New York: Twentieth Century Fund, 1944.

Committee on Race Relations. "The Negro in Portland," *Portland City Club Bulletin,* XXVI, No. 12 (July 20, 1945).

Conconi, Charles. "Toledo NAACP Stresses Legal Integration Efforts," *Blade* (Toledo), July 5, 1964.

Copeland, Lewis C. "The Negro as a Contrast Conception," in Edgar T. Thompson, ed., *Race Relations and the Race Problem: A Definition and an Analysis.* Durham, N.C.: Duke University Press, 1939.

"Court Upholds Validity of City's Housing Law," *Human Relations News of Chicago,* the Chicago Commission on Human Relations, VIII, No. 1 (January, 1966), 1.

Deutscher, Max, and Isidor Chein. "The Psychological Effects of Enforced Segregation: A Survey of Social Science Opinion," *Journal of Psychology,* XXVI (1948), 259–287.

Doolittle, The Honorable James R. "Homestead Exemption from Taxation," an address delivered before the Chicago Real Estate Board at 5th annual banquet, Chicago, quoted in *Call Board Bulletin,* I, No. 3 (February 4, 1888), 39–45.

Dunbar, Ruth. "Board Unit OKs S. Side High School Cluster Plan," *Chicago Sun-Times,* August 12, 1964.

Fenton, John H. "20,571 Pupils Out in Boston Boycott," *New York Times,* February 27, 1964.

Folsom, Merrill. "White Plains Big Problem," *New York Times,* April 25, 1956.

Ford, Harvey, "NAACP Aide Says Harlem, Cleveland East Side Alike — Peace Corps Volunteers Given Report on Status of Race Relations in U.S.," *Blade* (Toledo), July 24, 1964.

———. "Neighborhoods Guide Own Integration in Detroit," *Blade* (Toledo), October 25, 1962.

Fowler, Glenn. "President of Realtors Puts Property Rights First," *New York Times,* November 11, 1964.

Francis, E. K. "Multiple Intergroup Relations in the Upper Rio Grande Region," *American Sociological Review,* XXI, No. 1 (February, 1956), 84–87.

Frazier, E. Franklin. "Race Contacts and the Social Structure," *American Sociological Review,* XIV, No. 1 (February, 1949), 1–11.

Frey, Donald S. " 'Freedom of Residence' in Illinois," *Chicago Bar Record,* XLI, No. 1 (October, 1959), 9–21.

Geyer, Georgie Ann. "Realtors Hire Lawyers to Fight City Housing Law," *Chicago Daily News,* September 19, 1963.

Gilbreth, Edward S. "Leaders of Boycott Call It Big Success," *Chicago Daily News,* February 25, 1964.

Givins, Robert C. "Ownership *vs.* Communism," an address delivered before Chicago Real Estate Board at 5th annual banquet, Chicago, quoted in *Call Board Bulletin,* I, No. 3 (February 4, 1888), 50–53.

Goldhammer, Herbert, and Edward A. Shils. "Types of Power and Status," *American Journal of Sociology,* XLV, No. 2 (September, 1939), 171–182.

"Hauser Discusses Negro," *Chicago Maroon* (University of Chicago), LXX, No. 86 (April 25, 1962).

Bibliography

Helper, Rose. "Neighborhood Association 'Diary' Records History of Citizen Effort to Adapt to Racial Change," *Journal of Housing*, XXII, No. 3 (March, 1965), 136–140.

"Housing Segregation Called Worst Problem," *Human Relations News of Chicago*, the Chicago Commission on Human Relations, II, No. 5 (September–October, 1960), 1, 4.

Hughes, Everett C. "The Ecological Aspect of Institutions," *American Sociological Review*, I, No. 2 (April, 1936), 180–192.

Jedlicka, Albert, Jr. "The Realtor: Real Estate Dealer, Plus," *Chicago Daily News*, May 17, 1963.

Kendall, Patricia L., and Paul F. Lazarsfeld. "Problems of Survey Analysis," in Robert K. Merton and Paul F. Lazarsfeld, eds., *Continuities in Social Research: Studies in the Scope and Method of "The American Soldier."* Glencoe, Ill.: Free Press, 1950.

Kennedy, Tolbert Hall. "Racial Survey of the Intermountain Northwest," *Research Studies of the State College of Washington*, XIV, No. 3 (September, 1946), 163–246.

King, Morton B., "The Minority Course," *American Sociological Review*, XXI, No. 1 (February, 1956), 80–83.

Knight, C. Louis. "Blighted Areas and Their Effects upon Urban Land Utilization," *Annals of the American Academy of Political and Social Science*, CXLVIII, No. 237 (March, 1930), 133–138.

Krock, Arthur. "Proposition 14's Chances of Survival in the Courts," *New York Times*, November 6, 1964.

Laurenti, Luigi M. "Effects of Nonwhite Purchases on Market Prices of Residences," *Appraisal Journal*, XX, No. 3 (July, 1952), 314–329.

Lewin, Kurt. "Frontiers in Group Dynamics: II. Channels of Group Life; Social Planning and Action Research," *Human Relations*, I, No. 2 (1947), 143–153.

Lewis, Anthony. "Civil Rights Suit over Imbalance in Schools Fails," *New York Times*, May 5, 1964.

Littlewood, Tom. "Kerner Defends Open Occupancy," *Chicago Sun-Times*, June 14, 1964.

Loftus, Joseph A. "Chester Attacks Racial Problems," *New York Times*, August 9, 1964.

Lohman, Joseph D., and Dietrich C. Reitzes. "Note on Race Relations in Mass Society," *American Journal of Sociology*, LVIII, No. 3 (November, 1952), 240–246.

McClure, James. "Realtors Loom as Strongest Open Housing Foe," *Austinite*, March 12, 1964.

Malinowski, Bronislaw. "Culture," *Encyclopaedia of the Social Sciences*, IV (1931), 621–646.

———. "Introduction," in H. Ian Hogbin, *Law and Order in Polynesia*. New York: Harcourt, 1934.

Marciniak, Edward. "Breaking the Housing Barrier," *Commonweal*, LXXVII, No. 23 (March 1, 1963), 588–591. (Author is Executive Director, Chicago Commission on Human Relations.)

Marx, Karl. "The Eighteenth Brumaire of Louis Bonaparte," in *A Handbook of Marxism*, ed. by Emile Burns. New York: International Publishers, 1935.

Merton, Robert K. "Discrimination and the American Creed," in R. M. MacIver, ed., *Discrimination and National Welfare*. New York: Institute for Religious and Social Studies, 1949.

Miller, Harry. "Race Strife: A Tale of Two Cities: Rochester and Chicago," *Chicago Daily News*, July 28, 1964.

373

Mills, C. Wright. "Language, Logic, and Culture," *American Sociological Review*, IV, No. 5 (October, 1939), 672–673.

Monthly Summary of Events and Trends in Race Relations (Fisk University), III, No. 10 (May, 1946), 304.

Moore, Elizabeth. "I Sold a House to a Negro," *Ebony*, XVIII, No. 12 (October, 1963), 92–100.

Nathanson, Neal, William J. Hall, Lauri D. Thrupp, and Helen Forester. "Surveillance of Poliomyelitis in the United States in 1956," *Public Health Reports*, LXXII, No. 5 (May, 1957), 381–392.

NAREB. *Educational Letter*, IX, No. 6 (October, 1957).

———. "Statement of Policies," approved by Resolutions Committee and adopted by Board of Directors, NAREB, Chicago, January 27, 1945, *Headlines*, XII, No. 6 (February 5, 1945), Pt. II, contained in NAREB, *Policy Handbook*, Vol. III.

———. "Statement of Policy of the National Association of Real Estate Boards," submitted by Resolutions Committee at 41st annual convention, New York, 1948, in NAREB, *Policy Handbook*, Vol. I.

"The Negro Housing Market from a Real Estate Broker's Point of View: An Illinois Survey," in Alfred Avins, ed., *Open Occupancy vs. Forced Housing under the Fourteenth Amendment*. New York: Bookmailer, 1963.

Nelson, Herbert U. "The Objectives and Content of Real Estate Courses," in NAREB, *Annals of Real Estate Practice*, Vol. I, *General Real Estate Topics: Proceedings of General Sessions and Special Conferences at Eighteenth Annual Convention*. Chicago: the author, 1925.

———. "The Real Estate Code of Ethics," *Journal of Land and Public Utility Economics*, I, No. 3 (July, 1925), 270–275.

"New York City in Trouble: Story of a Rising Fear," *U.S. News and World Report*, LVI, No. 23 (June 8, 1964), 72–77.

"New York City in Trouble — Another Chapter," *U.S. News and World Report*, LVI, No. 24 (June 15, 1964), 43–45.

Newman, M. W., Norman Glubok, and Betty Flynn. "Teachers' Tale of Terror," *Chicago Daily News*, March 7, 1964.

Ogburn, William F. "Social Trends," *American Journal of Sociology*, XLV, No. 5 (March, 1940), 756–769.

Park, Robert E. "News as a Form of Knowledge: A Chapter in the Sociology of Knowledge," *American Journal of Sociology*, XLV, No. 5 (March, 1940), 669–686.

Pomfret, John D. "Milwaukee Poles in Johnson Camp," *New York Times*, August 12, 1964.

Poston, Ted. "This Happened in New York," *New York Post*, August 22, 1951.

Powell, Richard R. B. "The Relationship between Property Rights and Civil Rights," *Hastings Law Journal*, XV, No. 2 (November, 1963), 135–152.

Powledge, Fred. "New White Group Asks Integration — Seeks Common Front with Negro and Puerto Rican Rights Leaders Here," *New York Times*, February 21, 1964.

Preusser, Serena B., compiler. "Color Question in California Reveals Many Problems," *California Real Estate*, July, 1927.

"Race Friction — Now a Crime Problem?" *U.S. News and World Report*, LIX, No. 9 (August 30, 1965), 21–24, 58–62.

"Realty Brokers Asked to Back Fair Housing," *Human Relations News of Chicago*, the Chicago Commission on Human Relations, VII, No. 1 (January–February, 1965), 2.

"Rent Strike in Harlem — Fed-up Tenants Declare War on Slum Landlords and Rats," *Ebony*, XIX, No. 6 (April, 1964), 112–120.

Robinson, Corienne K. "Relationship between Condition of Dwellings and Rentals,

Bibliography

by Race," *Journal of Land and Public Utility Economics*, XXII, No. 3 (August, 1946), 296–302.

Rodwin, Lloyd. "The Theory of Residential Growth and Structure," *Appraisal Journal*, XVIII, No. 3 (July, 1950), 295–317.

Rose, Arnold M., Frank J. Atelsek, and Lawrence R. McDonald. "Neighborhood Reactions to Isolated Negro Residents: An Alternative to Invasion and Succession," *American Sociological Review*, XVIII (October, 1953), 497–507.

Roucek, Joseph S. "Minority-Majority Relations in Their Power Aspects," *Phylon*, XVII, No. 1 (1st Quarter, 1956), 24–30.

"Schools Boycotted," *Senior Scholastic*, LXXXIV, No. 4 (February 21, 1964), 19–20.

Scott, Robert V. "Residential Value," *Appraisal Journal*, XX, No. 3 (July, 1952), 343–356.

Sengstacke, John. "Our Segregated Schools," *Chicago Daily Defender*, December 10, 1962.

Shaw, Frank A. "The Negro in Harlem," *Real Estate Bulletin* (pub. by Real Estate Board of New York), I, No. 6 (February, 1914), 21–23.

Silberman, Charles E. "Give Slum Children a Chance: A Radical Proposal," *Harper's*, CCXXVIII, No. 1368 (May, 1964), 37–42.

Silver, Roy R. "J.J. Negroes Fight Panic Home Sales," *New York Times*, June 20, 1961.

Slocum, John W. "Teaneck Revives Anti-Bias Board," *New York Times*, November 26, 1961.

———. "Teaneck Unit Files Complaints Charging Race Bias in Housing," *New York Times*, August 10, 1962.

Taeuber, Karl E., "Negro Residential Segregation," *Social Problems*, XII, No. 1 (Summer, 1964), 42–50.

"Twenty Cities Adopt Fair Housing Laws in Past 17 Months," *Human Relations News of Chicago*, the Chicago Commission on Human Relations, VI, No. 5 (September, 1964), 3.

Urban League of Portland, Oregon. "Portland Balance Sheet on Race Relations," *Interracial Progress*, I, No. 3 (December, 1952).

Vitchek, Norris, told to Alfred Balk. "Confessions of a Block-Buster," *Saturday Evening Post*, CCXXXV, No. 27 (July 14, 21, 1962), 15–19.

Weaver, Robert C. "Class, Race, and Urban Renewal," *Land Economics*, XXXVI, No. 1 (August, 1960), 235–251.

———. "The Effect of Anti-Discrimination Legislation upon the FHA- and VA-Insured Housing Market in New York State," *Land Economics*, XXXI, No. 4 (November, 1955), 303–313.

Wendt, Paul F. "Real Estate Education at Colleges and Universities," *Journal of Property Management*, XX, No. 4 (June, 1955), pp. 226–235.

Wirth, Louis. "The Problem of Minority Groups," in Ralph Linton, ed., *The Science of Man in the World Crisis*. New York: Columbia University Press, 1945.

Znaniecki, Florian. "Social Organization and Institutions," in *Twentieth Century Sociology*, ed. by Georges Gurvitch and Wilbert E. Moore. New York: Philosophical Library, 1945.

OTHER PUBLISHED MATERIALS

American Jewish Congress, Commission on Community Interrelations, *Northtown Survey on Human Relations*. New York, 1947.

American Missionary Association, Department of Race Relations. *Minneapolis Community Self-Survey on Human Relations, Racial Problems in Housing*. Nashville, Tenn.: Fisk University, 1947. (Mimeographed.)

Baltimore Urban League. *Civil Rights in Baltimore: A Community Audit.* January, 1950. (Pamphlet.)

Black, Algernon D. *Who's My Neighbor?* New York: Public Affairs Committee, 1958.

Brown v. Board of Education of Topeka, 347 U.S. 483, 494–495, 74 S. Ct. 686, 691–692, 98 L. Ed. 873, 38 A.L.R. 2d 1180 (1954); op. supplemented 349 U.S. 294, 75 S. Ct. 753, 99 L. Ed. 1083 (1955).

Campbell, Clifford J., and Edward Marciniak, *A Report to the Mayor and the City Council of Chicago on the Present Status and Effectiveness of Existing Fair Housing Practices Legislation in the United States as of April 1, 1963.*

Chicago, City of, City Council. Minutes of the Committee on Judiciary, August 6, 1963, A.M. Session, hearing for the opponents to the pending "open occupancy" ordinance and real estate brokers ordinance. In the files of the Council.

Chicago Commission on Human Relations. "First Annual Report of Complaints Received under the Chicago Fair Housing Ordinance." Chicago: the author, January 27, 1965. 1 p. (Mimeographed.)

———. *Mortgage Availability for Non-Whites in the Chicago Area.* A report prepared by the Division of Housing and Community Services. Chicago: Chicago Commission on Human Relations, April, 1963.

———. "Report on Complaints Received under the Fair Housing Ordinance for the Period Ending June 30, 1964." Chicago: the author, July 2, 1964. 1 p. (Mimeographed.)

———. *Selling and Buying Real Estate in a Racially Changing Neighborhood.* Chicago: the author, June, 1962.

———. Summary of testimony at public hearing on August 9, 1962. Chicago: the author, 1962. 6 pp. (Mimeographed.)

———. "Survey to Determine the Extent of Negro Membership on Local Boards of the National Association of Real Estate Boards," completed November, 1962. Re-issue, March 1, 1963, including Chicago. 1 p. (Mimeographed.)

Chicago Community Inventory, University of Chicago. *Population Growth in the Chicago Standard Metropolitan Area 1950–1957.* Report to the Department of City Planning, Chicago, February 1958. Chicago: the author, 1958.

Chicago Fair Housing Ordinance, Ch. 198.7-B, in *Journal of the Proceedings of the City Council of the City of Chicago, Illinois,* regular meeting, Wednesday, September 11, 1963, pp. 977–980. Chicago: City Council, 1963.

Chicago Housing Authority, report, March 31, 1957.

Chicago Real Estate Board. *1800 of Us Invite You.* 6 pp.

Committee for Yes on Proposition 14 to Abolish Rumford Forced Housing Act. *Some Questions and Answers Demonstrating the Need for a "Yes" Vote on Proposition 14.* Los Angeles: the author, n.d. 2 pp.

Committee on Civil Rights in East Manhattan. "Survey of Apartment Rentals through Applications to Brokers," *Summary of Procedures and Findings in Housing Surveys,* January, 1953–April, 1955. (Mimeographed.)

Ennis, H. R. "Annual Report of the President," in NAREB, *Annual Reports of the President, the Officers and the Chairmen of the Divisions.* Dallas, Tex.: the author, January 16, 1925. 64 pp.

Evans, William L. *Race Fear and Housing in a Typical American Community.* New York: National Urban League, 1946. 44 pp.

Goldblatt, Harold S. *Westchester Real Estate Brokers, Builders, Bankers and Negro Home-Buyers.* Report to Housing Council of the Urban League of Westchester County, on *Opportunities for Private Open-Occupancy Housing in Westchester County.* November, 1954.

Hewes, Laurence I., Jr. *Intergroup Relations in San Diego.* San Francisco: American Council on Race Relations, 1946.

Bibliography

Illinois, Department of Registration and Education. *Real Estate Brokers and Salesmen Law.* Springfield: State of Illinois, July 1, 1957.
———. *Registered Real Estate Brokers.* State of Illinois, 1957.
———. *Registered Real Estate Brokers — 1963.* State of Illinois, 1963.
Illinois Commission on Human Relations. *Tenth Biennial Report.* State of Illinois, May, 1963.
Johnson, Charles S. *Negro Housing.* A Report of the Committee on Negro Housing to the President's Conference on Home Building and Home Ownership. Washington, D.C.: Conference, 1932.
Kirk, James H., and Lane D. Spano. *Private Housing Boom — For Whites Only.* 1955, 24 pp. (Mimeographed.)
Lichtenstein, M. R. *M.T.S. Annual Medical Report — 1961.* Chicago: Municipal Tuberculosis Sanitarium, 1961.
Montclair Civil Rights Audit. Report at Montclair Forum, December 11, 1947. (Mimeographed.)
NAACP. *Civil Rights Crisis of 1957.* NAACP 49th annual report. New York: the author, June, 1958.
National Association of License Law Officials. *1963–1964 Summary on License Law Statistics.* Totals for 48 states and District of Columbia. Pittsburgh: the author, 1965. 2 pp.
NAREB (at first, National Association of Real Estate Exchanges). *Ethics of the Real Estate Profession.* Adopted by the Association in 1913. 4 pp. "Exchanges" was changed to "Boards" in 1916. 2nd Code (n.d.), 8 pp. 3rd Code, *Code of Ethics,* 1915, adopted at 8th annual convention, Los Angeles, June 21–24, 1915. The present *Code of Ethics* was adopted in 1913, put in final form in 1915, and amended at annual conventions in 1924, 1928, 1950, 1951, 1952, 1955, 1961, and 1962. 2 pp.
———. *NAREB Policy on Minority Housing.* Chicago: the author, June 4, 1963. 1 p.
———. *Property Owners' Bill of Rights.* Chicago: the author, June 4, 1963. 1 p.
———. "Realtors Membership Progress Report." Report No. 8, August 31, 1956.
———. "Realtors Membership Progress Report 1964." Report No. 6, June 30, 1964. 2 pp.
———. *Report of the Resolutions Committee: Statement of Policy.* 48th annual convention, New York, 1955. 6 pp.
———. *Statement of Policy.* Submitted by Resolutions Committee at 49th annual convention, St. Louis, Mo., November 14, 1956. 6 pp.
———. *Statement of Policy of the Resolutions Committee.* 45th annual convention, Miami Beach, Fla., 1952. 4 pp.
———, Build America Better Council. "Ten Principles of Neighborhood Conservation." Adopted by Council on May 22, 1955, Chicago. Bulletin No. 55-4, May 27, 1955. (Mimeographed.)
NAREB, Committee on Education. "Highlights in Activities of NAREB Department of Education, 1951." Report to Executive Council, NAREB Committee on Education at meeting, November 12, 1951, Cincinnati, Ohio.
NAREB, Committee on Resolutions. Report to annual convention, San Francisco, June 3, 1922, quoted in NAREB, *Policy Handbook,* Vol. I, p. 7.
———. Report to annual convention, Washington, D.C., 1924, quoted in NAREB, *Policy Handbook,* Vol. I, p. 31.
NAREB, Department of Education. Report on use of real estate textbooks in universities and colleges, November 1, 1951. (Photo-offset.)
———. *Study of Real Estate Courses Offered for College Credit at Universities and Colleges throughout the U.S.* Chicago: the author, October 12, 1955. (Photo-offset.)

National Association of Real Estate Brokers. *Your Future and the N.A.R.E.B.* The author, n.d. 8 pp.

National Conference of Christians and Jews, Brotherhood Week Audit Committee of the New York Region. "Human Relations in New York City — Assets — Liabilities — Balance." New York, 1949. (Mimeographed.)

National University Extension Association. *Guide to Correspondence Study.* February, 1954.

National Urban League. *Building for Equal Opportunity.* Report for 1956–1957. New York: the author, 1958.

Ohio Civil Rights Commission. *A Survey of Discrimination in Housing in Ohio.* Columbus: the author, January, 1963.

Price, William L. *Factors Influencing and Restraining the Housing Mobility of Negroes in Metropolitan Detroit.* Detroit: Detroit Urban League, 1955.

Property Owners Coordinating Committee. *Bulletin — The Chicago Forced Housing Lawsuit and the Petition-Referendum Campaign.* Chicago: the author, n.d. 2 pp.

———. "Petition to the Secretary of State, Springfield, Illinois, to place the question of 'Open Occupancy' before the voters of the State in a statewide referendum at the General Election to be held on the third day of November, A.D., 1964."

Senn, Milton A. "Report on Efforts in the Los Angeles Area to Circumvent the United States Supreme Court Decisions on Restrictive Covenants." Memorandum to Anti-Defamation League of B'nai B'rith, December 31, 1948. (Mimeographed.)

Toledo Board of Community Relations. *Program for Progress 1956–1960.* Report on activities of the Board. Toledo: the author, 1961.

United Citizens Committee for Freedom of Residence in Illinois. *About Fair Housing.* Evanston, Ill.: the author, n.d. (Pamphlet.)

U.S. Commission on Civil Rights. *Civil Rights '63: Report of the United States Commission on Civil Rights.* Washington, D.C.: Government Printing Office, 1963.

———. *Housing: 1961 Commission on Civil Rights Report.* Washington, D.C.: Government Printing Office, 1961.

———. *Report of the United States Commission on Civil Rights, 1959.* Washington, D.C.: Government Printing Office, 1959.

U.S. Department of Health, Education, and Welfare, Office of Education. *School-Home Partnership in Depressed Urban Neighborhoods.* Washington, D.C.: Government Printing Office, 1964.

U.S. Department of Health, Education, and Welfare, Public Health Service. *Tuberculosis in the United States — Status of the Disease in the Early Sixties.* Publication No. 1036. Washington, D.C.: Government Printing Office, 1963.

U.S. Federal Housing Administration. *Underwriting Manual.* Underwriting and valuation procedure under Title II, National Housing Act, FHA Form No. 2049, rev. to April 1, 1936. Washington, D.C.: Government Printing Office, 1936. Rev. to February, 1938; Washington, D.C.: Government Printing Office, 1938.

———, National Housing Agency. *Underwriting Manual.* Underwriting analysis under Title II, Section 203, National Housing Act, FHA Form 2049, rev. January 1, 1947. Washington, D.C.: Government Printing Office, 1947.

U.S. Federal Housing Administration, Housing and Home Finance Agency. *Underwriting Manual.* Underwriting analysis under Title II, Section 203, National Housing Act, FHA Form 2049, rev. March 15, 1955. Washington, D.C.: Government Printing Office, 1955.

U.S. Housing and Home Finance Agency. *Our Nonwhite Population and Its Housing: The Changes between 1950 and 1960.* Washington, D.C.: Government Printing Office, July, 1963.

———. *Sixth Annual Report 1952.* "Special Problems and Approaches in Housing

Bibliography

of Minorities and the Role of the Racial Relations Service." Reprint, August, 1953.

————. *State Statutes, and Local Ordinances and Resolutions Prohibiting Discrimination in Housing and Urban Renewal Operations,* rev. Prepared by Intergroup Relations Service and Office of the General Counsel. Washington, D.C.: Government Printing Office, December 1961.

University of Michigan. *The State-wide Certificate Program in Real Estate, Fall, 1957.* Offered by School of Business Administration and University Extension Service with Michigan Real Estate Association and local real estate boards. 8 pp.

White, Walter, and Thurgood Marshall. *What Caused the Detroit Riot?* New York: NAACP, July, 1943.

UNPUBLISHED MATERIALS

Bouma, Donald H. "An Analysis of the Power Position of the Real Estate Board in Grand Rapids." Ph.D. thesis, Department of Sociology, Michigan State College, 1952.

Davies, Pearl Janet. "Real Estate Achievement in the United States." MS. by historian of NAREB, 1957.

Fulton, Robert L. "Russell Woods: A Study of a Neighborhood's Initial Response to Negro Invasion." Ph.D. thesis, Department of Sociology, Wayne State University, 1959.

Hughes, Everett C. "A Study of a Secular Institution: The Chicago Real Estate Board." Ph.D. thesis, Department of Sociology and Anthropology, University of Chicago, 1928.

Kramer, Bernard. "Residential Contact as a Determinant of Attitudes toward Negroes." Ph.D. thesis, Department of Social Relations, Harvard University, 1950.

Mikva, Zorita W. "The Neighborhood Improvement Association: A Counterforce to the Expansion of Chicago's Negro Population." M.A. thesis, Department of Sociology, University of Chicago, 1951.

National Committee on Segregation in the Nation's Capital. "Residential Segregation: Discriminatory Housing in the Nation's Capital." Joseph D. Lohman, Director of Research. MS., 1948. (Mimeographed.)

Nelson, Herbert U. "A History of the National Association of Real Estate Boards as a Factor in Modern Business Advance." May, 1929, Chicago. (Mimeographed. Author was Executive Secretary, NAREB.)

————. "The Objectives of Real Estate Organization." Address before Realtor Secretaries Division, Washington, D.C., June 5, 1924. 21 pp. (Mimeographed.)

Schietinger, Egbert F. "Racial Succession and Changing Property Values in Residential Chicago." Ph.D. thesis, Department of Sociology, University of Chicago, 1953.

"Some Main Dates and Circumstances of NAREB's Founding and Early Development." Document in vertical files of NAREB library, Chicago. (Mimeographed.)

Star, Shirley A. "Interracial Tension in Two Areas of Chicago: An Exploratory Approach to the Measurement of Interracial Tension." Ph.D. thesis, Department of Sociology, University of Chicago, 1950.

Thezan, James W., Chairman Pro Tem, Property Owners Coordinating Committee. Remarks at official opening of POCC Open Occupancy Petition-Referendum Campaign, February 10, 1964, Chicago. 2 pp.

Urban League of Seattle. "Investigation of Discrimination in Housing 1955." (Typed.)

Wallace, David A. "Residential Concentration of Negroes in Chicago." Ph.D. thesis, Department of Planning, Harvard University, 1953.

Williams, Robin M., Jr. "Factors Affecting Reactions to Public School Desegregation in American Communities." Paper read at 14th annual meeting, Society for the Study of Social Problems, Montreal, P.Q., Canada, August 30, 1964.

Winder, Alvin E. "White Attitudes towards Negro-White Interaction in an Area of Changing Racial Composition." Ph.D. thesis, Committee on Human Development, Division of Social Sciences, University of Chicago, 1952.

Wolf, Eleanor P. "Changing Neighborhood: A Study of Racial Transition." Ph.D. thesis, Department of Sociology, Wayne State University, 1959.

Youngstown Interracial Clinic, "Report of the Sub-Committee on Negro Residence and Property Values." (Mimeographed; n.d.)

Index

Abrams, Charles, 16, 296
Akron (Ohio) Real Estate Board, 291
Alinsky, Saul D., 297, 298
American Institute of Real Estate Appraisers: definition of homogeneity, neighborhood, 197; educational program, 243; factors affecting value, 201; right to own property, 193; *Underwriting Manual*, 203; value, how created and modified, 196–197
Anderson, Frank Ray, 212–213
Ann Arbor (Mich.) Board of Realtors, 282
Apartment buildings: effect of Negro approach and entry on, 92–93; Negro buys to control block, 93
Atkinson, Harry Grant, 198, 213–214, 244
Atlanta (Ga.) Real Estate Board, 231

Babcock, Frederick M., 202–203, 215–216
Baltimore (Md.) Board of Real Estate Brokers and Property Agents, 220–221
Benson, Philip A., 195, 196, 203, 244, 320
Berkeley (Calif.) Realty Board, 226
Birmingham (Ala.) Real Estate Board, 227
"Block Method" of Negro settlement: recommended by Chicago Board committee, 225
Block organization of owners: recommended by Chicago Board committee, 226
Blumer, Herbert, 20, 348n. 5
Bontemps, Arna, 352
Buffalo (N.Y.) Real Estate Board, 231

California Real Estate Association: initiated Proposition *14*, 281; integration through education and persuasion, 284; racial restrictions revealed in survey by, 229
California Supreme Court, 281
Canton (Ohio) Real Estate Board, 227
Case, Frederick E., 215, 242
"Changing neighborhood" ("changing area"): broker's belief in racial succession, 108–109; lending agencies will not lend in, 170–171
Chicago Commission on Human Relations, 277, 282, 288
Chicago Conference on Religion and Race, 294
Chicago Real Estate Board: against fair housing and open occupancy legislation, 277, 278; Code of Ethics of, 188, 261; committee investigates effects of Negro inmigration, 224–226; dealing with Negroes, 45; distribution of respondents by membership in, 219; drafts residential restrictions, 229–230; educational program of, 187, 243; establishes trust with public for Realtor, 199–201; formation of, 221; ideological influence of, 190–217; ideology of NAREB accepted as that of, 191; importance of ideological control of, 258–262; initiates lawsuit to test Ordinance, 279, 280; integration through education and persuasion, 284; interdependence with members and non-members, 188–190; lack of control over deviant broker, 254–258; member of, sells unrestrictedly, 162–163; moral authority of, 247–249; moral

381

Index

Racial real estate ideology: of brokers and institution distinguished, 19–20

Racial real estate ideology, of brokers: changes in, 271–273; Component 9 as part of, 57–58; components of, 56–58; content of components of, 58–151; determination of types of, 142–143; in preliminary interviews, 19–20, 56, 142; sources of, 58
— main ideas: exclusion, 143–145; integration, 146–147; intermediate, 145–146

Racial real estate ideology, of institution: 19–20, 201–217; in textbooks, 202–216

Racial real estate practices, brokers: changes in, 271–273

Racial restrictive covenants: development of, in Chicago, 358–361; U.S. Supreme Court decision on, 210, 211, 212, 232, 235

Ratcliff, Richard W., 213, 242

Real estate board: and real estate men, relation of, 23–24; study of, 16

Real Estate Boards of NAREB: acts of, to protect property values, 223–235, 277–287; Chicago nonmember Boards oppose Fair Housing Ordinance, 283; educational programs, 243; Negro members in, 237–238, 287

Real estate brokers (respondents of the study): adherence to institutional ideology, 258–262; adjustments to Negro entry, 36–38; approval/disapproval of organizations' programs, 159–160; belief that racial succession inevitable, 107–109; blamed for discrimination in housing, 15; characteristics of, for study, 29; conceal dealings with Negroes, 44–45; concern for Negroes, 120; decisions about racial policy, 36; determine when selling to Negroes permitted, 109–112; "deviant behavior" of, 26; emphasize conservation, 198; future plans about dealing with Negroes, 54; influence in racial occupancy change, 54; influence on and influenced by trend, 33–35; integration if Negroes improve, 104–105; management of property for Negro owners, 38–39; participation in programs of organizations, 158–160; personal reaction to Negroes' entering white areas, 129–132; policies and

practices, 4, 5, 38–55, 288–292; possibility of residential integration, 94, 102–107; reasons for selling to Negroes in white area, 127–128; refusal to sell to Negroes, methods of, 42–45; restrictions in management, 46; restrictions in selling, 39–42; results of racial practices, 140–141; sales of homes to white buyers after Negro entry, 94; secret deals with bad speculators, 182–184; terms used to describe Negro movement, 141–142; training, 246; treat Negroes as individuals, 58; typology of, 265–271; unrestricted sales unethical, 117–123, 275, 276; views of, distinguished from Board, 293–294; will not sell to Negroes in white area or block, 39–42, 274, 275. *See also* Exclusion ideology, brokers; Profit
— consequences of: dealing with Negroes, 161–162; unrestricted selling, 162–164; unrestricted selling, unconcern about, 139–140
— exclusion practice, reasons for: business consequences, 135–137; consequences to others, 112–116, 120; danger of physical harm, 138–139; ordering of, 263–265; relation to community, 25; social consequences, 137–138; uphold community standard, 132–134
— influence from: community, 23, 24–25, 152–156, 275; factors revealed in preliminary interviews, 18–19; lending agencies, 23, 25–26, 166–172; organizations, 155–159; other sources, 156–157; particular sources of gain, 23, 25; real estate board, 23–24
— restrictive policy, justification of: absolute values, 123–124; higher authorities, 124–125; principles of "American life," 125–127; principles of conduct, 117–123

Real Estate Brokers Ordinance, Chicago, *see* Fair Housing Ordinance

Real estate Gresham's law (Hoagland), 208, 210

Real estate ideology: comparison of brokers' with that of institution, 19–20, 217–218

Real estate ideology, of brokers: 19–20, 147–150; relation of exclusion to real estate, 150–151

Real estate ideology, of institution: 191–

385